Cities of North America

Cities of North America

Contemporary Challenges in US and Canadian Cities

EDITED BY
LISA BENTON-SHORT

ROWMAN & LITTLEFIELD
Lanham • Boulder • New York • Toronto • Plymouth, UK

Published by Rowman & Littlefield
4501 Forbes Boulevard, Suite 200, Lanham, Maryland 20706
www.rowman.com

10 Thornbury Road, Plymouth PL6 7PP, United Kingdom

British Library Cataloguing in Publication Information Available

Library of Congress Cataloging-in-Publication Data

Cities of North America : contemporary challenges in U.S. and Canadian cities / edited by Lisa Benton-Short.
     pages cm.
  Includes bibliographical references and index.
  ISBN 978-1-4422-1313-5 (cloth : alk. paper) — ISBN 978-1-4422-1315-9 (electronic) 1. Urban policy—United States. 2. Urban policy—Canada. 3. Cities and towns—United States. 4. Cities and towns—Canada. I. Benton-Short, Lisa.
  HT122.C57 2014
  307.760973—dc23
                                                                                                    2013028531

Printed in the United States of America

Contents

Illustrations

FIGURES

BOXES

TABLES

1

An Introduction to Cities of North America

THREE CITIES, THREE STORIES

Washington, DC

January 20, 2009. They came to the National Mall in Washington, DC, by the hundreds of thousands. They came from around the country, endured frigid weather, security checkpoints, and long lines. The entire two-mile stretch of the mall was a carpet of nearly two million people—an unprecedented crowd of astonishing size and spirit. They were there to bear witness to history—the inauguration of Barack Obama. That day, the Mall was quite visibly a stage for and of democracy.

The National Mall in Washington, DC, is one of the most recognized and visited public spaces in the United States. It is where presidents are inaugurated and where the country has commemorated important people and events. It is a stage on which we act out the meaning of the nation, where protests challenge us to rethink what constitutes citizenship, justice, and the promise of democracy. It is where American society expresses its national ideals of democracy, liberty, and freedom in the built form and the physical landscape. The power of the Mall derives not from its stoic architecture, inspiring memorials, or grassy open spaces but from the people who visit, who use the space in celebration or protest, and who, ultimately, use the Mall as a stage for the expression of democratic ideals.

New York City

In the fall of 2011 dozens, then hundreds, then thousands of people gathered in Zuccotti Park, in the heart of New York City's Wall Street financial district. The protest movement became known as Occupy Wall Street. Activists rallied against the increasing corporate influence on democracy, the lack of legal consequences for those who brought about the global recession, and the increasing disparity in wealth. The Occupy slogan "We are the 99%" refers to the income inequality and wealth distribution in the United States between the wealthiest 1 percent and the rest of the population.

The protest led to media awareness that inspired similar Occupy protests in numerous US and Canadian cities, including Los Angeles, Detroit, Buffalo, Baltimore, Montreal, San Diego, Toronto, and Vancouver. By late November, city officials announced they would close Zuccotti Park to the protesters. Since the closure of the park, the Occupy Wall Street movement has focused on protesting and occupying space at banks, corporate head-quarters, and college and university campuses.

Vancouver

In February of 2010, millions of people around the world turned their attention to the city of Vancouver. For the next seventeen days, the city played host to the Winter Olympic Games. The city spent hundreds of millions—perhaps as much as two billion dollars—to upgrade facilities, build new venues, and create the Olympic Village. It was estimated that the Olympics brought $2.5 billion to the Vancouver economy and generated 45,000 jobs.

Hosting the Olympic Games involves not only a creative vision but also a physical restructuring of the city, an opportunity for urban renewal. The construction of the Olympic Village and projects, such as the construction of new roads and sewer system, and the creation or improvement of parks, plazas, and streets links the games with urban renewal. Often this involves an upgrade of the city's infrastructure and transportation networks, the renovation of the seafront, and/or the organization of the historic center. Hosting the games leaves a physical legacy that has longer-term development potential. Perhaps the largest infrastructural legacy is the upgrade of airports, telecommunications, mass transit schemes, and road networks that quite literally better connect the city to global flows of people, ideas, and commerce.

The games are a catalyst for urban renewal, environmental remediation, and improvements to a city's infrastructure that can make the city more competitive on the world stage. Vancouver is betting that the games will reposition the city in the global imaginary by promoting a positive global image of the city and stimulating tourism and investment.

These three cities and the three recent stories that occurred there remind us of the powerful and central role that cities play in our political, economic, and social lives. They are where we gather to celebrate. They are where we gather to protest. They are often the sites of important events. They are also where millions of us live daily, navigating the streets of our neighborhoods, commuting to work, raising families. Americans and Canadians live in a highly urbanized society, where what happens in our cities informs not just our local lives but our national political, economic, and social discourses.

In this book, we use the regional term "North America" to refer to cities in the United States and Canada. Although geographers include Mexico in North America, we chose to focus this book on just US and Canadian cities because these cities share so much more in common economically, politically, and socially. For example, US and Canadian metropolitan areas face complex issues that include the redistribution of economic activities, the continued decline of manufacturing, and a global growth in services, all of which have rapidly changed the look and experience of cities. Inner cities have experienced both gentrification and continued areas of segregation and poverty. Downtown revitalization has created urban spectacles that include festivals, marketplaces, and sports stadiums. Older, inner-ring suburbs now confront decline and increased poverty, while the outer-ring suburbs and exurbs continue to expand, devouring green space. While it is true that some Mexican cities have experienced these changes, most have not. As a result,

Mexican cities confront different economic, political, and social challenges from their US and Canadian counterparts. We do, however, acknowledge the linkages and networks that comprise US, Canadian, and Mexican cities and have included a chapter that examines critical trends among border cities.

URBANIZATION TRENDS

The world passed a major milestone in 2010: more than one-half of the world's residents now live in urban areas. This event is impressive when we consider that less than 10 percent lived in urban areas in 1900 and only 30 percent lived in urban areas in 1950. This major demographic shift marks a century of accelerating urbanization. It is now a fact that in many areas of the world, a majority of the population lives in urban areas, and this trend is only growing. In the United States and Canada, a majority of the population has been urban throughout most of the twentieth century and into the first decades of this century (table 1.1). Today, more than 80 percent of the US and Canadian population lives in urban areas. The three largest cities in North America are New York, Los Angeles, and Chicago, but there are some forty-eight cities that have a population of more than one million. Figure 1.1 shows the major cities of the United States and Canada.

Many urban scholars have noted that we are in the midst of the Third Urban Revolution. The first began over six thousand years ago with the first cities in Mesopotamia. The First Urban Revolution, independently experienced in Africa, Asia, and the Americas, was a new way of living in the world. The Second Urban Revolution began in the eighteenth century, spurred by the twin processes of urbanization and industrialization. These forces created the industrial city and resulted in unparalleled rates of urban growth and transformation. The Third Urban Revolution began in the middle of the twentieth century and is marked by a significant increase, in both absolute and relative terms, in urban populations, the development of "megacities" of more than ten million people, the growth of giant metropolitan regions, and the global redistribution of economic activities as former manufacturing cities in Europe, the United States, and Canada decline, while new industrial cities emerge in the developing world. This revolution has had major impacts on transforming the urban landscape: inner cities have become the site of redevelopment and gentrification as well as poverty and decline; urban planners have turned to high-density development along public transportation routes such as bus lines, subway systems, and light rail; suburbs have exploded and have transformed once agricultural areas and open space; gated communities and business parks now sprawl into

Table 1.1   Percentage Urban Population in the United States and Canada, 1900–2010

	1870	*1900*	*1950*	*1975*	*2000*	*2010*
Canada	19.5%	37%	62%	76%	77%	80%
United States	22%	45%	64%	70%	79%	81%

Source: US Census Bureau and Statistics Canada.

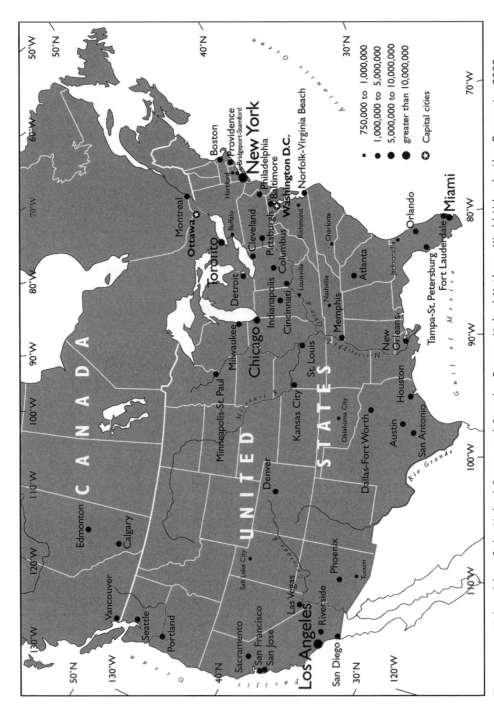

Figure 1.1 Major cities of the United States and Canada. *Source:* United Nations, *World Urbanization Prospects: 2009 Revision*, http://esa.un.org/unpd/wup/index.htm.

the former countryside. All of these changes have led to new terms to describe cities. These new terms include "postmodern," "global," "networked," and "fractured" and attempt to capture the complexity and contradictions of urban change. Whatever terms are used, the impacts of this Third Urban Revolution are complex and often contradictory. The latest urban revolution is not only a redistribution of population: it is also a fundamental change in the spatial organization of society and the social organization of space.

The cities of the United States and Canada embody the dynamic and challenging trends of this Third Urban Revolution. In both countries, a rising percentage of the population resides in cities, as shown in tables 1.2 and 1.3. In Canada, 81 percent of the population lives in urban areas, and half of this population lives in the three largest urban areas: Toronto, Montreal, and Vancouver. In the United States, 82 percent of the population lives in cities. Experts predict that by 2030, urbanization could be as high as 87 percent. Yet despite the urban

Table 1.2   Twenty Largest Metropolitan Cities in the United States by Population, 1950–2010

Rank	1950	1970	1990	2000	2010
1	New York, NY	New York, NY	New York, NY	New York, NY	New York, NY
2	Chicago, IL	Chicago, IL	Los Angeles, CA	Los Angeles, CA	Los Angeles, CA
3	Philadelphia, PA	Los Angeles, CA	Chicago, IL	Chicago, IL	Chicago, IL
4	Los Angeles, CA	Philadelphia, PA	Houston, TX	Houston, TX	Houston, TX
5	Detroit, MI	Detroit, MI	Philadelphia, PA	Philadelphia, PA	Philadelphia, PA
6	Baltimore, MD	Houston, TX	San Diego, CA	Phoenix, AZ	Phoenix, AZ
7	Cleveland, OH	Baltimore, MD	Detroit, MI	San Diego, CA	San Antonio, TX
8	St. Louis, MO	**Dallas, TX**	Dallas, TX	Dallas, TX	San Diego, CA
9	Washington, DC	Washington, DC	San Antonio, TX	**Louisville-Jefferson Co., KY**	Dallas, TX
10	Boston, MA	Cleveland, OH	Phoenix, AZ	San Antonio, TX	San Jose, CA
11	San Francisco, CA	**Indianapolis, IN**	**San Jose, CA**	Detroit, MI	Jacksonville, FL
12	Pittsburgh, PA	Milwaukee, WI	Baltimore, MD	San Jose, CA	Indianapolis, IN
13	Milwaukee, WI	San Francisco, CA	Indianapolis, IN	Indianapolis, IN	San Francisco, CA
14	Houston, TX	**San Diego, CA**	San Francisco, CA	San Francisco, CA	Austin, TX
15	Buffalo, NY	**San Antonio, TX**	**Columbus, OH**	Jacksonville, FL	Columbus, OH
16	New Orleans, LA	Boston, MA	**Jacksonville, FL**	Columbus, OH	**Fort Worth, TX**
17	Minneapolis, MN	**Memphis, TN**	Milwaukee, WI	**Austin, TX**	**Charlotte, NC**
18	Cincinnati, OH	St. Louis, MO	Memphis, TN	Baltimore, MD	Detroit, MI
19	Seattle, WA	New Orleans, LA	Washington, DC	Memphis, TN	**El Paso, TX**
20	Kansas City, MO	**Phoenix, AZ**	Boston, MA	Milwaukee, WI	Memphis, TN

Note that there is some stability as New York, Los Angeles, Chicago, and Philadelphia keep their position in the top five. Others have only recently joined the list. Bold denotes new to the top twenty.

Source: J. R. Short. 2012. "Metropolitan USA: Evidence from the 2010 Census." *International Journal of Population Research*, 1–6.

Table 1.3   The Ten Largest Metropolitan Areas in Canada, 2011

Rank	City	Population	
1	Toronto, Ontario	2,615,060	
2	Montreal, Quebec	1,649,519	
3	Calgary, Alberta	1,096,833	
4	Ottawa, Ontario	883,391	
5	Edmonton, Alberta	821,201	
6	Mississauga, Ontario	713,443	
7	Winnipeg, Manitoba	663,617	
8	Vancouver, British Columbia	603,502	
9	Brampton, Ontario	523,911	Brampton's first appearance on the list
10	Hamilton, Ontario	519,949	

Source: Statistics Canada.

nature of these two countries, North American cities vary in size, form, and fortune. The New York metropolitan region has twenty-two million people, Los Angeles has eighteen million, and Chicago has ten million. Atlanta, Houston, Miami, Philadelphia, Toronto, and Washington, DC, have five million or more, while Baltimore, Denver, Ottawa, Portland, and Vancouver have about two million people.

MODELS OF URBAN STRUCTURE

Although there is no single model to explain why things are located where they are within cities, we can generalize about the structure of North American cities. There are two general features that characterize most North American cities. The first is that most North American cities are built on the grid system. The second feature is "sprawl," or the horizontal spread of development from the center city. This is different from many other world regions, such as Europe, where cities have remained densely developed.

The average city in the United States and Canada has a land-use pattern that breaks down as follows:

- residential (30 percent)
- industrial/manufacturing (9 percent)
- commercial (4 percent)
- roads and highways (20 percent)
- public land, government buildings, and parks (15 percent)
- vacant or undeveloped land (20 percent)

The layout of these various land-use categories differs according to the age of the city. For example, cities established prior to 1840 tend to have very dense or compact cores. For cities such as Los Angeles or Vancouver that developed later, during the twentieth century, industrial activities might be located outside the core area to take advantage of advances in transportation facilities such as railroads. Still other cities that saw development occur after 1950, such as Phoenix, have more deconcentrated cores with expansive residential zones due to the automobile and the emergence of suburbs. The majority of US cities, however, have both high-rent and low-rent residential areas in the inner core, and moving outward, into the suburbs, the price (and size) of single-family homes tends to increase. Here patterns of expansion and land use often follow the concentric zone model.

The pattern is different for most Canadian cities, where the price of single-family homes actually increases as one moves closer to the city center. In Canadian cities, the inner-ring suburbs consist of smaller-sized houses built on larger lots, while the largest homes tend to be in areas on the suburban fringe, where the lots are actually smaller (box 1.1).

Box 1.1 Classic Models of Urban Structure

In the twentieth century, urban scholars developed models to help explain urban growth patterns. Three models, in particular, have informed how geographers have explained why things are located where they are within cities (figure 1.2).

The Concentric Zone Model: This model was developed in the 1920s by urban sociologists Robert Park and E. W. Burgess at the University of Chicago. What Burgess wanted to model was Chicago's spatial structure with regard to the usage of "zones" around the city. Burgess was particularly interested in how waves of immigration and innovations in transportation altered the internal structure of the city. The center of the model—the first zone—is the central business district (CBD), from which other zones radiate concentrically outward. The second zone was the belt of factories that were directly outside of the Loop, the third zone included homes of laborers who worked at the factories, the fourth zone contained middle-class residences, and the fifth and final zone hugged the first four zones and contained the homes of the suburban upper class. Burgess observed the farther from the CBD, the better the quality of housing, but the longer the commuting time. The concentric zone model is simple and elegant, but it has several weaknesses. First, it was developed when American cities were growing very fast in demographic terms and when motorized transportation was

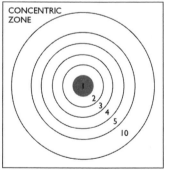 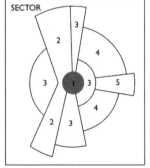

1 Central business district	5 High-class residential	8 Residential suburb
2 Wholesale light manufacturing	6 Heavy manufacturing	9 Industrial suburb
3 Low-class residential	7 Outlying business district	10 Commuter zone
4 Medium-class residential		

Figure 1.2   Three models of urban structure. *Source:* Stanley D. Brunn, Maureen Hays-Mitchell, and Donald J. Zeigler, eds., *Cities of the World: World Regional Urban Development*, 5th ed. (Lanham: Rowman & Littlefield, 2012).

still uncommon as most people used public transit. Expansion thus involved reconversion of existing land uses. The model does not adequately explain urban growth post-1950, when highways enabled urban development to escape the reconversion process and to take place directly in the suburbs. A second limitation is that the model assumed a spatial separation of place of work and place of residence, which was not generalized until the twentieth century. Finally, the model did not work for European cities, where the elite resided closer to the center of the city and the poor were on the periphery. However, the Burgess model remains useful as a concept explaining concentric urban development, as a way to introduce the complexity of urban land use, and as an explanation of urban growth in American cities in the early to mid-twentieth century.

Hoyt Sector Model: Because the concentric zone model was not applicable to many cities, other scholars attempted to further model the urban environment. One of these was Homer Hoyt, a land economist who was mostly interested in taking a look at rents within a city as a means of modeling the city's layout. The model (also known as the Hoyt model or sector model), developed in 1939, took into account the effect of transportation and communication on a city's growth. Hoyt's thoughts were that rents could remain relatively consistent in certain "slices" of the model, from the downtown center all the way to the suburban fringe, giving the model a pie-like look. Instead of concentric zones, Hoyt conceived of the city as having a central business district with zones that expanded in wedges or "sectors" that formed along major transportation corridors such as railways and waterways. This model accounted for the movement of households of different income and ethnic groups toward the outer edge in the pre-established direction. For example, his model of Chicago shows the movement of upper-class residential areas evolved outwards along the highly desirable Lake Michigan shoreline north of the CBD, while industry extended southward in sectors that followed railroad lines. As with the Burgess Model, Hoyt's sector model also has limitations. The model is based on early twentieth-century rail transport and does not make allowances for private cars that enable commuting from cheaper land outside city boundaries. Second, freeways built in the postwar years do not conform to the predicted locations assumed in the Hoyt model.

Multinucleated Model: A third model, called the multinucleated model, was developed in 1945 by two geographers, Chauncy Harris and Edward Ullman, to try and further describe a city's layout. Harris and Ullman made the argument that the city's downtown core (CBD) was losing its importance in relation to the rest of the city and should be seen less as the focal point of a city and instead as a nucleus within the metropolitan area. The automobile had become increasingly more important during this time, which made for greater movement of residents to the suburbs. The model sought to better explain land-use patterns in the late twentieth century and particularly the outward growth of cities such as Los Angeles. The theory was formed based on the idea that people have greater movement resulting from increased car ownership and that this increase of movement allows for the specialization of regional centers (e.g., heavy industry, business park, retail areas). As a result, there is no "single" central business district but rather a number of nuclei around which the city expands. Instead, the city expands by peripheral spread, creating separate districts that eventually coalesce at the margins. This creates nodes, or nuclei, in other parts of the city besides the CBD—thus the name multiple nuclei (or multinucleated) model. For example, regional shopping centers became an anchor point, like the CBD. In some ways, this model helps explain "edge cities" that emerged in the 1960s and 1970s. However, this model, too, has its critics. First, while the aim was to produce a more realistic model, in fact, it was a more complicated model. For example, it consisted of nine different sections that each had separate functions.

All three models are products of their time, and as such, they all have limitations. In addition, none of these models considers the influence of physical relief and government policy. Despite the fact that models have weaknesses, these models are a fundamental part of the history of urban geography and continue to explain some land-use decisions in cities. For example, the models foreshadow the concept of zoning, which categorizes land use into residential, commercial, and industrial zones or functions. Attempts at creating models of the way cities function serve to enhance our understanding of the urban environment.

The grid plan, which imposes a rectangular street grid on urban space, dates from antiquity. Some of the earliest planned cities were built using grids; it is by far the most common pattern found in a variety of political societies from absolute monarchies to democratic societies. The grid provides a simple, rational format for allocating land by setting streets at right angles to one another. Despite a multitude of geographies, topographies, altitudes, and latitudes, many North American cities on the grid share common design features: a lack of sensitivity to the physical environment, the imposition of the grid regardless of topography, a focus on straight lines (geometry over geography), and an underlying sense of the ability to control urban space. San Francisco, which bears the Spanish imprint, nevertheless imposed a grid on what must be considered among the most dramatic topographies of North American cities (see figure 1.3).

The grid plan was nearly universal in the construction of new towns and cities in the United States and Canada. In part, the dominance of the grid was due to the influence of the European system. Adopting the grid plan, however, also allowed for the rapid subdivision of large parcels of land. As US cities have grown outward, particularly after the mid-twentieth century, the grid has become less prevalent. The suburbs present a more organic pattern of growth, often designed with cul-de-sacs and winding lanes. As a result, many suburbs provide a purposeful contrast to the gridironed city. When cities and suburbs merge, as many have, the grid merges into a series of loops, curves, and open spaces, and its rigidity begins to disappear, as shown in figure 1.4.

In contrast, some recent suburbs have returned to the grid system under the influence of New Urbanism. New Urbanism

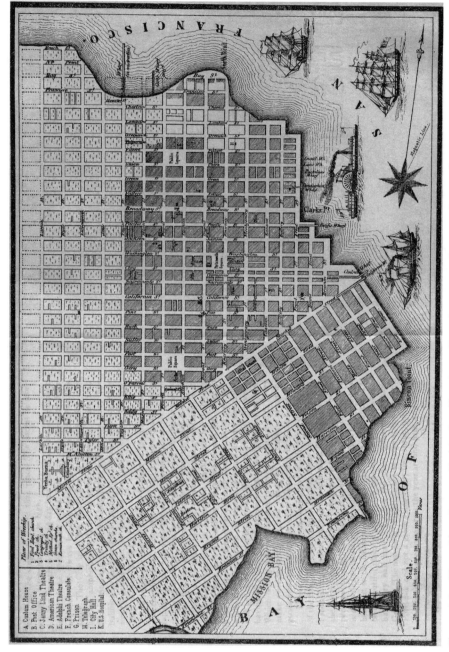

Figure 1.3   The grid system applied in San Francisco. Map circa 1852. *Source:* Library of Congress.

Figure 1.4   Suburban forms offer a contrast to the grid system by introducing curvilinear streets and cul-de-sacs. (Photo by Lisa Benton-Short)

nostalgically longs for lost community and the older high-density cities of the past. New Urbanism design principles emphasize walkable, mixed-use "town centers" and higher-density residential areas. Ironically, New Urbanism, which is a response to suburban sprawl, has had less impact on redesigning cities than it has had on the redesign of suburbs. The most cited example of New Urbanism is the town of Celebration in Florida, a community initially planned and built by the Disney Corporation. Celebration has all the design elements of New Urbanism: low-rise, high-density residential areas where garages are at the back of the residences, walkways and porches allow pedestrian movement, and a vibrant, car-free mixed-use downtown is available.

The emergence of *edge cities* provides yet another model of urban structure. Edge cities consist of predominantly large-square-footage office space located beyond the downtown on the urban fringe. Journalist Joel Garreau

coined the term "edge cities" and defined them as:

- Having more than five million square feet of office space. This is enough to house between twenty thousand and fifty thousand office workers (as many as some traditional downtowns).
- Having more than six hundred thousand square feet of retail space, the size of a medium shopping mall.
- Having more jobs than bedrooms.
- Looking nothing like a city before 1960.

These newer urban forms attract large numbers of service-sector workers during the day but are empty at night as residential areas are scarce. Garreau identified 123 places as being true edge cities, including two dozen in greater Los Angeles, twenty-three in metro Washington, DC, and twenty-one in greater New York City. Other examples are found in Dallas-Forth

Figure 1.5   The edge city of Buckhead in Atlanta. Hotels and office buildings line the streets, but several lanes of roads make this edge city unfriendly to pedestrians, as noticed by the lack of people on the sidewalks during the lunch hour. (Photo by Lisa Benton-Short)

Worth, Orlando, and Atlanta. Figure 1.5 shows the edge city of Buckhead in Atlanta.

Edge cities, however, may become a phenomenon relegated to the twentieth century.

Because edge cities are built in and around major highway intersections, traffic congestion has become a problem. Pedestrian access is poor, and public transportation is nearly absent. Ironically, edge cities may stimulate redevelopment of the downtown core as people seek to leave their cars and commute by public transportation. Additionally, as development continues in and around edge cities, they may "merge" into megalopolitan areas with nodes of residential areas and nodes of commercial and/or business activity (see box 1.2).

TWENTY-FIRST CENTURY URBAN TRENDS

Contemporary urban scholarship encompasses a variety of approaches to the study of cities. The evolution of ideas and theories has shaped the way scholars study cities and

Box 1.2 New York City: A Global Metropolis

New York City is the largest city in the United States and the one most frequently identified as the cultural and financial capital of the country. At 8.4 million people and more than 19 million in the consolidated metropolitan statistical area, or CMSA, New York is the only metropolis in North America to rival the megacities of Asia and Latin America in terms of population. A true "world city," New York is a point from which global and economic trends diffuse outward. Recent events, however, have also shown that New York—like any other city—is far from invincible. The World Trade Center attacks of September 2001, the blackout of August 2003, and the real-estate crisis of 2008 and 2009 have shown that New York, perhaps because of its global connectedness and prominence, can also be brought to a halt by external actors.

Despite these setbacks, New York continues to lead the world in commerce and industry. The port of New York/New Jersey, once the main connection between the Atlantic Ocean and the St. Lawrence Seaway (via the Erie Canal), now handles the third-highest tonnage in the United States and falls within the global top twenty of busiest ports. New York—along with Los Angeles—continues to dominate the United States' manufacturing-based industries, with more than twenty thousand establishments, but has especially thrived in the so-called creative industries that have gained popularity in the past two decades. These sectors tend to be spatially concentrated in different portions of the city, with music and theater in Times Square, fashion in the Garment District, interior design and architecture in Chelsea and SoHo, and advertising on Madison Avenue. These industries often draw from the talent pools of nearby educational institutions, such as the Julliard School (music), the Pratt Institute (design), and the Fashion Institute of Technology. The city government has also contributed by boosting tax incentives for the television and film sectors.

First inhabited by the Algonquin Indians, Manhattan Island was purchased and settled by the Dutch in 1626. By 1800, New York City, with its sixty thousand residents, had become the largest city in the country. It has maintained this position since then, forming the center of the Boston-to-Washington conurbation that geographer Jean Gottmann later called the Megalopolis. Along with Tokyo and London, New York is one of the three powerful "world cities" that anchor global trade, commerce, banking, and stock markets.

Even as New York becomes further globally interconnected, the city is in many ways socially, economically, and spatially fragmented. Despite its world-city status, New York has always struggled with its reputation for poor sanitation and high crime. Many geographers have argued that these problems, rather than being truly corrected, have merely been suppressed or relocated and confined to particular areas of the city. New York has frequently located environmentally hazardous projects, such as expressways and incinerators, in poor and racialized neighborhoods (e.g., South Bronx, Sunset Park), where public visibility is reduced and resistance is less likely. The city has also tried to reconfigure itself as a safe, livable city and tourist destination. Under the administration of Mayor Rudolph Giuliani (1994–2001), New York implemented "quality of life" laws that criminalized panhandling and homelessness while policing and securitizing (e.g., through closed-circuit cameras) highly trafficked and visible public spaces. Even places that have previously served as important sites of public protest, such as the steps of City Hall, are now frequently fenced off or guarded.

Gentrification has undoubtedly driven the fragmentation of New York City. Although gentrification is commonly understood as the product of gradual, localized, ground-up improvements to neighborhood properties, much of the gentrification in New York since 2000 has been driven by corporate developers and municipal interests. The New York Urban Development Corporation, for example, has forcibly purchased many Times Square properties for redevelopment. Privately managed business improvement districts (BIDs) are now responsible for many of the public space improvements (e.g., beautification, signage) in New York. Rapid gentrification of previously decaying neighborhoods such as the Meatpacking District (Manhattan) and Williamsburg (Brooklyn) have expanded the living space available for the upper class and upwardly mobile, but they have priced out the middle-class residents of neighborhoods such as Park Slope (Brooklyn), Harlem, and the Lower East Side of Manhattan.

Immigration has been central to both the identity of New York and the individual identities of its neighborhoods. More than twelve million immigrants from Ireland, Germany, Italy, Poland, Greece, and elsewhere arrived in New York City during the late 1800s and early 1900s. During the past three decades, however, immigrants from Latin American and Asia make up the bulk of newcomers to New York. Despite being one of the United States' most ethnically diverse areas, it is still highly segregated. Real-estate agents, who serve as gatekeepers to the city's properties, often sort new immigrants toward neighborhoods dominated by their particular ethno-racial group. Such practices, however, reinforce self-segregating tendencies, ethno-racial ghettos (e.g., Puerto Ricans in the Bronx, Dominicans in Washington Heights), and mutual antipathies among groups. New York thus remains a city of extremes. In a relatively small area, extreme wealth meets with extreme poverty, global integration encounters local fragmentation, and individualistic economic opportunity sits side by side with the increasing management and regulation of public space. These dichotomies, however, are likely to guarantee New York's place as a fascinating site of geographic study for years to come.

Source: This material draws on Lisa Benton-Short and Nathaniel Lewis, "Cities of the United States and Canada," in Stanley D. Brunn, Maureen Hays-Mitchell, and Donald J. Zeigler, eds., *Cities of the World: World Regional Urban Development*, 5th ed. (Lanham: Rowman & Littlefield, 2012).

is the subject of **chapter 2**. This chapter examines the ways in which urban geography has been influenced by various approaches to the study of cities. Today, scholars have a range of interpretations about urbanization, including neo-Marxian, globalization, postmodern, critical, and feminist approaches. More recently, new digital technology and geographic information systems (GISs) have allowed urban scholars to better analyze connections, distribution, and spatial patterns. None of these approaches by themselves tells us the full story of urbanization. The task for urban geographers is to sift through the array of ideas presented with an awareness of the boundaries that are drawn, the histories, characters, and places that are excluded, and the power that has been mobilized.

Geographers approach the study of cities through the discipline's major subfields:

historical geography, economic geography, political geography, cultural geography, and environmental geography. These are also the main organizing themes of this book.

Urban History

The contemporary North American city is primarily the product of industrial developments of the nineteenth and twentieth centuries. As explored in **chapter 3**, the era of industrial capitalism marked the transformation of the US and Canadian economies from ones based on trade in natural resources to ones that processed raw materials and manufactured products. New York, Philadelphia, and Baltimore became main industrial cities in the United States, while Toronto and Montreal dominated in Canada. Cities along rivers and lakes used new advances in transportation such as canals and railroads to become important hubs in the distribution of goods. St. Louis, Chicago, and Cincinnati emerged as key gateways, while Winnipeg, Edmonton, and Calgary developed as major centers.

Industrialization was more than just factories and jobs. Key inventions changed the look of cities. The introduction of iron and then steel in construction launched the era of skyscrapers. By the end of the nineteenth century, electric street trolleys laid the foundations for twentieth-century suburbanization by allowing people to live farther from the city center. Urban planning and architecture, particularly in the downtown core, reflect industrial capitalism at its peak and remain key features of the urban landscape today.

The twentieth century saw cities such as Los Angeles, Phoenix, Dallas, and Vancouver grow in population. But a reliance on private vehicles and a nearly absent investment in public transportation meant that cities in the West grew more horizontally than vertically, and a distinctive pattern of sprawl resulted.

Economic Transformations

Urban scholars generally agree that three major forces have played pivotal roles in recent economic changes in North American cities. Deindustrialization, globalization, and suburbanization have combined to radically transform these cities. The impact of globalization on North American cities has affected economic restructuring, downtown redevelopment, neoliberal urban politics, and social polarization. These processes have restructured urban economies in profound ways and are the subject of **chapters 5 and 6**, although these changes weave their way throughout most of the chapters in this book.

Chapter 5 details deindustrialization in the United States and Canada that began in the 1970s and has continued for nearly forty years. Many corporations began moving out of North America to developing countries, lured by lower labor costs and tax breaks that promised higher profit margins. Starting in the 1970s but increasing during the 1980s and 1990s, in cities such as Pittsburgh, Syracuse, Buffalo, Cleveland, and Detroit, companies fired or relocated workers, closed factories, and left the region or country. These cities, many of which were located in the Northeast corridor or the Midwest, were transformed from vibrant manufacturing centers to "Rust Belt" cities of despair. This decline marked a critical shift in the North American economy, and these impacts reverberate today. Detroit, for example, was once home to both General Motors and Ford and was dubbed "Motor City" or "Motown." At its peak, Detroit was home to 1.8 million residents in 1950. Today, its population is around seven hundred thousand. During the 1980s and 1990s, drug-related violence and property crimes, along with high unemployment, gave Detroit a bad reputation as one of the most crime-ridden cities in North America. Detroit's woes have continued. Today it is estimated that about one-third of the city, some forty square miles (one hundred square kilometers), consists of vacant or abandoned structures. The current joke is that the only growing business in Detroit is demolition.

While many industrial cities have experienced a reversal of fortunes, the rise of the service sector have played critical roles in urban development in North America. Cities such as Seattle, Orlando, Miami, Phoenix, Calgary, and Vancouver have grown primarily through the expansion of the service sector. This has also helped to create new city-regions such as Atlanta, Charlotte, Dallas-Fort Worth, and Silicon Valley (between San Francisco and San Jose). These cities have grown from increased jobs in wholesale and retail trade, finance, insurance, real estate, information and communication technologies, education, and medical services. The service sector is highly diverse; some jobs offer low-level pay and include those in data entry, cleaning services, retail sales, and waitstaffing. Other jobs generate higher wages and often require graduate degrees. These include research and development, banking, medicine, law, advertising, computer engineering, and software development. Jobs in the service sector have replaced manufacturing jobs as key components of a twenty-first-century urban economy. The twin processes of deindustrialization and the growth of the service sector have fundamentally restructured the economies of North American cities.

Chapter 5 also discusses the rise of a new political-ideological apparatus: neoliberalism. Neoliberalism emphasizes deregulation, privatization, and free-market operations; it also involves a disengagement with social welfare programs such as public housing, shelters, and other social services. Recent neoliberal policies have focused on service-sector jobs as cities have fervently sought to cultivate their relocation and retention of service companies through tax subsidies and other incentives. As a result, North American cities have restructured economically and spatially—increased segregation, the rise of "parasite economies," and the refashioning of certain city areas have deepened polarization between the haves and have-nots.

Another major factor generating urban change is the link of cities to global trends, the subject of **chapter 6**. Globalization has restructured cities in numerous ways. Urban boosters, once concerned about securing and recruiting domestic firms, now focus on attracting international investment. The presence of international banks, department stores, and foreign firms provide a visual clue that most global cities bear the imprint of globalization. As a result, spatially, the most competitive and successful global cities have financial districts, luxurious residential areas, gated communities, and, of course, a nearby Starbucks (figure 1.6).

Cities in both the United States and Canada have been fortunate in that key globalization arenas have so far been concentrated in Europe, North America, and East Asia. Cities in these regions have dominated the global urban hierarchy.

Miami, Phoenix, San Diego, Los Angeles, San Francisco, Washington, DC, Toronto, and Vancouver have become key urban centers in the global economy and North American urban hierarchy. Some cities have benefited from globalization and have eclipsed their rivals. For example, many corporate headquarters have moved from Montreal to Toronto, which has become the major conduit between Canada and the international capital markets, while Calgary and Edmonton serve as crucial links to the more specialized international petroleum industry. Quebec City has also transitioned to a more diverse, postindustrial economy. The North American Free Trade Agreement of 1993 has resulted in an increase of exports from Quebec City to the United States. In addition to a fairly robust aerospace industry, tourism, information technology, and biotechnology compose some of the economic growth sectors for Quebec City. Table 1.4 lists some of the key urban North American cities in the global economy.

Figure 1.6   Ubiquitous Starbucks in Times Square, New York City. In many cities, Starbucks are found in many neighborhoods and areas, a sign of globalization. There are more than one hundred Starbucks in Manhattan. *Source:* Google Maps.

Table 1.4   US and Canadian Cities in the Global Urban Hierarchy

Top-Tier Global City	*Second-Tier Global City*	*Third-Tier Global City (often have specialized roles)*
New York	Chicago	Atlanta (international airline hub)
	Los Angeles	Miami
	Toronto	Montreal
	Vancouver	Dallas (petroleum)
		Phoenix, Seattle (information technology/ aerospace)
		San Diego
		San Francisco
		Wilmington, DE (banking)
		Washington, DC (political)
		Calgary, Edmonton (petroleum)
		Quebec City

Other cities have fallen further down in the hierarchy. Detroit, Cleveland, Buffalo, and Pittsburgh have experienced a decline as manufacturing has left the region. These cities struggle to compete for coveted global linkages and networks that promise to reinvigorate their economies. In Canada, Thunder Bay, St. John's, and Halifax contend with the challenges of an urban economy based on natural resources.

There are various articulations of the urban hierarchy. Some cities compete for financial command functions—stock markets, banks, multinational corporate headquarters, and other forms of capital exchange. New York is the most important city in this regard, followed by Chicago and Toronto. Other articulations include multicultural command centers such as Vancouver, Miami, and Los Angeles, which make important linkages to other regions via their immigrant populations. Some cities have found a niche in the hierarchy by establishing important air-route connections through the global airline network. These cities include Toronto, Los Angeles, Seattle, Memphis (home to Federal Express), Atlanta (home to United Parcel Service and Delta Airlines), and Anchorage, a stop along military and cross-Arctic air routes. Some cities are resurrecting their place in the urban hierarchy. Cleveland and Pittsburgh, which experienced economic decline and massive job losses associated with deindustrialization, have successfully realigned their economies with the global market. While some of the old industrial companies remain, revamped economies in these cities now capitalize on health-care facilities that have gained national reputations. To some extent, Cleveland and Pittsburgh have moved back up the hierarchy—albeit in more specialized roles.

The North American urban hierarchy reflects and embodies social, economic, and demographic changes associated with globalization (figure 1.7). As competition within the

Figure 1.7   Signs of globalization in Cincinnati. Throughout the Cincinnati airport, signs of sister-city relationships across the globe. This one features Taipei. (Photo by Lisa Benton-Short)

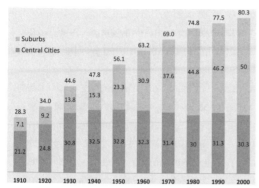

Figure 1.8 Percentage of total population living in US metropolitan areas, 1900–2000. The graph reveals that metropolitan growth is caused by population growth in the suburbs, while central cities have seen a decline in population. *Source:* US Census Bureau.

urban hierarchy continues, a city's perceived position within the hierarchy can drive local urban development.

Suburbanization, the subject of **chapter 11** documents the rise of North America as a suburban society. This process has been

both an economic and social restricting. For example, in 1950, 23 percent of the US population lived in suburbs; by 2010 more than 46 percent did. And yet the center city population has generally remained relatively fixed during this time. In 1950, for example, about 30 percent of the US population lived in city centers; in 2010 it was 36.9 percent (figure 1.8). The trend of overall metropolitan population growth while center city population has remained the same or declined has been referred to as decentralization (see table 1.5). The last decades of the twentieth century saw decentralization increase (see box 1.3).

Table 1.5   Percentage of US Population Living in Metropolitan Areas, 1950 and 2010

Year	City Center	Suburbs
1950	35%	23%
2010	36%	47%

Source: US Census.

Box 1.3 Los Angeles: Fifty Suburbs in Search of a City

Los Angeles is a city that contrasts sharply with New York. The large, sprawling city covers 498 square miles (1,290 square kilometers), has multiple business districts (e.g., Hollywood, Beverly Hills), and depends on complex, often congested networks of roads to connect the various "nuclei" of the city. The sprawl of the city, typified by concrete structures, superhighways, and low-lying residential and commercial developments (e.g., strip malls) extends north through the San Fernando Valley ("the Valley") and eastward into the "In-land Empire" of San Bernardino and Riverside Counties. Within Los Angeles County, there are some eighty-eight cities, including the City of Los Angeles, which contains about four million residents. The metropolitan region has a population of thirteen million people, and the Greater Los Angeles region has about eighteen million. Like New York, Los Angeles is also a city of extreme contrasts. Both the immense wealth of Beverly Hills and the endemic poverty and disorder of South Central Los Angeles have been fixtures in the US media and the American cultural imagination. A young, politically liberal population in the arts and entertainment sector stands in stark contrast to the Republican families (and the conspicuous consumption featured in the *Real Housewives* television show) of Orange County. Gated communities—intended to protect and contain wealth—abound in many areas. Finally, the extent and rapidity of man-made development is intermittently interrupted by the natural forces of the region: earthquakes, wildfires, and mudslides.

Today, Los Angeles is known for being a national leader in manufacturing—especially clothing and luxury goods—and a global leader in aerospace, film, and television. The city's port handles more trade with Japan, Southeast Asia, Oceania, and Latin America than any other US port, and Los Angeles International Airport is the third-busiest airport nationwide (after O'Hare in Chicago and Hartsfield in Atlanta). The strong industrial base and transportation networks situated in Los Angeles have also attracted several ancillary sectors, including tourism and conventions, federal government contract work, and medical services, including plastic surgery.

Although Los Angeles has a shorter history of international immigration than New York—most of the city's migrants were from within the United States before the 1960s—the city is one of the most diverse in the United States. More than a third of the city's population is foreign-born, with the most recent waves of immigrants coming from Latin America—particularly Mexico—and Asia. Yet the newness of immigration also poses challenges for Los Angeles. Most immigrants are not English speaking, and both Los Angeles and California have debated whether to continue integrating foreign languages (especially Spanish) into school curricula and signage or to make English the sole official language. New immigrants in the Los Angeles area also tend to be poor and experience discrimination in housing, employment, and education. While these immigrants help support the quintessentially "southern California lifestyle" by working in services ranging from gardening to dry cleaning, they often live in spatially and economically marginalized neighborhoods such as East Los Angeles and Compton.

Los Angeles is also marked by a number of environmental problems, such as traffic congestion and pollution. In this sprawling, automobile-dependent city, most residents commute, and more than seven out of ten workers drive to work alone. All of the streetcar lines in Los Angeles were closed in 1963 in favor of freeway development. Although the city reinstituted a commuter rail system in 1990, its five lines—designed mostly to transport riders from downtown Los Angeles to the surrounding suburbs—are insufficient to provide an adequate alternative to car transport. The traffic congestion, coupled with an unfavorable basin location and dry climate, has made Los Angeles the smoggiest city in the country. Although smog alerts in Los Angeles have decreased since the 1970s—when there were almost one hundred alerts per year—the National Lung Association has consistently ranked Los Angeles as the first- or second-most polluted city in the United States. Los Angeles also has insufficient water resources to support its population. Transfers of water from northern California and the Colorado River have reached their limits, and when combined with the frequent droughts, the only alternatives seem to be conservation and a turn toward the sea. In 1990, the first desalinization plant opened along the California coast. Finally, the ever-present threat of an earthquake is announced by several low-grade tremors each year. The potential for devastation is real, and emergency planning is a priority item for schools, businesses, and police.

Source: This material draws on Lisa Benton-Short and Nathaniel Lewis, "Cities of the United States and Canada," in Stanley D. Brunn, Maureen Hays-Mitchell, and Donald J. Zeigler, eds., *Cities of the World: World Regional Urban Development*, 5th ed. (Lanham: Rowman & Littlefield, 2012).

Geographer John Short has written that the story of center-city metropolitan statistical areas (MSAs) is complex. For some cities, steady decline has been the trajectory since the 1970s. Cities that have experienced steady decline include Detroit, Cleveland, Baltimore, and Pittsburgh. On the other extreme, some cities have seen a continuous increase and, along with it, land annexation, creating a larger city area. Cities such as San Jose, California, San Diego, Orlando, and Las Vegas have followed this trajectory. A third pattern has been that of interrupted growth. Cities such as New York, San Francisco, Chicago, and Seattle saw center-city population decline during the 1970s and 1980s but have experienced a return of population growth, surpassing their previous population peaks. In Atlanta, there was rapid growth from 1950 to 1970 followed by thirty years of decline before population began to experience an uptick again after 2000.

Whether center cities gained or lost population, their overall MSAs added suburban counties to their metropolitan regions since 1950. Between 2000 and 2010, for example, the Pittsburgh MSA added Armstrong County, with a population of nearly 67,000. Atlanta MSA, experiencing more dynamic growth, added eight new counties with a combined population of almost 160,000 and a total area of 2,250 square miles. These patterns show the continuous outward march of the suburban frontier.

Suburbs of North America have become sites of immense change that include continued growth (sprawl), the creation of new spatial forms (edge cities, exurbs, boomburgs), and even the rise of suburban poverty (see figure 1.9 and box 1.4). In addition, the suburbs have become much more ethnically and socioeconomically diverse than many people realize.

Figure 1.9   An exurb is often characterized by development on the urban fringe and intrusion into farmland. (Photo by Lisa Benton-Short)

Box 1.4 The Foreclosure Crisis: The Case of Stockton, California

The US housing market peaked in 2006 and began a major decline. The housing foreclosure crisis that began in 2008 has resulted in a wider economic recession. The crisis was a combination of a housing bubble, excessive homeowner debt, and subprime mortgages. An increase in loan incentives, such as easy initial terms, and a long-term trend of rising housing prices had encouraged borrowers to assume difficult mortgages in the belief they would be able to quickly refinance at more favorable terms. However, by 2007–2008 refinancing became more difficult. As adjustable-rate mortgages began to reset at higher interest rates (causing higher monthly payments), mortgage delinquencies soared. Securities backed with mortgages, including subprime mortgages, widely held by financial firms, lost most of their value.

By 2012, it was estimated that more than two trillion dollars had been lost in housing values. Foreclosures continue to impact housing values, housing sales, and the local economies of most US cities. The housing foreclosure crisis has impacted certain regions in the United States more than others. Cities in Florida, Arizona, Nevada, and California have been most impacted, although recently Illinois and Pennsylvania have seen increased foreclosures.

We can also scale down to the urban level. Many of the fastest-growing cities in 2000, such as Las Vegas, Nevada, or Charlotte, North Carolina, have seen a bust in the construction business and a plummeting of housing prices. Scaling down more, it is the suburban areas of the urban fringe that have experienced the greatest numbers of foreclosures. Many are newer, upscale exurbs and boomburgs in which houses were purchased with near-prime or subprime mortgages. (Near-prime mortgages are loans generally aimed at people with mediocre but not poor credit histories and at people who are perhaps buying more home than they can afford; subprime mortgages are aimed at those with poor credit but charge much higher interest rates.) Such loans often adjust after a couple of years and result in monthly payments that are hundreds or even thousands of dollars higher than what homeowners initially paid. Homeowners who have been paying only interest or "picking their payment" may find that in a time of declining home values, they owe more on their mortgage than their house is worth.

In addition, recent reports show that African American and Hispanic neighborhoods were hit especially hard, losing some one trillion dollars in housing values. A report by the nonpartisan Center for Responsible Lending noted that most Americans lost $21,000 in household wealth, representing 7 percent of home values; however, in minority neighborhoods, the average loss is (or will be) $37,000, or 13 percent of median home values in those neighborhoods. One reason for this is because minorities have been particularly subject to predatory lending. The foreclosure crisis affects more than just homes: communities have lost tax revenue and yet must also deal with vacant properties, increased crime, and lower school performance.

Stockton, California, is among the US cities hit hardest by the crisis. It began to boom in the early 2000s by offering lower-priced housing for those priced out of the San Francisco Bay area. New suburbs were built by the thousands. The map in figure 1.10 shows the significant impact of foreclosures and how some of the hardest-hit areas are in the outer, newer suburbs. At the height of the crisis, about one in ten houses fell to foreclosure. Houses that sold for more than $500,000 before the crash now go for $200,000. Whole neighborhoods have been decimated by the mortgage disaster. The city's tax base has shrunk. City services and municipal jobs have been cut. Unemployment hovers at about 16 percent. Economists predict it will take years for Stockton to recover from the housing bust.

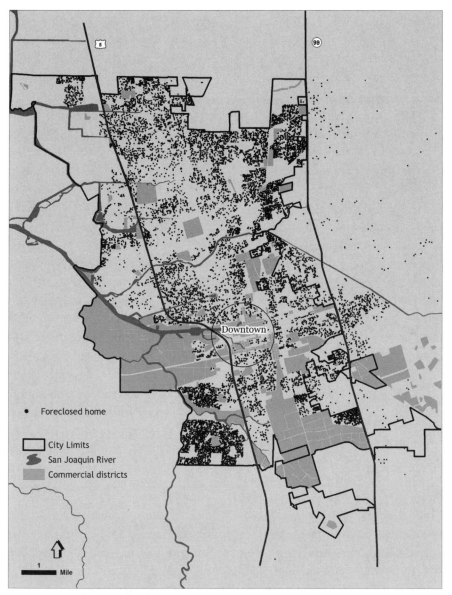

Figure 1.10   Foreclosures in Stockton, California. The map shows a heavy concentration of foreclosures in the urban fringe. *Source:* Maianna Voge, using data from ForeclosureRadar.com and the City of Stockton.

It is also important to recognize that North American cities operate within a system of networks and flows that connect some cities in profound ways. **Chapter 4**, for example, discusses the relationship between border cities in North America. The relationship between border cities such as Seattle/Vancouver, Detroit/Windsor, San Diego/Tijuana, and Nogales, Arizona/ Nogales, Sonora, is one of continual interaction. The flows of both people and goods among border cities reveal the diverse cultures that inform everyday processes in North America. While cities in Mexico are in many ways experiencing urbanization processes very differently from cities in the United States and Canada (for example, cities in Mexico are industrializing, while cities in the United States and Canada have largely experienced deindustrialization), this examination allows an appreciation of these connections and flows with the North American regional context. Although these border-city flows are often fragmented and complicated, the everyday landscapes of the border regions reinforce the interconnectedness of North American governments, economies, environments, and populations.

Political Approaches

How cities are governed and who governs them is examined in **chapter 7**. The cities of North America can be characterized by the decentralization of population and economic activity from the urban core to the suburban fringe. The globalization of the economic functions of cities, suburbs, and regions resulted in the decline of the manufacturing sector, the rise of a service economy, and demographic restructuring. These social, economic, and spatial transformations have reshaped the politics of governing local spaces. The decline of the city center and the phenomenal growth of suburbia played an important role in refocusing the question of who governs the city to who governs the suburbs—and then to who governs the region. The contemporary metropolitan area is fragmented and composed of numerous jurisdictions, including cities, towns, special districts, and planning organizations. The political fragmentation in urban regions makes it difficult to address economic development, service provision, or democratic voice at the regional level.

Chapter 8 considers the politics of planning and highlights how planning reveals struggles over land and resources, which ultimately are struggles over what the city should look like and how it should function. For this reason, planning is an intrinsically political act. This chapter also considers key trends in planning likely to influence North American cities for the next several decades. One major trend is the growing gaps in income equality between the rich and poor and how this often plays out in city services, infrastructure, and amenities. Another major trend is the increased fortification of our cities as a result of heightened security efforts. Since 9/11, many cities have added security cameras, bollards, bunkers, and barriers (see figure 1.11). This raises serious issues about mobility and public access, particularly to urban public spaces. A third major challenge is that of sustainability, a theme explored in more detail in chapter 14.

Social and Cultural Changes

North American cities have not only transformed their economies and their fortunes, they have transformed the lives of those who live in them. Economic changes have created social and cultural outcomes such as population growth, residential segregation, and increasing diversity. Demographically, socially, and culturally, cities in the United States and Canada have become highly diverse places (see box 1.5).

Figure 1.11   Watching you. This very visible police panopticon closely monitors crowds at major events such as July 4 in Washington, DC. (Photo by Lisa Benton-Short)

Box 1.5 Toronto's Diver*city*

While we tend to think of immigrants as coming from and going to countries, most immigrants go to cities. At the dawn of the twentieth century, nearly all the immigrants coming to North American cities were European. But by the 1980s and 1990s, immigrants began to arrive from all corners of the world. Because of the globalization of migration, there is a tendency for immigrants to come from a broader range of sending countries and, in the process, create cities that are more racially and ethnically diverse. Immigrants can add to a city's global competitiveness by enhancing a city's diversity and talent, thus making such places better able to compete in a global age. With birthrates declining in both Canada and the United States, migration is now a more important determinant of differential urban growth (or decline).

While it is true that immigration is a global phenomenon, it is also true that some regions of the world receive significantly more immigrants than others. North America, long an established region of immigrant settlement, is among the highest. Although the three largest immigrant destinations in the region are New York City, Toronto, and Los Angeles, sixty other metropolitan regions have more than one hundred thousand foreign-born residents. In Canada, nearly 75 percent of all immigrants primarily go to one of three cities: Vancouver, Montreal, and Toronto. But smaller Canadian cities such as Ottawa and Calgary are places where well over 20 percent of the population is foreign-born. Similarly, in the United States, immigrants are targeting newer gateways such as Washington, DC, Phoenix, Charlotte, and Atlanta, where the relative increase in the foreign-born population is much higher than in traditional gateways.

Yet crude measurements of the foreign-born in urban North America tell us little about the composition or distribution of the foreign-born within cities. Some cities are home to a "hyperdiverse" foreign-born population, and others are home to a large number of foreign-born but are not particularly diverse. Two of the most hyperdiverse cities in the world are New York and Toronto, home to millions of foreign-born that come from every region of the world. As North American immigrant destinations go, Toronto is often overshadowed by the dominance of New York City. Yet Toronto's percentage of almost 50 percent foreign-born actually far exceeds New York City's, and, according to some measures, Toronto is more diverse. Toronto's proportion of immigrants is more than twice as high as Canada's national average and is higher than any US city.

Between 2000 and 2010, estimates were that Toronto saw an influx of some 55,000 new immigrants each year. From Armenian to Urdu, more than 140 languages and dialects are spoken in the city. Today almost 50 percent of the city's population is foreign-born, one of the highest percentages for any major metropolitan area. No one group dominates Toronto's immigrant stock. As the major destination city for new immigrants to Canada, Toronto also has a large black population arriving from both the Caribbean and Africa, which distinguishes it from other Canadian cities. While Toronto's immigrant population is concentrated in the urbanized part of the Census Metropolitan Area, it is not evenly distributed. Affluent neighborhoods in the heart of Toronto and along the prestigious waterfront areas have a smaller proportion of immigrants, especially immigrants of color. Figure 1.12 is a map of Sri Lankans in metropolitan Toronto, clustering in some neighborhoods in the eastern part of the city. Settlement patterns before 1980 saw immigrants living in "traditional immigrant neighborhoods" or enclaves, such as Chinatowns or Little Italies. However, recent immigrants tend to settle in the suburbs, often dispersing. Immigrants from Hong Kong and Taiwan, for example, have settled directly in the outer suburbs, whereas immigrants from Sri Lanka and Vietnam have settled in preexisting inner-city ethnic enclaves or in the inner-ring suburbs.

The increasing diversity led to the Canadian government officially endorsing multiculturalism as a policy that celebrates diversity while treating all people equally, regardless of race or ethnicity. Toronto is heralded as one of the most multicultural cities in the world, and it trumpets its rich and varied cultural mosaic. In 1998, the City of Toronto adopted the motto "Diversity Our Strength" (figure 1.13).

However, this diversity has created obstacles and challenges, and some immigrants find themselves increasingly excluded from the larger Toronto society and economy. Research by Canadian geographer Lucia Lo has shown that the city has experienced an increase in racial inequality, neighborhood poverty, and increasing segregation and alienation among some immigrants. She says that while Toronto's cultural diversity makes it a vibrant and exciting place, that same diversity has helped produce a bifurcated labor pool with visible-minority immigrants serving subordinate roles. Ironically, immigrant poverty among city prosperity has actually strengthened Toronto's role in the global urban hierarchy.

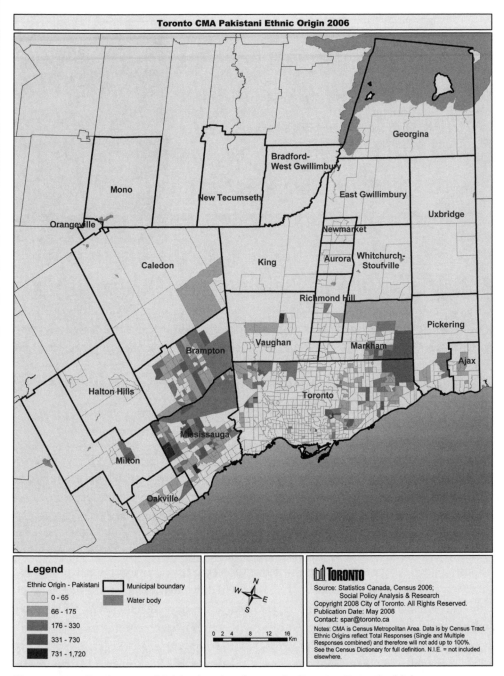

Figure 1.12   Settlement of Sri Lankan immigrants in Toronto. Note the high concentrations in the eastern-area neighborhoods of Rouge, Malvern, and Highland Creek. *Source:* Map by Census Canada, 2006.

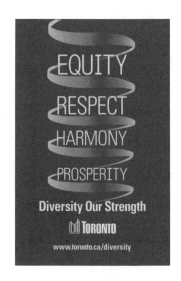

Figure 1.13 The city of Toronto has adopted the motto "Diversity Our Strength" in order to promote equity and intercultural understanding among its diverse residents. *Source:* City of Toronto.

Chapters 9 and 10 explore contemporary social and cultural challenges, including issues of inequality, homelessness, gender, and race. **Chapter 9** explores the concepts of difference and inequality in cities. Contrasts between wealth and poverty, between those who are successful and those who struggle, often invisibly offer a more polarized view of the urban landscape. This chapter looks at some of the social and economic processes that have produced inequality in North American cities. For example, land use, explored initially in the chapter on urban planning, contributes to inequality, as do government policies regarding public housing. The focus on segregation and housing provides the lens through which inequality is explored in finer detail.

Urban geographers, along with cultural geographers, have demonstrated that identities such as male and female—as well as white, black, gay, straight, and others—not only precipitate very different experiences of the city but are themselves *constructed* through the dominant discourses and narratives of media, institutions, and day-to-day social interactions. The recent emergence of downtown food trucks, shown in figure 1.14, attests to

such growing diversity. Identity is not just something associated with cities or their residents but something that is actively shaped, reshaped, and inscribed in processes of urban development. These ideas are explored in **chapter 10.**

The Urban Environment

In many urban textbooks, the city has been treated as only a social or economic phenomenon, and the natural environment has largely been ignored. Yet every city is part of a natural ecosystem and is subject to environmental constraints and opportunities. At the same time, environmental processes are filtered through social arrangements of political and economic differences. Cities also face different environmental challenges based on site. For example, Las Vegas, a city located in the desert, has been shaped by the desert but also continues to impact it. Despite its desert location, Las Vegas extravagantly displays water in lakes, water fountains, and water shows that belie this truth. The building of the Hoover Dam brought cheap water to Vegas and allowed the city to grow. Las Vegas is a

Figure 1.14　A relatively recent sight in many North American cities are these food trucks, often featuring ethnic cuisine. This food truck serves Lebanese food. Patrons can use online apps to find the closest truck. (Photo by Lisa Benton-Short)

desert city with the highest per capita water consumption in the United States, at just over four hundred gallons per person, in defiance of its desert setting. Similarly, New Orleans has been shaped—both literally and figuratively—by water. The flow of the Mississippi River and the city's low-lying location has subjected the city to floods throughout its history. The city responded to floods by trying to out-engineer the physical environment by designing a system of levees and pumping stations and trying to channel the river. The problem is that that the river is dynamic: it will shift its position over and over, and while engineers might take flood prevention measures, they will never be able to control nature. Annapolis, Maryland, has also been shaped by its relationship to water, celebrating its long history as home to the US Naval Academy (see figure 1.15).

The last three chapters, chapters 12, 13, and 14, discuss the visible connection between nature and the city. **Chapter 12** examines the role of the city as an ecosystem with inputs of energy, water, and food and outputs of noise, climate change, sewage, garbage, and air pollutants. The chapter focuses on the impact of human activity on the natural system and looks at four key areas of pollution: land (in the form of brownfields), water, air, and climate. The chapter explores the sources of pollution, how pollution is manifested in the city, and how policy makers and planners are seeking to address the challenges. How cities deal with pollution today sets the broader context for understanding how cities perceive the need to respond to risk and vulnerability and to plan for long-term sustainability.

Chapter 13 examines one of the most visible connections between cities and their natural environment: hazards and disasters. In the twenty-first century, North American cities are susceptible to many environmental hazards, including droughts, floods, heat waves, earthquakes, ice storms, and volcanic eruptions. At first glance, many "natural

Figure 1.15   Annapolis, which is also home to the US Naval Academy, is defined by its relationship to water and its Chesapeake Bay location. (Photo by Lisa Benton-Short)

disasters" in cities seem like a force of nature. But these events have impacts and effects that were mediated through the prism of socioeconomic power structures and arrangements. While there are certainly physical forces that can wreak havoc on our cities, disasters are first and foremost social experiences that often affect the poor more than the rich and reveal economic inequality, social injustice, and poor planning efforts.

We end on an optimistic note in **chapter 14**, which looks at how cities are planning for a more sustainable future. Sustainability is not just about living our lives in a way that is more environmentally benign. It is about a new way of seeing the world and our place in it. This new concept involves taking advantage of new economic opportunities and, equally important, ensuring that environmental and economic benefits are distributed equitably among all citizens. Urban sustainability is organized into "three e's"—environment, economy, and equity. Cities, especially those that are densely settled, permit us to utilize resources more efficiently, generate economic activity more effectively, and enjoy healthy, meaningful lives.

CONCEPTS AND DEFINITIONS

Studying cities requires an understanding of concepts and definitions commonly used in urban geography. The following are some critical concepts and definitions in contemporary urban geography.

Center city: The central business district or, more colloquially, the "downtown."

City: A political designation that refers to a large, densely populated place that is legally incorporated as a municipality. Today, we use the term "urban area" as it better describes the spatial forms of the twenty-first century.

Deindustrialization: The decline in industrial activity and jobs in a city or economy.

Gentrification: The restoration of run-down urban areas by the middle class, resulting in the displacement of low-income residents.

Urban area: As cities have expanded, the boundary between urban and rural is less distinct. In both the United States and Canada, automobile transportation has allowed suburbanization and sprawl. The urban area thus includes the city and its suburbs.

Urbanism: A broad concept that is the result of urbanization. It refers to all aspects—political, economic, social, and environmental—of the urban way of life. It suggests that living in urban areas is a different way of life than living in rural areas.

Urbanization: The complex processes of urban growth in demographic, social, political, behavioral, and economic terms. In the United States and Canada, urbanization growth rates are relatively low, at 1.2 percent annually, compared with rates of countries undergoing significant annual urban population growth of 2 or 3 percent. At the same time, US and Canadian society is highly urbanized.

Megacity: A city with a population of at least ten million. Megacities are magnets for people, business, and organizations, and they consume vast amounts of resources such as water and food. They are not merely cities of a large size; they are a new, distinctive spatial form of social organization, economic production, and political governance.

Metropolitan area: A metropolitan area includes a center city plus all surrounding territory (urban and rural) that is somehow integrated into the urban core. This is usually measured by commuting patterns. In other words, a metropolitan area consists of a substantial population nucleus surrounded by adjacent counties that have significant commuting linkages. This implies that not all the land is built up; rather, a metropolitan area has a mixture of open and built-up land on the periphery. In the United States, the term "Metropolitan Statistical Area" (MSA) is the official moniker designated by the US Bureau of the Census and is defined as an area that has an urban core of at least fifty thousand people and includes surrounding urban and rural territory that is socially and economically integrated with the core. Generally, MSAs can be divided into central cities and suburbs. In Canada, the official term is "Census Metropolitan Areas" (CMAs), which must have an urban core of at least one hundred thousand people. This means that the United States and Canada have different definitions of what a metropolitan area is. To complicate matters, the US Bureau of the Census has been designating metropolitan areas since 1950, but the criteria and types have changed over time. Since the 2010 census, however, the US census distinguishes between two types of urban areas (see figure 1.16):

- Urbanized areas (UAs) of fifty thousand or more people; and
- Urban clusters (UCs) of at least 2,500 but less than 50,000 people.

These are important geographies because, unlike metropolitan areas or incorporated cities, they are based on the results of the census. They are not arbitrary lines on the map but a description of the facts on the ground. According to the 2010 census, there are 486 urbanized areas in the United States

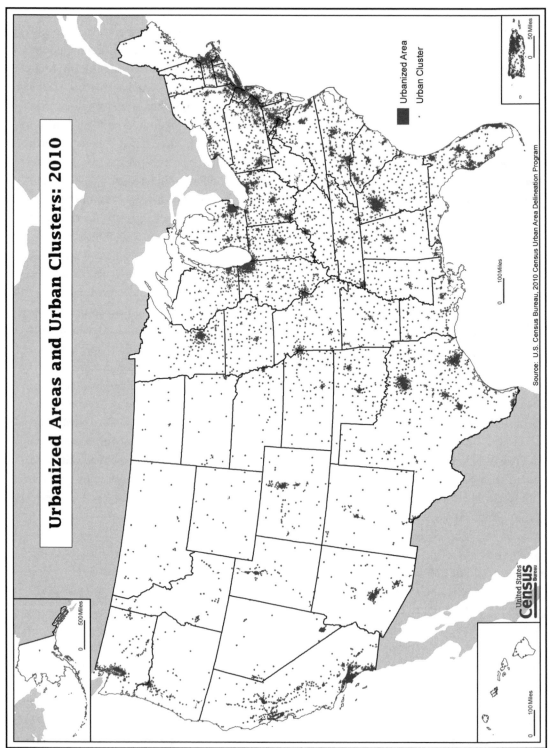

Figure 1.16 This map shows the urbanized areas and urban clusters in 2010. *Source:* US Census Bureau.

and 11 urbanized areas in Puerto Rico, for a total of 497 urbanized areas. A total of 71 percent of the US population today lives in an urbanized area. The census also counted 3,087 urban clusters.

Urban landscapes: The manifestations of the thoughts, deeds, and actions of human beings. They offer "clues" to the economic, cultural, and political values of the societies that built them. Geographers have looked at city skylines, architectural styles, signage, graffiti, street activities, and public spaces as ways to interpret, analyze, and critique the values of those who built the landscape.

Urban regions: One spatial outcome of twentieth-century urbanization in North America has been the emergence of large city-regions. The largest one in the United States is the urbanized Northeastern Seaboard, a region named Megalopolis by geographer Jean Gottmann in the 1950s. Megalopolis stretches from south of Washington, DC, north through Baltimore, Philadelphia, and New York, and north to Boston (see figure 1.17). This region is responsible for 20 percent of the nation's gross domestic product. In 1950, Megalopolis had a population of almost thirty-two million people; by 2010, it had increased to almost fifty million, about 15 percent, or almost one in six, of the US population. Today, Megalopolis consists of 52,300 square miles stretching across twelve states, the District of Columbia, and 124 counties. The dynamics of Megalopolis are interesting and complex; compared with earlier decades, the distribution in 2010 of center-city to suburban population seems more stable as years of rapid suburban growth and center-city decline have been replaced by more varied patterns of growth. Cities such as New York and Washington, DC, have enjoyed rising center-city populations, but Baltimore

Figure 1.17   The cities and counties of contemporary Megalopolis. *Source:* Map courtesy of John Rennie Short.

has continued to lose population. Suburbs such as Camden, New Jersey, have seen rising levels of poverty and deteriorating housing, while Chevy Chase, Maryland, saw its median household income increase from 2000 to 2010.

In addition to the obvious demographic significance, Megalopolis reminds us of the environmental impact of such population growth: more people, more suburban development and loss of farm land, and more people driving cars, running dishwashers, flushing toilets, running showers, and living in bigger houses. It is estimated that Megalopolis generates approximately one hundred thousand tons of garbage each day.

North American megalopolitan regions are defined as clustered networks of metropolitan regions that have at least ten million. Geographically, they comprise at least two contiguous metropolitan areas, which include city centers and their surrounding suburbs. In North America, there are eleven megalopolitan regions (see table 1.6). Collectively, the megalopolitan regions constitute

Table 1.6   Megalopolitan Areas of the United States and Canada

Area	Anchor Cities
Cascadia	Vancouver, Seattle, Portland, Eugene
NorCal	San Francisco, San Jose, Oakland, Sacramento
Southland	Los Angeles, San Diego, Las Vegas
Valley of the Sun	Phoenix, Tucson
I-35 Corridor	Kansas City, Oklahoma City, Dallas, San Antonio
Gulf Coast	Houston, New Orleans, Mobile
Piedmont	Birmingham, Atlanta, Charlotte, Raleigh
Peninsula	Tampa, Miami, Orlando
Midwest	Chicago, Madison, Detroit, Indianapolis, Cincinnati
Northeast	Richmond, Washington, DC, Philadelphia, New York, Boston
Main Street	Windsor, Toronto, Montreal, Quebec City

Source: Adapted from the Metropolitan Institute at Virginia Tech University.

only 20 percent of the nation's land surface yet comprise 67 percent of the population. On a smaller population scale, geographer Stanley Brunn has identified numerous urban regions in the United States (see figure 1.18).

Global city-regions: Cities in the United States and Canada have been shaped by the intensification of economic globalization and heightened competition in the global urban hierarchy. Another term to describe the ways that

Figure 1.18   Possible urban regions in 2050. *Source:* Stanley D. Brunn, Maureen Hays-Mitchell, and Donald J. Zeigler, eds., *Cities of the World: World Regional Urban Development*, 5th ed. (Lanham: Rowman & Littlefield, 2012).

globalization is transforming cities in North America into a new type of urban form is the global city-region. Global investment, information technology, and widespread corporate and personal mobility have transformed North American cities. Increasingly, many function as the nodes of the global economy and play leading roles in finance, investment, tourism, and culture. Los Angeles, San Diego, Seattle, Vancouver, New York, and Toronto are making a transition from national or regional economic capitals to more integrated cities of the world. Global city-regions feature the socioeconomic elite, globally oriented locations that contrast sharply with more insular cities.

Sustainability: The most widely accepted definition of sustainability is the 1987 Brundtland Report, which stated, "Sustainable development is development that meets the needs of the present without compromising the ability of future generations to meet their own needs." Seen as the guiding principle for long-term global development, sustainability consists of three pillars: economic development, social development, and environmental protection. These are often referred to as the "three e's"—economy, ecology, and equity. Sustainability has been applied in the urban context. Herbert Girardet, for example, defines a sustainable city as "a city that works so well that all its citizen are able to meet their own needs without endangering the well-being of the natural world or the living conditions of other people, now or in the future."

SUGGESTED READINGS

Anisef, P., and M. Lanphier, eds. 2003. *The World in a City*. Toronto: University of Toronto Press.

Auch, R., J. Taylor, and W. Acevdeo. 2004. *Urban Growth in American Cities*. US Geological Survey, Circular 1252. Denver: US Geological Survey, EROS Data Center. *This book is a visual feast showing urban transformations over several decades. Cities profiled include one image from the 1970s and one image from the 1990s.*

Berry, B. J., and J. O. Wheeler, eds. 2005. *Urban Geography in America, 1950–2000: Paradigms and Personalities*. New York: Routledge.

Blais, P. 2010. *Perverse Cities: Hidden Subsidies, Wonky Policy, and Urban Sprawl*. Vancouver: UBC Press.

Florida, R. 2005. *The Flight of the Creative Class: The New Global Competition for Talent*. New York: Harper Business.

Fogelson, R. M. 2003. *Downtown: Its Rise and Fall*. New Haven: Yale University Press.

Glaeser, E. L. 2011. *The Triumph of the City*. New York: Routledge.

Gottman, J. 1961. *Megalopolis: Urbanization of the Northeastern Seaboard of the United States*. New York: Twentieth Century Fund.

Greenberg, M. 2008. *Branding New York: How a City in Crisis Was Sold to the World*. New York: Routledge.

Hanlon, B., J. R. Short, and T. Vicino. 2010. *Cities and Suburbs: New Metropolitan Realities in the US*. New York: Routledge.

Harvey, D. 1989. *The Urban Experience*. Baltimore, MD: Johns Hopkins University Press.

Jacobs, J. 1969. *The Economy of Cities*. New York: Random House.

Kahn, M. 2006. *Green Cities: Urban Growth and the Environment*. Washington, DC: Brookings Institution Press.

Knox, P. 2011. *Cities and Design*. New York: Routledge.

Mumford, L. 1989 [1968]. *The City in History*. Orlando, FL: Harcourt.

Power, A., J. Ploger, and A. Winkler. 2010. *Phoenix Cities: The Fall and Rise of Great Industrial Cities*. Bristol: Policy Press.

Sassen, S. 2001. *The Global City: New York, London, Tokyo*. 2nd ed. Princeton, NJ: Princeton University Press.

Vale, L. J., and T. J. Campanella, eds. 2005. *The Resilient City: How Modern Cities Recover from Disasters*. New York: Oxford University Press.

Venkatesh, S. A. 2006. *Off the Books: The Underground Economy of the Urban Poor*. Cambridge, MA: Harvard University Press.

CITIES ON THE WEB

City Population, www.citypopulation.de: presents population statistics and maps for cities around the world.

GaWC—Globalization and World Cities, www.lboro.ac.uk/gawc/: includes numerous scholarly studies, data presentations, and an inventory of "world cities."

Planetizen, http://www.planetizen.com: is a website and public-interest information exchange for the urban planning and development community. Its weekly newsletter highlights newspaper articles on cities and urban issues from around the world.

Statistics Canada, www.stancan.gc.ca: data on towns and cities in Canada can be found here; however, urban-level data for the 2011 census will not be released until 2013.

US Bureau of the Census, www.census.gov/: data on towns and cities in the United States can be found here; urban-level data released as of June 2012.

2

Changing Approaches to Urban Geography
KATIE WELLS

One recent summer night, I found myself lost driving around a neighborhood in Washington, DC. The new city map I had purchased from Barnes and Noble did not turn out to be much help. It did not include my intersection or, as I slowly realized, a large swath of the city. What was wrong with this map? The map, it turns out, was not defective—just selective. Like nine free maps that I subsequently gathered from hotels and the tourism industry (i.e., the Convention and Visitors Bureau), the map I had purchased excluded without explanation particular areas of the city. Not one of the free maps advertised itself as a partial, selective, or incomplete representation of Washington, DC (see figure 2.1). As I dug deeper, I found a correlation between the presence of pervasive poverty and the areas excluded from the tourist and visitor maps. Tourist maps, as geographers Laura Pulido, Wendy Cheng, and Laura Barraclough have demonstrated, typically reproduce hegemonic views of cities. As a corrective, Pulido and colleagues compiled *A People's Guide to Los Angeles*, which highlights the forgotten and marginalized stories of Los Angeles—especially stories from the viewpoint of minorities. This alternative history exposes the power imbued in tourist guides and pushes for challenges to the status quo in travel-oriented publications.

What I experienced in Washington, DC, was not an anomaly. As all representations do, the maps of Washington, DC, helped to shape how and where visitors traveled, giving value to certain areas of the city through inclusion and dismissing others through omission.

REPRESENTING "THE URBAN" IN POWERFUL WAYS

Theories are like maps in this way. They highlight certain ideas and hide others. Theories about the city give prominence to certain aspects of the built environment, social relations, or economic processes while minimizing the relevancy of other elements. Just as a traveler must be careful about whose map of the city she uses as a guide, so, too, must urban geographers be careful about whose approach to the city they integrate into their studies. It matters in important ways how we describe what's happening in the city. Geographical language and categories are descriptive, but they are also representative. Geographical writings and representations carry powerful currencies about how the world is organized and how it should be organized. A description of poverty as inevitable rather than natural shapes whether we see poverty as something

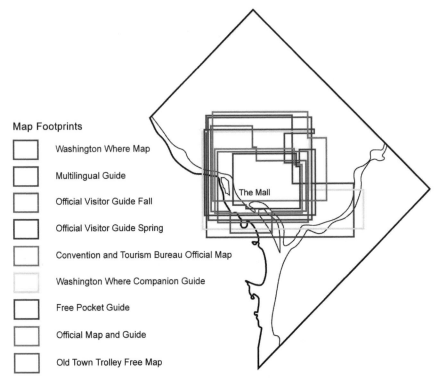

Figure 2.1   Washington, DC, map footprints. Different interest groups offer various interpretations of the National Mall and the monument core of Washington, DC. *Source:* Map by Kathryn Wells.

that necessitates intervention or something that should be left alone. Representations, which can come in visual (i.e., maps) or textual (i.e., theories) forms, have serious implications for the way we understand problems and imagine solutions.

Even movies convey powerful images about cities. Think of *Crash, Blade Runner, Chinatown, American Beauty, City of God, Boondock Saints, Lost in Translation,* and *Annie Hall.* Each of these movies, which reflect social perceptions, portrays the city in a different light and to a different effect. These representations in popular culture are no different from theoretical ones in academia. Films—whether they take place in suburbia, downtown centers, or the countryside—shape our understanding about how places exist and

function. This textbook, too, is a selective and political representation of knowledge about the city. A quick scan of the first few pages of other urban geography textbooks at the library can reveal a host of differences among which topics authors include and exclude. A comparison of tables of contents can suggest which aspects of urban geography get privileged. This textbook, for instance, includes a section on the relationship between cities and their physical environment, something atypical of most urban textbooks. But these inclusions, of course, come at another topic's expense. The task for urban geographers, like the readers of this book, is to sift through the array of ideas presented in any study, conversation, or representation about urban and non-urban processes with an awareness of the boundaries that are drawn, the histories, characters, and places that are excluded, and the power that is mobilized.

WHAT IS THE CITY?

The way urban geographers talk about cities and study cities has changed significantly over time. These changes, however, are not only a result of changes in the structure of buildings, transit systems, and technologies. Transformations in the beliefs, norms, and politics of urban scholars have affected how cities have come to be understood and imagined. What one researcher finds important about a certain place or event may be quite different from what someone else thinks is the foundational basis of social life. As a result, definitions of what constitutes "the city" or "the urban" vary dramatically across time, space, and social conditions. These differences in what "the city" is are the outcome of periodic reactions and revolutions—theories about the city do not form a straightforward story of linear evolution. What "the city" is and what counts as a legitimate subject of study about "the city" have been contested for more than 150 years, and no one expects these issues to be resolved anytime soon. Knowledge about cities, like any subject matter, is a work in progress. This history of approaches to urban geography reveals that some of the ideas about cities have been debated at length, while others have been swiftly relegated to the sidelines.

That the category of "the city" has been used to signal so many different factors and forces does not mean that the category itself is useless. On the contrary, the subdiscipline of urban geography encompasses a swath of diverse, relevant, and important inquiries

into many of North America's most pressing social issues. That the category of "the city" shifts so much means simply that we need to be attentive to the context in which it is being invoked and to the ideas it excludes. How the category is used—what it represents and what it excludes—offers important insights into the assumptions, priorities, politics, and methods of research projects. Geographers today are interested in not only studying what cities are, how they function, and what they mean but how and from where *ideas* about the city actually come to be.

RESPONSES TO URBAN INDUSTRIALIZATION

During the second half of the nineteenth century, horrific images of the industrializing cities of England set the stage for almost a hundred years' worth of middle-class revulsion and academic unease about the city in North America. The work of journalists, reporters, novelists, and researchers such as Frederick Engels and Charles Booth depicted the manufacturing hubs of the Industrial Revolution, such as London and Manchester, as breeding grounds for disease, disorder, and a host of social ills. Factories replaced agriculture as the dominant economic activity at record speeds. Alexis de Tocqueville in 1835 described the effects of this seemingly overnight economic transformation: "From this foul drain the greatest stream of industry flows out to fertilize the whole world." Newly industrializing cities like Manchester became known as "shock cities" because of their rapid population growth and impacts on sanitation, health, and housing. While watching such rapid industrialization and urbanization unfold in the nineteenth century, Karl Marx and Frederick Engels created some of the earliest urban theories. They argued that the modern city and all of its new class formations were intimately connected to the new capitalist mode of production. Though Manchester's rapid transformation was atypical of changes occurring in other cities at the time, the dominant narrative held that cities had been turned into places of danger and chaos. The notion that cities need to be sanitized and *ordered* was an idea that prevailed in western Europe and North America. The landscape of Paris, for instance, was redesigned by planners at the end of the nineteenth century to create a more orderly society. Small streets were replaced by wide boulevards, which were thought to limit the possibility of revolutionary acts and to make city life run more efficiently. In the United States, the City Beautiful movement brought these massive changes to the urban landscape under the belief that orderly cities with—literally—beautiful architecture would breed healthy, productive, and moral communities. The path of Philadelphia's Ben Franklin Parkway, for instance, cut through dense working-class neighborhoods under the guise of this Beaux-Arts way of thinking.

THE CHICAGO SCHOOL

The idea that the city, if left to its own devices, would breed mayhem was challenged at the beginning of the twentieth century by a group of scholars whose studies of the city, more than any other, established urban scholarship as a distinct field. These scholars from the University of Chicago's sociology department believed that underlying urban space were a set of laws, principles, and patterns that gave a city its uneven and, to them, exotic texture. The city had its own kind of order, even if it was an undesirable one, and the city's chaos was, upon closer examination, actually logical. At the time, Chicago was undergoing massive change. Industrialization had stimulated rapid population growth and significant immigration. The University of Chicago sociologists, the majority of whom had small-town or rural backgrounds, were fascinated by these changes and sought to create a coherent theory about the dynamics of their new industrial city.

These sociologists were not interested in simply describing the physical site of Chicago or charting its growth in phases. These scholars pushed against traditional studies of places and expanded the notions of what *is* the city and what exactly constitutes urban studies. In one of their most widely cited writings from the 1920s, sociologists Robert Park, Ernest Burgess, and Roderick McKenzie broadly defined the city as "a state of mind" rather than as a narrow, physical entity or political jurisdiction with distinct boundaries. By taking this approach, they expanded the scope of social inquiry to include culture, neighborhood organization, crime patterns, and other aspects of social life. They sought to uncover the sustenance of relationships and encounters among people in a city. They were trying to define the traits that made a city like Chicago what it was. What can largely be seen as a reflection of their rural backgrounds was their belief that social life in a city is fundamentally different from that in other places. It was a place of isolation, detachment, anonymity, and social distance, whereas the countryside was home to another kind of kinship and another set of (better) social relations. Louis Wirth, a researcher at the Chicago School, referred to this new and "modern" way of life, which he contrasted against the supposedly more traditional relationships of rural settings, as *urbanism.* Through detailed case studies and extensive fieldwork, Wirth and others documented the disastrous effects of urban life, specifically the experience of mobility on European and African American immigrants. The city, to Wirth, was flooded with crime, disease, and erratic human behavior that did not resemble anything like his conception of a good, moral, and functional society.

As a result of this focus on the so-called breakdown of social relationships in the city, the Chicago School developed a strong set of ideas about how the urban environment shaped human behavior. Their concepts about everyday life, decisions, and practices contrasted with popular ideas that put the root cause of racial conflicts in cities in biological differences rather than social contexts. The Chicago School stressed instead that racial differences were mental differences of identity and consciousness and that the urban environment could directly affect the identity and consciousness of individuals. It is important to note that their understanding of the link between the urban environment and human behavior can be diagrammed as a one-way arrow: environment → human behavior.

At the same time as the Chicago sociologists sought to expand the definition of the city, they tried to bring legitimacy to their work as a "real" science. They embraced some of the investigative tools used by the hard sciences (e.g., biology, chemistry, and ecology). Their goal was to make sociology a subject that others would see as objective and rigorous. Inspired by Darwin's recent theories about evolution, they adopted ecologists'

language of invasion and succession for their social inquiry into the "natural" evolution of cities, using terms such as "immigrant invasions" to describe the changing urban demography. The city became, in their eyes, a living, evolving organism subject to decay and growth just like any other plant or animal that may have bouts of disease or episodes of good health. Similarly, like organisms that obey biological patterns and principles, the city was understood to be undergirded by a set of unseen laws.

This ecological turn resulted in two developments of note. First, the tradition of urban ecology produced a narrative of linear urban change that would become the prototype for urban theory in North America. Second, a series of models that had been created at the University of Chicago and that promised to reveal the relationship between industrialization and individual human behavior were widely adopted by other urban scholars. The most well known of these models, the concentric circles model of the 1920s (figure 2.2) and the sector model of the 1930s—discussed in the previous chapter—mapped the city as a commercial core surrounded by rings or sectors of distinct spaces that had homogenous purposes (e.g., a ring of industry is separate from a ring of working-class housing). Figure 2.3 is a view of Chicago from the air, showing the downtown core surrounded by lower-density neighborhoods. Unfortunately, these models hid more than they revealed about the complexity of forces that shape cities and the differences that exist within and among cities. Despite the fact that models have weaknesses, they remain a fundamental part of the history of urban geography and continue to explain some land-use decisions in cities. The Chicago School influenced a generation (or two)

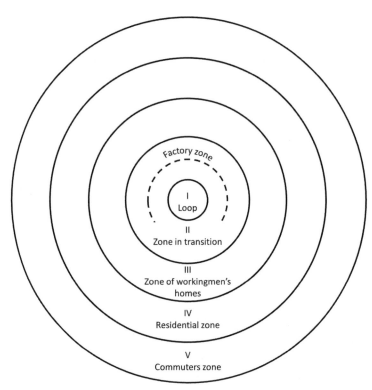

Figure 2.2   The concentric zone model from Ernest Burgess and the Chicago School. *Source:* Created by the George Washington University Department of Geography.

Figure 2.3   A view of Chicago from the air. *Source:* Wikimedia.

as they were the products of a well-funded, increasingly decorated academic department with a brood of young graduate students who took the traditions of the Chicago School to urban research programs across the country.

ACTION-ORIENTED RESEARCH

While the ideas of the Chicago School circulated far beyond Chicago, another set of ideas about cities failed to gain as much traction with academics and planners. At the turn of the twentieth century, Jane Addams, a social activist and the founder of the settlement house movement in the United States, was also trying to theorize what was happening in Chicago and make a plan for how to respond. Her ideas combined urban investigation with direct social reform. Inspired by settlement houses in London in the 1880s, Addams opened the Hull House in Chicago in 1889 as a way to help immigrants improve their living and working conditions and become US citizens. Whereas the Chicago School saw the city as a place of delinquency and vice, Addams saw the promise of a more equal, democratic society with welfare for all. Her reports and campaigns, which would form the basis of almost all US housing-reform legislation in the early twentieth century, were based on research undertaken within communities and *with* settlement-house residents. Unlike the Chicago School, who analyzed the city through a distanced, sociological eye, Addams immersed herself in the city and its people. As a progressive, she was convinced that democracy could thrive even in terrible conditions. The city was not a laboratory but a place where people actually lived and could live better. The problems of the city were caused by capitalism and its inherent inequality—not

problems of city life itself. Addams, along with Jacob Riis, who drew attention to the poor in his dramatic photographs, continued to advocate for urban reform. The conservative Chicago School had little patience for this kind of utopian vision of the city. Although they were well aware of Addams's work, the male sociology faculty dismissed her research and her call for social reforms, arguing that sociological theory should not be connected to the "feminine" practices of social work. To this day, the fields of urban geography and sociology remain plagued by a lack of convergence between urban theory and urban practice.

THE QUANTITATIVE REVOLUTION

By the mid-twentieth century, the Quantitative Revolution aimed to bring "scientific thinking" to geography, marking a dramatic change in methods and approaches. The Quantitative Revolution was not just restricted to geography but affected social-science fields from political science to sociology. In general, it involved the use of quantitative, statistical, or mathematical analysis to explain social phenomena. Some of the techniques adopted included political modeling and basic remote sensing, which relied on the use of new devices called computers. The Quantitative Revolution had its biggest impact in the subfields of economic and urban geography and their focus on land use, land values, and utility maximization. To these researchers, the city was described as a machine, while human behavior was discussed as something that could be reduced to rational decisions. This approach set the stage for a countermovement in the second half of the twentieth century: increasing attention to human agency, geographic difference, and power relations.

THE REVIVAL OF MARXIST THEORY

Beginning in the 1970s and largely in response to the quantitative approach, urban
scholars embraced questions about the complexity of human lives and urban space; the
growing problems of poverty, inequality, and
debt in postcolonial cities; and the relevancy
of the geographic discipline in general. Such
questions did not lend themselves as well to
quantitative analysis. Urban scholars turned
toward examinations of how urban patterns
were produced through the constraints of
broad social, political, and economic structures and the action and agency (i.e., will) of
individuals. It was these examinations about
where the line between structure and agency
should be drawn that occupied much of urban
geography's research agenda for the second
half of the twentieth century.

A new tradition of Marxist geography
took up questions about structure and agency
with gusto. The city, according to so-called
Neo-Marxians, was structured most by the
dominant mode of production and reproduction in society, which in North America
is capitalism. David Harvey, one of geography's most influential scholars, argued that
Marx's writings were more pertinent than
ever to an understanding of the contemporary
city. He made the case that cycles of urban
development were best understood through
economic restructuring and the cyclical crises
inherent to capitalism. The city was a built
form, and this built form reflected the social
form. The way of living in a city was not
something unique to cities but a reflection of
broader social, political, and economic processes. To Harvey, urbanism was the social
form of a particular historical epoch (i.e., advanced capitalism)—not an attribute of cities

themselves. The idea of the city as a product
of capitalism was markedly different from
that of the Chicago School, who saw life in
a city as distinct from other (better) ways of
being and not directly connected to economic
processes. Other Marxists, such as Manuel
Castells, pushed for geographers to abandon
Chicago School–like attempts to fetishize a
place and think instead about the qualities
and processes that produce the urban phenomenon in the first place. In Castells's eyes,
what happened in a city and how a city was
organized were less products of urbanization
than of capitalism. The city had been held
captive by capitalism and was not necessarily
a rotten phenomenon in and of itself. Social
alienation in cities, in other words, was tied
to political economy—not urbanization. This
view of the city echoed that of Jane Addams
and her notion that the way a city was, *was not*
the way it had to be.

Urban political economy approaches examine the ongoing tension between capitalism
and the city (i.e., does the city threaten capitalism, or is the city essential to capitalism's working?) and find opportunities to restructure and
even conquer this dominant mode of social
and spatial organization. The city was a material realization (or concrete manifestation) of
capitalism, and so the history of the city could
not be separated from the history of capitalist
production. From this perspective, the proliferation of cities in the industrial age occurred in
large part because cities were where (and still
are where) surplus concentrations of capital
and money are put to use to make more investments and profits. Similarly, gentrification and
the reinvestment of capital in the urban built
environment in the twentieth century were
symptoms of the decline in the manufacturing industry and the increasingly globalized,

service-based economy. As capital sought the highest rate of profit, it flowed into some areas and out of others. Therefore, the unevenness between and within places is an inevitable outcome of capitalism—not some disequilibrium that can eventually be returned to a natural and even state of affairs.

The introduction of French scholar Henri Lefebvre's work in the 1970s to North American geography refined thinking about urban space. Lefebvre helped to shift Marxist researchers from seeing space as a reflection of the social order to seeing space as deeply and actively engaged in a dialectic with society. The urban landscape is both mold and mirror to society, he explained. The city is not separate from what it contains or from what contains it. To understand the city, scholars must understand how the urban is produced—and how the urban produces us. This idea of a two-way relationship between the physical environment and people ($\leftarrow$ and $\rightarrow$) complicated earlier ideas about how the urban environment affects human behavior and how economic processes shape the layout of a city, and it quickly became a tenet of urban geography. Box 2.1 explores this concept in Atlanta's public schools.

Box 2.1 Urban Regimes and Public Education in Atlanta, Georgia

Urban regime theory, the most prominent paradigm of urban politics at the end of the twentieth century in the United States, emerged out of a case study of local development agendas in Atlanta, Georgia. In 1989, Clarence Stone published an analysis of urban power that sought to explain how governmental and nongovernmental actors mobilize and coordinate resources beyond formal institutional frameworks to achieve governance. Drawing on the idea of regimes from international relations literature and research in political economy, Stone argued that the kind of politics and policies that had unfolded in Atlanta could not be described as only the reflection of economic forces or the workings of formal institutions. Rather, the politics and policies of Atlanta are shaped by informal networks among various interest groups from neighborhood organizations representing middle-class African Americans to businesses. Decisions about the city's future had been made by an urban regime—an informal yet stable group of public- and private-sector leaders who had access to institutional resources. Power in American cities had become fragmented and decentralized, according to urban regime analysis, and urban scholarship needed to take notice of what was happening outside of formal boundaries of government. Stone, along with urban scholars Susan and Norman Feinstein, John Logan, Harvey Molotch, and Stephen Elkin, laid groundwork for geographic research into the different kinds of cooperation, negotiation, bargains, and collaborative arrangements that mediate the divide between popular control of government and private control of economic resources. They helped to secure the place of agency in studies of urban development.

Recent research by Katherine Hankins and Deborah Martin has explored how Atlanta's primary newspaper, the *Atlanta Journal-Constitution*, supported the expansion, deregulation, and consumer-choice-oriented flexibility of charter schools in Georgia in the late 1990s and early 2000s. In 1993, the Georgia state government passed a law to allow existing public schools to convert into charter schools, which are privately managed but publicly funded institutions. In 1998, the law was expanded to allow community groups and private corporations to create charter schools from scratch. During the subsequent years, despite national reports of poor student performance in charter schools, the Atlanta newspaper staff vigorously promoted this new model of public-private education. The vigorous support, which came in the form of exclusively positive editorials and generally favorable reports, established the newspaper as a prominent player in the city's education regime. An education regime—a type of urban regime—encompasses community members and policy makers who lobby for and enact public education policies and programs. It is not uncommon in North American cities for newspapers, which are often private and locally dependent actors with clear interests, to get involved in urban politics or to mobilize their influence on certain issues. Like any actor in an urban regime, newspapers can demonstrate ideological bents. In Atlanta, the charter school question revealed the newspaper's endorsement of privatized governance as the only valid policy solution to the city's problems of inequality and inefficiency in the public education system.

Source: Hankins, K., and D. Martin. 2006. "Charter Schools and Urban Regimes in Neoliberal Context: Making Workers and New Spaces in Metropolitan Atlanta." *International Journal of Urban and Regional Research* 30(3):528–47.

THE LOS ANGELES SCHOOL

Building on Lefebvre's theories on the production of space and Marxist political economy, a loosely affiliated group of interdisciplinary scholars in the 1980s unveiled a new set of ideas about the organization of the city. These scholars, who called themselves The Los Angeles School, argued that global economic restructuring had created a type of urbanization that could be understood only with a regional lens. The city as some single, coherent entity had been fractured into a sprawling, multicentered, and sometimes playful urban form, and researchers needed to take notice. Urban scholars such as Ed Soja, Mike Davis, Frederick Jameson, and others contended that the paradigmatic city of the industrial period might have been Chicago, but in the "postmodern" or advanced-capitalist age, the Rust Belt cities no longer held theoretical sway. It was now Los Angeles with its edge cities, security-obsessed designs, theme-park-like shopping malls, brand-making city boosters, car-oriented spaces, and centerless landscapes that best represented the shape of postwar urban America.

Global changes in immigration, transit, post-Fordist economies, and labor markets had transformed urban areas into regional agglomerations where the periphery mattered as much as—if not more than—the core. The L.A. School researchers, many of whom had ties to the UCLA School of Architecture and Planning, offered up the empirically neglected Los Angeles city-region as a counterpoint to contemporary urban theory. Michael Dear in particular characterized this new urban form as a checkerboard with fragmented patches (figure 2.4). Such an image was a stark contrast to the Chicago School's concentric zone

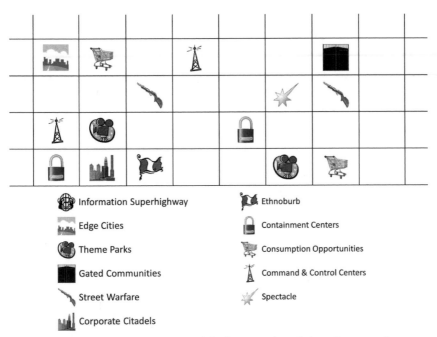

Information Superhighway
Edge Cities
Theme Parks
Gated Communities
Street Warfare
Corporate Citadels

Ethnoburb
Containment Centers
Consumption Opportunities
Command & Control Centers
Spectacle

Figure 2.4 "Keno Capitalism: A Model of Postmodern Urban Structure," by Michael Dear and Steven Flusty, presents the space of Los Angeles as a checkered and unordered gaming board—quite a contrast to the Chicago School's concentric circle model. This model stands as an antithesis of the industrial city. *Source:* M. Dear, ed., *From Chicago to LA: Making Sense of Urban Theory* (Thousand Oaks, CA: Sage, 2002), 80.

model of urban growth. Yet it was also similarly underdeveloped as a theoretical tool and did little to explain differences within and among cities. Moreover, the use of either of these places as the single basis for major theories about how all cities unfold and function has been questioned in recent years. How representative can one place be?

The L.A. School's attempts to show the underbelly of all the hyped glitz and glamour of tourist- and entertainment-oriented Los Angeles accomplished two tasks. First, this cadre of researchers generated a body of work that serves as a model for contemporary urban geography. The in-depth studies of Los Angeles demonstrated how an urban landscape is socially constructed and physically engineered and identified what forces gave

rise to the city's shape. Through deep histories, they largely avoided—apart from the claim that postindustrial urban forms have replaced industrial ones—creating a singular theory of urban growth. Second, the scholarship injected new life into the old notion of the city as dystopian. Not unlike the position of Chicago School sociologists, much of the work coming out of Los Angeles assumed that the local state and political institutions had failed and that the city as a place of democracy was impossible. In their writings, the city was not a place of possibility or a forum for social justice (see box 2.2). In part because of the view that postindustrial economic shifts so strongly shaped the form of the city, the possibility of human agency and progressive struggle was often marginalized.

Box 2.2 Selling Shelters in Washington, DC

After World War II, the development of Washington, DC, mirrored changes occurring in many other American cities. Mass out-migration of white middle-class families in the 1960s and then black middle-class families in the 1970s devastated the city's tax bases, curbed employment opportunities for those who stayed, and transformed the city into a majority black resident city for the first time in its history. By 1980, almost one in five residents lived below the poverty line. In response to these shifting demographics, local policy makers in the late 1970s and early 1980s began to use public policy to ease social welfare strains and expand the social safety net. One project to come out of this moment was the city's first shelter system and a strong base of homelessness advocacy that would garner international attention.

The meaning and use of the public shelter system in the city shifted in the late 1990s. For the first time, city residents elected a city council (the local governing body) whose majority was white—not black, like the population the council members represented—and a mayor who did not have a history of civil rights activism (the then-mayor, Anthony Williams, had an Ivy League finance background). In what amounted to a new municipal regime, pragmatic concerns over city services became dominant over larger issues of social and racial justice. Like the entrepreneurial shift under way in other American cities, the new legislators of Washington, DC, levied public monies (nearly a half-billion dollars) to build a stadium for Major League Baseball, privatized a city hospital, and set a goal to attract one hundred thousand new young professional and "empty nester" residents, who would contribute to the city's tax base and fiscal strength. Through tax increment financing programs, regionally competitive tax abatements, and reduced-priced public property sales, the city government of the twenty-first century became a facilitator, booster, and vendor for property market investments. Schools, libraries, firehouses, and public homeless shelters were sold to private developers and transformed into upscale hotels and luxury condos. DC has put up for sale almost three-quarters of all municipally held properties that had been used as homeless shelters between 1982, the year the public shelter system began, and 2012. These sales were pursued and secured despite increases in the number of the city's homeless population to more than twelve thousand and overflowing demand for the city's 1,300 public emergency shelter beds. The property sales occurred even after government agencies noted that limited facilities are the number one barrier to efficient operation for social-service provision.

For geographers, the adoption of privatization programs across political agendas and governance scales is evidence of the ideological purchase of gentrification—the conversion of working-class or vacant areas for consumption by progressively more affluent users—and its transformation into a generalized and global strategy for capital accumulation. Major real-estate development has become a centerpiece of contemporary urban economies and their free-market policies. Washington, DC's limited fiscal resources, property development dependency, increased demands on its social services, and urban development strategies that promote gentrification are not unique but illustrative of the tensions facing many North American cities. In the shadow of such changes to urban landscapes, public property's sociopolitical role has morphed. The disposal of public property in Washington, DC, is a transformation that affects not only the landscape of justice for homeless populations. Figure 2.5 shows the Franklin School, once a homeless shelter but now slated for development into market-rate condominiums. The elimination of physical spaces in which people are included threatens the existence of intangible and indispensible public spheres, which is where and how society gets ordered. Public property, according to geographers Don Mitchell and Lynn Staeheli, safeguards a space *for* political engagement at the same time that its existence *is* a form of political engagement. A lack of public property reduces opportunities for political engagement. The urban development strategy in Washington, DC, to sell homeless shelters limits the kinds of politics and justice possible in the city.

Figure 2.5   Franklin School is a former homeless shelter that the Washington, DC, local government has repeatedly tried to sell to a luxury hotel developer. Pictured here is a group of Occupy DC members who protested one of these attempts by occupying the building in November 2011. (Photo by Kathryn Wells)

Figure 2.6   This photo, "Cinematic New York City," depicts some of the social density, cultural richness, and constant street activity that have piqued the curiosity of New York City urban scholars. (Copyright © 2011 Alex Proimos)

THE NEW YORK SCHOOL

Another loosely affiliated and interdisciplinary group of urban scholars in New York City produced a set of research that focused on the role of human agency and the possibility of social justice. Writing in the second half of the twentieth century and at the same time as many of the L.A. School and Marxist scholars, the work of New York City scholars demonstrated that a purely economic explanation was not sufficient for understanding urban change. What social and cultural forces were at play in cities? What was it about certain cities, such as New York City, that make them so attractive decade after decade? In addressing these questions, their scholarship set the stage for examinations of the city as a place of unique culture, diverse neighborhoods, and utopian futures—rather than as a place of the capitalist economy alone. In an early study of gentrification and the cultural politics of local economic development, Sharon Zukin showed how culture was a powerful means of controlling cities

and a site of ongoing conflict (figure 2.6). Increasingly, entrepreneurial capital was intertwined in the making of cultural symbols and meanings (i.e., the culture industry) through art museums, restaurants, public festivals, and television networks such as MTV. For example, Kenneth Jackson and Richard Sennett research urban centers and the role of culture in urban centers. Scholars in New York City wanted to know why professional workers were moving back to urban areas and what was at stake with these downtown reinvestments. What had made the city so attractive to certain populations again?

THE CULTURAL TURN

Ideas about the role of culture in the city began to get traction in the late 1980s in geographic studies. The influence of literary theory led to the emergence of approaches such as poststructural, critical race, feminist, queer, and postcolonial theory. The reintroduction of German social theorist Max Weber's notion of culture by Canadian geographer David Ley is often used to signal the turn toward individual intentions and collective experiences that shape and are shaped by urban landscapes. By the 1990s, the so-called cultural turn had become prominent as research agendas moved from questions of class and the capitalist economy to the spaces, practices, and differences of everyday life. The work of feminist urban geographers such as Linda Peake, Susan Ruddick, Kay Anderson, and Geraldine Pratt were critical in moving from investigations into the politics of redistribution to the politics of recognition. Issues of redistribution such as structural inequality, poverty, income disparities, resource access, and taxes—the central concerns of the 2012 Occupy movement—were no longer more important than concerns about how gender, sexuality, nationality, and race were expressed, experienced, and enforced through urban space and how the omission of these differences compromised earlier (racist, sexist, and xenophobic) scholarship (see box 2.3). Implicit in this cultural turn was increased attention to mundane negotiations of the city, such as those of working-class African Americans rather than those of powerful elites, and the experience of heteronormativity (the dominance of heterosexual norms in urban spaces) on queer populations. For instance, how do transgender or gender-bending individuals deal with university campuses that offer only communal bathrooms designated for men or women rather than unisex options (figure 2.7)? The goal with this research shift was, and to a large extent still is, to see the city not as a text to be read or imprint of capitalist relations but as a set of processes that actively write and mediate social life.

Box 2.3 Constructions of Filipina Domestic Workers in Vancouver, British Columbia

In the Vancouver labor market, Filipinas—women from the Philippines—have been the most occupationally "ghettoized" or segregated of all women in the past two decades. More than any other ethnic group, Filipinas have been clustered into low-skill nursing, clerical tasks, medical assistance, housekeeping, and child-care jobs. They have made less money than the Canadian-born population despite having a higher rate of university degrees. Even though men who have immigrated to Canada have achieved wages at rates similar to those of Canadian-born men, the average earnings of female immigrants remained below that of their Canadian peers in 2001.

One program that has contributed to these disparities in the labor market (and to some extent benefited from them) is the Canadian federal government's Live-in Caregiver Program. The Live-in Caregiver Program, which began in 1992 and superseded the decade-long Foreign Domestic Movement Program, offered temporary visas to domestic workers to come to Canada on condition that they have a contract for employment as a live-in caregiver. After two years of employment, the domestic workers are eligible to apply for a more permanent visa and immigration status. The vast majority of immigrants through this program are women, and an increasing proportion (upwards of 86 percent in 1996) of these laborers are from the Philippines. Though these live-in workers have access to some rights, such as Employment Insurance, they are excluded from a number of regulations that govern overtime pay and hourly minimum wages because of their visa status. The federal government, by approaching these domestic workers as temporary visa holders rather than as actual employees and by prohibiting educational training for visa holders, contributes to a tenuous, often exploitative, downwardly mobile position for Filipinas in Vancouver. The Philippines national government, Canadian provincial governments, Canadian families, other Filipino immigrants, and nanny agents are also factors in the widespread de-skilling and marginalization of Filipinas in Canada.

Nanny agents—the brokers who match domestic workers with employers—have played an important role in framing Filipinas as inferior members of the Vancouver labor market and instilling racial and economic boundaries on certain immigrant women. As feminist geographer Geraldine Pratt has explored at length, many of the Filipinas who immigrated to Vancouver through the Live-in Caregiver Program have histories as registered nurses, high school teachers, trained social workers, and experienced bookkeepers. Still, nanny agents described Filipinas as housekeepers and servants who should be grateful to have been allowed entry to the country, whereas European women who come to Canada on the same visa program are discussed as professionals, nannies, and welcomed tourists. These stereotypes of Filipinas are similar to the images deployed by Americans during and after the colonization of the Philippines (from 1896 to 1946): Filipinos were portrayed as passive, inferior, uncivilized, childlike, and generally incapable of independent thought. Even though English was the primary language for instruction in schools in the Philippines until the late 1980s, domestic workers from the Philippines are consistently framed by nanny agents as incapable of providing intellectual stimulation to children of more than two years of age. Domestic workers in Canada live out the consequences of these notions held by nanny agents. There is, in effect, a two-tiered wage structure where European child-care providers make more money than Filipinas yet work fewer hours. The dynamics of race, gender, colonialism, and class cannot be separated from Vancouver's immigration patterns, labor markets, and household politics.

Source: Pratt, G. 2004. *Working Feminism*. Philadelphia: Temple University Press.

Figure 2.7   A gender-neutral bathroom.
(Photo by Kathryn Wells)

A RENEWED QUANTITATIVE REVOLUTION

It would be inaccurate to say that the quantitative revolution disappeared after the rise of Marxist geography and the cultural turn, although its prominence in urban scholarship certainly declined. In recent years, urban scholars have refocused on the ways in which large quantities of reliable socioeconomic data about cities and city neighborhoods have become available from sources such as the censuses. At the same time, new digital technologies, including geographic information systems (GIS) and remote sensing, have made contributions to understandings of cities (box 2.4). Many urban scholars now employ both a qualitative approach with some quantitative methods in order to allow these new digital technologies to uncover new spatial relationships.

Box 2.4 Geographical Perspectives on Participatory Action Research

Since 2000, participatory action research (PAR)—a method long used in social sciences for community development work in rural areas and supported by feminist scholarship—has been increasingly used by geographers as a different approach from mainstream research. Mainstream research often involves a researcher who goes to a "field," identifies a project, conducts a study, and leaves. PAR, by contrast, engages community members as collaborators in designing a research plan, implementing the plan, publishing the findings, and owning the data. The goal of PAR is not simply the production of knowledge but social change through education, empowerment, capacity building, and action. PAR prioritizes needs of certain communities over academic research agendas. This method is not research as community service, where the investigator presents research to a group that is supposed to benefit. This method is research as collaborative, complicated, and sometimes contentious.

It is the Jane Addams approach of the twenty-first century. In geography, this framework has been employed to explore questions of inequality, exclusion, and marginalization with, for instance, migrant and indigenous populations, children, and queer groups. Despite the popularity of this model, PAR is not without its shortcomings. Adherents to this more democratic model of research must remain vigilant and attentive to traditional issues of power imbalance between researcher and researched.

The exploding geographic subfield of geographical information systems (GIS) has cautiously embraced public participation methods like those of PAR. In the late 1990s, participatory GIS (PGIS) emerged in geography as a way to enhance community involvement in the making and using of spatial data. Like PAR, this approach seeks to decentralize control, ownership, access, use, and the terms of GIS. The goal is to make room for multiple geographical realities—multiple spatial knowledges—rather than some singular, objective body of knowledge that too many GIS research projects have tended to create. Similar in function to participatory mapping, PGIS has been used to help manage conflicts over natural resources and urban planning decisions on regional and neighborhood scales.

In Syracuse, New York, for instance, the Syracuse Community Geography Project has produced a forum for collaborative research and action among university faculty, students, and community partners. In response to the need for data on critical issues such as food deserts (neighborhoods without stores that sell fresh produce), elder transit, and the accessibility of bus shelters, the Syracuse Community Geography Project developed a model for using geographic resources to support local goals of positive change and initiatives for community development, public health, and social justice. One recent collaboration helped a local United Way group identify areas whose residents would benefit from access to free tax preparation services provided by United Way.

Another example of action-oriented GIS research that has challenged status-quo academic traditions is the Million Dollar Blocks project. The Million Dollar Blocks project, undertaken by architects at Columbia University and criminal justice policy makers at the JFA Institute and the Justice Mapping Center, created maps of single city blocks in the United States for which more than a million dollars a year was spent by governments to incarcerate the block's residents. While the compilations of city-to-prison-to-city-to-prison migration flows toured the country as art exhibits, the primary goal of this spatial and statistical analysis of socioeconomic data was to raise awareness about US incarceration and to affect public policy. The maps suggested—and often with success—that prisons and jails have become the predominant government institution and public investment for too many urban communities and that state and local leaders should take action. Nonetheless, such innovative GIS projects—and PAR in general—account for a small percentage of all contemporary research initiatives in geography.

Source: Kindon, S., R. Pain, and M. Kesby, eds. 2007. *Participatory Action Research Approaches and Methods: Connecting People, Participation and Place.* London: Routledge.

GLOBALIZATION, CITIES, NETWORKS, AND FLOWS

Another major approach to understanding the city has been to contextualize the city within the networks and flows of globalization. Since the 1990s, geographic interest in cities has broadened from spatial patterns within cities to global connections across cities. In the 1990s, a strand of urban research began to approach the city as supralocal and embedded in large-scale processes outside of traditional boundaries. In a shift away from focusing on the internal dimensions of a single city, scholars sought to situate a city's formation within wider networks and flows. Most famously, sociologist Saskia Sassen's idea of a "global city" repositioned some cities as multiscalar—places that have influence at local, regional, national, and international scales. According to Sassen, global cities were a setting for new types of political operations and a new global grid of politics and engagement. New York City, London, and Tokyo, for instance, were seen as the top (or command centers) of a global-economy hierarchy and of growing importance to their countries. Such global cities, according to urban theory, were nodes in sprawling circuits that connected one city directly to another and made the relationships among cities often more important than those between a city and a nation-state. For instance, the connection between Vancouver and Seattle—through trade agreements, transit, finance, food, and television programs—is increasingly more important to the lifeline of each city than each city's position within its respective state.

It was not until the 2000s that the idea of all cities as integrated into this circuit of global connectedness was articulated in urban geography. In response to an understanding of the city as a global place, some geographers began to rethink the lines between "the global" and "the local." How are cities connected together? How do ideas, commuters, commodities, airplanes, and viruses move between cities? How does "globalness" manifest in places like Detroit, where an increasing majority of its industry is dependent on parts, pieces, and labor from Canada and China? For example, when urban geographers John Rennie Short and Yeong Kim examined airline passenger information to construct flow data among global cities, they found that Los Angeles is less a global city and more a Pacific Rim city and that Miami is less a major North American city than a hub of the Caribbean and Central and South America.

By thinking relationally about cities and how local-global relations affect the spaces in which we live, more recently urban geographers have turned away from hierarchies of powerful cities to focus on the everyday "globalness" of all cities. Global networks do not exist in the ether, somewhere "up there," but are made and remade down here on the ground in the everyday actions and lives of people in cities. Consider the next example.

From Tahrir Square to Madison, Wisconsin:
Blurring the Lines between Urban
and Non-urban Processes

In February 2011, protestors at Tahrir Square in Cairo, Egypt, ordered pizza for protestors at the state capitol in Madison, Wisconsin. To understand what celebrations over the toppling of a thirty-year autocrat in Egypt have to do with labor debates about public employee bargaining rights in the United States, urban geographers might have asked the following questions: How is Cairo connected to Madison through Facebook, online media sources, and financial resources? How are these connections organized? How are each of these cities (unevenly) integrated into the processes of globalization? How are the spaces of the state capitol and Tahrir Square situated within each city? To understand the connection, city geographers seek to understand what is going on within it—the very local processes—as well as the global context in which it is situated. The long-distance pizza order was not a "global" event that happened to Madison, nor was it a "local" event in Cairo. For productive analysis of either of these places in the twenty-first century, the boundaries between global and local need to be muddied. Geographers Eugene McCann and Kevin Ward have specifically argued in recent years that the connections between cities—like that of the protesters' pizzas—are not supplements to how cities exist but are fundamental to their very dynamics. Cities are amalgamations of very mobile entities (like policies) *and* very static, stuck-in-place, or fixed entities (like environmental watersheds). In other words, cities exist as tensions. They are unbounded—as a set of flows, translations, transmissions, and mobilities—and yet unavoidably bounded— as specific sites. There are no easy answers to questions about where "the urban" begins and where it ends.

As geographers moved over the course of the past hundred years from studying cities as bounded sites to studying urban processes, the line between "the urban" and "the non-urban" has blurred. Recent approaches to urban geography have stressed the arbitrariness of "the urban" as a category. What geographers refer as "the urban" could not exist without a host of other forces that operate in a variety of places and at a variety of scales. To understand "the urban," it is necessary to place urban processes within a broad context of other dimensions of human society and the natural environment. What the city is has much to do with what the state does, where transit corridors are built, and how individuals negotiate the constraints of the capitalist economy. These kinds of factors are not place-specific and travel across traditional jurisdictional boundaries. What makes something "urban" anyhow? Struggling with this question, geographers have adopted the idea that the city is not something "out there," separate from the messiness of everyday life, decisions of politicians, or performances of artists. The city is *constituted by* and *constitutive of* the set of processes, routines, and conditions that extend far beyond metropolitan census districts as well as those that are entangled in the intimate details of how we live our lives. "The urban" and thus "the non-urban" are not, and never have been, helpful or even clean-cut descriptions of spatial patterns and processes. Much contemporary urban geography is concerned with reuniting the separate spheres of "urban" and "non-urban" to create a more integrated understanding of how urban processes are actually lived and experienced.

The embrace of complexity by urban geographers has sometimes meant a rejection of a singular, unifying theory for how cities are shaped and how they shape us. Model-like approaches from the Chicago School and even the L.A. School advance our understanding only to some degree. Instead, urban geographers have been encouraged to forgo an illusion of unitary logic for a reality of dynamism, plurality, and partiality in cities. Scholars Nigel Thrift and Ash Amin have encouraged urban researchers to embrace multiple theoretical lenses and different ways of knowing. Thrift and Amin, as well as others, have rightly questioned why ideas from North America should carry such theoretical weight in other contexts, such as the Global South. Given where cities have been studied—Manchester, Chicago, L.A., New York City—where do other cities fit into the production of ideas about cities? Whose experience counts? By recognizing the limits of North American and western European studies, geographers have come to see the danger of extrapolating from one culturally specific case of urban development to a radically different cultural, economic, and political scenario. Still, the problem of how to represent American and Canadian cities remains.

The call to reject an all-encompassing theory is useful. Why not explore the world through various disciplines and ideas? Why not open up room for dialogue between different ideas and allow for the emergence of new forms of knowledge? In reality, some scholars retreat to their comfortable corners and speak only with like-minded thinkers. And a multitude of approaches to the city means more complex and theoretically demanding debates. The trend to avoid singular truths and logics about urban experiences and the tolerance for multiple views has unfortunately been accompanied by a minimization of debate, dissent, and productive criticism. There are additional worries that this new emphasis on complexity obscures the importance of actually existing issues of inequality and injustice that demand a response. If we focus on the varieties of urban experiences at the expense of commonalities, how can we build coalitions across places and make joint efforts at reducing injustices? In the push to explore difference, variegations, and the shifting ter-

rain of connections among places, geographers have sometimes forgotten the blaring inequities of the capitalist economy that undergird "urban" and "non-urban" processes. Others, in rallying against principles or grand theories, have failed to contend with the reality that some ideas like that of spatial-social interaction unite a wide swath of contemporary research. A task confronting current and future urban geographers is to contend with the tensions among various approaches—between those that embrace multiplicity and those that prioritize commonalities, between those that see the city as a space of possibility and those that see it as a space of doom, between those that engage the blurriness of urban and non-urban processes and those that draw clear boundaries. This project of contending with tensions across approaches to urban geography is one that undergirds the rest of the book.

SUGGESTED READINGS

Anderson, K. 1991. *Vancouver's Chinatown: Racial Discourse in Canada, 1875–1980*. Montreal: McGill-Queen's University Press.

Blomley, N. 2004. *Unsettling the City: Urban Land and the Politics of Property*. New York: Routledge.

Davis, M. 1990. *City of Quartz: Excavating the Future in Los Angeles*. London: Verso.

Engels, F. 2010 [1892]. *The Condition of the Working-Class in England in 1844*. New York: Cambridge University Press.

Fincher, R., and J. M. Jacobs. 1998. *Cities of Difference*. New York: Guilford Press.

Harvey, D. 1998 [1973]. *Social Justice and the City*. Cambridge, MA: Blackwell.

Ley, D. 1983. *A Social Geography of the City*. New York: Harper and Row.

Low, S., and N. Smith, eds. 2006. *The Politics of Public Space*. London: Routledge.

Peak, L., and M. Rieker, eds. 2012. *Interrogating Feminist Understandings of the Urban*. London: Routledge.

Short, J. R. 2006. *Urban Theory: A Critical Assessment*. New York: Palgrave Macmillan.

Zukin, S. 1995. *The Cultures of Cities*. Cambridge, MA: Blackwell.

CITIES ON THE WEB

The Atlantic Cities: www.theatlanticcities.com

Michigan's Cool Cities: www.coolcities.com

Million Dollar Blocks: www.spatialinformation designlab.org/projects.php

Open Street Map: www.openstreetmap.org

Syracuse Community Geography: www.community geography.org

Ted City 2.0: http://thecity2.org

3

An Urban History

ROBERT LEWIS

The United States and Canada are metropolitan societies. More than a quarter-billion suburban and city inhabitants account for four out of every five Americans. The story is the same in Canada. The four largest metropolitan areas—Toronto, Montreal, Vancouver, and Ottawa—account for more than a third of Canada's population of thirty-two million. This has not always been the case. Until recently, few people lived in cities. Less than a century ago, more people lived in the countryside. Two hundred years ago, only one in twenty lived in urban places. The modern metropolis is new, a product of the past seventy years. What is not new, however, is that cities have always faced challenges. In some cases, the challenges have changed. The issue of clean drinking water that so bedeviled the inhabitants of the nineteenth century, for instance, is of little concern today. In other cases, the challenges are the same. The modern metropolis continues to face deep-seated problems that have characterized cities from the very beginning of urban development in the Americas four hundred years ago. Whether this is social discrimination, from racism to homophobia, economic disparities along the lines of class, race, and gender, or uncontrolled real-estate speculation, today's capitalist urban areas face many of the same challenges as in the past. To deal effectively with these it is necessary to know their origins and to appreciate their dynamics over time. Despite the enormous changes since the early seventeenth century, cities of the past have a great deal to tell us about the cities of today. As Aristotle said, "If you would understand anything, observe its beginning and its development." History matters. This chapter provides a window into the urban past so as to throw light on the problems confronting the contemporary metropolis.

THE COMMERCIAL CITY, 1565–1840

The origins of the Canadian and American city lie in the expansion of competing European powers overseas and the development of global commercial trade from the fifteenth century. The English, French, Spanish, Portuguese, and Dutch set down trading posts, missionary centers, slave camps, and fortresses in most parts of the world, including what would become the United States of America and Canada. The first permanent settlement, the Spanish town of St. Augustine, was established in 1565. In 1608 the Frenchman Samuel de Champlain founded Quebec City, and Montreal was established three years later. Over the next hundred years, many other permanent settlements were founded, including New York City (1614), Boston (1630), Charleston (1670), Philadelphia (1682), and Savannah (1733). By the 1770s, a system of urban places had been created, running from the southern states through the Mid-Atlantic and New England regions to the eastern portion of modern Canada.

Commercial cities in the United States and Canada were nodes in a wide-flung international system of trade. The establishment and growth of these small coastal or riverine places that hugged the Atlantic Seaboard were driven by the expansion of global mercantile capitalism, a system of profit centered on the trading of commodities. European expansionism overseas rested on long-distance trading of goods, most of which were made under noncapitalist production methods, orchestrated by urban import-export merchants. Trade, the dynamic motor of commercial urbanization, depended on international transportation and communication. An Atlantic trade triangle consisting of the Americas, the Caribbean, Europe, and Africa framed the local urban economies (figure 3.1). City docks

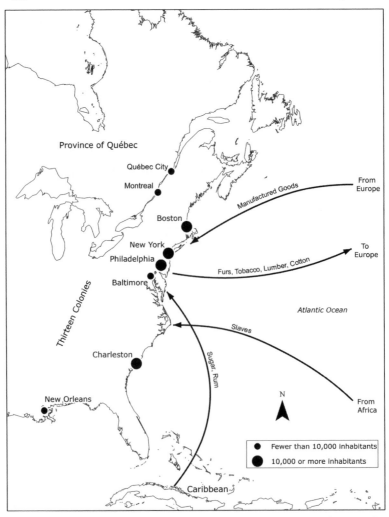

Figure 3.1   The Atlantic triangle of trade. *Source:* Map by Robert Lewis.

linked North America with the European imperial powers. Colonial Philadelphia, for example, exported furs, lumber, staves, iron, wheat, and flour from the continental interior to Europe and imported Caribbean rum and sugar, southern European wine, African slaves, and English manufactures.

Commercial cities were small. In 1690, Boston, the largest city, had seven thousand persons. Growth was slow over the eighteenth century. By the time of the revolution, New York City and Philadelphia were home to about 25,000 and 24,000 persons. A growing integration into international trading networks and an expanding rural economy quickened population growth. By 1842, five cities had populations of more than one hundred thousand (table 3.1). New York City, with one-third of a million, was the largest.

Table 3.1   Population of Selected Cities, 1690–1800

City	1690	1742	1775	1800
Philadelphia	4,000	13,000	24,000	62,000
New York	3,900	11,000	25,000	61,000
Baltimore	—	—	6,000	26,000
Boston	7,000	16,400	16,000	25,000
Charleston	1,100	6,800	12,000	19,000
Quebec City	1,345	4,100	7,300	14,000
Montreal	1,150	4,200	5,500	9,000
New Orleans	—	—	4,000	8,000

The city's physical size reflected the small population. Philadelphia in 1774, for example, stretched one mile along the river and half a mile inland. New York was hemmed into a small area at the bottom of Manhattan

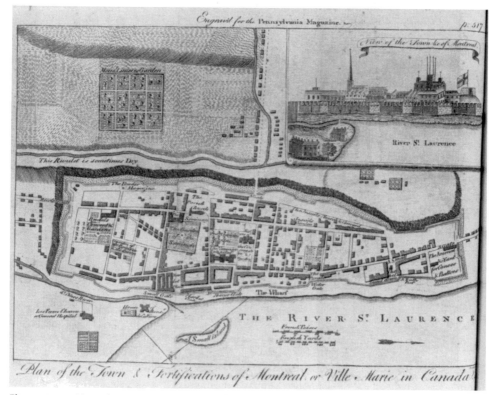

Figure 3.2   City of Montreal, 1775. *Source:* Library of Congress.

Island. The vast majority of city inhabitants were European in origin. Surrounded by fortifications, Montreal was a French-speaking city (figure 3.2). Philadelphia in 1750 largely consisted of English speakers, such as Quakers fleeing persecution. By 1820, Scotch-Irish and German immigrants were common. This remained the case for Philadelphia and most other cities until the 1880s. The one exception to this was Quebec, where a French-speaking population was the majority in Montreal and Quebec City (box 3.1).

Box 3.1 Quebec City: Social Inequality and Urban Space

Like many cities in Canada, Quebec City was a place of great economic inequality. It was established as a colonial French trading and military settlement in 1608. Over the next two hundred years, the town grew slowly, reaching 31,500 in 1842. It was integrated into a set of French and, after 1795, British economic and military networks. By the late 1700s, the city's economy was centered on a supply chain in which city timber merchants shipped large amounts of squared timber taken from the rural hinterland to Britain (see figure 3.3). The population consisted primarily of people of English and French backgrounds, with a sprinkling of First Nations people and European immigrants. Under both the French and British regimes, religious, military, and economic power was in the hands of a small elite: religious leaders, military officers, and long-distance merchants. With wealth garnered from profits made from the difference between the buying and selling of commodities, merchants controlled the city government and used their ability to regulate the local economy to pro-

Figure 3.3   Quebec City, 1768. *Source:* Library of Congress.

tect their global networks. The rest of the population consisted of a handful of well-to-do retail storekeepers and skilled craft workers and a much larger number of laborers, servants, and dockworkers. A handful of men controlled the city's social, economic, and cultural life. Between one-fifth and one-sixth of the population would have owned between two-thirds and three-quarters of the city's wealth. In contrast, laborers, widows, and servants had little to no property (land or otherwise), earned wages that frequently did not cover the basic costs of living, lived in abysmal housing conditions, and suffered indignities at the hands of their social superiors. Wealth and the economic and political power that came with it was concentrated in the hands of Anglophone men. Life for women was at best difficult, with little control over their everyday life and over the legal structures of the city.

The social geography of the city reflected these economic disparities. Quebec City's social geography in the late eighteenth century featured a high degree of residential and nonresidential intermixing. New forms of class and ethnic relations forged new social geographies. By 1842, elements of both the commercial city's traditional pattern and modern forms of social segregation were evident. The Upper Town, which looked down on the bustling shipping and industrial river area below, had lost a great deal of the earlier mix. It was now the prestigious residential core, home to the military, religious, landowning, and merchant elites, and the center of the city's key political and economic institutions. Lower Town, which hugged the St. Lawrence River, featured an assortment of warehouses, manufacturing workshops, and shipbuilding yards as well as the residences for all social classes. Merchants lived cheek-by-jowl with laborers and dockworkers. In relative terms, these older districts' share of the city's population declined as new suburban districts developed. Stimulated by the growth of the timber industry and shipbuilding, St. Roch, an extension of Lower Town, had a mix of residences and workplaces and was home to a large artisan and laborer population. St. Jean, on the other hand, was home to the well-to-do who could not afford the expensive Upper Town but were looking for better housing than found in the Lower Town and St Roch. A new class-based and functionally differentiated social geography had been implanted on the city's landscape by 1842.

Commercial cities had deep inequalities along the lines of class, occupation, and gender. At the top of the class system were male merchants such as John Hancock (1737–1793) and John Jacob Astor (1763–1848), who gained economic wealth and political power through long-distance trade. Hancock was a Boston merchant who signed the Declaration of Independence and was governor of Massachusetts. Raised by a wealthy uncle, he attended Harvard, went into his uncle's merchant business, and became partner and sole heir. Hancock fused his economic position within the international circuits of trade with local political power to became one of America's leading patricians. Astor, on the other hand, made a fortune from the fur trade, creating a massive North American empire that supplied Europe's urban bourgeoisie and royalty. He used his fortune from the international economy to buy huge amounts of Manhattan property and to amass a second fortune from urban land development. When he died, he was the richest person in America. Hancock and Astor were representatives of an elite wealthy class who controlled an overwhelming proportion of their city's resources. In Boston in 1771, the top 15 percent of the population had 66 percent of the city's wealth. Three years later, in Philadelphia, the top 10 percent of taxpaying households owned 89 percent of the taxable property. About five hundred men controlled economic life.

Most of the city's population had little income, property, and social status. The most substantial group was the small coterie of well-to-do male storekeepers, professionals, landowners, religious leaders, and civil and military administrators making up the urban middle class. Working mainly in the retail, government, or service sectors, they had a decent income, owned some property, and employed a few servants and perhaps a slave or two. They were men of substance. Less prosperous, but with some standing, were a small number of master artisans who operated the city's manufacturing workshops. The basic commodities necessary for everyday life, from barrels and ships to shoes and flour, were made in small workshops that employed from two to twenty-five mainly skilled workers. The vast majority of the population consisted of a despised laboring and servant class. Most laborers had insecure, poorly paid, low-status work. Many were employed on short-term contracts working as casuals on the docks, digging holes for public works, or removing human waste. Servants, the vast majority of whom were female, worked in the home, the store, and the workshop. Working long hours under the most exploitative conditions, the servant and the laborer were close to the bottom of the commercial city's class and occupational hierarchy. At the very bottom were prostitutes, petty criminals, and transients.

The merchant elite had tight political control over urban life and urban spaces. By the early 1700s, American male freeholders eligible to vote accounted for 10 percent of the urban population. Men of substance were able to use their wealth to consolidate their social power, control policy making, and take advantage of economic opportunities. Urban politics had two key features. First, the major axis of political power was deference. Political alliances tended to be vertical, across classes rather than within them. Leadership and direction issued from the top down, and politics represented more a competition between elites than between classes. This started to fragment by the late eighteenth century as a result of increasing ethnic diversity, the introduction of new ideas from Europe, and the transition to industrial capitalism. Second, the local government played a minimal regulatory role. Its prime role was to ensure that the local economy was best set up for long-distance trade. As cities became bigger, civic leaders imposed low property taxes and introduced measures to control crime, fire, and contagious disease.

The defining geographic feature of the commercial cities was the mixture of functions throughout the city. There was little land-use specialization other than at the waterfront. Businesses centered on the waterfront, which was the key connecting node for goods and people in and out of the city. Residences also crowded there, as merchants combined office, showroom, and warehouse close to their wharf. No other neighborhood was exclusively given over to economic, transportation, or residential functions. There was little residential separation, with minimal separation of class and occupational residences. Even though people of all classes were scattered through the city, living close to their place of work, there was a sociospatial gradient. The area adjacent to the waterfront had a concentration of wealthy merchants, landowners, and administrators. This area was surrounded by artisan workshops and stores. The poor and socially undesirable tended to reside on the urban fringe; the suburbs were in every way inferior to the city.

By the early nineteenth century, this mixed functional pattern was beginning to fragment, and new forms of social and economic segregation were appearing on the urban landscape. Increasing economic specialization led to greater land-use divisions. Manufactories working with bigger machinery, employing larger workforces, and producing more noxious products than the traditional workshop were banished to the periphery. Financial and legal professions clustered in locational niches close to one another and to ancillary trades in the growing city center. Social areas became more differentiated. Growing immigration, the rise of new, racialized identities of class, and the dock's incessant hustle and bustle combined to make the waterfront an increasingly undesirable locale for the status-driven middle class. By the last half of the eighteenth century, the wealthy and the respectable middle class were moving out from the wharf district to suburbs such as Germantown in Philadelphia and Roxbury and Cambridge in Boston. Some of the key features of the industrial city were clearly in view.

THE INDUSTRIAL METROPOLIS, 1820–1960

From the first half of the nineteenth century, a new economic regime came to dominate North American society. Industrial capitalism, an incremental process built over a long time and consisting of several interrelated dynamics, each of which had differential effects in different places, replaced commercial capitalism. Despite the gradual process of change, industrial capitalism was the major motor of economic growth, the dominant ideological belief system, and the primary basis of social position by 1850. The key development was increasing investment in manufacturing rather than trade. This occurred in two ways. First, small-scale artisans invested in new forms of labor processes, organizational structures, and machinery, with the result that the workshop became the factory. Second, wealthy merchants shifted capital from trade into manufacture. While this first took place in Great Britain after 1750, the dual process was well established across the Atlantic before 1850.

The emergence of industrial capitalism would transform the American and Canadian city. The industrial city—or, more properly, the metropolis (i.e., city and adjacent suburbs)—was at the center of capitalist industrialization (figure 3.4). New technologies supported an incredible spurt of industrial and urban growth. New forms of power, most notably steam and electric, drove new machinery and sped up work. Old industries (textiles, footwear) were transformed from artisanal to factory production, while new ones appeared (steel, petroleum, and electrical). Capitalist wage labor became generalized. Craft workers employed in small-scale, familial workshops were replaced by hourly wageworkers employed in increasingly large workplaces. A well-developed financial system developed that oiled the circulation of capital (box 3.2). The transformation of agriculture drove the demand for factory prod-

Figure 3.4   Pittsburgh, the Point, circa 1900. *Source:* Library of Congress.

Box 3.2 The Corporation and Corporate Capitalism: Swift and Company

By the 1880s, corporate capitalism had replaced competitive capitalism. Central to this was the rise of the oligopolistic corporation to economic, political, and social dominance and the development of modern industries (steel, chemical, petroleum, electrical, and automotive). The corporation is a large-scale business organization that is legally independent from the people who have shares in it. Corporations such as US Steel, Standard Oil, General Electric, and General Motors have several defining features. First, they are vertically and horizontally integrated. Vertical integration refers to a situation where different parts of the production chain are owned by the same company, while horizontal integration occurs when one company controls other firms in the same part of the production chain. Second, corporations have a large number of employees and assets and control vast amounts of economic wealth. In 1940, for example, 5 percent of US firms employed 70 percent of workers, while 0.2 percent of firms owned 52 percent of firm assets. Third, corporations were multi-unit institutions spread over a vast territory. Finally, corporate leaders exercised inordinate political power, either through their control over the levers of the economy or through direct access to political leaders.

One such corporation was Swift and Company. Established by Gustavus F. Swift, the Chicago firm quickly grew from a small butchering operation in the 1850s to a large corporation by the early twentieth century. Swift was a leader in mass-production techniques (the disassembling system), new technological innovations (refrigerated railcars), functional specialization (labor division), and a workplace hierarchy (by ethnicity and education) (see figure 3.5). By 1900, Swift's vertically integrated empire consisted of networks that included hundreds of production plants, warehouses, railroad companies, and offices spread across the nation. When Swift died in 1903, the corporation employed twenty-three thousand workers, owned five thousand refrigerated cars, slaughtered close to eight million animals, and had sales of $200 million. Its success was linked to a cartel with the three other big companies to fix prices, carve up markets, and restrict unions.

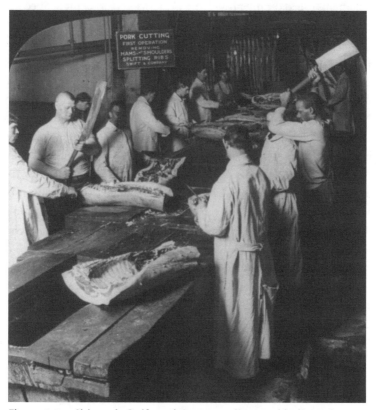

Figure 3.5   Chicago's Swift and Company disassembly line, circa 1905. *Source:* Library of Congress.

The urban implications of corporations such as Swift are enormous. With few exceptions, most corporate offices, production plants, branch houses, and warehouses are located in cities. A handful of corporations (industrial, retail, entertainment, financial) account for the vast majority of a metropolitan area's workforce. Corporations are locationally flexible, which means that urban areas can be held hostage to corporate spatial strategies. Corporate executive networks shape North America's urban system. It is no coincidence that the largest concentrations of corporate facilities are found in the major cities of the United States (New York, Los Angeles) and Canada (Toronto, Montreal), which are the centers controlling metropolitan and regional economies. Executive decisions regarding issues such as labor costs, business climates, and environmental policy have an enormous impact on cities. This was most evident in the industrial heartland of the United States and Canada when corporation after corporation closed shop and moved their plants to low-labor-cost areas in the southern United States and overseas.

ucts (farm implements, seeds) and provided cheap food for the urban working classes. The growing capacity of forestry and mining firms enabled them to exploit nature and provided the physical materials on which capitalist industrialization were dependent (wood, iron, oil, and gas). Newer, cheaper, and faster forms of communication (telegraph, telephone) and transportation (railroad, steamship, automobile) gave rise to space-time compression, the annihilation of space by time. A growing and wealthier population broadened the national market, which in turn promoted increased capitalist production.

Industrial capitalism transformed the United States and Canada into urban societies. Before the 1830s, most people lived in the countryside. Urbanization was slow, and only 5 percent of the population lived in cities in 1800 (table 3.2). By 1860, however, one in five Americans lived in places of more than 2,500 people. Sixty years later, the share living in cities had passed 50 percent; fifty-four million Americans lived in urban places. More than half of Canadians were urban dwellers by 1930. Metropolitan areas had become North

America's main centers of economic and population growth. The number of urban places increased. While there were only 392 urban places in the United States in 1860, there were 2,722 by 1920. More significantly, perhaps, cities became bigger. The number of cities of more than one hundred thousand grew from nine to sixty-eight in the same period. Individual cities expanded dramatically. New York City's population grew from 813,699 in 1860 to 5.6 million in 1920 and 10.6 million in 1960. Los Angeles's population of nine million in 1960 was larger than the entire population of the United States in 1800. A similar process of rapid urban growth was taking place elsewhere, in Canadian cities such as Montreal, Toronto, Winnipeg, and Vancouver.

Immigration has significantly contributed to Canada and US urban populations. In the first decade of the twentieth century, for instance, more than nine million people immigrated to the United States, most residing in the large industrial centers of the Northeast and the Midwest. In 1870, more than a quarter of Philadelphia's population was foreign-born, while more than a third of Toron-

Table 3.2   Population of Selected Cities and Metropolitan Areas, 1840–2000 (in Thousands)

City/Metropolitan Area	1840	1880/1881	1930/1931	1960/1961	2000/2001
New York	313	1,206	6,930	10,602	21,200
Los Angeles	1	11	2,319	6,669	16,374
Chicago	4	503	4,365	6,172	9,158
San Francisco	—	234	1,290	2,726	7,039
Philadelphia	220	847	2,347	4,301	6,188
Detroit	9	116	2,105	3,743	5,456
Toronto	13	86	810	1,919	4,683
Houston	—	17	339	1,237	4,670
Montreal	45	141	1,023	2,216	3,426
Phoenix	—	2	48	658	3,252
Pittsburgh	21	156	1,954	2,392	2,359
Vancouver	—	—	308	817	1,987

Note: The data for 1840 and 1890 refer to cities only. The 1930, 1960, and 2000 figures are for metropolitan areas as defined by the US and Canadian censuses.
Source: Various US and Canadian censuses.

to's population were between 1900 and 1930. The source of immigrants changed between 1800 and 1960. Before the 1880s, most were from northern and western Europe. Of the 9.2 million immigrants to the United States between 1820 and 1879, 8.2 million came from the British Isles, Scandinavia, and Germany. Illustrative of this is New York City in 1860, where more than half of the city's population was foreign-born, the vast majority coming from Ireland and Germany. Newcomers found work in the growing manufacturing trades or service sector and lived in areas populated by people from their home region. Beginning in the 1880s, immigrants were more likely to come from countries in southern and eastern Europe, such as Italy, Poland, and Russia. Despite differences in age, skill, and religion, foreign-born residents had several characteristics in common. First, the fact that the world they encountered in Canada and the United

States was culturally different from home led them to search for new forms of self-identity and to create a rich associational life in the New World. Second, even though some fled political repression, most immigrants were lured by economic opportunity. Third, immigrants tended to congregate in particular neighborhoods in New York, Montreal, and Atlanta. For example, the Lower East Side and Little Italy in New York City were immigrant enclaves (figure 3.6).

A second major migration stream to American cities was the move of rural-based, southern African Americans to northern cities. Between 1880 and 1970, in what is known as the Great Migration, six million African Americans fled the South for the promise of a new beginning in the North and the West. By World War II, large numbers had moved to northern industrial cities such as Detroit and Chicago to escape poverty and racism, look-

Figure 3.6   Lower East Side, New York City. *Source:* Library of Congress.

ing for work in the manufacturing, railroad, and service sectors. A much bigger surge after 1940 led to large increases in the number of African Americans moving to western cities such as Los Angeles and San Francisco as well as to northern ones. By 1960, there were more than 1.2 million African Americans living in New York City, while Chicago and Detroit had 920,000 and 564,000, respectively.

The industrial metropolis was divided by new forms of social distinction. There were three main classes. At one end of the class structure was the bourgeoisie. A small number of men such as George Pullman, Andrew Carnegie, and John D. Rockefeller amassed huge fortunes through their investment of industrial capital, control over a large wage-

labor force, and influence over social and political ideologies. At the other end, members of the working class, which constituted the vast bulk of the urban population, sold their labor power in order to exist. Even though they had little individual agency, workers gained collective power though unions (see box 3.3). Those in an intermediary class— the petite bourgeoisie—had a degree of control over their working and living conditions. Their place in society was acquired through education (lawyers, social workers) or small-scale business ownership (retailers, small-scale manufacturers). This basic class structure was complicated in several ways. Occupational differences centered on skill and trade created degrees of income and prestige

Box 3.3 Homestead, Pennsylvania: Class, Carnegie Steel, and the Amalgamated

Conflict between industrial managers and factory workers is endemic to urban industrial society. New class relations forged systemic conflict. Structural struggle between an industrial and financial bourgeoisie whose interests were directly linked to exploitation of labor and a working class whose interests lay in ending workplace exploitation and gaining a decent standard of living propelled ongoing clashes that took a variety of forms. One such struggle is the Homestead Strike of 1892.

Homestead, a small industrial town seven miles from downtown Pittsburgh, was a key node in the Andrew Carnegie steel empire (figure 3.7). The town, with its largely blue-collar population, was typical of many such places in the North American industrial heartland. In 1892, it was to become the center of a strike that would shape capital-labor relations for decades. In the spring of 1892, the Carnegie Steel Company and the Amalgamated Association of Iron and Steel Workers were at loggerheads over their collective agreement. Relations quickly spiraled downwards. While the union wanted a wage increase, Henry Clay Frick, the company manager, Carnegie's right-hand man, wanted to reduce wages by 22 percent. He was resolved to break the union. He locked the workers out of the mill and installed a high fence, several sniper towers, and water cannons around the plant. He also hired the notorious Pinkerton National Detective Agency to break the strike. By the time the collective agreement expired on June 30, the sides had hardened, with the union resolved to keep the plant closed and Frick to get the plant working, but with non-union workers. Tensions mounted during the first week of July.

Figure 3.7   Homestead mill, circa 1900–1910. *Source:* Library of Congress.

The situation exploded on July 6 to July 7, when a massive battle between workers and Pinkerton private security guards was touched off by the Pinkertons' attempt to capture control of the plant from the workers (figure 3.8). The fighting resulted in nine dead (six strikers and three guards). Even though the Pinkerton guards surrendered, the strike was broken as Governor Robert Pattison ordered six thousand state militiamen into the town to restore order. Over the next three months, all of the union leaders were charged with murder, treason, and various criminal offenses. Although only one was convicted, the legal proceedings pushed the union's finances and energy to the brink. No charges were brought against the Pinkerton Agency and Carnegie officials. Meanwhile, Frick brought in outside workers to replace the strikers. By September, the plant was in full operation. On October 13, the state militia pulled out, ending a ninety-five day occupation. Labor lost; capital won.

Figure 3.8   Homestead Strike featured in *Harper's Weekly*.
Source: Library of Congress.

The Homestead story is just one of hundreds of similar conflicts that shaped the everyday lives of North American city workers. The defeat at Homestead and the subsequent collapse of other steel-union actions in the first decades of the twentieth century were reversed with the 1935 Wagner Act and the 1947 Taft-Hartley Act. A combination of federal policy and the actions of organizations such as the Congress of Industrial Organizations (established in 1932) invigorated the union movement and worked to provide urban workers with some control over their work lives and better working conditions and wages.

among working-class males. Unequal gender relations operated to keep women in specific jobs (teaching, needlework, and domestics) that had the lowest income and status. Social and economic discrimination ensured that the majority of African Americans and foreign-born residents found themselves at the bottom of the lower socioeconomic scale.

Metropolitan social and economic divisions were accompanied by social inequality. Unemployment and poverty was rampant. Workers from the mid-nineteenth century onward shared little of the wealth generated by industrial expansion. Only skilled and white-collar workers met basic subsistence requirements. In Lowell in the 1860s, half of the Irish families did not have enough income to survive, while Italians in Buffalo between 1890 and 1916 earned only 50–80 percent of the income needed to support a family of five. Most families were unable to make a living income unless they had at least two wage earners. Even in times of full employment, workers faced low wages and long hours, terrible working conditions, and the absence of job security. They had little control over their work life. The urban labor force worked in a world where machine-dominated schedules were run by a hostile management. This was manifested through the increasing importance of scientific managerialism. Making ends meet was

very difficult for a significant share of the population in the industrial metropolis.

Until the 1960s most families survived the rigors of capitalist urbanization through a coping strategy centered on pooling resources and muting individual inclinations. The family economy's primary function was to assemble resources cooperatively for survival by sharing and reciprocity. These grew out of premigration class-based and gender-centered traditions of collective action and cultural solidarity. A set of formal institutions located in ethnic and working-class communities (unions, churches) supplied workers with places of worship, education, recreation, employment, charity, and credit. Kin relations determined both living and working arrangements and lay the basis for a family's economic and emotional stability. Cooperation at the family level took several forms: the centralization of family incomes; taking in of work (washing, sewing); and restrictions on education and leisure. Cooperation was gendered, with men doing paid work and women doing unpaid work at home. Families took in boarders, which often represented the margin between economic survival and catastrophe and helped subsidize a low-wage economy. Children, especially girls, were forced to leave school early to find paid work. Some working-class families invested whatever they could in buying a home as this was a viable alternative to high rents and one of the few hedges against unemployment and old age. Workers relied on the family economy to survive the precarious character of the urban economy.

For many, the fetid, squalid, and segregated industrial city was a difficult place to live and work. Unemployment was high, wages were low, and hours were long. Many people lived in poor to atrocious housing, where overcrowding, high rents, and poor conditions were the typical order of things (see figure 3.9). Awful environmental conditions, from coal-filled air to polluted waterways, were commonplace. Disease, frequently deadly, was rampant as housing squalor, poor nutrition, expensive health care, and the absence of decent public infrastructures combined to make death a frequent visitor to most households. By the last quarter of the nineteenth century, an urban reform movement emerged in order to find solutions to these problems. The movement had three main strands. Structural reformers believed that tinkering with local government and installing "good government" would make the problems dis-

appear. Moral reformers pushed legislative change aimed at controlling individual actions (Prohibition, 1919–1933) and limiting immigration (Johnson-Reed Act of 1924). Social reformers promoted change to a range of social and economic issues, including child labor, housing bylaws, bank regulation, and public health. All three strands had significant impacts on the everyday lives of North American city dwellers.

The industrial city was heavily segregated and functionally differentiated. Class, ethnic, and racial inequalities were translated into specialized and divided social spaces. The relatively intermixed residential geography of the commercial city was transformed into a set of homogenous social spaces defined along the lines of class, race, and ethnicity. Huge swaths of the city were home to immigrant and white native-born workers. These often featured ethnic concentrations, with Jews, Chinese, Italians, and Poles occupying different parts of the working-class areas, although there was a great deal of ethnic overlapping. The most divided areas were African American ghettos (box 3.4) and wealthy enclaves.

Figure 3.9   Housing in Camden, New Jersey, 1938. *Source:* Library of Congress.

Box 3.4 Chicago: Racial Divides and the Black Belt

In March 1919, Mr. and Mrs. R. B. Harrison moved to a new house on Grand Boulevard, Chicago. Two months later, their house was bombed. Eleven days later, the house was attacked again, this time by bombs lobbed from an adjacent vacant apartment house. On June 1, a bomb was hurled at the house of William Austin on Lake Shore Drive. Austin was the real-estate agent who sold the house to the Harrisons. Less than two months later, on July 27, Eugene Williams, a seventeen-year-old boy, was drowned at the 29th Street beach after being stoned by a crowd. Why? Williams had accidentally crossed an unmarked barrier that divided the beach. The death spawned a five-day riot. According to the Chicago coroner's report, the "five days of terrible hate and passions let loose cost the people of Chicago 38 lives, wounded and maimed several hundred, destroyed property of untold value, filled thousands with awful fright, blemished the good name of our city, and left in its wake fear and apprehension for the future."

The events of 1919 were not isolated. Between 1917 and 1924, more than fifty house bombings took place in Chicago. All of them had three things in common. First, they were all directed at African Americans (the Harrisons and Williams) and white realtors (Austin) who sold to African Americans. Second, their purpose was to stop the movement of African Americans into white residential areas. Third, they were geographically concentrated on the south side of Chicago along the border between white and black districts. These actions were taken to maintain social dominance through spatial control of black behavior. One effect of the cumulative actions in Chicago's racialized housing market was to create the South Side's Black Belt, the African American ghetto that has been a defining feature of the American city to the present day (figure 3.10). Homogenous neighborhoods and ghettos such as the

Figure 3.10   Children at the movies, Chicago, 1941. *Source:* Library of Congress.

Chicago Black Belt are produced by discriminatory housing and labor markets and the deep-seated and structural racism that pervades all elements of American urban society.

By World War II, most of Chicago's African American population lived in the ghetto. The Black Belt's housing and environmental conditions varied enormously. The professional and business classes living in substantially middle-class neighborhoods coexisted with the majority who lived in less than desirable conditions. Vast swaths of the area were overcrowded as population growth outpaced access to housing units, and multifamily households proliferated. Extortionate rents and the absence of reinvestment led to deteriorating housing conditions. African Americans typically paid higher housing costs, usually 10 to 15 percent higher, than whites for the same housing. Denied access to financial support and pushed to the lower echelons of the labor market, Chicago's African American population was confined to the city's worst housing and forcibly segregated from the rest of the city's population. Chicago was not unusual. By 1940, the ghetto had appeared all over the country, from Boston to Los Angeles. The situation has not become much better since then. Even today, the vast majority of US African Americans living in cities are also living in highly segregated neighborhoods.

While the former had few white residents, the latter had few low-income, black, or ethnic residents (other than servants). Segregation rested on the dynamics of the housing market (which produced unequal access), the labor market (which graded people by income and status), and social discrimination (which marginalized people by race and class).

Accompanying the formation of separate residential districts was the development of functionally differentiated economic districts. In the second half of the nineteenth century, the modern downtown was created. A central feature of the modern metropolis as we know it today was the emergence and growth of the central business district (CBD) and the downtown. Although a central business district had always been part of the North American city, the modern CBD and the adjacent downtown can be dated from the mid-nineteenth century. The CBD has two key features. First, it was a place of progress, modernity, and wealth. As the hub of financial, business, and

political decision making, it was the nexus of corporate power in an industrial capitalist society. Second, it was centrally located and distinguished by a specialized land-use pattern centered on four districts: financial, wholesaling and light manufacturing, civic institutions and entertainment, and retail. The relatively mixed central district of the commercial gave way to a highly differentiated economic landscape. Several forces, including the need to better coordinate the industrial economy, the demand for spatial proximity of allied functions, and rapidly rising land values, forced a refashioning of the central district.

Downtown was the home of two key defining institutions of the modern North American metropolis. Skyscrapers, which appeared in the 1880s, became the nexus of the nation's corporate economy. Towering above the street, from ten stories in the 1880s (Chicago's Montauk Building) to 102 stories in the 1930s (New York's Empire State), the skyscraper represented the economic and cultural power of the new economy. Even in smaller industrial cities such as Detroit, skyscrapers represented the power of manufacturing firms like GM and Chrysler (figures 3.11 and 3.12). The department store, which arrived on the urban scene in the middle of the nineteenth century, served the United States' and Canada's growing affluence. Emporiums of consumption, they anchored the retail district of the modern metropolis. While the downtown was home to a working-class population, the CBD had few, if any, homes. The industrial city was characterized by sharp land-use class divides.

This location and character of the social and economic divides separating the metropolitan population were controlled and orchestrated by an urban growth alliance. This alliance consisted of elites such as land developers, financial institutions, and local politicians who had strong interests in the city. While membership changed constantly and the relations among members were often conflictual, alliances worked together to devise land development and redevelopment projects, to promote the city as a place for outside investment, to reproduce a capitalist ideology of development and speculation, and to protect its own interests through its control over law and order, local bylaws, industrial relations, and so forth. The search for profits from land and locally based investments animated the actions of local land developers and financiers. Local politicians, on the other hand, worked with other members of the alliance to produce the services appropriate to the reproduction of social relations of place.

Figure 3.11   Detroit skyline, circa 1929. *Source:* Library of Congress.

Figure 3.12   New York City skyline seen from Brooklyn, 1900–1915. *Source:* Library of Congress.

These services were both hard (sewers, water mains, paved roads, public transit) and soft (ideological backing for land development and speculation, lackluster regulation of housing conditions).

One response to the escalating problems of the city was the development of modern planning. Planning was not unknown before 1900, although it differed from what emerged later. Modern, twentieth-century planning was rooted in a long tradition of ad hoc measures around sanitation, water, noxious industries, and segregation. What emerged after 1900, however, differed in the scale of intervention and comprehensiveness. Planning was a direct response to escalating urban problems and an attempt to maintain social and economic sta-

bility. Middle-class reformers sought to create a spatial order that was capable of sustaining the dynamics of capitalist development while minimizing its problems. The aim of planning was to manage urban growth in a scientific and efficient manner by regulating service provision and land use. By the 1920s, planning had been systematized and bureaucratized, and it consisted of two sets of experts: a governmental bureaucracy, which was to provide continuity and order to local government, and a technocratic system to plan and develop the city's physical reconstruction.

Suburban development, long a part of the North American city, became increasingly important after 1850. Suburbs were one of the solutions to the industrial city's problems. In economic terms, the suburb was a place for the making of profits, houses, infrastructure, and transit systems. Socially, the suburb was a place for the reproduction of social and economic divides. Suburbs allowed the upper and middle classes to escape the central city's growing social and economic disparities, escalating class and racial conflict, and deteriorating environmental conditions. Wealthy suburbs such as Riverside (Chicago), Llewellyn Park (New York City), Shaker Heights (Cleveland), and Westmount (Montreal) were based on principles of exclusion. The suburban housing market produced racial and class-based segregation.

A key element of the suburban housing market was the use of restrictive covenants. Structural covenants imposed minimum building values and acceptable construction material. Racial and ethnic covenants imposed restrictions on who could live in the development. One such covenant, used in the suburb of Westdale, just outside of Hamilton, Ontario, prescribed that "none of the land described . . . shall be used, occupied by or let or sold to negroes, Asiatics, Bulgarians, Austrians, Russians, Serbs, Rumanians, Turks, Armenians, whether British subjects or not, or foreign-born Italians, Greeks or Jews." These class and racial restrictions of the elite suburb were accompanied by new built forms. Elements such as the curved street and landscaped layout, detached homes on large lots, and, from the 1920s, wide roads and garages, appeared throughout North America. Landscape architects such as Frederick Law Olmsted sought to marry the advantages of the city with those of the country and to create a new bourgeois and middle-class world far from the turmoil of the central city.

The suburbs were also home to a substantial number of workers and factories. The majority of suburbanites on the eve of World War II were workers living in working-class suburbs. The defining elements of the hundreds of working-class residential suburbs that sprang up around most North American cities were a grid layout, small lots, modest, often attached, homes, and high densities. An array of developers opened up rural land for subdivision, while individual builders and relatively small building companies each built a small number of speculative houses. In some cases, as in Toronto in the first three decades of the twentieth century, owner-built housing was common. In others, a few company towns, such as the infamous Pullman (Chicago), were home to a large corporate workforce. Industrial suburbs became increasingly common after 1880. Some of these, such as Saint-Henri (Montreal) and Paterson (New Jersey; figure 3.13), were outgrowths of older artisanal and industrial towns, while others, such as Cicero (Chicago) and Fairfield (Birmingham), were built around corporate developments. The spatial sorting along the lines of class and race that had characterized the central city was being created in the suburbs as well. The industrial metropolis was a divided place.

POSTWAR HISTORICAL GEOGRAPHIES

Since the end of World War II, the urban population of Canada and the United States has grown enormously. In 1960, the central city, the suburbs, and the countryside were home to fifty-nine million Americans each.

Figure 3.13   Paterson, New Jersey, 1900–1906. *Source:* Library of Congress.

Forty years later, on the eve of the twenty-first century, 141 million and 85 million lived in the suburbs and the central city, respectively. The countryside's population had declined to fifty-five million. Both the United States and Canada are metropolitan societies. Much of this urban growth has taken place outside of the old industrial heartland of the Great Lakes and the Eastern Seaboard. Nearly two-thirds of the US population increase between 1900 and 2000 was in the West and the South. To the west, cities such as Vancouver, Calgary, and Edmonton in Canada, and Seattle, Los Angles, San Diego, Phoenix, and Denver in the United States have accelerated their increases in recent years. Similarly, southern cities such as Miami, Atlanta, and Houston have experienced large-scale development since World War II. There are

important differences between these postwar metropolitan areas and those that developed before 1900 in the northeastern part of the continent. The newer cities are more suburban places, with a greater proportion of their populations living outside the central city. Heavily dependent on the automobile, these suburbs tend to be of lower density, have a different housing profile, and cluster around new retail malls and business parks.

A key feature of the metropolitan population is the changing scale of immigration and the shifting origin of immigrants. In the immediate postwar period, there was a continuation of prewar patterns, with the vast majority of immigrants coming from different parts of Europe. The liberalization of immigration laws since the 1960s has caused a major shift away from European immigration in both countries. In the United States, for example, 83 percent of legal immigrants came from Asia and Latin America in the 1980s. It is estimated that there were more than eleven million illegal immigrants in the United States in 2008, two-thirds of whom are from Mexico. Close to half of Toronto's population is immigrant, and one in three residents speaks a language other than French or English at home. The large-scale flow of European immigrants has been replaced by a massive movement of people from all over the world. As a result, North American metropolitan areas are larger and more cosmopolitan than they have ever been.

The metropolitan economy has been transformed over the past fifty years. Deindustrialization has undermined the economy of most northern and midwestern cities, a change we explore in greater detail in chapter 5. Since the 1960s, North American cities have experienced large-scale manufacturing loss. This is especially the case in the northeastern and midwestern parts of the United States. Some Canadian cities such as Winnipeg, Montreal, and Brantford also have suffered a long-term structural decline of their manufacturing base. In general, though, Canadian cities were not as hard hit as American ones. Deindustrialization can be measured in two ways: absolute manufacturing job loss and falling share of national employment. The Great Lakes states, for example, lost 1.37 million manufacturing jobs, 16 percent of their total, between 1979 and 1985. The same area's share of national employment fell from 48 percent in 1960 to 33 percent in 1985. Structural industrial decline such as this has a reverse circular and cumulative causation effect. Once factory closings, plant downsizing, and job loss become a typical part of the urban regime, a negative process

is created that neutralizes existing capital and labor-force assets, stifles incoming investment and innovation, leads to declines in ancillary sectors (retail, construction), and undermines the local tax base. Spiraling downward growth becomes the order of the day.

Manufacturing, the city's key sector, has been replaced by a different set of sectors. Alongside the ever-present construction, transportation, and retail industries are a mix of new quaternary and tertiary service jobs geared to knowledge production and overseeing the expanding global corporate economy. While most cities continue to have a mix of work opportunities, high-end service jobs are concentrated in a few of the older metropolitan areas (New York, Chicago, and Toronto) and a small number of newer ones (Houston, Phoenix, and Vancouver). A growing share of employment is to be found in suburbs. This transformation has led to greater inequality as incomes have become increasingly polarized and a well-to-do blue-collar population has more or less disappeared. Median family incomes have fallen since the 1970s, while those of the wealthy have increased. Neoliberal policies have scaled back the welfare system, which has led to increasing levels of homelessness, unemployment, poverty, and crime. Social and economic disparities continue to haunt the American and Canadian metropolis.

Postwar metropolitan areas have been greatly shaped by the intervention of the federal state. Since the 1930s, the federal government has become increasingly involved in housing provision. In the United States and Canada, housing acts such as the National Housing Act (1934, 1937, and 1938) have been followed by a series of postwar acts that have greatly shaped the housing market.

Other than mortgage write-offs for (mainly middle-class) homeowners, the most important intervention had been the construction of millions of units of public housing, most of which were built in the central city. While providing housing for the less well-off, public housing has reproduced the same sorts of class- and racially based segregated enclaves created by the private housing market. Until very recently, immigrants, African Americans, and the white poor have been concentrated in the central city, while the upper and middle classes were to be found largely in the suburbs. The state has also been critical to suburban development. Accounting for 90 percent of the entire cost, the federal government built forty-one thousand miles of limited-access highway between 1956 and 1971. Connecting the nation's cities, the highway also facilitated the development of suburban retail, commercial, and industrial nodes, pushed a large-scale exodus of people from the central city to the suburbs, and underpinned the formation of a multicentric metropolitan pattern by linking what had previously been isolated suburban areas.

Social and economic divides continue to characterize the metropolitan landscape. Gentrification, which is defined as the restoration of run-down urban areas by the middle class that results in the displacement of low-income residents, has led to a revitalization of inner-city neighborhoods but has also resulted in the dismantling of working-class communities, higher land values, the undermining of an area's industrial fabric, and increased social segregation. Increased income polarization along with reduced federal expenditures on everything from food stamps to public housing have ensured that other parts of the city continue to be race- and class-based ghettos of deprivation. These social and economic divides are moving out to the suburbs. The postwar movement of the white population of all classes out of the central city led to a deeply entrenched city-suburban divide along racial lines. Large developers and governments have produced a series of housing submarkets that works to produce racial and income enclaves. Increasingly after World War II, the major divide was between city and suburb. Gated communities, and in a few places such as Canyon Lake (Los Angeles), gated cities, are spread throughout the suburbs. They are home to at least eight million people in the United States in the late 1990s. With their walls, gates, limited access, and security guards, they are a modern version of the strict exclusion practiced in the nineteenth-century bourgeois suburb. The suburbs are also becoming home to an increasing number of immigrants. Once corralled into the inner city, Asian and Latin American immigrants are moving to suburbs in search of work and housing. While there is a degree of social mixing in the new suburbs, the older patterns of segregation along the lines of class, ethnicity, and race continues to plague the North American metropolis.

While the contemporary American and Canadian metropolitan area is quite different from anything that has come before, it nevertheless faces a set of challenges that are not unique to the twenty-first century. Economic, social, and political issues that challenge the urban dweller today, such as the inequities of the housing market, the ongoing questions of racism and other forms of discrimination, the difficulty of many to navigate and survive the rigors of the capitalist labor market, the control of local politics by alliances of corporate, political, and financial elites, and the continued existence of divided and exclusionary spaces, have always haunted the city. It is true that the form, character, and dynamics of these issues distinguish the contemporary city from those of the past. Nevertheless, the Irish servant living in eighteenth-century Montreal or Boston, the East European Jewish immigrant and the African American from the American South who moved to New York City and Chicago in the late nineteenth century, and the migrants arriving in Los Angeles from the Dust Bowl in the 1930s have all encountered a complex, difficult, and bewildering urban world. While commercial, industrial, and modern forms of capitalism have created unprecedented wealth and power, they have also created enormous inequalities. The inequalities inherent to capitalism are embedded in the social, political, and economic spaces of the commercial city, the industrial metropolis, and the contemporary metropolis. A better understanding of the character and dynamics of the urban past can help us find solutions to the challenges of today's urban world.

SUGGESTED READINGS

Barrett, J. R. 1987. *Work and Community in the Jungle: Chicago's Packinghouse Workers, 1894–1922*. Urbana: University of Illinois Press.

Bauman, J., and E. Muller. 2006. *Before Renaissance: Planning in Pittsburgh, 1889–1943*. Pittsburgh: University of Pittsburgh Press.

Cronon, W. 1991. *Nature's Metropolis: Chicago and the Great West*. New York: Norton.

Freund, D. 2007. *Colored Property: State Policy and White Racial Politics in Suburban America*. Chicago: University of Chicago Press.

Harris, R. 1996. *Unplanned Suburbs: Toronto's American Tragedy, 1900 to 1950*. Baltimore: Johns Hopkins University Press.

High, S. 2003. *Industrial Sunset: The Making of North America's Rust Belt, 1969–1984*. Toronto: University of Toronto Press.

Hirsch, A. 1983. *Making the Second Ghetto: Race and Housing in Chicago, 1940–1960*. Chicago: University of Chicago Press.

Nicolaides, B. 2002. *My Blue Heaven: Life and Politics in the Working-Class Suburbs of Los Angeles*. Chicago: University of Chicago Press.

Scranton, P. 1989. *Figured Tapestry: Production, Markets, and Power in Philadelphia Textiles, 1885–1941*. Cambridge: Cambridge University Press.

Sugrue, T. 1996. *The Origins of the Urban Crisis: Race and Inequality in Postwar Detroit*. Princeton: Princeton University Press.

Warner, S. B., Jr. 1972. *The Urban Wilderness: A History of the American City*. New York: Harper and Row.

Zunz, O. 1982. *The Changing Face of Inequality: Urbanization, Industrial Development, and Immigrants in Detroit, 1880–1920*. Chicago: University of Chicago Press.

4

Border Cities
LINDSEY SUTTON

Although this book focuses on cities in the United States and Canada, these cities are bound together in networks and linkages with many cities in Mexico, constituting a broader regional relationship. These networks and linkages are found most notably among border cities, the subject of this chapter.

The greetings "Bienvenidos," "Bienvenue," and "Welcome" posted on signs alert border crossers at the Mexican, US, and Canadian borders of the political boundary they are crossing and briefly reveal the diverse cultures that inform everyday processes in North America (figure 4.1). In 2010, 80 percent of the Canadian population, approximately twenty-seven million people, lived within 160 kilometers of the Canadian-US border, and more than thirteen million Mexican and US residents lived in the US-Mexico border region (defined as one hundred kilometers south and north of the border). In Mexican and US border states, shoppers, families, businessmen, and tourists engage in conversations mixing English and

Figure 4.1   Welcome sign at US border near Columbus, New Mexico. (Photo by Lindsey Sutton)

Spanish, while in some Canadian and US border cities, border residents may use either English or French. In Canada, French and English are the national languages; in 2006, approximately 57 percent of the population learned English as a first language, and 22 percent learned French as a first language. In Mexico, Spanish is the national language, but in the northern border states, many residents also speak English. In US border cities such as El Paso, Texas, or Nogales, Arizona, where about 81 and 95 percent of the population are of Hispanic or Latino descent, families often speak Spanish at home.

Everyday landscapes, including graffiti and murals along border walls, bilingual advertisements in storefronts, and constant traffic flows, remind border-city residents of the extensive relationships and the contested spaces of border cities in North America (figure 4.2). Along the US-Mexico border, constructed

fences, border markers, and signage embody the contemporary political-economic context of heightened border security and migration flows from Mexico to the United States (figure 4.3). Infrastructure and facilities at crossing points also clearly mark the Canadian-US border, but political debate and news media focus far less attention on the border between Canada and the United States. Transborder exchanges occur within economic, social-cultural, political, and environmental dimensions and across urban, regional, and national scales. These border cities are significantly impacted by the ways in which individual experiences create multiple layers of simultaneously occurring transborder exchanges in particular places that span the length of the 5,500-mile border between Canada and the United States and the 1,900-mile border between Mexico and the United States (figures 4.4 and 4.5).

Figure 4.2   *Fronteras: Cicatrizes en la Tierra* (*Borders: Scars in the Landscape*). The graffiti on a border wall in Nogales, Sonora, states, "Borders: Scars in the Landscape." (Photo by Casey D. Allen)

Figure 4.3 Border vehicle, barrier fence, and drainage fence near Naco, Arizona, and Naco, Sonora. (Photo by Lindsey Sutton)

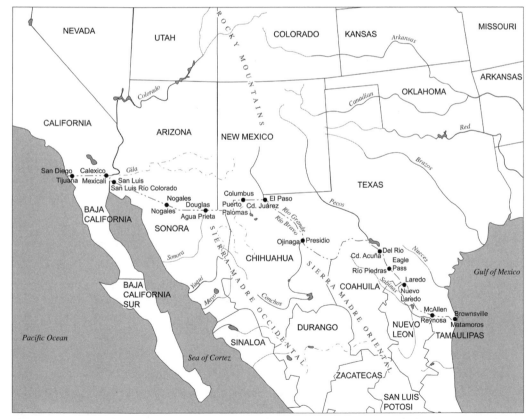

Figure 4.4 Map of US-Mexico border states and selected cities. *Source:* Lindsey Sutton and ArcGIS US Census files.

Figure 4.5   Map of US-Canada border states and selected cities. *Source:* Lindsey Sutton and ArcGIS US Census files.

MEXICO'S TWENTIETH-CENTURY INDUSTRIALIZING BORDER LANDSCAPE

As the three North American economies grew in the early twentieth century, newly built railroads in the southwestern United States and northern Mexico established trade routes that linked remote areas in Mexican border states to the US economy. In the state of Sonora, Mexico, railroad connections to the United States provided Mexican residents easier and closer access to goods and services that were hard to obtain from the distant national, political, and economic center in Mexico City. Railroad infrastructure also facilitated business opportunities for US companies seeking to develop mineral resources in Mexico and created a transborder network of copper routes, linking border cities such as Bisbee and Naco, Arizona, to towns like

Cananea in Sonora. This region, geographically defined as the "copper borderlands," attracted small time *gambusinos*, prospectors who claimed land stakes in search of gold, silver, and copper. Abandoned today, a few of these smaller mining claims remain visible in the Rio Sonora region and in the mountains of southern New Mexico and southeastern Arizona (see box 4.1).

Realizing the economic importance of the border, Mexico's national economic development strategies starting in the 1950s targeted the region as a means to boost employment and industrialize the national economy. As one of the most aggressive strategies, the Border Industrialization Program of 1964 sought to stimulate manufacturing sectors by funneling money into the construction of *maquilas*, factories, that would serve as assembly plants for US and other multinational corporations. In addition to Mexico's investment in border industrial infrastructure, the US Foreign-Trade Zone Act of 1934 and Tariff Law of 1965 provided policy infrastructure for bilateral trade by exempting general import duties on US goods assembled in whole or in part outside of the United States in foreign-trade zones. The exemption from import duties, combined with lower wages and operating costs, allowed US companies to cut overall production costs of manufactured goods. In Mexico, the Border Industrialization Program restructured a landscape that had been isolated and rural to one of industrial urban centers. By 2000, the number of *maquilas* in border towns reached 3,590 but decreased to approximately 2,800 in 2010 because of competition from China and global economic recessions.

In the early stages, *maquilas* manufactured basic textiles, but by the 1980s, more highly skilled workers enabled *maquilas* to produce parts for the automotive, domestic electrical appliances, and computer industries. During the peak years of manufacturing, from 1990 to 2002, employment in *maquilas* in the border cities increased some 150 percent. *Maquilas* were also built in cities such as Cananea, Sonora, approximately forty miles from the border but still close enough to engage in transborder trade. Although the work was labor intensive and often tedious, *maquila* workers earned 25 percent higher wages than workers in the other regions of Mexico in the early 2000s and also received health insurance and social security benefits. Both the type of

---

Box 4.1 A History of Mining in the Border Region

Some forty miles from the border, Cananea, Sonora, home to 32,936 people in 2010, is a key urban center in the borderlands region, in part because of its past and present mining ties to the United States. The city's mining history began in the seventeenth century when Spanish explorers founded several *minas reales*, or royal mines, in the area. These early ventures failed because of geographic isolation and conflict with Native American populations, but later, copper-mining operations formed transborder ties between Cananea, Sonora, and several southern Arizona towns. In the late nineteenth century, US investment in transborder mining economies expanded as a result of railroad networks. In early 1900 and 1901, US businessman Colonel William Greene, backed by other investors, formed the Cananea Consolidated Copper Company (CCCC), developing the mines and building smelters to process ore for export to southern Arizona. Although a successful export business, the company's lack of investment in the local economy and unequal treatment of workers led to conflict that tainted the early period of US mining operations in northern Mexico. By 1906, tensions between the company and employees erupted, mine workers went on strike, and skirmishes between miners, US volunteer armed forces, and the Mexican Rural Police resulted in several deaths. For the next two years, the mine was closed, and the CCCC restructured operations, updated technology, and improved worker conditions in order to reopen the mines in 1908. Meanwhile, Col. Greene expanded his mining investments in Sonora and Chihuahua, but he overextended company finances and bankrupted the mine.

From 1934 to 1982, the Mexican government nationalized the CCCC's holdings and began shipping copper ore to Mexico City to be smelted. Nationalization of copper resources as well as other natural resources corresponded to the Mexican revolutionary nationalistic sentiment that increased Mexican manufacturing through domestic industrialization. Today, Mexicana de Cananea, S.A., a subsidiary of Grupo Mexico, a holding company, privately owns the mines and is one of the major mining companies operating in Mexico, Peru, and the United States (figure 4.6). Evident by these extensive present-day multinational business investments in northern Mexico, the historical mining legacies contribute to a regional transborder mining identity.

Figure 4.6   The Grupo Mexico smelter in Cananea, Sonora. (Photo by Lindsey Sutton)

work and the benefits attracted a majority female workforce. The majority of *maquila* workers tended to be women because managers believed women were more adept at the type of work, had more patience, and were less likely to organize and strike. In 1975, women made up 80 percent of the *maquila* workforce in border states, but this number declined to 58 percent in 2000. Starting in the late 1970s, employment of women at the *maquilas* altered the social dynamics of traditional Mexican families, in which women typically were homemakers. Instead, steady employment at *maquilas* put women in the position of main income earner, often increasing tensions in couples. In cities such as Reynosa, Ciudad Juarez, Ciudad Acuña, and Tijuana, while wives, mothers, and daughters held steady jobs in *maquilas*, their male counterparts faced uncertainties searching across the border for work that was less stable and lower paid. Starting in the 1990s in Ciudad Juarez, such shifts in social dynamics incited domestic violence against women, and serial killings targeting women resulted in upwards of five hundred deaths from 1993 to 2010.

MACRO TRENDS—TRILATERAL TRADE AND NATIONAL ECONOMIES

Free trade agreements such as the General Agreement on Trade and Tariffs (GATT) in 1947 (later to be incorporated into the World Trade Organization in 1994), the Canada-US Free Trade Agreement in 1987, and the North American Free Trade Agreement (NAFTA) in 1994 decreased trade barriers, expanded free trade zones, and oriented US, Canadian, and Mexican national economies toward trilateral free trade. At the macro level, trade statistics describe growing economies and exchanges across boundaries since 2000. From 1993 to 2010, trilateral trade in North America increased by 200 percent, indicating greater economic cooperation among the countries of North America. This trade relationship has remained strong despite the 2008 global economic downturn.

Of the three North American countries, Mexico has experienced the largest growth in export trade in the past thirty years. In the 1980s, Mexico's exports totaled (US) $25 billion and made up less than 15 percent of Mexico's total gross domestic product (GDP), but by 2010, exports totaled $300 billion and made up 30 percent of total GDP. Mexico is now the United States' third-largest trading partner in goods; the total value of trade between Mexico and the United States has reached $600 billion. This increased trade has impacted Mexico as well as the United States; the six Mexican border states are among the top ten wealthiest states in Mexico, where people earn between $10,000 and $20,000 annually.

TRANSBORDER TRADE AND BORDER CITIES

Today, Canadian, US, and Mexican border cities comprise the main points of access to state and national markets in North America. At the urban scale, politicians and city planners consider the needs of populations, the opportunities that transborder commerce creates for cities, the logistics of managing transborder economies, and the infrastructure needed to maintain linkages to national economies. Commercial trucking transports the majority of transborder land-based trade in North America. In 2010, three million loaded truck containers crossed the US border from Mexico, and four million loaded truck containers crossed the US border from Canada. Regulations on vehicles, licensing, and pollution as agreed on by NAFTA oversee commercial trucks. Any truck crossing into the United States from Canada or Mexico as part of commercial trade must meet US standards as well as adhere to driving safety standards. Companies such as Transportez Olympic located in Monterrey, Chihuahua, approximately 136 miles from the border, are well aware of these standards and know that in order to maintain good business relations and make profits, they must follow US commercial trucking regulations. Because commercial trucking is an extremely important facet of North American trade, border ports of entry (POEs) must maintain up-to-date infrastructure. POEs are the physical customs facilities in the United States, Canada, and Mexico through which pedestrians, vehicles, and goods leave one country and enter the other. In places such as Santa Teresa and Columbus, New Mexico, where the majority of trucks bring in produce and livestock, border facilities need to ensure timely crossings as well as provide infrastructural capacity to deal with large quantities of agricultural imports. The two New Mexico POEs process one-third of all livestock imports from Mexico to the United States; the majority happens at the newer POE of Santa Teresa. These facilities were built in 1991 in order to redirect agricultural trade to a point of entry along the US-Mexico border that was nearer to the larger US cities of El Paso, Texas, and Las Cruces, New Mexico. At Santa Teresa, instead of transporting livestock between border port facilities, livestock, most often cattle, cross the border in the corrals that straddle the border, where they are inspected, dipped, and registered with the customs broker before being delivered to buyers.

At many bridge and highway border crossings, trusted traveler programs such as NEXUS expedite the border clearance process for cardholders entering Canada or the United States. Additionally, the Free and Secure Trade program (FAST) provides commercial clearance for businesses to trade between the United States, Mexico, and Canada. These programs along with updated and expanded physical infrastructure provide safe and quick travel routes for truck and personal vehicles into city centers and around congested areas. In Nogales, Arizona, and Nogales, Sonora, the Mariposa Bridge is a multilane highway bridge that crosses west of the cities, diverting traffic from busy downtowns where the interplay between shoppers, tourists, workers, and vehicles often create major traffic jams. Originally built in 1976 for freight traffic, it has recently added more vehicle lanes and two FAST lanes to accommodate increased vehicle flows and connect Mexico's Highway 15 directly to Hermosillo, the capital city and economic center of the state of Sonora. Similar bridge and highway infrastructure expedites traffic flows along the US-Canadian border in cities such as Detroit, Michigan, and Windsor, Ontario. Congestion, disjointed infrastructure, and community needs led to a nearly fifteen-year construction project to rehabilitate the Ambassador Bridge border crossing (see box 4.2).

Box 4.2 Gateways of the Industrial North American Border Region

Detroit, Michigan, and Windsor, Ontario, share similar histories in auto manufacturing. As part of Ontario's 260-mile-long automotive corridor, Windsor has one of the highest number of auto parts plants in the province, along with Toronto and Mississauga. In 2007, there were 107 auto parts plants in Windsor, 137 in Mississauga, and 169 in Toronto. In the United States, Detroit leads auto manufacturing and is home to the Big Three—General Motors, Ford, and Chrysler.

In an era of shrinking North American manufacturing, cities such as Detroit and Windsor consider tourism to be one possibility for rebuilding local economies. But when new security measures required all travelers from Canada, the United States, and Mexico to carry passports to enter the United States, business owners in Detroit worried about the impact on their sales and profits. Despite these new passport regulations, transborder commercial flows have actually increased, creating demand for improved infrastructure at the fifteen urban ports of entry between Windsor and Detroit. In 2010, commercial trade between Windsor and Detroit comprised over 40 percent of total trade flows between the United States and Canada.

In an effort to facilitate these vital economic links, the cities of Windsor and Detroit formed initiatives to address outdated border-crossing infrastructure. In Canada, the "Let's Get Windsor Essex Moving" strategy emerged as a cooperative effort between Canadian municipal, county, and province governments to address the needs of residential and commercial traffic flows at the city level. However, disagreements between Canadian municipal and province approaches delayed improvements. In the United States, the Ambassador Bridge Gateway Project in Detroit faced similar multilevel challenges to connect US Interstates 75 and 96 to the bridge crossing as well as reconnect the community of Mexicantown via the Bagley Street pedestrian bridge crossing over I-75 (figure 4.7). After years of legal battles, construction obstacles, and unexpected delays due to antiquated municipal infrastructure, the project was completed in 2011. Today, state-of-the-art infrastructure allows for trucks to transport the majority of the $73 billion transborder trade in goods that cross the Ambassador Bridge annually.

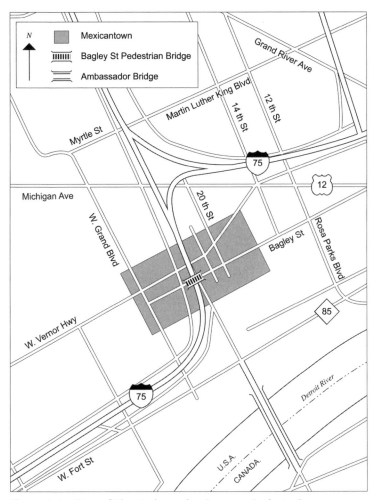

Figure 4.7   Map of the Ambassador Gateway Project. *Source:* Adapted from Michigan Department of Transportation.

The Great Lakes St. Lawrence Seaway System is one example of the binational water thoroughfares between the United States and Canada. The movement of goods along the waterway system exceeds 160 million metric tons in commercial trade annually, generating some $34 billion of economic activity in Canada and the United States. This deep-draft navigation system is the longest in the world and allows seaway traffic to transport goods from the Atlantic Gulf of St. Lawrence to ports on Lake Erie and Lake Ontario, bypassing the Niagara Falls. However, the St. Lawrence River is also a corridor for black-market economic transactions.

Higher taxes on tobacco and consequently higher-priced cigarettes in Canada have increased demand for lower-priced black-market tobacco products from the United States. Since the 1980s, cigarette smuggling from the United States into Canada has proven to be a lucrative illegal trade, generating annual profits upwards of $1.5 billion dollars in Canada. Smugglers transporting illegal cigarettes to Canada use speedboats to outrun Integrated Border Enforcement Teams patrolling the river. Much of this illegal trade passes through Cornwall Island, the Mohawk Native American territory of Akwesasne situated in Canadian river waters, where geographical and political boundaries complicate the apprehension of drug and human traffickers. The smuggling of illegal immigrants through the Mohawk territory was even the subject of a 2008 film, *Frozen River*, for which the actress Melissa Leo won an Academy Award. Sensitive jurisdictional boundaries between Canada and the Akwesasne Mohawk territory make catching smugglers difficult because in 2009, the Canadian Border Services Agency permanently closed its customs office on Cornwall Island. While some smugglers operate on a small scale, the multinational US-based company R. J. Reynolds Tobacco Company and Canadian-based firm JTI-Macdonald Corporation were involved with major smuggling operations in the 1980s and 1990s. In 2010, a nearly ten-year investigation by the Royal Canadian Mounted Police brought cigarette smuggling charges dating from 1992 against R. J. Reynolds and Macdonald that was settled when both companies pleaded guilty. Although the Canadian government estimated a loss of $10 billion in tax revenue, it settled for $550 million in fines. Despite this milestone achievement, profits from cigarette smuggling reached an estimated $2.2 billion in 2011, indicating that supply of and demand for black-market goods continue to transgress border restrictions.

At the US-Mexico border, escalating violence from drug trafficking exemplifies the devastating political and social impacts that illicit flows of goods can have on border populations. Recent media reports about drug mules, violence in Ciudad Juarez, and murder rates in Mexico draw attention to Mexican drug cartels' deliberate use of violence and the ways in which victims unknowingly participate or are forced into drug trafficking. The United States in 2010 alone spent $3.6 billion on drug trafficking interdiction efforts and invested $175 million in counternarcotics aid to Mexico.

In smaller US border towns, the increased rates of murders, kidnappings, and drug-use create fear. In Columbus, Las Cruces, and Deming, New Mexico, some residents hesitate to visit the nearby Mexican border town of Las Palomas, Chihuahua. In the past, Las Palomas was a popular day-trip destination for tourists, shoppers, and families, but today the town of approximately four thousand people experiences economic hardships as a result of fewer visitors crossing the border. As businesses close in town, decreasing work opportunities for younger generations in Las Palomas may lead some to turn to drug trafficking to earn money. In November 2009, the violence hit close to home when armed men kidnapped Dr. Ricardo Fierro, a dentist in Las Palomas who served both Mexican and US residents living in nearby New Mexico communities. Despite increasing violence, small businesses continue to advertise in the United States as well as cater to the local community in hopes of reviving economy and community and combating the perceived negative image of Mexican border towns. A locally owned and operated business, Palomas Oilcloth Designs, is one example of economic and gender development that resulted in a successful fair-trade transborder business. The business began when a few women in Las Palomas started creating and sewing bags, tablecloths, and other designs using oilcloth. With the encouragement and support of the nonprofit organization Border Partners, the women-owned business sells its products in stores in Las Palomas, Chihuahua, Silver City, Deming, and Las Cruces, New Mexico, and at small import stores in other US states.

CROSSING THE BORDER—
PEOPLE GOING PLACES

The population along the Texas-Mexico border region continues to grow and is home to two of the ten fastest-growing metropolitan areas in the United States, Laredo and McAllen. These cities' populations increased at twice the rate of the total population in the state of Texas. Estimates suggest that by 2030, the US-Mexico border region popula-

tion could reach twenty-five million. As population numbers increase, border residents continue to eat, shop, visit family, and make recreational outings across the borders to Canada, the United States, and Mexico.

At the US-Mexico border, the direct connection of border city to border city is evident by the significant amount of pedestrian traffic. Cities with the highest number of crossers (over one million) included Laredo, Hidalgo, El Paso, and Brownsville in Texas, San Ysidro, Otay Mesa, and Calexico in California, and San Luis and Nogales in Arizona (table 4.1). At the port level, the fewest number of pedestrians crossed at Sasabe, Arizona, where in 2010 some 1,127 people walked across the border. This small town of about 125 people is far from other urbanized areas in a remote desert region but has become a major corridor for unauthorized immigration from Mexico to the United States. Migrants begin their journey north in the town of Altar, Sonora, situated sixty miles south of Sasabe, Arizona, where they make preparations by filling backpacks with bare necessities. On the plaza, a mural of the Virgin of Guadalupe warns against the dangers

Table 4.1   US-Mexico Border Crossing Data

State	Number of POEs	2010 Border Crossers (Pedestrians)	% of Total 2010 Pedestrian Border Crossers
Texas	11	17,155,610	43.0
New Mexico	2	370,988	0.93
Arizona	6	7,648,107	19.2
California	6	14,740,276	36.9
Total		39,914,981	100

Source: Bureau of Transportation Statistics (BTS). 2010. "Border Crossing/Entry Data: Pedestrians." http://www.bts.gov/programs/international/transborder/TBDR_BC/TBDR_BCQ.html. Accessed February 17, 2012.

Figure 4.8   Migrants in Altar, Sonora, prepare with backpacks and water for their journey north to the border. (Photo by Lindsey Sutton)

of crossing the border, while hopeful migrants catch minibuses that drive recklessly along dirt roads and make scheduled stops where crossers will be met by a smuggler, called a *coyote* or *pollero* (figure 4.8).

Pedestrian traffic at the US-Canadian border is significantly less than at the US-Mexico border. This may be because the Canadian and US border cities are set farther away from the border and have downtowns and shopping districts that are more conveniently reached by vehicle. In 2010, almost 400,000 people crossed the Canadian-US border as pedestrians, most at Buffalo-Niagara Falls. This unique river border between Canada and the United States that joins Lake Ontario and Lake Erie attracts millions of tourists annually from all over the world and is advertised as the "Honeymoon Capital of the World."

Border Shoppers

Since 2009, the new security regulations require that US, Canadian, and Mexican residents carry passports in order to enter or re-enter the United States. Canadian residents do not need a nonimmigrant visa, but Mexican residents entering the United States at a land POE must obtain a nonimmigrant visa or border-crossing card, also known as a tourist visa. Despite concerns that the new regulations would negatively impact transborder exchanges, Canadian and Mexican residents continue to make shopping trips to major cities across the border for foodstuffs, clothes, electronics, pharmaceuticals, and home appliances. For example, in Tucson, sales to Mexican residents make retail chains such as Best Buy among the highest-volume stores in the nation. Along the Texas-Mexico border, Mexican shoppers spend an estimated two to three billion dollars on clothes, electronics, and other consumer goods. Most border shoppers make day or weekend trips in search of less-expensive consumer goods, brand-name clothes, and a larger variety of items. During the holidays, shoppers from the state of Sonora put up with wait times lasting several hours at border crossings in order to bring back presents for families and friends, driving as far as Tucson and Phoenix for shopping excursions. The Mexican *aduanas*, the customs office, allows residents to bring in goods valuing from $75 to $300 if traveling by land, depending on what type of exemption status the resident holds. However, during the holidays, in order to bring in more items whose value exceeds the maximum, shoppers will cut tags off merchandise, layer clothing, and find places to stash clothing in suitcases in hopes that if searched, these items will go undetected. Some shoppers also take advantage of bargain buys at dollar and department stores in the United States. They purchase in bulk to bring items back to smaller towns in Mexico where there are few other stores offering home wares, clothing, and other items and resell them to locals who cannot cross the border. This practice is illegal, and if Mexican customs agents find out about such operations, they fine individuals and confiscate the goods.

Canadians also visit the United States to shop, and various websites provide tips about prices, merchandise value limits, taxes, duty-free shopping, and border wait times. Lower sales taxes and prices make US cities popular shopping destinations for residents living in Canada. In 2010, changes in Canadian tax laws that resulted in tax exemptions in the State of Washington created confusion between retail businesses and local residents in the US border cities of Blaine and Bellingham. For a brief period, the Washington Department of Revenue exempted Canadian residents from sales tax in an effort to increase transborder shopping. But residents in Blaine and Bellingham argued that the exemption for Canadians would significantly decrease

tax revenue for the state and for Whatcom County since stores in these cities made up to 40 percent of their sales to Canadian residents. They also noted that the decrease in revenue would impact the Whatcom County transit system, which depended on sales tax for 85 percent of its revenue. In response to outcry from Washington residents, the state senate and house revoked the tax exemption for Canadian residents and ended the short-lived period of tax-free shopping for Canadians traveling to Washington. Despite this, Canadian shoppers continue to come to US border cities for shopping.

While Canadian and Mexican residents take advantage of shopping bargains in the United States, US residents seek out less-expensive health-care options in Canada and Mexico. Medical tourism between Canada and the United States as well as Mexico and the United States has fueled cross-border traffic for more than fifty years (figure 4.9). US border residents make trips across the border to Canada or to Mexico to seek out dental care and optometry services and to fill prescriptions at much lower costs than in the United States. In Nogales, Sonora, sixty dentist offices located in a three-block radius have inspired some to refer to the area as "Root Canal Street." Overall, the access to more affordable health-care services in Canada and Mexico attracts retired populations to settle in border towns along the northern and southern borders in the United States, but online medical prescription services also facilitate transborder pharmaceutical sales. In 2003, approximately 60 percent of the total dollar amount of undeclared prescription drugs that entered into the United States came from Canada, totaling $700 million. In southern US border communities, shuttles

Figure 4.9   Pharmacies in Naco, Sonora, ca. April 2006. (Photo by Lindsey Sutton)

from places such as Las Cruces, New Mexico, or Bisbee, Arizona, facilitate this connection by bringing individuals to border towns specifically to make pharmaceutical purchases or to see doctors, dentists, and optometrists.

LIVING IN BORDER CITIES

In the border regions, transnational networks connect families, economies, and political groups across borders, but these networks also extend beyond the border to cities such as Chicago, New York, Mexico City, Oaxaca, Montreal, and Toronto, creating hybrid landscapes of multiple nationalities and cultures. In these cities as well as border cities, restaurants, supermarkets, herbal and medicinal stores, hometown associations, churches, apparel shops, and radio stations provide familiar cultural settings and offer services and goods for migrant communities. These and other community infrastructures help

newly established immigrants and transient migrants maintain connections to their home country and offer transitional spaces in which people become comfortable with their new places of residence (see box 4.3). Additionally, efforts at the country level, such as the Mexican government's promotion of a "global Mexican nation" that extends voting rights to Mexican expatriates, indicate that sending countries may support transnational networks in an effort to keep emigrants in touch with the national identity and to encourage remittances. At the city level, shuttle-van companies offer services for workers or shoppers or long-distance transportation for families between cities such as Phoenix, Tucson, Los Angeles, San Antonio, Nogales, Durango, Chihuahua, and Monterrey (see box 4.4).

In addition to Anglo, French, and Hispanic identities, many other ethnic and cultural groups call the border regions of North America home. The case of Mormon and Mennonite people moving from the United

Box 4.3 Geographic Perspectives on Transnational Lives

Transnationalism is a theoretical approach that studies transborder activities and lifestyles that rely on networks and capital to maintain ties between a home country and a new place of residence. When people move from sending to receiving communities, they establish social institutions, political groups, everyday routines, and economic activities that help them adapt to life in their new places of residence while incorporating cultural practices and traditions from their home regions. Research within the field of transnationalism typically studies community and ethnic identities, political organizations, flows of goods and people across borders, and sociocultural identities. While some scholars argue that globalization and technological advancements have only recently resulted in transnational networks, other scholars argue that migrants have always led transnational lives. Despite the debate, discussions on transnational lives add new dimensions to the analysis of migratory patterns and sociocultural adaptation.

In some cases, the term "transcultural" is used in place of transnationalism to highlight the experiential aspect of a migrant's life. For example, while the term "transnationalism" emphasizes the roles of international borders in the migration experience, the term "transcultural" focuses on the person-to-person connection between sending and receiving communities. The differences between the terms derive from different methodologies used in sociology, anthropology, history, and geography studies. Because geographers ask the question of why here and not there or attempt to understand the ways in which spatial phenomena exist in more than one place, the socioeconomic, cultural, political, and physical borders constitute important units of analysis.

Transnational activities not only facilitate social reproduction for migrants away from family and friends but also create political-economic networks through the simple act of sending money back to family members or hometown associations, funneling aid to individuals, creating markets, and pressing for local government reforms. The spaces in which transnational networks arise may be formalized physical infrastructure (businesses, markets, or a town hall) but can also be less formal or temporary spaces created by celebrations, festivals, family gatherings, or demonstrations. One approach for studying transnational networks is to study the intensity or frequency of activities, the infrastructure and institutional frameworks that enable activities, and the cultural or symbolic meaning of activities. This allows researchers to examine the ways in which and the extent to which transnational networks occur, function, and endure and to better understand the broader socioeconomic and political implications of migration.

Box 4.4 Transportation Links:
Border Shuttle between Nogales and Phoenix

The growing Hispanic population in Phoenix is a relatively recent demographic trend result-ing from employment opportunities in construction and service industries that attract mi-grant laborers from Mexico. In 2000, 34 percent of the population in Phoenix was Hispanic or Latino, of which 28 percent was of Mexican descent. By 2010, 40 percent of the popula-tion was Hispanic or Latino, of which 35 percent was of Mexican descent. As people move from Mexico to the United States for work, they often establish homes in predominantly Hispanic communities that offer individuals the familiarity of their former home country as well as a space of transition to their new place of residency. In these spaces, businesses, events, celebrations, and social groups help migrants adapt to life in the United States while maintaining cultural and symbolic ties to their former home country.

In Phoenix, small (less than twenty employees) Mexican- and Mexican American–owned shuttle-bus services cater to the Mexican American and Mexican community in the metropol-itan area. These services provide the physical infrastructure through which individuals travel to Mexico, enabling them to maintain ties with family, place, and culture. A 2006 unpub-lished study of shuttle-bus services in the Phoenix metropolitan area surveyed twenty-one shuttle businesses and identified nineteen as small Mexican American–owned companies. Of the twenty-one companies identified, twenty were situated in or near census tracts where the percentage of Mexican foreign-born population of the total Hispanic population was 30 percent or greater (figure 4.10). In addition, the nineteen smaller companies were also

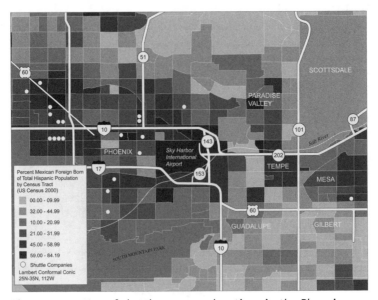

Figure 4.10   Map of shuttle company locations in the Phoenix metropolitan area. *Source:* Lindsey Sutton and ArcGIS US Census files.

relatively new, having operated from one to fifteen years. Both the location and length of time in business suggested that the shuttle-bus services catered to the growing Mexican American population in Phoenix.

The number of routes offered by the shuttle services to places in Mexico as well as US border towns demonstrated an extensive transportation network, giving people direct travel options to Mexico. Most shuttle companies had services every hour or every other hour, seven days a week, and traveled to Arizona and Sonora border towns.

Shuttle-bus services are a familiar part of Mexican culture. In Mexican cities and towns, people travel by *peseras* (also called *micros*), small vans or buses that are named for the short ride that costs only a few pesos. Also commonplace in Mexico is long-distance bus service that offers first-class travel with food and movie entertainment services. In many cases in Mexico, bus travel may be the only form of transportation to a specific destination. The shuttle services in Phoenix offer similar opportunities for individuals to travel to families and home countries and provide the network infrastructure for people to stay culturally and symbolically connected to Mexico.

States to Mexico is one example of a less well-known migration experience. In the 1890s, as a result of tensions over polygamous marriage practices, Mormons left Utah and migrated to the states of Chihuahua and Sonora, passing through Deming and Columbus, New Mexico, and Las Palomas, Chihuahua. In Chihuahua, they founded communities that continue to exist today, such as Colonia Juárez, southwest of the larger cities of Casas Grandes and Janos. Mennonites also founded homesteads mainly in Chihuahua in the early 1900s and continue living traditional farming lifestyles and trading with local Tarahumara indigenous peoples.

In the early twentieth century, Chinese immigrants also began to map new commercial landscapes in North America. Mexico initially welcomed Chinese immigrants to the northern border states, providing tax breaks and incentives in hopes they would establish commercial networks and businesses in what was at the time a vast and isolated border region. By the 1930s, the Chinese population was one of the largest minority groups in the state of Sonora, but in similar fashion to the 1920s anti-immigrant policies in the United States, Mexico passed anti-Chinese laws that forced people to leave the country. The North American Pacific Northwest region also shares a history of Asian immigration that produced long-standing cultural and socioeconomic patterns in urban landscapes. Despite strong anti-Asian sentiment in the early twentieth century, Chinese populations settled in the Pacific coastal areas of California, Oregon, Washington, and British Columbia. Contemporary demographic statistics indicate that Chinese populations in cities such as Seattle and Vancouver make up the majority of minority populations.

The US-Mexico border is a region of contrasts in which flourishing cultural exchanges bring people together while poverty in makeshift communities reveals harsh disparities between border communities. Transborder school-exchange programs such as Hands Across the Border, *Manos a Traves de la Fron-*

tera, founded by Gene Brust in 1981, facilitate cultural understanding and learning among younger generations. The program began as an exchange between the Palominas School District in Arizona and a school in Arizpe, Sonora, about 110 miles from the US border city Douglas, Arizona. During its most active period, more than one hundred middle and elementary schools participated in the program, providing opportunities for schoolchildren from Mexican and US communities to experience a one-week family stay exchange. Today, the program is on hold because of Arizona travel advisories for tourists and other visitors to Mexico.

In the border cities of El Paso, Texas, and Ciudad Juarez, Chihuahua, diverging socioeconomic experiences present a more exclusionary scenario. From US Interstate 10 in El Paso looking south into Ciudad Juarez, dirt roads, piles of tires, and makeshift houses precariously stacked on the outlying hillsides illustrate the realities of living on the urban fringe. From this view, rows of houses crowd around the alluvial fans of nearby mountain slopes; some of the houses are makeshift and clustered around dirt roads, but others have been transformed into two-level permanent homes lining paved streets (figure 4.11). Although the city is overcrowded and newcomers live in makeshift neighborhoods on the outskirts of the city, the possibility of work both in Ciudad Juarez and across the border attracts many migrants from the southern Mexican states hoping to find a better life. They migrate to the city and set up squatter housing in places such as Colonia Anapra, one of many *colonias* on the outskirts of Ciudad Juarez that exemplifies a landscape of making do with what is available. Here residents use whatever material they can find to build homes, patios, gardens, and play areas. Box 4.5 discusses the morphology (or layout) of Mexican cities.

TRANSBORDER URBAN GOVERNANCE

The boundary lines are one of the most visually defining landscape elements of the border

Figure 4.11   The outskirt *colonias* to the west of Ciudad Juarez, Chihuahua. (Photo by Lindsey Sutton)

Box 4.5 Geographic Perspectives on the Origins of US-Mexico Border City Morphology

The Laws of the Indies, a set of settlement codices, outlined specific landscape morphology for Spanish towns in the colonized territories of New Spain based on functionality and structural organization. New Spain included settlements that reached from the Central American isthmus beyond the present-day US-Mexico border as far north as Santa Fe, New Mexico, San Antonio, Texas, and Tucson, Arizona. The colonial city layout formed an extended grid pattern of north-, south-, east- and west-oriented streets that created a series of right-angled intersections. Although cities and towns in Spain were organized differently from this pattern, the Spanish crown mandated the gridiron layout in New Spain to better equip settlements for defense and to facilitate administration. As a result, the layout of Mexican cities is very different from those of the United States and Canada.

The colonial core centers almost always contained a plaza, a church, the local government offices, and centralized businesses. As a plain and open space in the urban center, the plaza provided a venue for troops to parade their military skills. Consequently, most plazas are named the Plaza de Armas, or the Plaza of Arms. Later, in the postcolonial era, plazas became community public spaces for celebrations and events instead of military exercises. In the mid-1800s, when Mexico fell under French rule, Emperor Maximiliano introduced European architectural style to the Mexican plaza that included a *kiosko*, gazebo, and bandstand, institutionalizing the plaza as a space for public celebration.

In addition to built urban form, the plaza dictated the demographic layout of towns. The populations living closest to the plaza comprised the wealthiest classes, including military officers, clergy, leading merchants, and artisans. Lower socioeconomic classes resided farther away from the plaza, and indigenous people lived on the outskirts of town, separate from the *criollo* (of Spanish descent and born in the New World) and peninsular (from Spain) populations. Many of these organizing structures persist in contemporary urban morphology in border cities. For example, remnants of the Spanish colonial historical landscape remain visible in street gridiron patterns, high population density, *barrios*, or segmented neighborhoods, neighborhood family-run stores, plazas, and core-periphery relationships between the urban core and suburban fringes.

In *The Mexican Border Cities: Landscape Anatomy and Place Personality*, geographers Daniel D. Arreola and Jim Curtis offer the most comprehensive assessment of border urban cultural landscapes. Their model draws on field research and landscape studies in eighteen Mexican border towns, presenting a comparative analysis of urban morphology (figure 4.12). The model contrasts with the concentric zone model and the sector models used to describe land use in US cities. Most importantly, the model distinguishes between premodern- and postmodern-era urban growth. In the model, prior to 1950, commercial, political, and social activity concentrated in the urban core, reflecting Spanish and French colonial characteristics in the presence of narrow streets, plazas, compact commercial spaces, and close living quarters. Postmodern-era growth reflected newer trends of wealthier families moving to suburban neighborhoods along major commercial spines. While lower-income families continue to live peripherally to the historical urban core in the postmodern era, after 1950 these populations have increased access to commercial centers as businesses relocate along newer commercial corridors. The presence of peripheral slums takes on a less structured form along the south edges of the model city and draws attention to more recent migratory patterns that correspond to post–World War II population booms, when migrants from other areas in Mexico made their way to the border in search of better wages and economic opportunity. In these slum areas, residents initially live without municipal services (water, sewage, electricity, paved streets), but over time, as these neighborhoods become integrated residential areas, they gain access to municipal services.

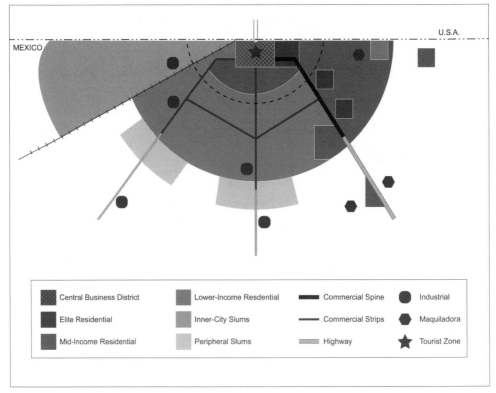

Figure 4.12   Arreola and Curtis's border city landscape model. Note how this differs from the three major US models of land use. *Source:* Adapted from D. Arreola and J. R. Curtis, *The Mexican Border Cities: Landscape Anatomy and Place Personality* (Tucson: University of Arizona Press, 1993).

regions and highlight a divided sense of transborder relationships in North America. Increased investments in border infrastructure such as border markers, fences, POE facilities, and bridge crossings limit the movements of transborder flows, assert national sovereignty, and promote unilateral policy making. Post-9/11 policies that tighten border security obscure the interdependence among Canada, the United States, and Mexico at the national level and make it necessary for states and municipalities to seek out ways to advance transborder commercial, political, and social networks at the local level.

At the national level, the Canadian Border Services Agency, the US Border Patrol (USBP), and the Patrulla Fronteriza Mexicana (Mexican Border Patrol) enforce national security policies on the ground by apprehending unauthorized crossers, monitoring flows through the POEs, and using surveillance techniques to secure border areas. Starting in 2008, USBP began storing data collected at the POEs about border crossers as part of a database of information used to identify suspicious activity and provide probable cause for conducting more extensive searches of border crossers. Other surveillance techniques include USBP checkpoints, the use of tethered aerostat radar systems, and unmanned aerial systems (UASs—often called "drones"). Agents at USBP checkpoints along US Interstate 10 and state highways near border communities stop, monitor, and inspect vehicles, asking passengers to state their citizenship. Six aerostats located along the US-Mexico border provide radar support for drug interdiction efforts, and six UASs deploy in the US-Mexico border region to provide visual support for interdiction efforts in remote areas. Yet these UASs are expensive, costing some $3,000 per flight hour. Critics argue that the high cost and low numbers of apprehensions using UASs make them impractical, but Border Patrol argues that UASs help in many other surveillance capacities beyond simple apprehension. In remote areas near places like Naco, Arizona, a town of only one thousand residents, UASs provide support to on-the-ground USBP agents that drive along the border fence and stand watch in mobile towers to spot border crossers (figure 4.13). In these

Figure 4.13   A scout looks out for US Border Patrol on the border fence just west of Naco, Sonora. (Photo by Lindsey Sutton)

Figure 4.14 Water stops placed in the desert by humanitarian groups. (Photo by Lindsey Sutton)

the arrest of forty-eight unauthorized immigrants from Latin America. These spot checks raised concerns about the ethics of profiling ferry passengers because plainclothes Spanish-speaking USBP agents appeared to be targeting Spanish speakers at the terminal. But, in 2008, new federal laws decreased the probable cause needed to conduct investigations of unauthorized immigrants and suspected drug activity. Such security measures in a post-9/11 era that allow increased surveillance and searching create major obstacles and serious consequences for the estimated 230,000 thousand unauthorized immigrants in the state of Washington. Some groups have begun to demand immigrant rights, especially for unauthorized immigrants.

remote desert regions, civil society groups, such as Humane Borders, leave flagged water stops for crossers who could potentially become lost and dehydrated as they head on foot to larger cities such as Tucson (figure 4.14).

Spot checks at POEs by USBP agents constitute another method for monitoring transborder flows, a method used at border checkpoints worldwide. In Anacortes, Washington, undercover USBP agents have carried out spot checks at the ferry terminal. The ferries are the main form of transportation to and from the San Juan Islands, located in the Pacific Coast waterways bordering Canada and the United States. Today the channels are used to transport illicit shipments, including marijuana, from British Columbia to the United States. Recent searches at the ferry terminal intending to interdict drug flows resulted in

SHARED ECOSYSTEMS AND ENVIRONMENTS

Border cities are also linked by shared physical environments, most notable in the similarities in wildlife and vegetation that traverse the boundaries but also in the less visible natural resources such as groundwater. Differing approaches, geographical proximity to natural resources, and the multiple governmental entities involved in management of natural resources create complex bilateral environmental situations. For example, sewage pollution of the Tijuana River and watershed from untreated sewage originating in Tijuana, Baja California, impacts residents living in both Tijuana and San Diego. As a result, the US Congress approved construction for the South Bay International Wastewater Treatment Plant in San Diego. The treatment plant is federally owned and operated and treats twenty-five million gallons per day of sewage from Tijuana, mitigating possible transborder problems of inadequate wastewater treatment facilities in Tijuana, such as dumping into and polluting river and ocean waters.

Bilateral cooperation via regional organizations and national committees, such as the Great Lakes International Joint Commission between Canada and the United States and the International Boundary and Water Commission between Mexico and the United States, helps border communities comanage and ensure the viability of transborder resources for future generations. Along both the north and south North American border regions, growing urban populations strain natural resources and require larger-scale comanagement of natural resources. In the tristate region of Texas, New Mexico, and Chihuahua, intrastate management of the Rio Grande, one of two major river systems that flow from the United States into Mexico, faces many challenges. Historical treaties allocate the state of Chihuahua 60,000 acre-feet a year out of the total 790,000 acre feet of water released to the tristate region from the Elephant Butte Dam Reservoir located north of Las Cruces, New Mexico. Since the state of Chihuahua, and specifically Ciudad Juarez, receives a smaller share of the water, municipal residents pump groundwater resources to meet water consumption needs. But pumping from groundwater resources is not a sustainable solution because of a lack of legislation, regulation, and oversight on the use of groundwater resources as well as agreements about the ways in which groundwater (aquifers) and surface water (rivers) interact. Additionally, differing governing approaches to water resources between Mexico and the United States complicate cooperation. In Mexico, regional watershed councils

manage water use of both surface water and groundwater. However, in the United States, water management is managed at the state level; some have called for the United States to establish watershed councils to manage binational water resources.

To the west of Ciudad Juarez, the two communities of Columbus, New Mexico, and Las Palomas, Chihuahua, face similar groundwater situations. Agricultural production, growing retiree populations, and increased migration flows in the region result in increased pumping from the Mimbres aquifer, a transborder aquifer that supplies water for residents in both cities. On both sides of the border, increased pumping has created cones of depression, a drawdown of water to the pumping sites, and reverse flows of water. Recently, the levels of groundwater pumping from the aquifer indicated that water use was greater than the rate of natural recharge, which makes long-term water sustainability a major challenge. Complicating this are the facts that groundwater resources in the tristate region remain unregulated and communities continue using unmonitored wells to pump water from the aquifer. Environmental educational efforts through the New Mexico school systems such as "water festivals" as well as the 2008 first binational Border-Wide Environmental Educators (EE) Conference held in Ciudad Juarez exemplified on-the-ground efforts to increase knowledge in local communities about water use and the state of shared water resources in the US-Mexico border region. Current grassroots efforts in Las Palomas, including the NGO Border Partners, support sustainable gardening projects and water recycling efforts that help provide fresh produce for local residents as well as conserve local water resources.

Migrant experiences, border infrastructure, transborder commerce and development, the impacts of illicit flows of drugs and people on small towns, binational natural water resources, and demographic changes reveal the ways in which national-level policies and trends transpire in border cities. Further investigative research, fieldwork, and case studies, as presented in the following chapters, help researchers and students identify specific details that emerge from the everyday processes in North American urban landscapes. At the urban level, a complex milieu of increased border security measures, expanding trilateral economies, and social networks merge, simultaneously incorporating and refuting border identities. In addition, the physical infrastructure of the borders, including bridges, POEs, and new regulations about border crossings and surveillance technologies, simultaneously facilitate and limit transborder flows of goods and people. Despite these dichotomies, border residents continue shopping in, visiting, commuting to and from, and living in Canada, the United States, and Mexico. Although these flows are often fragmented and complicated, the everyday landscapes of the border regions reinforce the interconnectedness of North American governments, economies, environments, and populations.

SUGGESTED READINGS

Anderson, J. B., and J. Gerber. 2008. *Fifty Years of Change on the US-Mexico Border: Growth, Development, and Quality of Life.* Austin: University of Texas Press. *Statistical study of economic, political, and social indicators for the US-Mexico border region.*

Arreola, D., and J. R. Curtis. 1993. *The Mexican Border Cities.* Tucson: University of Arizona Press. *Geographical study of the US-Mexico border and urban areas.*

Hern, F. 2011. *Yip Sang and the First Chinese Canadians.* Victoria, BC: Heritage House. *Socioeconomic contexts and Chinese Canadians in the late 1800s and early 1900s.*

Mattingly, D. J., and E. R. Hansen, eds. *Women and Change at the US-Mexico Border: Mobility, Labor, and Activism.* Tucson: University of Tucson Press. *Gender and sociopolitical contexts and development.*

Nabhan, G. 1985. *Gathering the Desert.* Tucson: University of Arizona Press. *An account of the human ecology of the Sonoran Desert environment.*

Truett, S. 2006. *Fugitive Landscapes: The Forgotten History of the U.S.-Mexico Borderlands.* New Haven: Yale University Press. *A historical account of the economic and political shaping of the US-Mexico border region.*

Urrea, L.A. 2009. *Into the Beautiful North.* New York: Little, Brown. *A fictional account of Mexican migration.*

CITIES ON THE WEB

Economy, Trade, and Development

US-Mexico Chamber of Commerce: http://www.usmcoc.org/

Texas Center for Border Economic and Enterprise Development: http://texascenter.tamiu.edu/texcen_services/border_crossings.asp

New Mexico Border Authority: http://www.nmborder.com/

Arizona-Mexico Commission: http://azmc.org

Palomas Oilcloth Designs: http://www.palomasoilclothdesigns.com/

Binational Urban Governance

Border Legislative Conferences: http://www.borderlegislators.org/

Lower Rio Grande Development Council: http://www.lrgvdc.org/

Windsor-Detroit Gateway Project: http://www.mto.gov.on.ca/english/engineering/border/windsor/; http://www.partnershipborderstudy.com/; http://www.michigan.gov/mdot/; http://www.dptv.org/ondemand/special/mdot.shtml

People and Places

Border Partners, Deming, New Mexico: http://s371539307.onlinehome.us/2012/wp-2012/

Chinatown International District of Seattle: http://www.cidbia.org/

Vancouver Chinatown: http://www.vancouver-chinatown.com/

US-Canada Cross-Border Shopping: http://www.crossbordershopping.ca/

Transborder Environments

Southwest Consortium for Environmental Research and Policy: www.scerp.org/

US-Mexico Sister Cities—EPA Border 2012: http://www.epa.gov/Border2012/framework/people.html

Viva Verde—Green Living in Southern New Mexico: http://www.vivaverdenm.com/

I

URBAN ECONOMIES

5

Urban Economic Restructuring

DAVID WILSON AND MATTHEW ANDERSON

North America's large cities, in all their complexity, today continue to be elaborate economic engines. Economic and political forces, today as before, seethe through their fabric and render them evolving and turbulent. In one dimension of this, these places persist as sites where businesses and companies seek to transform their cities to profitably produce goods and services. In this process, city governances (i.e., the actors and institutions involved in creating economic growth and land redevelopment) have continually updated the providing of the factors of production that alter the city's spatial form: land, pools of labor, stocks of money-capital, and access to raw materials. In a second dimension of this, these cities have also functioned as areal expressions of the interests of land-based elites. Such elites—collectivities of builders, developers, local government, and realtors—have strived to develop and redevelop a city element—land—to heighten its value.

But these multiple drives have been complicated by three realities. First, people live in these cities and desire a city form and city functionality that fulfill their deepest concern: decent qualities of life. Desirous of this, city residents of all classes, races, ethnicities, and lifestyle choices commonly create people-supporting institutions: tenant councils, block clubs, neighborhood associations, civic groups, and, most recently, Occupy Wall Street groups. Second, the intensification of land values can remove people from homes and communities, which frequently mobilizes them to "defend their turf." This reality is currently being acted out in many cities across North America, notably with organized opposition to gentrification and government-driven "ghetto clearance." Third, both real-estate capital and industrial capital are prone to systemic bouts of falling profit margins. As urban economies experience upturns and downturns that are endemic to any capitalist economy, these fractions of capital experience changing fates in their ability to achieve their goals.

Yet these two kinds of economic restructuring have complex roots. In particular, cities experience these in response to the broader rhythms of a capitalist economy that are mediated by the actions of local institutions and populations (see box 5.1). This "multiscalar" interplay, always at work, ceaselessly hits the ground of these cities in a complex interconnecting. A broader economy's ebbs and flows thus reverberate through these landscapes that set the stage for active institutions and populations to engage and

Box 5.1 Geographic Perspectives on Urban Political Economy

During the early 1970s a new way of thinking about and conceptualizing the city became popular: urban political economy. Drawing from the writings of Karl Marx, academics working in urban political economy, initially led by Manuel Castells, David Harvey, Richard Walker, Richard Peet, and Neil Smith, asserted that the city and the process of urbanization help spark national and global capitalist economies. Specifically, the built environment of the city functions as an engine for capitalist investment, profit making, and growth. City functioning, mediated by local political elites, institutions, and growth coalitions, ties city on-the-ground political dynamics with the logic and flow of broader capitalist structures and imperatives.

In cities, businesses and companies capitalize on concentrations of people, physical infrastructure, and resources to locate their production centers; and in cities, commodities are shipped and consumed. Therefore, the built environment and infrastructure of urban landscapes represents resources that are mobilized to service the interests of capitalist growth. Transportation infrastructure—streets, rail transit, and expressways—coordinates the circulation of products, people, and money necessary for capitalist growth to continue. Residential districts warehouse workers whose labor propels the production and consumption of commodities on which profits are realized. Schools, hospitals, and public amenities are erected to service and "reproduce" workers while real-estate development constructs these very physical structures. Downtown districts are sites where investment and resources are spatially concentrated to maximize production efficiency and where secondary businesses and industries locate to carry out production (i.e., legal, financial, paper, printing, etc.).

In this perspective, cities are core production nodes and spatial manifestations of the broader capitalist economies. They are humanly produced built environments, a resource base of social and physical structures through which capitalist investment flows are con-cretized, circulated, realized, and expanded. But a capitalist economy is a dynamic and perpetually changing formation. Urban landscapes, however, once erected, are constituted by relatively permanent fixtures of streets, roads, and warehouses. While appropriate to the demands of capitalism at a moment in time, they can soon become outdated and obsolete as "modes of accumulation" change.

The Fordist mode of production, for example, peaking around 1950, produced the large in-dustrial cities of North America to service its needs: the mass production and consumption of commodities. The expansionary dynamics of this mode of production, however, grew beyond the capacity of what this type of city could accommodate. These cities, once facilitators of capitalist growth, immediately became barriers to the continuation of this very growth. It is here that, as David Harvey has written, the urban process becomes a tension-ridden affair as capital must walk a "knife's edge" path between preserving the utility and value of a given landscape and destroying that landscape to create new infrastructural systems (i.e., new roads, houses, and office buildings). In this vein, geographer Richard Walker has noted that urban landscapes "are literally museums of the past and of past social relations."

This tension places immense pressures on businesses, companies, and political elites to either restructure urban landscapes to meet the evolving demands of capitalist growth or relocate to new spaces. Such spaces, it is posited, can be developed free of preexisting (and outdated) infrastructures and where land and labor is cheap. The second means of overcoming this barrier often becomes the reality, as massive postwar suburbanization attests to. Yet cities are increasingly being remade (i.e., new downtowns, swaths of gentrification) in efforts to economically reclaim these environments as sites for capitalist growth.

Yet these cities are not merely physical infrastructural systems. In political economy studies, they are also places where people live and seek to build decent qualities of life. Thus, people desirous of producing suitable lives often confront and collide with the dynamics of capitalist growth. It is here that these cities also become sites of social and political struggle as community groups resist the power of political elites, developers, and businesses to control the urban process and fashion cities according to the "use-value" interests of community, stability, and security. Cities thus become contested political terrains as the restructuring of these landscapes unfolds. Out of the complex interplay between capital and labor and each side's supporters, new possibilities and political economic trajectories come to the fore and stimulate unanticipated (and sometimes fundamental) change.

constitute everyday social, economic, and political life. These cities, we chronicle in this chapter, have seen remarkable changes in economic functionality and spatial form driven by the hidden hand of this multiscalar interlocking. From industrial powerhouses, to deindustrialized places, to reinvented tourist-leisure-service cities, city governances have adroitly responded to the changing political-economic times that we now detail.

THE FLOURISHING INDUSTRIAL CITY (1950–1974)

As briefly discussed in chapter 3, by 1950, US and Canadian cities had begun to experience a fundamental restructuring that was to render them modern facsimiles of today's urban environment. At this moment, the world economy had emerged from the depths of the Great Depression, with the United States leading the way as a global, industrial powerhouse. The resolution of World War II placed the United States in a privileged economic and political position in relation to the rest of the world, particularly a European continent decimated by the war. Between 1950 and 1974, US corporations experienced tremendous growth and prosperity, encountering modest global competition as they led the reconstruction of the European and Japanese economies (i.e., the Marshall Plan) and the expanding global economy.

In the process, Fordism—named after Henry Ford for his innovations in assembly-line production and efficiency—crystallized as the dominant mode of mass production in North America and beyond. This entailed substantial increases in both the volume of products (in the process lowering costs) and union-backed wages, thereby giving workers the means to become viable consumers of the very commodities they produced. Anchored by a sizable manufacturing sector and record-high employment levels, this mode of production stimulated the rise of a consumer society that propelled the most prosperous period in American history. Between 1948 and 1973, America's gross national product increased fivefold, the median income more than doubled in constant dollars, and homeownership rose by 50 percent.

The Canadian economy, although considerably smaller in scale, also experienced a remarkable postwar boom. Unemployment remained low, and manufacturing commanded a sizable force—29 percent of the Canadian workforce by 1944—as both the national and provincial economies experienced dramatic expansion. By 1953, gross national product in Canada was already 2.3 times that of 1938, a figure which continued to grow steadily through the 1950s and 1960s.

The great industrial cities of the American Northeast and Midwest—New York, Chicago, Philadelphia, Baltimore, Boston, Detroit, and Cleveland—were the core production centers of the US economy. By 1950, these cities had reached their peak in terms of population and economic vitality (table 5.1). Well-paying manufacturing jobs were in abundant supply in these cities, which fueled the growth of the modern middle class. Between 1946 and 1973, disposable personal income (in 1958 dollars) rose from $210 billion to $577 billion, while residential wealth, in aggregate terms, increased by 75 percent between 1952 and 1968. The result: these flourishing industrial cities were in impeccable fiscal health. In Chicago, for example, between 1958 and 1963, over a

Table 5.1   Largest Cities in the United States and Canada—1950*

City	Population
New York City	7,891,957
Chicago	3,620,962
Philadelphia	2,071,605
Los Angeles	1,970,358
Detroit	1,849,568
Toronto	1,176,622**
Montreal	1,021,520***
Baltimore	949,708
Cleveland	914,808
St. Louis	856,796

* Only Los Angeles is located outside the Northeast or Midwest.
** Census taken in 1951 and represents post-1998 amalgamated boundaries.
*** Census taken in 1951.

million square feet of office space was added to the city's central business district (CBD), and the number of city employees increased by 33 percent.

Canada's most industrial cities—Toronto, Montreal, and Hamilton—experienced similar growth trajectories. Montreal's population peaked in 1961 at 1,257,537 (Montreal's city boundaries expanded in 2002 through annexation, which accounts for the larger figures currently reported). Ontario's Windsor similarly flourished as part of the "automobile belt" that formed along the US-Canada border during the mid-twentieth century and centered on the Detroit-Windsor metropolitan agglomeration. Here an unbroken mass of heavy industry cut across two nations. Raw-material flows and aggregations of workers seamlessly moved through this automobile belt to tie this aggregation together.

But all was not totally rosy. By the mid-1950s, chinks in the urban armor had begun to appear. Signs came to the forefront that these cities were, first and foremost, having difficulty absorbing and assimilating growing populations into their economic bases. Class and racial discrimination, unresponsive and non-agile political governances, and urban aging were at the foundation of this problem. In US cities, profoundly segregated, aged and minimally expanded housing stocks were failing to accommodate the continued in-migration of people through the 1950s and 1960s. Growing levels of population density and congestion that isolated poor, racialized households had begun to overwhelm aging and fixed infrastructures. At the core of this, the Great Migration from the American South accelerated in the United States, increasing the in-migration of African Americans (and other minority populations) in search of employment and better lives. Fixed spaces that housed these minority populations became increasingly insufficient and intolerable, resulting in crowding and deepening sociospatial isolation that would spark waves of turbulent city strife in the 1960s.

In Canada, on the other hand, this period was marked less by this kind of socioeconomic segregation and racial tension. However, after immigration laws were relaxed in 1968 in response to the need for more workers (particularly at the lower economic end), levels of immigration accelerated through the 1970s and 1980s. The number of European and Asian immigrants dramatically increased in Toronto, Vancouver, and Hamilton, leading to the rise of something new: clearly discernible segregated enclaves of immigrant workers (the rate of immigration into Canadian cities has been roughly twice the rate experienced by US cities since the 1980s).

This growing segregation and balkanization in US and Canadian cities were facili-

tated by two other processes: urban renewal and mass suburbanization. Urban renewal, a government undertaking in both countries, entailed the demolition of many older, deteriorating buildings (including many residential structures in previously racial/minority districts) that were deemed "blighted." As a result, CBDs were able to answer the post-1960 growing demand for downtown office space by expanding into cleared areas. In the United States, the now infamous "modernist-style" public housing complexes (e.g., Cabrini-Green in Chicago, Pruitt-Igoe in St. Louis, and the Tilden Homes in New York City) were subsequently constructed and concentrated in strategic areas, which functioned to warehouse the predominantly poor African American populations that were displaced (figure 5.1). In Canada, much of the public housing was located in the suburban periphery and resulted in notably less displacement (although some projects did result in considerable displacement, such as Alexandria Park in Toronto). And only since the 1980s have these complexes been concentrated with racial minority populations (they previously housed

Figure 5.1 Public housing in the Bronx in New York City. The Betances Homes, a series of nine buildings, were completed in 1973. *Source*: Wikipedia.

mostly nonimmigrant populations), such as Caribbean blacks in Toronto and Montreal, but also various mixes of Pakistanis, Indians, and East Asians in different cities.

The form of the towering high-rise was selected as a means of collecting and containing this population in the smallest footprint of land possible, thereby preserving the swaths of vacant space cleared by demolition. Between 1949 and 1974, nearly $10 billion was spent in approximately 1,250 cities in the United States, with more than 500,000 housing units demolished and over 900,000 public housing units built. By 1975, New York City operated 116,000 public housing units; Philadelphia, 22,900; Chicago, 38,600; Baltimore, 16,200; and Atlanta, 24,700. In Pittsburgh, urban renewal demolished more than 3,700 buildings, displaced more than 1,800 businesses, and uprooted more than 5,000 families. In Toronto, similarly gutted by urban renewal, over 90,000 social (or public) housing units remain in operation, the second-largest public housing system in North America after New York City.

Urban renewal also produced space for linking the CBD to the burgeoning suburban periphery via the construction of high-volume expressways. The answer to the congested and overconcentrated conditions of the industrial city was the "suburban solution," the explosion of the metropolitan periphery in the form of suburban expansion. The completion of the federal interstate system made an abundance of cheap land easily accessible for development; the GI Bill provided returning veterans with incentives to purchase homes; and innovations in home construction and mortgage finance translated into thousands of affordable homes suddenly available for middle-class families in the suburbs of many American cities. The Canadian Mortgage and

Housing Corporation and construction of a similar high-volume expressway system stimulated this process in Canada.

Aided and abetted by the consumerist ideology of the "American and Canadian Dream," thousands of white, middle-class families and businesses in both countries relocated to the suburbs during the 1950s and 1960s, fleeing from the rising costs, congestion, and growing numbers of lower-income workers in the industrial city. Between 1945 and 1970, FHA-insured mortgage debt (in structures housing one to four families) in the United States increased from $5 billion to $45 billion, while twenty-four million new private housing units started between 1945 and 1960. In Philadelphia alone, nearly four hundred thousand new suburban housing units were built between 1954 and 1973. From 1945 to 1981, Canada's suburban population nearly doubled while total housing dwellings tripled. Toronto's suburban area, for example, grew in size by more than 60 percent and experienced a more than twofold increase in population. In perhaps the most extreme case, nearly 67 percent of residents in the Calgary metropolitan area came to reside in this city's suburban periphery.

The unsurprising outcome: the central cities of these rapidly expanding metropolitan regions began to experience population decline. In the 1950s and 1960s, New York City, St. Louis, and Boston all became smaller by more than one hundred thousand people, while Buffalo, Pittsburgh, and Camden, New Jersey, each shed from one-third to one-half of their residents. This was also the case in Canadian cities, with losses experienced in Montreal, Toronto, Hamilton, and Ottawa. Between 1951 and 1986, the twelve largest Canadian central cities declined in population by 37 percent, whereas their outlying suburbs increased by 200 percent. As a consequence of this trend, more than five hundred thousand jobs were lost in US central areas in the fifteen largest cities between 1960 and 1970, mostly in the Northeast and Midwest. In the suburbs, more than three million jobs were created (proportional central city losses and levels of suburban growth also marked Canada's industrial centers).

The steady loss of the middle class from these cities eventually led to a precipitous decline in the fiscal health of many central cities during the 1970s and 1980s, particularly in the United States. This was also accompanied by the onset of a steady shift from manufacturing to service-oriented employment: from 1945 to 1973, employment in goods production in the United States declined from about thirty million to twenty-five million, while employment in services rose from eight million to some fifty-seven million. Although Canada's manufacturing sector has been similarly affected, this was somewhat delayed in relation to the United States, hitting more severely in the 1980s and 1990s. Thus, jobs losses were minor in Toronto and Hamilton in the 1970s and 1980s. This loss accelerated thereafter as deindustrialization and suburbanization fully emerged to engulf these cities.

Moreover, toward the end of the 1960s, US and Canadian corporations started to experience increased competition from rising economies around the world, particularly Germany and Japan. Between 1965 and 1973, US manufacturing firms experienced a fall in rates of profit by a whopping 44 percent. Many Canadian-based corporations (Suncor Energy, Power Corporation of Canada, Imperial Oil) also experienced this profit plummet but at a lessened rate. To combat

this declining competitive advantage in the United States, the dollar was taken off the gold standard in 1971, which subsequently triggered a spike in inflation, which was further compounded by the effects of the 1973 oil embargo. Further industrial restructuring in these North American cities followed, with plant closures and plant outmigration its leading edges. In short, by 1975, the age of the flourishing industrial city in North America was largely over; times had changed.

DEINDUSTRIALIZATION AND THE AFFLICTED CITY (1974–1990)

By the 1970s, a dominant societal economic trend emerged that immediately affected the city and would haunt it for decades to come: a sharp and long recession. This downturn lingered for years (through the late 1970s) and effectively cut through every sector of the US and Canadian economies. By 1974, North American corporations (in the United States in particular) were experiencing sharp drops in profits in a now globally competitive world and in a reality of increased wages in the union-dominated manufacturing sector. At the same time, both US and Canadian economies were reeling from the emergence of stagflation, a combination of high rates of inflation and unemployment throughout the 1970s. The 1973 oil embargo systematically deepened these trends, shooting oil prices skyward and crippling the health of urban economies.

In this context, cities saw their economies wither, which intensified suburbanization. Industrial cities were hit hardest by this, a process called deindustrialization. There are three key reasons for deindustrialization. The first is the growing challenge to American global economic dominance. Once the supreme industrial nation, the United States has faced ongoing competition not just from old rivals such as France and Germany but also from Japan and low-wage countries in Asia and Latin America. The second is the ability of large corporations to shift capital from one area to another with growing ease. Corporations such as GM, Ford, and US Steel shifted investment in new plant from cities such as Flint, Detroit, and Chicago to new locales. In some cases it was to the American South and West, while in others it was to underdeveloped countries. This occurred because corporate executives sought higher profits, lower wages, a non-unionized workforce, and greenfield sites where they could build modern factories with minimum interference. The third key factor in deindustrialization was the policies of the federal government. On the one hand, massive defense expenditures have undermined industrial growth. On the other, domestic and foreign policies have given corporations unprecedented ability to make profitable rather than socially and economically responsible decisions.

The anchor of the industrial city—manufacturing jobs—experienced monumental losses during the 1970s and 1980s as jobs further fled to the suburbs, the American South and West, the Canadian west, and overseas. In the 1970s, estimates placed the total number of US jobs lost to capital mobility at 30 million (in the 1980s, the loss was from 1.5 to 2 million jobs a year). In Chicago, after city manufacturing employment grew from about 330, 000 to 390,000 between 1958 and 1972, the number fell by 130,000 between 1972 and 1983. From 1967 to 1987, Philadelphia lost 64 percent of its manufacturing base; Chicago, 60 percent; New York City, 58 percent; and

Detroit, 51 percent. In Canada, central city manufacturing employment declined nearly 10 percent from 1960 to 1972, with the most pronounced drops in the Quebec-Windsor axis—Quebec City, Montreal, Ottawa, Toronto, Hamilton, and Windsor—which had once accounted for roughly 80 percent of Canadian manufacturing output. With job losses came spatial consequences: abandoned factories and shuttered industrial areas (see figure 5.2).

Suburbanization, continuing through the 1970s and 1980s, left vast inner-city areas in ruins. In the 1970s alone, thirteen million more US residents left the central cities than moved there; more than twenty-six million people moved to the suburbs. Between 1950 and 1980, Philadelphia's population had dropped by four hundred thousand, the number of vacant housing grew fourfold, and the drop in real property values reached over $1 billion, pushing the city government into fiscal distress. In New York City, after losing nearly one million people between 1950 and 1980, the city's short-term debt rose from about zero to $6 billion between 1970 and 1975, pushing the city into bankruptcy.

Not surprisingly, these cities experienced an upsurge in unemployment and poverty. By 1982, Chicago's overall unemployment rate had risen to a postwar high of 17 percent, with the effects disproportionately impacting inner-city minority neighborhoods. In Chicago, of some eighty thousand jobs lost to capital mobility in the 1980s, 34 percent of those who lost their jobs were women, 27 percent were African American, and 23 percent were Latino, percentages that were higher than their participation in the workforce. The number of African Americans living in inner-city poverty across

Figure 5.2   Abandoned industrial landscape in Detroit. The structure was once part of the Packard Automotive plant. *Source:* Wikimedia.

the United States grew by more than one-third from 1980 to 1990, reaching nearly six million. The result was the production of what urban sociologist Loïc Wacquant has called the "hyperghetto." For example, Chicago's Bronzeville—a predominantly African American neighborhood—lost half its residents between 1970 and 1990 while male employment declined by 46 percent between 1950 and 1990, leaving the neighborhood (and many others like it) mired in conditions of what many refer to as "concentrated poverty." Detroit experienced a similar economic and demographic collapse (see figure 5.2).

Box 5.2 Deindustrialization in Cleveland

By 1950, Cleveland's population's reached a high of 914,808 and was anchored by one of the strongest industrial economies in North America. Specializing in steel, iron, and metal making, Cleveland's manufacturing sector constituted a particularly large percentage of the city's workforce and enjoyed high rates of employment and fiscal health. However, like other North American industrial cities, mass suburbanization resulted in a steady drain of middle-class residents, jobs, and resources from the city. This was further propelled by the African American civil rights movement in the 1960s, acutely felt in Cleveland's inner city, which culminated in the Hough riots in July 1966 and fueled the mainstream perception of Cleveland as a dangerous, disorderly city.

Combined with high wages and a particularly strong union base, Cleveland was hollowed out by deindustrialization. From 1960 to 1980, Cleveland suffered a loss of more than forty thousand factory jobs, which coincided with accelerated population decline. By 1983, unemployment had reached its peak, nearly 14 percent higher than the national average at the time. As it was in many other industrial cities, this was a politically tumultuous period for Cleveland. Mayor Dennis Kucinich, in the late 1970s, refused to cater to local pressure to privatize the city's electric utility company, Muni Light. In response, the Cleveland Trust Company required the city to immediately pay its outstanding and spiraling debt. This forced the city into default and, effectively, ended Kucinich's tenure as mayor.

Job loss continued to devastate Cleveland's economy through the 1980s, with sizable declines in its iron and steel industrial base. In an attempt to reverse Cleveland's evaporating industrial base, Kucinich's successors—George Voinovich and Michael White—mobilized an ambitious redevelopment agenda through the 1980s and 1990s that funneled over $350 million to finance the construction of the Rock and Roll Hall of Fame, the Gateway Complex, and the tourist-oriented Flats District. In the process, millions of dollars in tax abatements were given to corporations such as Ritz-Carlton, Tower City, and Key Corporation Center to attract middle- to upper-class jobs back to the city.

Unemployment, however, remained high through the 1980s, and poverty deepened in many low-income neighborhoods now cast to the margins of funding priorities. Cleveland's Hough and Fairfax neighborhoods, for instance, experienced a roughly 42 percent increase in high-poverty residents between 1990 and 2000. Moreover, during the 1990s, the city's median income ranked third lowest of America's one hundred largest cities. While this redevelopment did indeed reinvigorate Cleveland's economy, underpinning this deepening of poverty was continued manufacturing job loss: another ten thousand manufacturing jobs were lost between 1990 and 2000, a trend that has accelerated in recent years.

Since 1980, juxtaposed against a now dominant service sector, over 42 percent of Cleveland's manufacturing employment has been lost. Beyond the refurbished downtown, much of Cleveland's landscape remains littered with the relics of a bygone industrial era. Making matters worse is the city's continued loss of population: Cleveland's 2010 population of 396,815 represents a mere 43 percent of its peak mark in 1950. As the populations of many former industrial cities have leveled or even increased (e.g., Chicago, New York), Cleveland's half-century bout with deindustrialization ranks today among the worst casualties of capitalist destruction in North America.

Canadian industrial cities, notably those in the Quebec-Windsor axis, were afflicted with increased central city unemployment and impoverishment. This poverty also disproportionately hit minority populations. Between 1971 and 1986, the percentage of foreign-born residents in central cities doubled from 15 to 30. And roughly over the same period, median income in central cities declined from 70 to 62 percent of that reported in the burgeoning suburbs. Cities with the most sizable manufacturing losses were most affected, particularly Montreal, Winnipeg, and Quebec. Montreal suffered the highest levels of concentrated poverty: nearly 50 percent of Canada's population that was living in concentrated poverty resided in Montreal.

Yet the devastating social and economic impacts from deindustrialization were not evenly felt across North American cities. While the older Rust Belt cities in the Northeast and Midwest suffered sizable losses in population, jobs, and resources, cities in the South and West, or the "Sun Belt," continued to grow (see box 5.3). US firms were attracted to Sun Belt cities with their abundance of cheap land, newer infrastructures, lower taxes, and non-unionized labor. As geographer David Gordon has argued, these cities shared the significant advantage of never acquiring the now outdated physical infrastructure (roads, houses, etc.) of the older industrial era. Urban growth, in short, could progress in these new cities from scratch to fit the demands of a new period of capitalist development.

Box 5.3 Rust Belt and Sun Belt

The term "Rust Belt" gained popularity in the 1980s as a way to describe the geographical region of what once served as the hub of American industry. It is a symbolic name for devastating economic changes. Because the term describes a set of economic and social conditions rather than a specific region of North America, the boundaries are not precise (figure 5.3). However, what is called the "industrial heartland of North America"—once home to thriving coal, steel, and automotive industries—includes much of the American Midwest, the Great Lakes, and parts of the Mid-Atlantic. Illinois, Indiana, Michigan, Ohio, Pennsylvania, and New York were once dominant industrial manufacturing centers.

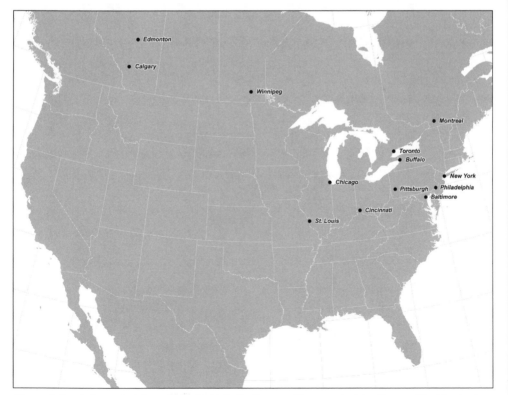

Figure 5.3   Selected cities of the Rust Belt. *Source:* Map created by George Washington University Geography Department.

Factories and plants for coal, steel, automobiles, automotive parts, and weapons dominated the industrial landscape of many of these cities. Detroit is often cited as the quintessential example of a Rust Belt city. In the 1950s and 1960s, the city became home to General Motors, Ford, and Chrysler. As postwar demands for cars increased, so, too, did automobile production, leading to a population boom. Detroit became the epicenter of motor vehicle and parts production. But during the 1980s, parts production moved overseas, and the city began a long, steady decline. It is important to understand that deindustrialization has been highly uneven in terms of geography and social class.

The term "Sun Belt" refers to the region in the United States that stretches across the southern and southwestern portions of the country, from Florida to California, and includes the states of Florida, Georgia, South Carolina, Alabama, Mississippi, Louisiana, Texas, New Mexico, Arizona, Nevada, and California (figure 5.4). The term "Sun Belt" is said to have been coined in 1969 by writer and political analyst Kevin Phillips to describe the area of the United States that included industries such as oil, military, and aerospace. The region enjoyed milder winters and fewer labor unions and in the 1970s and 1980s began to attract immigrants and retiring baby boomers. In contrast to the Rust Belt, the Sun Belt represents the major areas of growth in the past twenty-five years, particularly through an expanding service sector. In more recent decades, Sun Belt states are home to many of the technology centers, such as Silicon Valley near San Jose, California. While many Rust Belt cities have confronted population decline, Sun Belt cities have been among the fastest-growing areas.

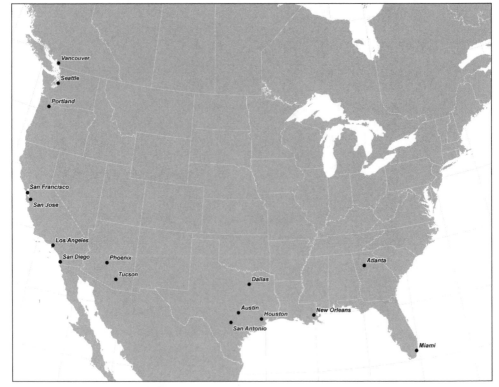

Figure 5.4   Selected cities of the Sun Belt. *Source:* Map created by George Washington University Geography Department.

Table 5.2   Largest US and Canadian Cities—1980

New York City	7,071,639
Chicago	3,005,072
Los Angeles	2,966,850
Toronto	2,137,395*
Philadelphia	1,688,210
Houston	1,595,138
Detroit	1,203,339
Montreal	980,354**
Dallas	904,078
San Diego	875,538

* Census taken in 1981 and represents post-1998 amalgamated boundaries; while Toronto's population doubled since 1951, the population of the "Old City of Toronto" declined from 675,754 to 599,217, marking a loss proportional to Montreal.
** Census taken in 1981.

Four of the ten most populous cities in 1980 were in fact Sun Belt cities (table 5.2). Only one city outside the Rust Belt, Los Angeles, appeared on this list in 1950. Houston's population grew from 596,163 in 1950 to 1,595,138 in 1980, while Phoenix exploded from 106,818 to 789,704 over the same period. In Canada, Calgary experienced the sharpest growth in population, from 129,060 in 1951 to 592,743 in 1981. Edmonton's population similarly increased from 159,631 to 532,246 over the same period. Moreover, between 1960 and 1978, manufacturing employment in US urban areas increased by 42 percent in the South and 21 percent in the West. The Midwest, however, lost 9 percent of its manufacturing employment, and the Northeast suffered a staggering 54 percent decline. Similar trends marked Canada in its east and west, with Quebec experiencing the steepest manufacturing decline. Cities like Vancouver, Calgary, and Edmonton, on the other hand, experienced growth in nearly all sectors.

This loss in manufacturing employment is only half the story. At the same time, the US and Canadian economies after 1980 experienced substantial growth in service-sector employment. Specifically, this service-oriented employment included job growth in the FIRE industries—finance, insurance, and real estate—as well as legal services, retail, and tourism. Between 1979 and 2000, service-sector growth exploded in Hamilton, Toronto, Windsor, and Calgary. The bulk of these service-sector jobs paid either high wages or low wages; there was little in between. Salaries for lawyers, accountants, and high-tech engineers were substantial. Alternatively, wages for hotel workers, fast-food restaurant workers, and public-sector maintenance operatives were typically minuscule. In the United States, the percentage of the Illinois workforce employed in manufacturing declined from 27 to 15.7 percent while the percentage employed in service industries increased from 17 to 30.8 percent. Between 1975 and 1990, the proportion of private investment in the FIRE industries doubled in the United States. This growth in service-sector employment ultimately polarized both US and Canadian workforces between high-wage, white-collar jobs (i.e., finance and legal) and dead-end, low-wage jobs. In North American cities, it follows, the gulf between the haves and the have-nots widened. Social polarization, not surprisingly, spawned accelerated spatial polarization.

This transition to a service-oriented economy also corresponded with the rise of a new dominant political ideology: neoliberalism. This emergent ideology represented a deepening of and building upon of neoconservative political thought rooted in American political conservatism. Neoliberalism, seizing this conservative conceptual terrain, spoke force-fully and bluntly of a new social, moral, political, and economic reality—the need to organize society and its cities around the tenets of deregulation, privatization, and free-market operations. Here was the answer to the supposed burdens of "welfare statism," lax entrepreneurial climates, and inadequate city, regional, and national economic growth. First implemented by the Reagan and Thatcher ad-ministrations in the United States and United Kingdom (i.e., the assault on unions, inter-est-rate hikes, tax cuts for the wealthy, cuts in funding to purportedly wasteful social programs), neoliberal policies were subse-quently "downloaded" through the 1980s to the urban scale as a way to resuscitate cities as sites for capital accumulation. While the neoliberal turn similarly impacted Canadian cities, it was comparatively slow to do so; the transition was first implemented during the 1990s, notably by the Mike Harris Conserva-tive Party government in Ontario, the Gordon Campbell Liberal Party government in British Columbia, and the Ralph Klein Conservative Party government in Alberta (Canada's "wel-fare-state" system is managed more at the pro-vincial scale). The least impacted Canadian province has been Quebec.

In the process, federal funding to cities in the United States was more incisively re-duced, falling from 18 percent to 6.4 percent from 1980 to 1990 (funding to Canadian cities comes from the provincial level and was also severely cut during the 1990s). Cities were suddenly placed in precarious positions, forced to secure new sources of revenue to balance faltering budgets. City governments were forced to be less concerned with redis-tributive social-welfare programs; they had to more strenuously compete for private capital investment and white-collar professionals to restore economic health and city vitality. Be-tween 1966 and 1979, over 90 percent of debt financing in US and Canadian cities was used for public facilities; by 1985, about 80 percent was used to promote private-sector activity in areas such as business development and upscale housing. Thus, many North American cities began to rebuild their central areas by in-vesting in downtown redevelopment projects, constructing upscale consumption spectacles, and "gentrifying" many low-income, strategi-cally located central city neighborhoods.

This restructuring was also accompanied by a significant decline in unionized jobs, the suppression of real wages, and rising levels of inequality. The US federal minimum wage, which stood on par with the poverty level in 1980, had fallen to 30 percent below that level by 1990. More than two million people were thrust beneath the poverty line between 1980 and 1988. Between 1977 and 1989, the top 1 percent of all families by income secured no less than 70 percent of the total national wealth, while the next 9 percent se-cured virtually all the rest. While this trend has not been as severe in Canada, there has also been notable polarization: between 1980 and 2005, earnings increased over 16 percent for the top third income group, stagnated in the middle, and fell by roughly 20 percent in the bottom third.

These trends, in neoliberal times, were justified by civic elites (businesspeople, may-ors, city council members) as unfortunate but necessary realities in a new tumultuous era of ominous globalization. All of this, ironically, emerged against the backdrop of capital beginning to return to industrial cities after decades of flight away from them. Capital's return took the form of new residential investment in real estate (the ascendancy of substantial gentrification) and select corporate relocation into these cities (particularly high-tech and information-based companies). Now these cities were beginning to be remade and fashioned—in accordance with the temporal rhythms of capitalist growth—into what urban scholar Manuel Castells has called "informational cities." These cities now incorporated a select number of new functions: as globally connected centers for financial coordination, mass consumption, marketing, commerce, and privileged sites for real-estate capital in a rapidly evolving postindustrial or knowledge-based economy.

THE SERVICE-SECTOR NEOLIBERAL CITY (1990–2013)

The post-1990 North American city has continued to be restructured, especially in response to meeting the latest needs of two historically powerful city groups: real-estate capital and service-sector capital. Privileging these groups, political governances have steadily moved away from supporting their traditional staple—heavy industry—which had become dramatically reduced in size and economic importance. One more time, these cities have been refashioned in response to the changing rhythms of the national and global capitalist economies. As St. Louis city council member G. Rodds noted to us, "Industry today in our city . . . has simply become less important . . . it's [industry] really a thing of the past . . . now our business is business . . . to build up a city that has the people, culture,

and amenities to compete globally for investment, jobs, and goodies." Councilperson T. Keyes of Chicago concurs: "We now live in an era where things have to be changed . . . everyone realizes this . . . we have to remake our image, our downtown—we have to if Chicago is going to weather the storm of globalization." Globalization, in many North American cities, became ironically situated as both the new threat to city survivability and the new supposed instrument for economic possibility. Competing effectively with other cities was the new mantra: hypermobile business that brought in high-wage-earning workers was the supposed anecdote to new ominous global times.

Catering to the "No Decent Jobs Available" Economy

This post-1990 speeded-up transition from an industrial to postindustrial economy has meant a city functionalized, on the one hand, to more profoundly support service providers. Service headquarters and establishments, in all their diversity and types, have come to more deeply supplement heavy industries as the major economic staple of these cities. Thus, while Chicago lost more than 26 percent of its manufacturing jobs and one-quarter of its factories between 1985 and 2005, its service sector grew by nearly 13 percent. The Chicago region lost 35,700 manufacturing jobs in this five-year period, which accelerated to a loss of 46,300 manufacturing jobs (a 22 percent decline) over the next five years. Similarly, Cleveland lost nearly 40 percent of its manufacturing base (approximately 87,000 jobs) but gained 14 percent more service jobs. Baltimore lost almost one-third of its manufacturing jobs but gained 13 percent new service jobs. Many of these new service jobs (more than 65 percent) were of the low-wage variety—for example, fast-food restaurant employment, bank teller operations, landscape maintenance, temporary labor jobs. The other kind of new service job—high-paying, educationally intensive work—has had a different kind of effect, that is, it has generated a new type of economic dynamism and prosperity centered in the rapid growth of high-income professionals and high-income corporate service firms.

It follows that this job substitution has not been a simple, innocent replacement in city economic functionality. Manufacturing jobs have tended to pay decent, living wages, averaging $17.01 per hour in the United States in 1990. Alternatively, low-wage service jobs—significantly less unionized—paid an estimated

$8.20 per hour in 1990. For those displaced from one kind of job to the other, this has meant a significant decline in purchasing power, job stability, and access to health care. High-wage services jobs, of course, have enabled some to prosper and partake in a "culture of recolonizing" their city for middle- and upper-middle-income populations. Across North American cities, this has entailed the remaking of city space oriented to the consumption desires of this more affluent population: new, ritzy downtown shopping, entertainment districts, upscale condo living, and safe and "sanitized" leisure space (figure 5.5).

Both broader economic trends and government policy have propelled this new city catering to the service sector. On the broader economic front, the North American economy was coming out of a widespread restructuring (the United States in the 1980s

Figure 5.5   The postindustrial landscape of Baltimore's Inner Harbor District, revitalized during the 1970s and 1980s: once the locus for industrial production and now entertainment destination for tourists and affluent consumers. (Photo by John Rennie Short)

and Canada in the 1990s) that was manifest in massive technological change and a tsunami of corporate layoffs as firms downsized to meet the prerequisites of bone-crushing global competition. This transition, acutely painful for millions of households, also laid the foundation for a sustained recovery in productivity, wages, and, to a lesser extent, employment. After 1990, the US economy experienced a kind of long, jobless recovery rooted in service-sector expansion. Initially (1990–1991), the economy lost one million jobs in this period (US cities shed more than one hundred thousand jobs), many of them in the industrial sector. In Canada, GDP fell by more than 3 percent, unemployment reached as high as 11 percent, and household spending plummeted by nearly 6 percent. But growth in the US and Canadian service sector at the same time was unmistakable. Between 1990 and 2000, the US economy gained more than 1.1 million new service jobs . Because of this, corporate profits in these economies (and cities) were sufficiently strong to fuel a modest economic expansion (this coming later in Canada during the 2000s).

In the United States, however, this narrow kind of national and city growth turned into a brief major economic downturn in 2001. This recession in the United States was significant (Canada was notably unaffected). In short order, job loss was substantial. Between 2001 and 2003, the US economy lost a total of 650,000 more jobs. But again, the manufacturing sector took the brunt of the hit. Total manufacturing jobs in the United States plunged to fewer than three million, the lowest total in more than forty years. Amid this, Chicago-area employment declined by more than forty thousand jobs

(5 percent of total employment); Cleveland lost twenty-five thousand jobs; Detroit lost twenty-three thousand jobs; and Philadelphia lost twenty-one thousand jobs. Still, service-sector job growth in both national and city economies in the United States offset the magnitude of this manufacturing job loss. By 2005, it was clear that the national and urban economies in both the United States and Canada had become dependent on service producers. Both of their dominant forms—high-wage and low-wage components—were exploding across cities and regions, which paralleled the countervailing trend of continued industrial jobs loss. Services, in short, had evolved as the new "resource for cities" that ostensibly held the key to future city employment and growth.

City policy, unsurprisingly, has been wielded to be responsive to these trends. This policy has fervently sought to cultivate the relocation and retention of service companies. Thus, service companies are now regularly provided large tax subsidies to locate their headquarters and their establishments in these cities. In St. Louis, multinationals Cortex and Solae received tax abatements of more than $1.2 million apiece to relocate there after 2002, a city record. In Philadelphia, businesses in the city's massive Navy Yard complex were guaranteed extremely generous tax abatements to relocate and stay there. Service companies are also routinely provided generous land write-downs to foster their relocation and retention. In Boston, economically dynamic Genzyme (a biotechnology producer) was provided $1.5 million in land and tax write-downs to remain in the area. In New York, Toronto, Baltimore, Detroit, Indianapolis, Los Angeles, and Vancouver, the story is the same. Since 1990, no other economic sector or urban class has been provided nearly the same level of government support.

Federal policy, in a different way, has furthered this select kind of government assisting in the United States and, to a lesser extent, Canada. This policy, most notably, has reduced its support to many once-reliant government recipients (e.g., social-service providers, health-care clinics). In this process, neoliberal sensibilities and norms have advanced over North America and these cities; government aid to cities in general has been frowned on for the past twenty years. The George H. W. Bush and George W. Bush administrations set the stage for this, which has continued during the Obama years. In Canada, the significant cuts to provincial and urban jurisdictions first set by Jean Chrétien's Liberal Party in the 1990s have been continued by Stephen Harper's Conservative Party.

George W. Bush's rhetoric was particularly influential; his national policy discourse led with the view that little public policy should be explicitly urban. His repetitious message-was this: policy should lift all boats rather than focusing on lifting an urban boat or any other "special-interest" boat. In this theme, government policy should not be about "urban giveaways" or playing politics with powerful constituencies but about making the United States more competitive and compelling in new global times. Public policy, it was declared, was to cope with a changing world (globalization) and the need to re-entrepreneurialize the United States. Cities, now, were cast as a special interest that had no rightful claim to the government's largesse.

This new economic function also became inscribed into the city's spatial form. Most dramatically, many cities have experienced a dramatic growth in "neoliberal parasitic economies" as distinctive urban spaces. These economic swaths—amalgams of temporary labor agencies, day labor sites, payday lenders, check-cashing outlets, pawnshops, and convenience stores—now blanket many low-income racialized areas (figure 5.6). They provide shoddy jobs, overpriced services, and expensive goods to dependent, immobile populations. These economies today prove enormously profitable. This has occurred, ironically, while these same neighborhoods have experienced reduced purchasing power and declined wage-labor possibilities.

There are now an estimated 250 neoliberal parasitic economies in major US cities, with doubtless many more across Canada. They typically take advantage of two spatially immobile populations: long-term poor African Americans and recently arrived Latino households and families. This subeconomy deepens local poverty and inequality. While temporary labor agencies and day labor sites deliver inexpensive bodies using a just-in-time process, payday lenders service economically depressed populations and provide short-term loans at high interest rates. Pawnshops operate by providing fixed-term loans to consumers who use collateral to guarantee such loans. Check cashers service those paid by check who lack access to banks and who need to pay bills. These providers and their principal spokespeople, community and city chambers of commerce, offer an elaborate rationale for their existence, boldly speaking of reversing a community malaise by providing needed goods and services, operating under unfettered competition, and promoting free markets (box 5.4).

Figure 5.6   Pawnshops are a common feature in low-income communities and are part of the "parasitic economy." (Photo by Lisa Benton-Short)

Box 5.4 Neoliberalism and Gentrification in Toronto

Postwar Toronto has followed a growth trajectory similar to that of other North American cities: industrial centralization, deindustrialization and suburbanization, and central city revitalization. Amid Canada's neoliberal turn in the 1990s, Ontario's provincial government helped create municipal-scale neoliberal programs. The Progressive Conservative government of Mike Harris, elected in 1995, embraced the shift toward neoliberalism. Harris's government drastically reduced provincial funding to cities, significantly impacting Toronto and other Ontario cities. Funding for public housing, public transit, and other social programs, now the responsibility of the City of Toronto, compounded already existing budget pressures produced by suburban flight.

Toronto, like many other North American cities, now had to secure its own revenue streams. However, unlike the North American experience, the city was amalgamated in 1998 with its adjacent municipalities—Scarborough, York, North York, East York, and Etobicoke. Opposed by these former outlying municipalities, the City of Toronto—through its now centralized municipal governance—received a boost in its resource base that became prioritized as subsidies to the city's real-estate community. The erosion of growth and zoning controls, privatization of municipal utilities, arrest of public housing construction, and enactment of "workfare" were coded into urban policy as gentrification was embraced as the means of transforming Toronto from a supposedly declining industrial landscape into a "vibrant," service-oriented, global financial center.

At the same time, Toronto's bid for the 2008 Summer Olympics was announced and led to a series of "megaproject" plans on the city's waterfront. This proposed waterfront revitalization, led by the Toronto Waterfront Revitalization Corporation, initially entailed new entertainment districts, upscale condominiums, and new sports facilities to accommodate the Olympics. The bid eventually failed as increased resistance from a range of grassroots groups—the Ontario Coalition against Poverty, Green Work Alliance, and Metro Network for Social Justice—shut down the city's financial district and forced Harris's resignation and the collapse of Ontario's Progressive Conservative government.

But gentrification—fueled by the speculative investment that was stimulated by the bid and now neoliberalized municipal governance—was well under way and continued to progress through the 2000s. Expanding urban spaces "fit" for middle- to upper-class colonization, gentrification unfolded in the form of new condominiums and loft conversions, "historic" districts and new sanitized waterfront public spaces, and upscale consumption and entertainment complexes in formerly underutilized warehouse districts surrounding the city's restructured "knowledge-based" CBD. Thousands of low-income residents were displaced to clear the way for new white-collar professionals. Coinciding with this gentrification has also been the "revival" of numerous ethnic commercial and residential districts. The branding of Greektown, Little Italy, and Gerrard India Bazaar—as in Chicago, New York, and Philadelphia, where correlative sites function similarly—has led to new spaces of ethnic consumption and tourism as part of the "reculturalizing" of Toronto's neighborhood fabric to align with middle- to upper-class sensibilities. As such, much of the old City of Toronto is now gentrified. And with poverty displaced elsewhere, it now represents one of the most upscale and affluent housing markets in North America.

This parasitic economy differs from previous predatory economies in key ways: in its intensity of affliction imposed, its base of resources drawn upon, and its goals for social engagement. At the core of this difference, these economic formations often have a sheer size and dominance that reduce possibilities for residents to purchase alternative goods and services and to obtain alternative occupations. They have spread rapidly from core incipient blocks of occupancy and now typically dominate local retailing. Today, these economies all but annihilate competitive retail, service, and employment opportunities. Moreover, these economies are typically more durable and flexible than before. In many areas, they are heavily capitalized by large doses of multinational investment from Asia, Europe, and beyond, as many establishments are branches of multinational companies. Given this base of capital and expertise, many establishments can stay with a pattern of resource provision (e.g., making loans at high interest rates) and strategically adjust this pattern when local market conditions are determined to have changed.

Finally, this parasitic economy is a more robust intervention into local lives than before (see box 5.5). While the establishments supposedly provide needed goods and services in downtrodden communities, they now strike out with another purpose: to insert a deeper social responsibility into local life. Embracing neoliberal values and drives, many of these institutions now advertise themselves as offering goods, services, and what Peter Ehrenhaus has called a "therapeutic motif." The ethos of neoliberal values, the new tonic for the supposed correct way to see and act in the world, penetrates the sensibilities, goals, and directives of these parasitic institutions. In the process, made problematic are the cultural values and social mores of nearby residents that can supposedly be reengineered by imposing more fiscal responsibility, social promptness, and heightened individual-competitive sensibilities. This economy's actions thus purportedly enhance lives in the economic, social, and cultural realms with an unapologetic stated goal: to constitute a more responsible, productive, and civic person.

Box 5.5 Neoliberal Parasitic Economies in Chicago

The rise of neoliberal parasitic economies in the 1990s coincided with the sharp increase in Latino immigration to North America in general and US cities in particular. Chicago's experience is notable as its Latino population has risen from essentially nonexistent in 1970 to 753,644 in 2005. Latinos are now 27 percent of Chicago's total population. The historic points of entry for this population—Pilsen, Near West Side, and Wicker Park/Bucktown—are now significantly gentrified, pushing low-income Latinos and new arrival destinations outward to neighborhoods such as Little Village, on Chicago's southwest side. While concentrations exist in Humboldt Park, Albany Park, and East Garfield Park, Little Village has become an epicenter for this parasitic economy formation in Chicago, particularly along 26th Street with extensions along Cermak Road, Kedzie Avenue, and Pulaski Road. Now, profits from these stores and businesses (measured by gross receipts from 26th Street) rank second only to Michigan Avenue in Chicago.

This formation is termed "parasitic" because it targets spatially immobile people and operates by plundering them despite their limited base of resources and wealth. In the domains of retail provision, housing provision, and work, people are exploited in similar ways as the subprime mortgage market has targeted other low-income (i.e., African American) populations. With Mexican-origin residents alone occupying roughly 30 percent of the jobs in Chicago's formal and informal service sector, this pool of immigrant labor has provided local businesses with an abundant and expanding source of dependable low-wage labor over the past ten years.

Embedded in this landscape, along with day labor sites, temporary agencies, and convenience stores, is a host of parasitic institutions, such as payday lenders, pawnshops, and check cashers. Payday lenders service populations in need of credit through short-term cash loans (i.e., $200–$300) typically at high interest rates, often as high as 15 to 20 percent. With bills (e.g., rent, gas, heat) often due before payday, these loans are in high demand as few other options are afforded this spatially confined population. However, due to the high interest rates, many are unable to pay and are forced to refinance, repeating and deepening their indebtedness. Pawnshops also provide fixed-term loans to customers who use assets as collateral to back the loan (thus credit checks are not necessary). These loans are also often renewed at high interest rates to avoid appropriation of the collateral by pawnshop owners.

Check cashers, perhaps the most parasitic of these institutional forms, serve those paid by check but who lack bank accounts (because of bad credit, indebtedness, etc.). These agencies cash checks for fees that range anywhere between 3 and 10 percent of the check's value. These businesses also write checks for customers (for $10–$15 fees) as a means of paying bills. With no bank access, this has become a particularly popular service. The largest of these in assets and number of stores are Western Union, Segue, and Money Express, together numbering nineteen stores in Little Village and representing the penetration of global financial capital into this local formation's operation.

Residents who repeatedly use these services (i.e., turning checks into cash and/or other checks), because of having few other options, accumulate additional costs in fees that often amount to thousands of dollars annually. Yet with employment typically at $8 per hour, many have no realistic way to pay off these loans, which keep them perpetually indebted and struggling to economically subsist. Arriving in the United States with dreams of a better life and returning money to households in Mexico, they often become disillusioned with their new circumstances.

Figure 5.7   Liquor stores such as this one in Washington, DC, offer a range of services, including check cashing, but charge exorbitant fees. (Photo by Lisa Benton-Short)

*Catering to Real-Estate Capital
and the New Segregation*

More than before, North American cities are also functionalized to meet the aspirations of developers, builders, and public-private development partnerships. This group's actions—to remake urban space—purportedly hold the key to future city successes in navigating supposed punishing and turbulent global times. Their efforts to remake city form, it is suggested by mayors and city councils, address a struggling-for-business and struggling-for-investment city that needs to be "re-entrepreneurialized" in order to energize job creation and declining tax bases and economic fortunes. In this context, local governances sanction them to "breathe new life into these cities," that is, to upgrade downtowns, sculpt showy middle- and upper-middle-class livable spaces, and build vibrant cultural facilities and spaces that communicate a new aesthetically sensitive and culturally dynamic city. Real-estate capital, of course, has always

been one privileged entity in North American cities, but its status is now further elevated.

Given this focused upgrading, a dominant outcome has been anything but surprising: a deepened socioeconomic balkanization of these cities. These cities, always marked by pronounced economic and racial divides, now experience a sharpening of this that is most visibly reflected in two trends: expanding gentrification and deepening poverty in poor, minority communities in both the United States and Canada. This trend is ominous: while downtowns and near-core gentrified enclaves are "condoed" and "themed," vast numbers of communities across these cities are essentially ignored (figures 5.8 and 5.9). Downtowns are "culturally revamped" and aestheticized along upper-middle-class lines; nearby working-class and poverty enclaves are brutally written off. Governances apply a select visibility: one area is illuminated and privileged, and the other is cast into the shadows and concealed by the planner and policy gaze. Now energy, vitality, and

Figure 5.8 Affluent townhomes in Chicago's drastically redeveloped South Loop District, once a deindustrialized landscape of abandoned warehouses, rail yards, and vacant lots. (Photo by David Wilson and Matthew Anderson)

Figure 5.9   Poverty in Chicago's Bronzeville, only two miles away from Chicago's glitzy CBD. (Photo by David Wilson and Matthew Anderson)

resources are selectively allocated across these cities and exacerbate an uneven development that is keenly felt by many. Such policies are grounded and rationalized as a kind of shock treatment—of city recommodification, reregulation, and acute targeting of planning and policy actions—that visibly splinters these cities.

One pole in this balkanizing, deepening gentrification is now increasingly fostered by city programs: tax increment financing (TIFs), business improvement districts, historic preservation, and urban beautification projects. In short, gentrification has been centered as explicit urban public policy. Once treated as an urban aberration, a trend that was ambiguously understood, gentrification is now seized by local governances as a key policy centerpiece in the tool kit to progressively restructure these cities to meet supposedly new challenging global times. "Gentrification," to St. Louis Planner M. Kipe, "allows us to forge ahead . . . to remake our city [St. Louis] in a way that can help us bring in new jobs, creative people, creative firms . . . that will strengthen St. Louis and allow us to compete." Moreover, gentrification as urban policy fits this scheme perfectly: it does not involve government subsidies or

resources, it is a private market process, and it "reculturalizes" the city via the remaking of new neighborhoods, public spaces, and downtowns. Gentrification post-1990, then, has increasingly been accepted as something efficient and progressive (figure 5.10).

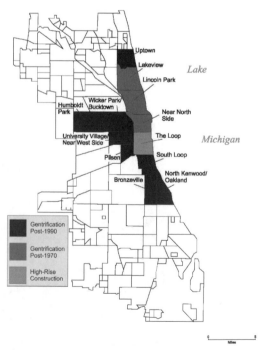

Figure 5.10   Gentrification in Chicago. *Source:* Map by Matthew Anderson.

This restructuring has also been propelled by something crucial: a bold but subtle rhetoric. At its core has been a pro-gentrification theme now well chronicled across urban North America: the "urban pioneer." Urban pioneers are cast as brave and courageous gentrifiers renewing physically decayed neighborhoods. These neighborhoods supposedly need something fundamental—replenishing resettlers—to transform dilapidated communities. A class-based "recolonizing" of the inner city is made a laudable and important city-renewing goal. Local newspapers and magazines across urban America, for example, widely tout the restorative aspects of this population and the need for gentrification in these neighborhoods. At the same time, the post-1990 plethora of arts festivals, street fairs, and redevelopment initiatives in these neighborhoods reinforces this rhetoric. Such festivals and street fairs, now a cottage industry in these locations, relentlessly (if benevolently and gently) extol the creation of a new kind of space rooted in humanly nourishing place-sensitive aesthetics and mores.

This theme profoundly disciplines and commodifies aesthetics in these cities. Culturally upscaling and fortifying neighborhoods and public spaces (e.g., turning them over for residency by "the creative class," building townhouses and gated communities, creating discerning-consumption retail blocks and districts) is to be seen as a civic undertaking. Culture, in this sense, is to be judged for its class-based content as well as functionalized to meet city needs. It is offered as a new source of civic anxiety and attention. Culture, in this sense, is not simply something to be lived through: it must be carefully organized, strategically used, and made functionally utilitarian. This means obliterating a wealth of

cultural forms (e.g., "underclass culture," "industrial aesthetics") and encouraging others (e.g., "aesthetic-livable communities," culturally progressive civic subjects). Citizens become as much prisoners to culture as masters of it. These cities, supposedly constrained by the need to put their best cultural forms forward, ostensibly have no other choice.

It follows that in the shadows of sparkling downtown skyscrapers and showy gentrified neighborhoods, many impoverished neighborhoods in these cities have worsened. Thus, leaders and residents in these communities struggle more than ever to obtain resources to upgrade their spaces as they contest formidable obstacles. The first fundamental obstacle is the accelerated institutional drive to produce and defend downtown revitalized landscapes of pleasure, what urban scholar Gordon MacLeod has called "the new cathedrals of consumption." Expanding gentrification and new redeveloped spaces have become luminous, upgraded icons for what these cities supposedly can and need to become. They are to be bolstered and vigorously defended (via zoning, surveillance and policing, being identified as growth nodes, and built around). The second obstacle is an emergent federal push to "entrepreneurialize" cities and places. This has been deepened via an arsenal of programs, particularly workfare, No Child Left Behind, and the HOPE-VI program of public housing demolition and reform (initiated by the Clinton administration in 1992) in the United States.

The poor and their communities in this emergent "entrepreneurial city" too often fail to meaningfully rate; these are spaces and populations that become tangential to the city building drive. These residents supposedly suffer from making an insignificant contribution to the "city competitive project" and purportedly need to practice more sound self-initiative, lessen their reliance on the "welfare state" and its dependency creation, and be more effective contributors to making their cities hardworking and entrepreneurial. Through HOPE-VI, cities apply for federal grants to demolish their public housing stock and replace it with "mixed-income" redevelopments. Subsidized residents are to be instilled with better cultural/family values and work ethics via living in close proximity to wealthier, successful residents. In this philosophy, very-low-income families will learn from the working families when they see people getting up at the crack of dawn and heading to work. Likewise, workfare is designed to replace a welfare system that supposedly encourages laziness and culturally pathologic behavior. Here, government assistance requires that low-income residents must perform waged work (typically in dead-end fast-food types of jobs). In the process,

they are to sharpen their work ethic and boost their motivation to pull themselves up by their bootstraps. These programs, deeply embedded within local (neoliberal) frames of knowledge, constitute the new attempt at social welfare.

Much evidence documents that poor black and Latino communities in the United States have worsened in recent years. Most immediately, windshield surveys in the poorest neighborhoods of Baltimore, Chicago, Detroit, Cleveland, Pittsburgh, Philadelphia, and other cities reveal a swell of the standard markers of persistent neglect and disinvestment: unbroken blocks of abandoned and foreclosed homes, acres of derelict buildings, and vast tracts of vacant, weedy lots (See figure 5.11). In Canada, this deepening of urban poverty is not as notable (although just as concentrated). While many of the same policies are in place, their poverty-exacerbating impacts have not been as drastic (i.e., while some public housing has been demolished, most of it is still

Figure 5.11   Abandoned structures in a poor neighborhood in Baltimore. Today, there are more than forty thousand vacant homes in Baltimore. (Photo by Lisa Benton-Short)

funded and in operation). The streets in these communities reflect the reality of unrelenting economic hardship and material deprivation: one readily sees homeless men and women dotting the streets, roaming panhandlers, clusters of unemployed and underemployed youth, and a plethora of crumbling houses.

In short, these neighborhoods, often only a few minutes from downtown, seem consigned to a different reality. And, as discussed, retail strips in these communities are now dominated by plundering, exploitative shops and outlets that are broken up only by barely surviving groceries, disinvested day-care facilities, struggling dry cleaners and banks, marginal hardware stores, and the like. Daily buying and working in these areas have become routinized human-ensnaring experiences; lack of spatial mobility is the ticket to being plundered (see box 5.6).

Box 5.6 Poverty in Philadelphia

Philadelphia, following the path of other large industrial cities, has been decimated by the flight of middle-class residents, jobs, and resources that continues today. By 1980, Philadelphia's population had plummeted to nearly 20 percent of what it had been in 1950, from 2,071,605 to 1,688,210. More than one hundred thousand jobs were lost during this time period, mostly manufacturing in orientation. The consequence was an increasingly unemployed, poor, and disproportionately African American population left behind in an urban landscape outmoded by the evolving broader capitalist economy (42 percent of the city's 2010 population was African American).

This poverty was compounded by the neoliberal turn in the 1980s. As city center revival and gentrification became prioritized urban policy, resources were directed away from an already starving (figuratively and literally) inner city. This spread of poverty, concentrated mostly in North and West Philadelphia, stimulated national media attention in 1985 with a dramatic confrontation between the anti-poverty resistance group MOVE and the Philadelphia Police Department. The incident resulted in the bombing of the group's headquarters by police forces, killing eleven and wiping out entire blocks in West Philly. The incident drew mainstream criticism against police brutality across the United States.

Affluent gentrification in neighborhoods such as Society Hill and Northern Liberties, set against widening and deepening poverty in the 1990s, rendered Philadelphia a modern-day "tale of two cities." Traditional manufacturing jobs continued to decline while the rising service sector split the city's workforce between high-wage professional jobs and dead-end menial service jobs. About fifty thousand further jobs (6 percent of the city's workforce) were lost between 1990 and 2000, with another twenty-six thousand from just 2000 to 2003. And the erosion of funding to social programs, such as public housing and community block grants, worsened already declining material conditions for the city's most marginalized residents. During these years, in North Philly's Fairhill and Hartranft neighborhoods, the official percentage of those living in poverty rose to an astounding 57 percent, with unofficial marks hovering above 80 percent, as the city's total population bottomed out at 1,517,550 in 2000.

As of 2009, roughly 25 percent of Philadelphia's residents lived below the poverty level (nearly 12 percent lived below 50 percent of the poverty level). Nearly two hundred thousand of these residents were African American, with eighty thousand Latino and eight thousand white. Nearly 67 percent of these residents lived in single-female-headed families, and about 73 percent were unemployed. Only 2 percent of this population, in fact, worked full-time jobs, with over half living in housing structures that were built before 1939. Philadelphia now ranks as the poorest US city among the nation's ten largest cities. Much of this poverty remains concentrated in North and West Philly and has led to worsened degrees of homelessness, hunger, and crime. The city's homicide rate also ranked the highest of the ten largest US cities in 2006. Philadelphia's experience has been emblematic of the plight of the contemporary US city. While this restructuring has returned middle-class people, jobs, and resources to once depressed landscapes, it has been a starkly uneven process, with poverty both deepening and numerically growing.

And this is accompanied by another exacerbating development: an increased stigma cast upon these neighborhoods and populations. Police departments often exacerbate this. New crime crackdown procedures and stepped-up surveillance now mark many of these urban areas and engender a widespread notion among the general public of problematic, anti-civic communities. This trend also parallels an acute rise in incarceration. Between 1970 and 2000, a 400 percent surge in prison building across the United States was accompanied by a 60 percent increase in the rate of black incarceration. In Illinois, during this same time period, inmate numbers increased from roughly 7,500 to more than 43,000. In Chicago, eighty surveillance cameras were recently placed across the city; sixty of them were located in such community "hot spots." Operation Disruption Surveillance, initiated in 2003, has spent $3.5 million to detect street crime and monitor the activities of these residents. And with the recent election of Chicago's current Mayor, Rahm Emanuel, ninety-two patrollers have been added to the streets to meet a supposedly growing crime and safety concern. Children and adults are constantly watched in the city's proclaimed "high-pathology neighborhoods," which leaves many unsettled and feeling impugned. On the one hand, this "soft" use of electronic surveillance helps reduce crime. On the other hand, funneled through established understandings and meanings, it reinforces the notion of a problematic, anti-civic group of neighborhoods and populations.

CONCLUSION

This chapter has chronicled the evolving economic functionality and changing correspondent spatial form of the North American city. We document that these cities have been sculpted especially by a dominant process: the complex legacy of city-based institutions and people mediating the powerful rhythms of the broader national and global economies. From an intensively industrial, to a service-based, to a neoliberal, balkanized city, urban environments have evolved in structurally conditioned but historically distinctive ways. People and institutions, on the ground, have mattered, but so, too, have regional, national, and global forces.

In this context, North American cities today bear the legacy of the past as they continue to be economically and spatially restructured. Currently, the rise of neoliberal political doctrine (bolstering the construction of the service-sector neoliberal city) paves the way to functionally revamp the afflicted deindustrialized city around global financial coordination, affluent consumption, and gentrified living. But all is not so innocent: this sociospatial restructuring has unleashed a host of deleterious consequences. It has especially afflicted lower-income and marginalized urban spaces and their populations, who still reel from the punishing effects of deindustrialization. New layers of uneven development now blanket these cities as newer spaces of disinvestment (i.e., peripheral urban neighborhoods and older inner suburbs) are produced by the wrath of a creatively destructive capitalist economy. New inequalities, in effect, are superimposed on existing inequalities. In short, the service-sector neoliberal city, while refashioning central city areas for upper-income aesthetics, consumption, and work, has also produced a deepened polarization between the haves and have-nots.

Yet the brief reign of the neoliberal city may have reached its zenith, particularly in the United States. As an acutely felt subprime mortgage crisis and the broader post-2008 financial collapse threaten their orderly sociospatial functioning, high-rise and condo construction have slowed down amid economic uncertainty. Moreover, stagnant service-sector growth (particularly in high-wage, educationally intensive jobs) in this crisis period parallels continued manufacturing job loss (condo construction and service-sector growth in Canada, however, has spiked since 2008). Time will tell whether the Canadian economy will follow the US pattern (as it has often done before), but across urban America, the middle and upper-middle class now feel the sting of material insecurity that has long marked the urban working class and poor. At the same time, city spatial form seems aged, many gentrified enclaves seem defensively retreatist and inward looking, downtown consumption play spaces seem unduly balkanized and exclusionary, and poor residential zones appear dominated by afflicting, contentious parasitic economies.

The crisis—effectively a crisis of neoliberal capitalism—suggests the potential for a new round of urban restructuring whose form is currently unknown. As Chicago mayor Rahm Emanuel recently noted about his city's plight, "Much has changed . . . new times demand new answers," yet these answers are still being developed and will require enormous institutional mobilization. We believe, then, that more rounds of tumultuous city restructuring (which will change this urban milieu's economic functionality and spatial form) are around the corner. City governments and business communities one more time must rethink their circumstances, spatial forms, and public policies for the profit-production enterprise to continue. We all need to stay tuned for the details; they will assuredly soon unfold.

SUGGESTED READINGS

Beauregard, R. 2006. *When America Became Suburban*. Minneapolis: University of Minnesota Press.

Bognar, S., and J. Reichart, dirs. 2009. *The Last Truck: Closing of a GM Plant*. DVD. New York:

Home Box Office. *This film highlights how deindustrialization continues in the twenty-first century with a look at a 2009 GM plant closing in Moraine, Ohio.*

Brenner, N., and N. Theodore. 2002. *Spaces of Neoliberalism: Urban Restructuring in North America and Western Europe.* London: Blackwell.

Gordon, D. 1984. "Capitalist Development and the History of American Cities." In *Marxism and the Metropolis: New Perspectives in Urban Political Economy*, 2nd ed., edited by W. Tabb and L. Sawyers, 21–54. Oxford: Oxford University Press.

Hackworth, J. 2007. *The Neoliberal City: Governance, Ideology, and Development in American Urbanism.* Ithaca, NY: Cornell University Press.

Harvey, D. 1989. *The Urban Experience.* Baltimore: Johns Hopkins University Press.

Jonas, A. E. G., and D. Wilson. 1999. *The Growth Machine: Critical Perspectives Two Decades Later.* Albany: SUNY Press.

Moore, M., dir. 1989. *Roger and Me.* DVD. Burbank, CA: Warner Home Video, 2003. *The film examines the regional negative economic impact of General Motors CEO Roger Smith's summary action of closing several auto plants in Flint, Michigan, costing thirty thousand people their jobs at the time (and cumulatively about eighty thousand by 2013).*

Ranney, D. 2003. *Global Decisions, Local Collisions: Urban Life in the New World Order.* Philadelphia: Temple University Press.

Smith, N. 1996. *The New Urban Frontier: Gentrification and the Revanchist City.* New York: Routledge.

Wilson, D. 2007. *Cities and Race: America's New Black Ghetto.* New York: Routledge.

Wilson, D., D. Beck, and A. Bailey. 2009. "Neoliberal-Parasitic Economies and Space Building: Chicago's Southwest Side." *Annals of the Association of American Geographers* 99(3): 604–26.

CITIES ON THE WEB

To learn more about how businesses see opportunities in urban restructuring, try the US Chamber of Commerce website at http://www.uschamber.com and the Canadian Chamber of Commerce web site, http://www.chamber.ca.

One trend under neoliberalism has been the rise of public-private partnerships. Learn more about these at http://www.ncppp.org.

Many cities have development authorities or comprehensive plans for urban redevelopment. For example, you can learn about individual development plans in Pittsburgh at http://www.ura.org, in Vancouver at http://www.vancouvereconomic.com, or in Washington, DC, at http://dmped.dc.gov/DC/DMPED.

You can follow automobile plant closing at autonews.com.

6

Globalization and the City
YEONG-HYUN KIM

Much has been written and said lately about the urban impact of globalization, as the world witnessed and continues to witness call-center cities in the Global South, waves of new immigrants to globally oriented cities, and financial clusters that serve global markets. People, firms, industries, and countries are greatly affected by the process of globalization, and so are cities. Globalization is believed to have led to increased competition not only among North American cities but also between North American and foreign cities. To put it simply, we are living in a world where cities of all sizes and regions compete to get the attention of international business investors, skilled talent, tourists, and event organizers, among others. Globalization is the new reality.

Different kinds of urban change are often linked to the same global forces and trends. Whether it involves an extensive economic restructuring of a city or a short-term policy change made by the city council, globalization and competition are the two words used time and again to describe all recent and important changes in the contemporary city. It is not uncommon to see in both academic and media accounts that various urban problems and solutions are explained through, and reduced to, the city's competitiveness

and visibility at the global level. A lot is expected of city governments to maintain and strengthen their city's competitive positions and performances in global marketplaces. This chapter explores the effects of globalization on the city and the changing competitive positions of North American cities, particularly traditional industrial cities in the Rust Belt of the United States. Finally, we look at their governments' new development initiatives designed to remedy old weaknesses and to develop new strengths in the face of increasing globalization.

GLOBALIZATION AND URBANIZATION

Neither globalization nor urbanization is a new story, but they have been fairly recent phenomena of urban research. During the late 1980s and early 1990s, a then-emerging research field called world (global) cities research began to take a global perspective on urban change, with a particular focus on the effects of economic globalization on large cities. Although cities change for various reasons and in different ways, their change—economic, demographic, political, and spatial—has increasingly been viewed in relation to the globalizing world

Figure 6.1   The global commercial city of Las Vegas. (Photo by Yeong Kim)

economy. Recently, another urban perspective on globalization has also gained attention, one that analyzes globalization with a focus on cities and their impact on global issues such as climate change and environmental risk, international (im)migration, and political movements. Although it is clear that urban issues can force changes in the course of global events, this chapter focuses instead on the significant impact the current process of globalization has had on the city.

Three globalization-related urban changes have received much of the academic attention in recent years. First, the globalization of urbanization has been identified as one of the most significant developments in recent urban history, as more than half of the world's population now lives in urban areas. The term "global urbanism" not only illustrates the dramatic growth of urban population across the globe, including developing countries, but also highlights broadly shared urban experiences and practices, such as corporate office buildings, postmodern architecture, youth

consumer culture, and commercialized public spaces among large, globalizing cities (figure 6.1). Few things would prove the globalizing world more clearly than the fact that cities in different places and different conditions offer a similar look and feel.

Second, an indiscriminate adoption of neoliberal urban policies—as discussed in chapter 5—has been implicated as a leading cause of global urbanism, in which many cities around the world undergo comparable, if not identical, changes that are predominantly market led and business friendly. When multitudes of elected city officials readily use corporate words like "competitiveness," "benchmarks," "best practices," and "strategic planning" in envisioning their respective cities' future, it is becoming more and more clear that different cities converge toward a set of recognized policy tools, such as business tax incentives, public-private partnerships, mega-infrastructure projects, and creative knowledge industries. It is still debatable whether globalization causes city governments to act in certain ways or whether cities are the sites of a bottom-up process of global convergence. But one thing is certain: that more cities submit themselves, willingly or unwillingly, to competition and cooperation beyond their traditional borders.

And third, the growing importance of global cities in the world economy has been another heavily researched topic with relation to globalization. The simple definition urban scholar Saskia Sassen gives to global cities, like London, New York, and Tokyo, as the sites "where the work of globalization gets done," brilliantly sums up how urban changes in this handful of cities shape and are shaped by globalization (see box 6.1). Financial services, for

example, remain concentrated in top global cities such as New York and London, where the economics of agglomeration and the ability to provide face-to-face contact are of great importance. The rise of global cities captures the idea that some cities have more influence and power than others in today's globalizing world. While these emergent global cities' importance as the world's economic centers, cultural meccas, and tourist destinations has been well documented, "other" cities and their urban changes remain largely underresearched and are frequently assumed to feel a similar but less pronounced impact from global forces and trends.

Box 6.1 Geographical Perspectives on World Cities

Patrick Geddes first used the term "world cities" in *Cities in Evolution* (1915) to illustrate urban and suburban growth outside of the United Kingdom. His list of world cities included not only Paris, Berlin, and New York, but also some of the fastest growing cities at that time such as Dusseldorf and Pittsburgh. Fifty years later, British geographer Peter Hall reintroduced the term in *The World Cities* (1966) to explain the growing concentration of the world's political and economic power in a handful of world cities, namely London, Paris, Randstad, Rhine-Ruhr, Moscow, New York, and Tokyo.

After John Friedmann published "The World City Hypothesis" (figure 6.2) in 1986, urban geographers started paying attention to the connections and competitions among cities beyond their national borders. Friedmann's argument, that worldwide processes affect urban change, has inspired many to take a global perspective on economic, cultural, and spatial restructuring in their study areas. Although urbanization and poverty in postcolonial and developing societies have long been contextualized in international political and economic processes, the global framework was rarely used, prior to Friedmann's work, to investigate the form and function of major cities in the developed world, particularly those in North America. Instead, most of the earlier studies on intercity relations, such as analyses of central place, urban systems, spatial diffusion, and transportation network, set urban centers at the national or even subnational scale.

While the notion of a world-city system as a research framework has been well accepted among urban scholars, the research methods that Friedmann used to rank cities have been questioned extensively. Much of the criticism has centered on the empirical data, or the lack of them, used in establishing his world city hierarchy, as is well demonstrated in John

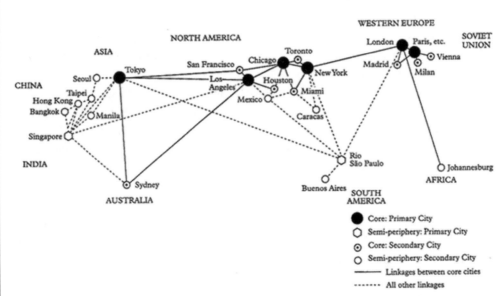

Figure 6.2   John Friedmann's hierarchy of world cities. *Source:* George Washington University Geography Department. Adapted from John Friedmann, "The World City Hypothesis," *Development and Change* 17 (1986): 69–83.

Rennie Short and colleagues' article titled "The Dirty Little Secret of World Cities Research." Friedmann's list of first-tier world cities includes London and Paris in Europe, New York, Chicago, and Los Angeles in North America, and Tokyo in Asia, but with better data and more sophisticated techniques, different cities for different functions and different levels of geographical coverage have been suggested in later research. For example, geographer Peter Taylor's world city hierarchy puts Miami, Hong Kong, and Singapore right behind New York and London as major regional centers, while Tokyo is slated as a minor regional center. Another criticism includes Friedmann's exclusive focus on economic functions of cities while neglecting cultural and political centers around the world. Some have also questioned the relevance of this hierarchical approach to our understanding of ordinary cities that do not feature in any of these world city hierarchies.

Along with the research endeavor to draw a comprehensive hierarchical mapping of major cities across the globe, a great deal of scholarship has focused on the unique nature of top-tier world cities at the apex of the hierarchy. Drawing heavily on Saskia Sassen's *The Global City: New York, London, Tokyo* (1991), this group of researchers has paid particular attention to the financial institutions and advanced businesses services that have separated the top three from all other cities in the contemporary world. The increasing global dispersal of economic activities has created a huge demand for expanded central control and management functions, which are disproportionately concentrated in these few cities. In addition to their importance as the world's economic command and control centers, global cities are also the hubs of global networks of transnational business elites, immigrants from developing countries, high-skilled talents, and international tourists.

Undoubtedly, large global cities have captured and indeed dominated the imagination of urban researchers in the past two decades. Sitting at the top of the global urban hierarchy, these cities are the very sites where globalizing networks of corporations, finance, telecommunications, and immigration develop and grow. Not only that, the wider world is often affected by the actions of various key institutions and individuals based in these cities. Cities like London, New York, Tokyo, Paris, and Frankfurt are the sites where global financial crises (and recoveries) are set in motion, where new fashions and styles are introduced on a seasonal basis, and where innovative business methods are put forward and tested. Simply, the work of globalization is both experienced and practiced literally at the workplaces, stores, streets, neighborhoods, and homes of global cities and other "almost there" cities.

As is the case with other globalization research, global cities research is criticized for its heavy focus on the economic aspect of the globalization-urbanization nexus, leaving other aspects of the nexus—such as sociocultural and demographic factors—overlooked and often undervalued. For example, the Globalization and World Cities (GaWC) Research Network, the world's best-known research group for global cities research that has conducted extensive data collection and quantitative network analysis to map out the global urban hierarchy, has paid a great deal of attention to where major financial and business service firms are located. But limited work exists on where the world's premier religious, geopolitical, and cultural institutions are and how they contribute to globalization. Criticism is also directed at current research's lack of focus on smaller cities and those in the non-Western world. Indeed, the impact of globalization on midsize cities in North America has not received much attention from global cities research either. Although urban decline in the old Manufacturing Belt of the US Northeast and Midwest has been directly linked to a global shift in manufacturing, economic troubles in cities like Youngstown, Cincin-

nati, and Cleveland, Ohio, have rarely been discussed in the context of the cities' loss of connections to global production networks or deteriorating positions in the global urban hierarchy. Canadian industrial cities, such as Windsor and Hamilton, fare similarly, as little research exists on how globalization has affected their urban fortune over time. Instead, their falling urban fortunes have been discussed in terms of their respective cities' local politics, civic entrepreneurship, and workforce flexibility. Recognizing the gap in the current academic research on the globalization-urbanization nexus, the remaining sections in this chapter examine how North American cities have struggled to maintain their competitive edge in the face of economic globalization and how they now attempt to revitalize their fortunes by reglobalizing their local economies and peoples.

GLOBALIZATION AND COMPETITIVENESS OF NORTH AMERICAN CITIES

Cities in North America have long been linked to the wider world through the networks of people, firms, governments, and other organizations. Ever since the first European settlements, North American places and towns have been exposed to and engaged in the forces and influences that originated far beyond the national borders. In an age of increasing globalization, however, their ties to the outside world have grown ever more numerous and more intense. Globalization now has more profound and visible effects on North American cities.

In the mid-1990s, urban geographer David Wilson declared that "under the onslaught of globalization, North American cities are changing dramatically. . . . Cities become victims, beneficiaries, or survivors in this new reality." An important question is why and how some cities benefit from the current process of globalization while others lose businesses and population and undergo further decline? For example, New York continues to be one of the preeminent cities in the world economy, but cities like Cleveland have suffered the loss of their connectivity to the rest of the world and their once-dominant position in global industries. In 1900, Cleveland was among the top three cities for corporate headquarters, behind New York and Chicago; today it ranks far below the top ten, according to the location of Fortune 500 companies. The question becomes even more relevant when we consider that not all traditional manufacturing cities in North America suffer from the aftermath of deindustrialization. A recent *Economist* article praises Pittsburgh, the "Steel City," for its aggressive attempt at reinventing itself as a global financial center in the past decade, while Cleveland's determination to become the "Comeback City" of the Midwest has not brought as much success to the local economy.

Certainly it is not an easy task to navigate the complex geography of the globaliza-tion-urbanization nexus in North America, as cities are never passive in the face of globalization but mediate, rework, and often resist the process in unique and multifaceted ways. While one might assume that cities in the Sun Belt grow fast with waves of immigrants and companies from overseas, the sobering reality is that many Sun Belt cities, such as Stockton, California, continue to struggle with economic woes after the 2008 subprime mortgage crisis. In contrast, Allentown, Pennsylvania, is located in the heart of the Rust Belt, but it has successfully defied the odds by emerging as a biotech city in the heart of the Rust Belt. As part of the effort to explain and predict stories of urban success and decline, various measures and indicators of city competiveness have been developed in recent years. It is widely suggested that globalization puts our cities under added pressure to be efficient and competitive to attract investment and jobs and that cities should develop and occupy power niches in global marketplaces. Otherwise, they may just not survive or thrive. Today, being global and being competitive are interchangeable in an era where we constantly hear about how globalization pits American cities against international cities in the battle for business.

While most of the global city indicators are used to simply demonstrate how US and Canadian cities fare against other major international cities in terms of the number of corporate headquarters, financial firms, or international airline connections, some sophisticated composite indices assess individual cities' connectivity, competitiveness, and creativity on a global scale. Table 6.1 shows three of the most cited lists of the world's top thirty cities identified, respectively, by their global engagement (according to A. T. Kearney's "Global Cities Index"), global competitiveness (*Economist* Intelligence Unit's "Global City Competitiveness Index"), and global network connectivity (Peter Taylor's "Global Network Connectivity Rankings"). According to these measures, New York, Chicago, Los Angeles, Toronto, and San Francisco are the only five North American cities that are deemed truly globally engaged, competitive, and connected, while Washington, DC, Boston, and Montreal are ranked in two of the three lists of global cities (See box 6.2). With more debates over how to "measure" globalness—whether through attributional measurements or linkages between specific cities—few would debate that most of the cities listed in table 6.1 are indeed global cities, serving as economic powerhouses and international gateways for other smaller and less influential cities across the continent. Yet it remains debatable whether and how their globalness and success can be replicated in hundreds of other North American cities. Despite the growing interest in urban competitiveness and the future, there has not been sufficient clarity and agreement on what indicator(s) would accurately measure urban competitiveness at the global level and even less on what needs to be done by whom to strengthen a city's competitiveness and overall economic health in the face of globalization.

However, one thing is very clear: cities are now firmly back in the forefront of the national economic agenda. The new global reality means that cities are now at the center of the discussion on national economic health and competitive strength. A look at recently published book titles, such as Martin Boddy and Michael Parkinson's *City Matters* and Mario Polese's *Why Cities Matter*, suggests that cities do matter a great deal for the prosperity and global success of the nation and its citizens and their economic interest.

Much of this new thinking on the importance of building globally competitive cities in national economic development efforts reflects the rapid transition from an industrial economy to the so-called New Economy, which draws largely on a growth surge in new ideas and innovations, creative high technologies, new kinds of investment and infrastructure, advanced business services, and, most importantly, highly skilled workers. As this global transition has created new challenges and opportunities for national economies, they look to the cities that can adapt swiftly to and excel in the new economic environment with the right mix of policies for businesses and workers that are deemed desirable. Cities such as San Jose, Seattle, and Colorado Springs are often cited as the nation's top-ranked cities for high-tech, high-wage jobs. Miami has created a global niche for itself as "the capital of Latin America" (see box 6.3). In Canada, for example, Ottawa has become a new tech pole now known as "Silicon Valley North." The Ottawa-Gatineau high-tech sector focuses on information technology, telecommunications, and nanotechnology and now employs between fifty thousand and eighty-five thousand workers. Their success is celebrated not only for the local businesses, residents, and other stakeholders, but also for their contributions to the national economy and competitiveness. These cities instantly become model cities for others to follow, and the methods their governments have used are accepted as best practices for growth. The New Economy Initiative that Detroit launched in 2008 makes a good example of how declining industrial cities attempt to

Table 6.1   The World's Most Globally Engaged, Competitive, and Connected Cities*

A. K. Kearney's Global Engagement	Economist's Global City Competitiveness	P. Taylor's Global Network Connectivity
New York	**New York**	London
London	London	**New York**
Paris	Singapore	Hong Kong
Tokyo	Paris	Paris
Hong Kong	Hong Kong	Tokyo
Los Angeles	Tokyo	Singapore
Chicago	Zurich	**Chicago**
Seoul	**Washington DC**	Milan
Brussels	**Chicago**	**Los Angeles**
Washington DC	**Boston**	**Toronto**
Singapore	Frankfurt	Madrid
Sydney	**Toronto**	Amsterdam
Vienna	**San Francisco**	Sydney
Beijing	Geneva	Frankfurt
Boston	Sydney	Brussels
Toronto	Amsterdam	Sao Paulo
San Francisco	**Vancouver**	**San Francisco**
Madrid	**Los Angeles**	**Mexico City**
Moscow	Stockholm	Zurich
Berlin	Seoul	Taipei
Shanghai	**Montreal**	Mumbai
Buenos Aires	**Houston**	Jakarta
Frankfurt	Copenhagen	Buenos Aires
Barcelona	Vienna	Melbourne
Zurich	**Dallas**	**Miami**
Amsterdam	Dublin	Kuala Lumpur
Stockholm	Madrid	Stockholm
Rome	**Seattle**	Bangkok
Dubai	**Philadelphia**	Prague
Montreal	Berlin	Dublin
	Atlanta	

* North American cities in bold.

Box 6.2 Toronto as a Global City

Toronto is the fourth-largest city in North America, behind only New York, Los Angeles, and Chicago. According to Canada's 2011 census, the city has a little more than 2.6 million people, accounting for nearly 46 percent of the total population of its metropolitan area, called the greater Toronto area. This ratio of central city population to metro population is a lot higher than that of most US cities depleted by decades of mass suburbanization—for example, Cleveland and Cincinnati each account for less than 20 percent of their metropolitan area's population.

Though not explicitly cited as a global command and control center in world cities research, Toronto has been noted for its fast-growing financial industry and ethnically diverse population. This profile of Toronto focuses on these two newly developing aspects of the city. Toronto has long been regarded as the financial capital of Canada, but it has recently become one of the three top-tier global financial centers in North America, New York and Chicago being the first two. While US and European financial centers were hit hard by the 2008 financial crisis and the 2012 euro crisis, Toronto has continued its strong performance in the past decade. Financial services are now the leading economic sector in the city, contributing around 14 percent of Toronto's gross domestic product. The first signs of Toronto's success in the global financial industry can be seen in its financial district on Bay Street, where the Toronto Stock Exchange is located along with scores of bank head offices and life insurance companies. Within the next ten years, as some financial media predict, Toronto may surpass London to become the world's leading financial center.

Toronto also boasts of its cosmopolitan atmosphere, a key element in the city's globalness (figure 6.3). More than one hundred thousand immigrants arrive in Toronto every year,

Figure 6.3   Toronto as a cosmopolitan city. (Photo by Yeong Kim)

as nearly one in four immigrants to Canada settles here. As a result, the foreign born now account for 49 percent of the city's population—not as high as in Miami, but much higher than in New York, Los Angeles, and Vancouver. As shown in figure 6.4, the city has a highly diverse ethnic and racial makeup, and its diversity has increased dramatically with the recent stream of immigrants from literally all over the world. The number of Asian immigrants, including Chinese, Indians, Pakistanis, and Filipinos, continues to grow rapidly. African and Caribbean communities also expand quickly in the neighborhoods of Kingsview Village and Rexdale. According to the city government's survey, more than half of these new immigrants have a bachelor's degree or higher. The large inflows of skilled and educated immigrants are likely to help drive up Toronto's global competitiveness even further.

Like many other second-tier world cities, Toronto has aggressively promoted itself as a global city. The city government's official website sets aside a section for "Toronto in World Rankings," listing various international city rankings and reports that show the city's secured position on the world stage. Some of the latest listings include Toronto being the world's fourth-ranked technical hub, twelfth-ranked globally competitive city, second-smartest city, tenth-ranked global financial center, and fourth most livable city. Based on its impressive showings in these rankings, Toronto's claim as "one of the most livable and competitive cities in the world" seems warranted.

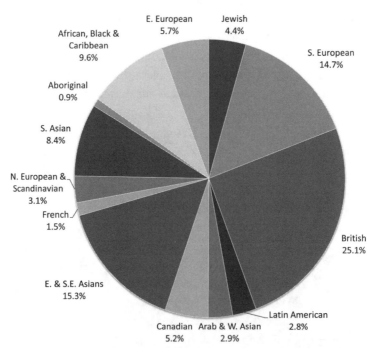

Figure 6.4   Toronto's ethno-racial composition. *Source:* City of Toronto, "Youth and New Immigrants in Toronto," 2006, http:// www.toronto.ca/demographics/presentations.htm.

Box 6.3 Miami: A Sun Belt City

Miami is a metropolitan area that grew throughout the twentieth century. But the real growth occurred during the past forty years, when it transformed from a quiet resort town at the periphery of the United States to a dynamic metropolis in the center of an emerging region that spans North and South America and the Caribbean. Such rapid growth earned Miami the nickname "Magic City" because winter visitors remarked that the city grew so much from one winter to the next that it was like magic.

Geographer Jan Nijman has written about Miami's transformation as a result of two factors: economic globalization—primarily growth in the service sector—and massive immigration from Latin America and the Caribbean during the 1970s onward. Because of its geographical proximity to Latin America and the Caribbean, Miami has earned another nickname: "Capital of Latin America." New immigrants created a new business elite that capitalized on Miami's international economic opportunities. Miami has been marketed to the North as a subtropical and exotic place, while it has been marketed to the South as haven of stability and opportunity. Nijman calls Miami one of the most "foreign" of any large metropolitan area in the United States and notes that Miami is a showcase of the forces of globalization. Its designation as "Capital of Latin America" has proven to be a powerful sales pitch to bring regional headquarters of many global firms and banks to the city.

Cultural globalization is certainly a visible element in the city. In 1960, Latin Americans made up only 5 percent of the foreign born. By 2012, the foreign born constituted nearly 51 percent. Neighborhoods such as Little Havana, West Flagler, and Flagami are home to many of the city's immigrant communities. Today, Miami is the second-largest US city (after El Paso, Texas) with a Spanish-speaking majority and the largest city in terms of Cuban Americans. It is also home to many Caribbean immigrants, many from Haiti. The Spanish version of the *Miami Herald, El Nuevo Herald*, is the largest Spanish-language newspaper in the United States. Businesses such as Telemundo, Telefónica USA, and Espirito Santo Financial Group are also headquartered in the city. Both the Port of Miami and Miami International Airport are among the nation's busiest ports of entry, especially for cargo from South America and the Caribbean. These Latin American connections have allowed Miami to continue to grow both economically and demographically.

A glance at the downtown skyline reveals much about Miami's connections to the global economy (figure 6.5) . It is very much a Sun Belt city, with an economy that relies on finance, culture, entertainment, and tourism. Take tourism, for example. The beaches, conventions, and festivals annually draw more than thirty-eight million visitors who spend nearly $17 billion. The central business district is home to a large concentration of international banks. Other corporate headquarters include Burger King, CompUSA, Bacardi, and US Century Bank. For more than two decades, the Port of Miami has been the number one cruise passenger port in the world, earning the city yet another nickname: "Cruise Capital of the World."

Figure 6.5   A view of Miami, looking toward the high-rise hotels on the beach, reinforces its image as a recreational playground and tourist destination. (Photo by Lisa Benton-Short)

Not surprisingly, Miami is home to the headquarters of Celebrity Cruises, Carnival Cruise Lines, Royal Caribbean Cruise Lines, and Norwegian Cruise lines. In the past decade, Miami has experienced a large building boom, with more than fifty skyscrapers built or currently under construction. According to the ranking of world cities undertaken by the Globalization and World Cities Study Group & Network (GaWC) in 2010 and based on the level of presence of global corporate service organizations, Miami is considered an "alpha minus world city."

In contrast to the old industrial cities, Miami's rise has been relatively recent and is connected to the service economy. Its growth continues to be robust, and it has become a major global center linking North America and Latin America.

Source: Nijman, J. 1997. "Globalization to a Latin Beat: The Miami Growth Machine." *Annals of the American Academy of Political and Social Science* 551: 164–77.

upgrade their manufacturing base by offering business incentives to new and existing high-tech firms. Although it is not clear whether and how this incentive eventually leads to those firms bringing in more skilled and educated workers to the city, Detroit might see it as one of its few remaining options for restoring competitiveness.

Is globalization forcing all North American cities to undertake such economic development initiatives as the Smart Globalization Initiative and skills- and knowledge-based capacity building? Can they truly gain competitive strength in the globalizing economy by benchmarking those leading global cities, high-tech cities, and other best new cities? Would this be the ultimate effect of globalization on urban North America? Given the different urban settings and economic and geographical constraints of each individual city, it is highly unlikely that the success of innovative solutions in a coastal city would be replicated in a midwestern industrial city. Moreover, if all cities take the same innovative approach to tackle their social and economic problems, it would not be innovative at all. How do we then explain the promise almost all city mayors make to keep their city globally competitive? Besides the apparent fact that

politicians benefit from promoting positive views of their city buoyant with new, global businesses, the lack of academic research on the globalization process of nonglobal, non-high-tech cities should be pointed out as another reason. When few alternatives are presented to local politicians and policy makers about good governance in the age of globalization, they will continue to take a neoliberal, business-friendly approach to the urban economy while promising to make their city globally competitive and successful under the onslaught of globalization.

Although small and medium cities present a more typical urban American experience and thus are fertile ground for research, they have been vastly underresearched in terms of the changes they undergo with relation to globalization (see box 6.4). As noted before, it has been commonly accepted among urban scholars that most American cities would and should act and react differently to the forces of globalization from the few high-flying global cities and high-tech cities on the coast. While much is known about how the United States' and Canada's most successful cities embrace, exploit, and resist globalization, little is known about how other cities, such as declining industrial cities, do.

Box 6.4 Muncie, Indiana—America's Middletown

Muncie is located in east-central Indiana, approximately sixty miles northeast of Indianapolis. The city's current population is approximately seventy thousand. Up until the 1970s, Muncie and its immediate suburbs had gained population, but since then, the city's population has stagnated. Although Muncie is now best known as the home of Ball State University, its economy had been established around manufacturing since the late nineteenth century, when the Indiana gas boom attracted such firms as Ball Corporation to the area. The city's official website notes that the corporation was founded by the Ball family, who moved their company from Buffalo, New York, to Muncie in 1887 to take advantage of abundant natural gas reserves essential to making glass.

The city's manufacturing-dominated workforce continued until the 1970s, when factory jobs still accounted for nearly 40 percent of the city's total employment. However, the number has since decreased dramatically, and its current manufacturing employment is at an all-time low, below 9 percent of Muncie's workforce. Like many other traditional manufacturing towns in the US Midwest, Muncie suffered greatly from massive deindustrialization and rising unemployment in the second half of the past century. Based on his in-depth case study of economic restructuring in Muncie, geographer Aaron Malone argues that while much of the job loss that occurred in the 1970s had been the result of increased automation in the factory, the steep decline of factory jobs from the late 1990s onward has been caused mostly by factory relocation and closure. Indeed, the city saw more than six thousand factory jobs disappear when several automotive firms, like Borg Warner, Delco Remy, and Westinghouse, decided to close down their Muncie-based plants in the 2000s.

Unlike other small industrial cities in the Rust Belt that continue to decline long after the closure of local manufacturing firms, however, Muncie has been extremely fortunate to see the growth of new employers replacing the old. Ball State University and Cardinal Health Systems have emerged as the top two employers for local workers, and they have played an integral role in transforming this traditional manufacturing town of the Midwest to a city with vibrant education and health-care industries.

In the 1920s, Muncie was called the "Middletown," as it was the site for an academic research project on the impact of industrialization on small American cities. Columbia University sociologists Robert and Helen Lynd conducted a series of personal interviews with Muncie residents to ask about their work, family life, and community in the face of industrialization (see *Middletown: A Study in Modern American Culture*, 1929; *Middletown in Transition: A Study in Cultural Conflicts*, 1937). That Muncie is now viewed as a success story for its ability to transition to a service-oriented economy warrants new research focusing on how its residents adapt to deindustrialization and globalization.

GLOBAL COMPETITIVENESS OF INDUSTRIAL CITIES IN THE NORTHEAST AND MIDWEST

The effects of deindustrialization on traditional industrial cities across the US Northeast and Midwest have been well documented over the years for having suffered from factory closure, high unemployment, urban fiscal crisis, and social decay. Although a lot of local politicians and business leaders of these Rust Belt cities would persuasively argue that their city's economic fortune has finally bottomed out after years of decline, in fact, the deep and lingering effects of deindustrialization continues into the twenty-first century, further contributing to a longer-term urban decline throughout the region. Of the bottom ten US metropolitan areas ranked by percentage of change in median household income during the 2000s, according to the US Census Bureau, five are located in the state of Ohio (Toledo, Youngstown, Dayton, Cleveland, and Akron) and two in Michigan (Detroit and Grand Rapids). These metropolitan areas, particularly their central cities, continue to post steep losses in population and business. In the case of Canada, medium-sized heavy manufacturing cities such as Sarnia and Sault Ste. Marie, Ontario, have posted population loss in the past decade, as have smaller cities such as Saint John, Thunder Bay, and Sudbury, which proves the point that on both sides of the US-Canada border, deindustrialization leads to multiple experiences of loss. It is unfortunate but understandable when these cities are found near the top of the annual lists of America's worst cities for jobs and worst cities to live in, although city ratings and reviews in the mass media are rarely based on empirical data and research. The struggling industrial cities of Ohio show how large and small cities all across the Rust Belt have lost their competitive edge to such an extent that many have wondered whether they could ever come back and thrive in this ever more globalizing world economy.

The industries of aerospace, automotive, chemical, machinery, and steel manufacturing had played a significant role in urbanizing and modernizing cities in Ohio during much of the twentieth century. Many Ohio cities still carry nicknames that remind us of the once prosperous benefits of their industrial specialization, and they include the "Rubber Capital of the World" (Akron), the "Queen of the West" (Cincinnati), the "Birthplace of Aviation" (Dayton), the "Glass City" (Toledo), and the "Steel Valley" (Youngstown). However, their attractiveness and competitiveness began to deteriorate as early as in the 1960s, when the aforementioned industries entered a period of intense automation, technological and operational restructuring, and foreign competition. The decades of the 1970s and 1980s witnessed a long, painful decline of industrial cities throughout Ohio and beyond.

The reorganization and restructuring of those heavy manufacturing industries has been further intensified by the participation of newcomers from emerging markets, such as Brazil and China, in recent years. To make matters even worse for Ohio cities, American companies have intensified and focused their survival efforts on relocating local production facilities overseas and outsourcing local jobs. According to the state government's statistics, General Motors (GM) and Ford Motors were Ohio's top two employers in 1995, when they had 63,200 and 24,000 in-state employees, respectively. But continuing its aggressive downsizing in the United States, GM has since closed several of its Ohio-based facilities, including the Moraine assembly plant in the suburbs of Dayton. The 2008 closure of the Moraine assembly plant was even featured in a documentary film titled *The Last Truck: Closing of a GM Plant*. The number of GM jobs in Ohio has been reduced by more than 80 percent over the years, to ten thousand in 2012. Ford now hires a mere 5,800 Ohioan workers, a great contrast to the 1960s, when Ford's casting plant in Brook Park of Cleveland alone employed fifteen thousand people. Ohio's new major employers include retailers such as Wal-Mart Stores and the Kroger Company, but the number of jobs and wage levels that formerly working-class families and their communities once relied on have long disappeared with those closed plants. As manufacturing activities continue to leave or be pushed away from Ohio, its statewide unemployment rate hovers at over 10 percent, and its median household income has taken a sharp fall.

The shattering effects of deindustrialization on Ohio cities are clearly seen in their population loss. Table 6.2 shows population

Table 6.2	Population Decline in Major Cities in Ohio						
	Akron	Cincinnati	Cleveland	Columbus	Dayton	Toledo	Youngstown
1900	42,728	325,902	381,768	125,560	85,333	131,822	44,885
1910	69,067	363,591	560,663	181,511	116,577	168,497	79,066
1920	208,435	401,247	796,841	237,031	152,559	243,164	132,358
1930	255,040	451,160	900,429	290,564	200,982	290,718	170,002
1940	244,791	455,610	878,336	306,087	210,718	282,349	167,720
1950	274,605	503,998	914,808	375,901	243,872	303,616	168,330
1960	290,351	502,550	876,050	471,316	262,332	318,003	166,689
1970	275,425	452,524	750,903	539,677	243,601	383,818	139,788
1980	237,177	385,457	573,822	564,871	203,371	354,635	115,436
1990	223,019	364,040	505,616	632,910	182,044	332,943	95,732
2000	217,074	331,285	478,403	711,470	166,179	313,619	82,026
2010	199,110	296,943	396,815	787,033	141,527	287,208	66,982
Change (2000–2010)	**−8.3%**	**−10.4%**	**−17.0%**	**10.6%**	**−14.8%**	**−8.4%**	**−18.3%**

Data source: US Census Bureau.

trends in seven major cities of Ohio since the beginning of the past century. Cincinnati, once the largest city of the Midwest, with large streams of immigrants, has been losing population since the mid-twentieth century, while Cleveland, the nation's fifth-largest city in 1920, now houses fewer than four hundred thousand residents and is ranked forty-seventh. Cleveland's current population amounts to far less than half of its all-time high in 1950, when the city was home to almost one million people. Reporting the extent and effects of population loss in Cleveland, local newspaper *The Plain Dealer* estimated that every day at least forty-two local residents move out, while few move in. Actually, all Ohio cities except Columbus continued to lose population in the first decade of this century. Youngstown sustained a punishing 18.3 percent loss during the period, while Cleveland attracted, again, national media attention

for having recorded the largest population loss among major cities around the country. In contrast, Columbus has managed not only to avoid this statewide trend of losing jobs and people but also to gain population on a yearly basis. Along with the continued expansion of its administrative boundaries by annexing neighboring towns, its diversified economy, not relying heavily on heavy manufacturing industries, has helped this state capital city weather economic downturns better than most other cities in the Rust Belt region.

As the global competitiveness of US industrial cities has continued to deteriorate, plenty of blame has been placed on their local governments for not doing enough to stop the downward spiral and put the economy on a better footing. Some blame the companies that left; others blame the workers who failed to adapt to the changes. As a matter of fact, much effort has been made by those governments to reverse the destructive process of deindustrialization and depopulation and to reclaim their city's competitive position in the national and international markets. The problem is that very little of it has paid off. Ohio's two major cities, Cincinnati and Cleveland, are iconic examples of how city governments try hard but fail harder in revitalizing their manufacturing base. Both cities have offered tax incentives and other business-friendly spurs to entice local businesses to stay put and expand at home and to attract new businesses. For example, the GO Cincinnati: Growth and Opportunities project was launched in 2007 to increase the city's tax revenues by helping to develop new business in health and financial industries as well as helping traditional industries like aerospace and chemical manufacturing firms to be more productive. The city has pursued both old and new industries with very little success. Downtown revitalization projects have also been implemented in these cities in an attempt to bolster inner-city neighborhoods and tax revenues. In the case of Cleveland, a series of megasized urban renewal projects were initiated under former mayor George Voinovich, who also began a nationwide city marketing campaign to shed Cleveland's negative image, highlighted by a moniker given during the 1960s of "The Mistake by the Lake." The "Cleveland's a Plum" logo was designed to put Cleveland's economic development endeavor on par with New York's Big Apple campaign.

Cleveland's drive to restructure and reinvent itself appeared to have paid off in the mid-1990s, when the city was chosen as one of the nine cities to receive the Clinton administration's Empowerment Zone grant and hailed as the "Comeback City" of the Midwest in the national media. Geographers

Barney Warf and Brian Holly wrote about this in their article "The Rise and Fall and Rise of Cleveland." The city's ability to build a strong public-private partnership became an instant model for other cities to emulate, as it played a key role in promoting and rebranding Cleveland as a shining example of revival in North America's industrial heartland. Several downtown construction projects, including the Rock and Roll Hall of Fame and Cleveland Browns Stadium, seemed to have helped make downtown Cleveland more inviting to suburban residents and visitors alike (figure 6.6). However, the high hopes for Cleveland making its long-awaited comeback have not been realized, as few of the programs and projects implemented during the "comeback" years have delivered their promised growth spurt, let alone the old competitive edge.

The Cleveland comeback has stalled. The lived realities of Clevelanders have not improved significantly, and the city now lags behind other industrial cities such as Milwaukee and Pittsburgh as the economic gap between Clevelanders and the national average has further widened since the 1990s. The severity of Cleveland's urban problems was clearly evident when local newspaper *The Plain Dealer* ran a special series in 2001 titled "The Quiet Crisis," about how Cleveland had fallen behind other industrial cities in the Midwest, let alone booming cities in the Southwest. Today, ten years later, the 2010 census data reveals that another round of depressing comparisons is being made between Cleveland and other North American cities. But while some point to the further decline and decay of the city and the spread of its problems into the suburbs, others notice positive signs in the city's development strategy regarding the promotion of health and

Figure 6.6   Cleveland Browns Stadium on the south shore of Lake Erie. (Photo by Yeong Kim)

cultural industries and the opportunity for renewed connections with the outside world. In what follows, this chapter looks at some of the new attempts that have been proposed to improve declining industrial cities' competitiveness in the globalizing economy.

GO GLOBAL AND STAY LOCAL WITH CULTURAL INDUSTRIES

The long and storied struggle of US and Canadian industrial cities for economic recovery proves vividly that few urban initiatives for development, however well intentioned and well designed, have resulted in bringing sustainable growth to their local economies. City halls across the Rust Belt have unveiled a host of new strategic initiatives and action plans to reinvent their cities and be part of a great urban success story (see box 6.5). However, few development strategies have been able to turn their cities into compelling comeback stories, which prompts many elected officials and policy advisers to continue to explore newer models of the economically dynamic city. Although the past has taught us that newer, innovative strategies might not necessarily bring a better outcome to the city than previous ones, local politicians, business leaders, media, and even researchers, all alike, want to be recognized and appreciated for their forward-looking vision that embraces the challenges of globalization.

One of the new visions that have been suggested for the revitalization of old, declining cities is to develop the creative cultural economy—along with economies of information technology as well as knowledge and business services. While some still staunchly argue that American cities need to have a strong manufacturing base, such as Richard McCormack's *Manufacturing a Better Future for America* (2009), many suggest accepting the globalization of manufacturing industries as inevitable and turn to postindustrial and postmodern economic sources, such as cultural industries. Cultural activities were

Box 6.5 Cleveland, Ohio—The Global Cleveland Initiative

Along with Buffalo and Detroit, Cleveland has been America's fastest-declining major city not hit by a natural disaster. The three cities topped major US cities in population loss during the past census period. Few would now remember that Cleveland was among America's top ten largest cities from 1890 to 1970. It is well known that manufacturing industries have had a lot to do with the city's population growth and decline over the years. But the ebbs and flows of immigration have also been another key factor in Cleveland's population change. During its boom years of 1870–1920, much of the needed labor supply was generated by the influx of immigrant labor, as large numbers of southern European and eastern European immigrants arrived here. As shown in figure 6.7, the foreign born accounted for greater than a third of the city's population during this period. The strong presence of substantial and diverse immigrant communities in the city resulted in the formation of some famous ethnic neighborhoods, like Little Italy, Little Bohemia, Slavic Village, and Warszawa. Clevelanders often proudly tell visitors that at one time their city was home to so many Slovenian immigrants that it was the largest Slovenian city in the world, to so many Hungarian immigrants that it was the second-largest Hungarian city in the world after Budapest, and to so many Slovak immigrants that its Slovak population was three times as big as Bratislava's.

However, large-scale European immigration ended soon after World War II. Steady streams of Appalachians and African Americans followed, but once the city's manufacturing industries began to falter, Cleveland ceased to be an attractive destination of either international or domestic migrants. Its foreign-born share of the population dropped to less than 5 percent in 2010, well below the national average of 12.9 percent. Although many large cities around the country, particularly coastal cities and border cities, began to receive large numbers of new immigrants from the 1990s onward, Cleveland has not been able to attract many.

In 2011, the city government launched the Global Cleveland Initiative as a new economic development plan (figure 6.8). While this city has announced an array of development plans

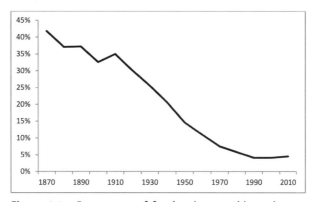

Figure 6.7   Percentage of foreign-born residents in Cleveland, 1870–2010. *Source:* US Census Bureau.

Global Cleveland Shouts Welcome **to the World**

What is Global Cleveland?

Global Cleveland is an organization focused on regional economic development through actively attracting newcomers, and welcoming and connecting them both economically and socially to the many opportunities throughout Greater Cleveland. Global Cleveland will provide a point of contact for all newcomers, both domestic and international, to help them establish greater organizational and individual connection within the Greater Cleveland community.

Global Cleveland's goal is to help attract newcomers who will support the growth of burgeoning industries, establish roots in our vibrant neighborhoods, and help foster and promote a universally inclusionary and welcoming community.

Figure 6.8   Global Cleveland Initiative. *Source:* Global Cleveland, http://www.globalcleveland.org.

over the years, this is its first time to look to attract immigrants to make up for its ongoing population loss. The city seeks to attract at least one hundred thousand new residents by 2020 by targeting three groups of people: foreign students, immigrant entrepreneurs, and Cleveland natives who moved away. This initiative certainly benchmarked Philadelphia's recent success in reclaiming itself as an immigrant gateway. Detroit and St. Louis are among many other declining cities that have launched a similar initiative to target immigrant newcomers who could bring entrepreneurship and cosmopolitanism to the city and, equally importantly, fill the depopulated urban core.

Considering the severe population loss that the city has experienced in recent decades, it might be a daunting task to attract as many as one hundred thousand new residents to Cleveland. Given its small number of foreign-born residents, the city government's efforts to utilize local ethnic communities and their transnational networks in attracting immigrants may not pay immediate dividends. However, it is also a clearly positive sign for the future in that the city looks to restore its cosmopolitan past and recognizes the economic benefits of diversity.

previously considered to have marginal effects on the urban economy in terms of jobs and tax revenues, but they have increasingly been recognized as an important economic asset for competitiveness. Although there is no definite list of cultural industries that promise to create the largest multiplier effects for declining cities, it is now the norm that city governments fund arts and cultural institutions as part of economic development. The many ethnic festivals and other cultural events that cities sponsor are invariably linked to government subsidies to downtown businesses and developers. And street banners advertising museum exhibits and historical heritages have become a familiar sight on the main streets of North American cities.

Culture and the arts have long played into urban redevelopment and gentrification, as many inner-city neighborhoods have been gentrified with art museums, historical districts, and professional sports stadiums. That is to say, it may not be the case that the newly fashioned urban cultural strategy launched across the United States would create an imminent sea change in the government's intervention in the urban economy. Nonetheless, public funding for the arts has come to be defined in ever more explicitly economic terms. Cultural elements have been added to many declining industrial cities' development strategies on the grounds that culture contributes to the urban economy and that northeastern and midwestern cities have a wealth of culture and tradition. Desiring to capitalize on their rich heritage and long history, these cities have begun to invest a large sum of public money in restoring local arts and cultural institutions. For example, in 2010 Cleveland launched the "Global Cleveland Initiative," yet another economic development plan, which

includes a project called "Remix Cleveland" to link its century-old classical music tradition to the city's economic recovery. The Cleveland Museum of Art, located in the University Circle of Cleveland, has been renovated under the project name of "Building for the Future." In fact, many of the art museums that were founded at the heart of Ohio's industrial cities during the early years of the twentieth century have undergone a makeover in recent years in pursuit of economic growth. The Akron Art Museum, in downtown Akron, undertook in 2007 a major expansion and renovation that has tripled the institution's size. Celebrating its new art museum, the city ran a nationwide advertisement of its Andy Warhol collection in travel and business magazines. Toledo had its own grand-opening ceremony in 2006 for the Glass Pavilion at the Toledo Museum of Art. In the case of Cincinnati, the city government purchased downtown property to build its new Contemporary Arts Center that was designed by internationally renowned architect Zaha Hadid. Its Music Hall (figure 6.9) is scheduled for a major renovation within the next few years, and so is Dayton's Art Institute.

These urban cultural strategies have been greeted by both enthusiastic supporters and cynical skeptics. Local business and art communities in general support the recent cultural turn in urban development policies, as the promotion and growth of locally based cultural activities are one good way for the city to highlight its uniqueness and, at the same time, go global in the age of globalization. Compared to the traditional business incentives used to attract Fortune Global 500 firms from outside, government plans to grow jobs and tax revenues from within by tapping into the already established local cultural industries would seem a lot more community

Figure 6.9   Cincinnati's Music Hall and May Festival. (Photo by Yeong Kim)

oriented and locally operated. In doing so, they could help cultivate a softer, more inclusive image for the city that has long suffered from negative perceptions associated with manufacturing decline and inner-city problems. But some serious concerns have been raised about the long-term effects of cultural initiatives on developing an attractive and competitive business environment for the city. *Plain Dealer* journalist Mark Naymik wrote an article mocking the city's new cultural initiative as "writing a new chapter in Cleveland's never-ending Comeback City story" and reminds his readers that there is not much real hope for a better future anytime soon:

> The plot goes like this: The under-appreciated town is in the midst of a major building boom that could help turn around the region, so city leaders rally to capitalize on it by better engaging tourists from both inside and outside Ohio. Leaders meet, write a plan, add a catchy slogan and try to convince the world that Northeast Ohio is a great place. The effort ends with limited success.

> In the end, though, it always feels like it's a campaign to convince ourselves. Northeast Ohio is a great place. But the Comeback City story always nags me for this reason: The town's cheerleaders only recognize our greatness when we have something to show for it such as a new stadium, a new museum, a new casino.

It remains to be seen whether cultural industries and, in general, the New Economy can truly restructure and reinvent the old industrial cities of the Rust Belt and improve their competitiveness in today's global marketplaces. The correct mix of government initiatives, private entrepreneurship, and civic leadership might do the trick. If so, both urban policy makers and researchers will have to explore the best options for individual urban settings. Or globalization may create new success stories, without leaving much room for traditional industrial cities of North America to improve their global competitiveness. However, conventional wisdom tells us that cities that remain connected to the wider world tend to do better than those that are closed or limitedly connected. North American cities, particularly declining ones in the Rust Belt, will have to expand and deepen their connectedness and globalness through trade, investment, and immigration in order to be part of a great urban success story.

SUGGESTED READINGS

Beaverstock, J. V., R. G. Smith, and P. J. Taylor. 2000. "World City Network: A New Metageography?" *Annals of the Association of American Geographers* 90(1): 123–35.

Brenner, N., and R. Keil. 2006. *The Global Cities Reader*. London: Routledge.

Davis, D. E. 2005. "Cities in Global Context: A Brief Intellectual History." *International Journal of Urban and Regional Research* 29(1): 92–109.

Gold, J., and M. Gold. 2005. *Cities of Culture: Staging International Festivals and the Urban Agenda*. Aldershot: Ashgate.

Hall, P. 1984. *The World Cities*. London: Palgrave Macmillan.

Harvey, D. 2005. *A Brief History of Neoliberalism*. New York: Oxford University Press.

Knox, P. L., and P. J. Taylor, eds. 1995. *World Cities in a World System*. Cambridge: Cambridge University Press.

Markusen, A., and G. Schrock. 2006. "The Artistic Dividend: Urban Artistic Specialization and Economic Development Implications." *Urban Studies* 43(10): 1661–86.

Polese, M. 2009. *The Wealth & Poverty of Regions: Why Cities Matter*. Chicago: University of Chicago Press.

Robinson, J. 2006. *Ordinary Cities: Between Modernity and Development*. New York: Routledge.

Safford, S. 2009. *Why the Garden Club Couldn't Save Youngstown: The Transformation of the Rust Belt*. Cambridge, MA: Harvard University Press.

Sassen, S. 2012. *Cities in a World Economy*. 4th ed. London: Sage.

Short, J. R., and Y. Kim. 1999. *Globalization and the City*. Harlow: Longman.

Taylor, P. J. 2004. *World City Network: A Global Urban Analysis*. London: Routledge.

Zelinsky, W. 1991. "The Twinning of the World Cities in Geographic and Historical Perspective." *Annals of the Association of American Geographers* 81(1): 1–31.

Zukin, S. 2011. *Naked City: The Death and Life of Authentic Urban Places*. Oxford: Oxford University Press.

CITIES ON THE WEB

City of Cleveland, "Global Cleveland, Our Future: One Talented Person at a Time," http://globalclevelandinitiative.com.

City of Toronto, "Toronto in World Rankings," http://www.toronto.ca/progress/world_rankings.htm.

Atlantic Online, "The Atlantic Cities: Place Matters," http://www.theatlanticcities.com. *The Atlantic Cities explores some innovative ideas and pressing issues facing today's global cities and neighborhoods.*

Globalization and World Cities Network (GaWC), www.lboro.ac.uk/gawc/. *This site has a variety or reports and data on numerous cities, including many in North America.*

II

URBAN GOVERNANCE

7

Urban Governance
THOMAS J. VICINO

Chicago Mayor Richard M. Daley served as mayor of Chicago for twenty-two years until 2011, following in the footsteps of his father, Richard J. Daley, who governed the same city for twenty-one years, from 1955 to 1976. Thomas Menino, the five-term mayor of Boston, has governed for nearly two decades. Vincent "Buddy" Cianci governed Providence for an unprecedented five terms from the 1970s to the 2000s. The longevity of the mayoralty is not unique. A century prior, planner Robert Moses held informal power over New York City politicians for nearly seven decades, controlling transit, planning, and redevelopment in the city. Israel Durham held political power over the governance of Philadelphia for much of the late nineteenth century, and Thomas Pendergast held power over Kansas City for some twenty years during the early twentieth century. These are but a few examples of concentrated political power in local government. The persistence of this power was facilitated by the creation of organizations—machines—that ensured the reelection of the political executive. Indeed, there is a long history of individuals and organizations holding onto the political power of their cities. Whether we look at social elites, business leaders, civic and political organizations, or simply politicians, we can inquire about who has power. In other words, who governs?

In 1961, political scientist Robert Dahl asked this simple question about political power in cities in his seminal book *Who Governs?* Dahl was interested in who held power and why. In his study of New Haven, Dahl contended that power was pluralistic in nature; that is, many individuals and groups competed in the political realm for the power to govern. The role of government is to mediate a wide range of competing individuals and groups that influence the governance of the city. Politics, then, is a process for determining winners and losers. It is also the process of determining who gets what, when, and how. Still others hold that politics determines how society authoritatively allocates its values, which thus become the goals of public policy. The politics of governing cities is no exception to these definitions.

One of the great, enduring questions in urban politics is simply, "Who governs?" The question of who governs cities is also a question of geography, or the scale of governance (see box 7.1). An inquiry into who governs cities must also consider who governs suburbs and who governs metropolitan regions. In particular, the cities of North America can be characterized by the decentralization of population and economic activity from the urban core to the suburban fringe. The

Box 7.1 Geographic Perspectives on Metropolitan Governance

What makes urban politics and the question of governance of cities and regions distinct? The simple answer is geography. The territories, or spatial boundaries, of local and metropolitan jurisdictions matter for a variety reasons. These are the bodies of government that carry out public policies and planning decisions that directly impact communities. The characteristics of the populations and relationships among these local governments within a region determine the flow of public resources and services. The politics of space guides the local decision-making processes and outcomes.

The actions of urban and regional governments directly impact the lives of citizens. These local governments function to provide services to their residents. First, they collect resources, typically through local residential and commercial property taxes, and then by pooling these resources together, they redistribute resources. Cities maintain infrastructure such as roads, sewers, and stormwater drains. They build schools to educate children. They ensure public safety through police, fire, and health services. They keep neighborhoods clean through trash pickup and green space maintenance. Cities provide these services to varying degrees of quality and quantity based the input of residents' voices.

The politics of space determines how public decisions are made—and where. The source of NIMBY ("not in my backyard") politics rests squarely in location decisions by local managers, policy makers, and planners. Questions about the provision of service and public infrastructure provide an interesting lens on the politics of space. For example, where will new schools be built? Where will the next city dump be located? Where will public transportation routes be located? Where will police enforcement be located? The answers to such questions are spatial in nature. Land-use location decisions are a political part of the policy-making process.

The intersection of the local economy and politics is another distinctive aspect of local and metropolitan governance. As the regional and national economy ebbs and flows, cities are particularly sensitive to these changes. Local governments are generally funded based on their geography. Sources of revenue include property, income, and sales taxes of entities within the boundaries of a city's jurisdiction. Downturn in the economy might dramatically shift the ability of the city to provide public services because the jurisdiction is dependent on its residents and businesses for revenue.

The relationships that local governments have with one another are important aspects of governance. Cities maintain close contact with other nearby jurisdictions, and in some cases, they coordinate activities or govern jointly on issues of mutual interest. Regional transit systems of subways, commuter rails, and bus networks require the participation of numerous cities to implement. Similarly, the regulation of pollution mandates that the cities cooperate to lower levels of output. Governance on these issues typically occurs through regional organizations such as metropolitan planning organizations, county governments, or regional governments. In the federalized political system in the United States, cities also maintain intergovernmental relationships with states and the federal government.

Thus, the geography of local policy issues is an important dimension of metropolitan governance. A spatial perspective of cities and suburbs demystifies the complex network of political relationships among these governing systems.

globalization of the economic functions of cities, suburbs, and regions resulted in the decline of the manufacturing sector, the rise of a service economy, and demographic restructuring. Thus, these social, economic, and spatial transformations shape the politics of governing local spaces. Power is contested, and politics determines who governs.

THE POLITICAL MACHINE AND REFORM MOVEMENT

From the peak of the Industrial Revolution until the Great Depression, political machines governed big cities. These organizations maintained power by providing support and jobs to neighborhoods and immigrants; in return, it was expected that residents would vote for the politicians that led the organization. At the beginning of the twentieth century, the Progressive Era ushered in a period of much-needed institutional reforms to local urban politics. Let us first consider the rise of the political machine and then turn to the reform period.

The Political Machine

The birth of the political machine dates to the original period of urbanization of cities during the late 1800s. By definition, the political machine is an informal system of

political organization that is based on maintaining control of local power. Typically, the organization maintains control through patronage, or the spoils system. As millions of immigrants settled in big cities, the machine welcomed them to join the civic life of the city by providing jobs and life necessities in exchange for political support. As a result, local politicians and bureaucrats maintained "behind-the-scenes" control of government. The growth of cities ensured the machine's longstanding political ties within the structure of a representative democracy.

The political power that machines wielded was due in part to the hierarchical nature of the organization. Figure 7.1 provides a flow chart of the political machine. The boss served as head of the machine. The boss was generally the mayor or head of the local political party. Captains of wards, districts, and neighborhoods reported to aldermen or city

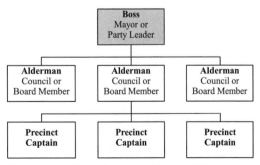

Figure 7.1 Organization of the political machine. *Source:* Tom Vicino.

councilors. They oversaw the distribution of rewards and ensured that voters supported the machine. Dedicated public sector workers also supported the machine because they, too, depended on the patronage system for government contracts and jobs. Political machines steered away from issues-based politics, favoring instead a quid pro quo politics. The boss and captains did favors for the constituents, and in return, voters supported the machine by reelecting bosses and captains. Thus, power was consolidated and reinforced each election cycle.

A system of clientelism supported the machine's organization. The machine's wealthy patrons promised to provide poor clients with jobs, economic security, and other benefits in exchange for votes and loyalty. These relationships were exploitative, and they often resulted in the perpetual indebtedness of the clients. Patrons employed coercion, intimidation, sabotage, and even violence to maintain power. Bosses and captains were unaccountable for their actions, which left few checks and balances on urban governance. For example, William "Boss" Tweed maintained a stronghold on urban politics in New York City's Tammany Hall for nearly four decades. Figure 7.2 shows a *Harpers Weekly* satirical illustration of Boss Tweed's political victory at the Rochester Democratic Convention in 1871. Political corruptness like this was commonplace.

The urban political machine built on its staying power by taking advantage of the ethnic solidarity of new immigrants. The machine's distribution of material benefits empowered ethnic groups to govern together. Immigrants' common goal of achieving the "American Dream" meant that ethnic groups, especially the Irish, Italians, Jews, and Germans, governed together to create upward

Figure 7.2   Caricature of Boss Tweed. *Source:* Thomas Nast, "The Brains," *Harper's Weekly,* October 12, 1871, 992.

mobility. For example, an Italian mayor and Irish city councilperson might serve together. While the machine created new opportunities for immigrants, some argue that it impeded immigrants' assimilation into American society. Patronage was actually spread as thinly as possible to maximize electoral advantage. The benefits of patronage were meager. Police officer jobs were plentiful, for instance, but wages and benefits were suppressed for many years. Other immigrants, typically new immigrants, were excluded from the patronage system. So the urban working class did not fully benefit.

In many US cities, machine politics dominated civic life from about 1875 through 1950, but the remnants of some machines are still present today. Some postwar examples include Chicago's Daley machine and Newark's James machine. Yet by the arrival of the Great Depression, many political machines had died as Progressive Era reformers sought to clean up urban government and prevent further abuses of power.

In Canadian cities, machine politics played a notably lesser role than in the cities of the United States. But in the cities of Toronto and Montreal, the political machine was active in municipal affairs. For example, during the second half of the nineteenth century, mayors who were members of the Orange Order governed Toronto for five decades. As members of a society for Protestant men, mayors fraternized with citizens and rewarded faithful members with jobs in city government through a patronage system. Similarly, in Montreal, the city's political machine had its roots in the election of mayor Raymond Préfontaine, who maintained control of the electorate by providing public utilities to the city's poor districts in the 1880s. Whereas many Canadians echoed the same demands for urban reform as Americans, some rejected the reforms in favor of a socialist politics, as in the case of Democratic Socialist Party leader James Shaver Woodsworth of Winnipeg. Still, in the American and Canadian experiences, Progressive Era reforms were aimed at instilling a sense of good and ethical government.

The Reform Movement

The Progressive Era reform movement grew during the early 1900s and came to fruition in the roaring 1920s. For the muckrakers, the journalists who made a career out of exposing the abuses of corporations and politicians, the urban political machine was a popular target. The muckrakers wrote scathing attacks about the politics and governing of the big cities. In the well-known book published in 1904, *The Shame of Our Cities*, journalist Lincoln Steffens exposed corrupt political leaders in St. Louis, Minneapolis, Pittsburgh, Philadelphia, Chicago, and New York. A national outcry

ensued, providing fertile ground for a reform movement. Progressives, as they were called, sought to change the legal institutions and political climate to weaken the political machine.

One of the earliest influential Progressives was Andrew White. In an article titled "City Affairs Are Not Political," White, the first president of Cornell University, promoted the idea that cities should be run like businesses. To end the corruption and inefficiencies of the city, he held that cities should be nonpartisan and apolitical. Accordingly, he supported the removal of party labels to help break up the political machines and the linkages of immigrant loyalty to the machine. White was determined to rid society of "our evil history of the American city."

Urban historian Samuel Hays echoed White's ideas. He argued that business leaders and the upper class should spearhead the Progressive Era of municipal reform. The idea of good government, which was intended to trump special interests, was born. To protect political actors from corruption, a centralized decision-making process was necessary. The idea of governance through bureaucracy took hold. A professionalized, bureaucratic organization would create a new generation of professional public sector managers.

We can turn to a theoretical framework of local government structure to develop an understanding of the rationale for and types of reform that Progressives advocated. Political scientist David Easton's systems perspective illuminates the effect of government structure on public policy making (see figure 7.3). First, the system is interdependent and cyclical. Next, the system's inputs are the demands of citizens and groups for policy action as well as the resources needed for them. Then, the system's outputs are public policies to address

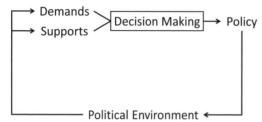

Figure 7.3   A systems approach to reform.
Source: Adapted from David Easton, *A Systems Analysis of Political Life* (New York: John Wiley & Sons, 1965).

the inputs. Last, a feedback loop addresses the influences of inputs and outputs. Reformers employed a systems approach to change the structure of government. On a basic level, the institutional structure of local government is to provide an organization to arrange *authority* and *responsibility* to carry out public functions for the state. Reformers advocated for political changes that made government more responsive, efficient, and effective.

The Progressives spearheaded the municipal reform movement to address key problems in urban governance. At the beginning of the twentieth century, it was not clear who governed cities. There were confused lines of authority because of separated powers. Legislative districts were large. Independent executive departments created an overlap of duties. Mayors were institutionally weak and did not put forth policy agendas. These characteristics created a political environment that bred corruption. Table 7.1 lists the specific reforms that Progressives achieved in many cities throughout the nation.

The Progressives' ethos demonstrates that they were influenced in distinct ways on their views of the role of local government and its structure. The public regarding, or unitary ethos, holds that government should provide for a common good through a rational process and then efficiently implement

policy in a professional, neutral bureaucracy. In contrast, the private regarding, or individualist ethos, stresses individual gain and views politics as a resolution of competing interests. Ultimately, the reform of urban government is a question of whether urban government primarily exists as a mechanism for discovering and implementing the public interest and the common good or whether it primarily exists as a public power to resolve competing political interests and to resolve externalities. Indeed, this question of who governs challenged the machine politicians and Progressives alike.

Table 7.1   Municipal Reforms

Reform	Effects
Strong mayor	Appointment power; accountability; implementation
Nonpartisan elections	No party affiliation diminishes bias and loyalty
At-large districts	Limits parochial interests of wards
Council-manager form	City manager serves the council; strict distinction between policy making and administration
Civil service and bureaucracy	Decision-making body; professionalizes public sector
Direct democracy	Recall; referendum; initiative; short ballot

GOVERNING THE POSTWAR CITY

After World War II, governing cities in the reformed setting became increasingly complex. It was clear that cities were not only governed exclusively by political elites who held political power. Coalitions of important stakeholders in the future of the city formed groups, or regimes, to govern. In this era, the dominant understanding about urban politics is that of regime theory. It seeks to explain the multiple relationships among politicians and private-sector individuals who influence their decisions. Who influences politicians, and how, and why? How do they build either short-term or enduring coalitions to effectively govern the city? We can ask how and under what conditions different types of governing coalitions develop and evolve over time by looking at the interdependence of the public, private, and nonprofit sectors.

In 1981, political scientist Paul Peterson, following in the footsteps of Dahl, wrote the influential book *City Limits*. Peterson states that "urban politics is above all the politics of land use." Indeed, as political actors seek to gain control of land use, they do so based on an economic imperative to compete with other cities to attract private investment. Cities are limited in their ability to address social concerns such as poverty and welfare; therefore, they need to balance the needs of all residents by improving the economic status of the city. Thus, Peterson argues that it is necessary to pursue public policies that improve the economic position of the city.

Next, in 1989, sociologists John Logan and Harvey Molotch respond to Dahl and Peterson in their classic book *Urban Fortunes*. Drawing on work that showed that elite coalitions have a strong influence on urban politics, Logan and Molotch argue that a powerful pro-development coalition, composed of business interests and pro-growth local politicians, generally favors new forms of economic development policies. The members of this coalition, or the machine, share a special emphasis on their common motivation for new urban growth. Table 7.2 shows that the members of the coalition are part of a wide variety of pro-growth sectors, including local

Table 7.2   The Growth Machine

Machine	Auxiliary Players
Politicians	Elected politicians; bureaucrats; campaign donors
Local media	Newspapers; television stations; radio stations
Utilities	Power; telephone; other
Cultural institutions	Universities; museums; sports; labor

Source: John Logan and Harvey Molotch. 1987. *Urban Fortunes: The Political Economy of Place*. Berkeley: University of California Press.

politicians, real estate, media, utilities, and cultural institutions. They share a mutually beneficial relationship of growth.

Later, in 1989, political scientist Clarence Stone wrote the classic book *Regime Politics*, in which he argues that cities serve important public purposes by assembling coalitions of political, business, and community elites— from all three sectors of the economy. For example, in Dallas, private business leaders and local politicians made political decisions and held power through the Dallas Citizens Council in the form of an entrepreneurial regime. The regime made decisions about the city's budget, school system, city council, and civic activities. Members of the regime included business executives at companies such as Texas Instruments and American Airlines, real-estate agents, and editors of the local newspaper. This group worked with the mayor and city council to govern the city, making important decisions about zoning, transportation planning, school desegregation, and downtown redevelopment. Similarly, in Miami, the governing regime included more than the mayor and county executive. Members of the banking industry, higher education institutions, hospitals, and Haitian and Cuban civic leaders all had a seat at the table. These regimes consisted of private, public, and non-profit-sector leaders who gathered informally to govern their cities.

GOVERNING THE FRAGMENTED METROPOLIS

Local government in the United States is fragmented. Today there are more than eighty thousand governmental units, and they are characterized by their separated and disparate nature. As a result, the governance of localities reflects the complexity and repetition of the political institutions. First we consider the formation of local governments, and then we turn to the legal standing of local governments.

Political Economy of the Metropolis

The metropolitan landscape is composed of a vast network of local and regional governments. This echoes the spatial development of urbanization and suburbanization of metropolitan areas. As regions grew outward, suburbanites created new local institutional units to govern their jurisdictions. In fact, there are five principal types of local government. Municipalities are general-purpose governments that provide public services. Counties are similar to municipalities, but they generally encompass larger areas and include unincorporated areas. Towns, townships, and villages provide a limited range of services in unincorporated areas. Regional governments generally encompass large territories across metropolitan areas and provide a wide range of services. Special-purpose districts operate governmental units for public services such as schools and water delivery. The prevalence of these types of units only adds further to the fragmented nature of local government (box 7.2).

In 2007, the Census of Governments showed that there were 89,476 local governments in the United States. Approximately half were general-purpose, and the other half were special-purpose governments. Of the general-purpose units, there were 3,033 counties, 19,492 municipalities, and 16,519 towns or townships. Of the special-purpose units, there were 37,381 special districts and 14,561 school districts. Political fragmentation refers to the prevalence and degree to which local units of government overlap. Geographic fragmentation is the spatial separation of multiple local jurisdictions that govern the same territory. Functional fragmentation is the duplication of responsibilities to provide similar public services to the area. Consider the case of the City of Chicago and surrounding Cook County, Illinois. There are more than one thousand local units of government, including taxing school districts; transit district; county, municipalities, villages, and townships; sanitary district; health district; and even a mosquito abatement district. In a region as highly fragmented as Chicago, there is a redundancy of public services and diseconomies of scale, but residents may have a greater number of choices.

Likewise, local government is fragmented in Canada. However, there are substantially fewer political units. As in the United States, Canada's local governments are administrative units of the country's ten provinces. In 2006, there were 199 counties, regions, and districts as well as 3,731 cities, towns, villages, and townships. The powers and responsibilities of local governments are set

Box 7.2 The Diversity of Local Government in the United States

There are many local governments in the United States, and they are an enduring feature of the nation's political geography. According to the Census of Governments conducted in 2012, there are 89,004 local governments. In these many forms of government, there are 37,203 special districts, 19,522 municipalities, 16,364 towns or townships, 12,884 school districts, and 3,031 counties. These many governments represent a mosaic of localities that provide voice, representation, and services to residents in their communities.

Similarly, many varied forms of local government abound. The mayor-council form of government has a council or board of representatives that are elected to a legislative body. A political executive, generally a mayor, is elected as the head of government. This position holds important administrative authority. Approximately 38 percent of local governments are structured this way. Next, the council-manager form of government is composed of an elected council and a political executive, generally a mayor. They jointly are responsible for adopting and implementing public policy. A professional administrator maintains full responsibility for the day-to-day operations of the jurisdiction. Approximately 38 percent of local governments are structured this way.

The town meeting or representative town meeting is a form of government whereby either voters convene to choose a board of selectmen or residents themselves adopt and implement public policies. Approximately 7 percent of local governments are structured this way. Last, the commission form of government, the rarest (1 percent), is a form in which a board of commissioners govern the city's administrative units and legislative bodies together.

All forms of local government hold elections and grant appointments to individuals and organizations to govern. In reformed cities, at-large elections are held on a citywide basis such that all residents vote for the same political executive or legislative representative. In contrast, single-member district voting divides the city vote into smaller areas such that only a portion of the city votes for the same public representative. In many cities, nonpartisan elections remove party affiliations from local elections. Strong mayors central-ize responsibilities and allow the political executive to play a larger role in adopting and implementing public policy. Last, council-managers allow cities to create an apolitical man-agement environment to professionalize the operation of local government.

forth in various statutes of the provinces, generally known as municipal acts, the local government acts, or cities and towns acts. They provide services such as police and fire, transportation, planning and development, public utilities, welfare services, and recreational amenities. For example, the province of British Columbia contains 160 municipalities and 27 regional districts. They provide a variety of regional and local services through a representative board of directors from the municipalities. But the provinces have a significant impact on Canadian cities, whereas US states do not significantly impact their cities. What is different is the culture of governance in the provinces. States intervene less in the affairs of cities because of the political culture of home rule, while Canada's provinces derive from the British colonial administrative culture of control and regulation. As a result, provinces play a much larger role in the political agenda of cities, whereas the US states are less likely to be so involved. Thus, with this heavy-handed oversight, provincial governments do not allow most Canadian cities to make the kinds of decisions that would be taken for granted in US cities. For example, Vancouver cannot decide to add stops to its light rail system or to tax residents without provincial approval; Toronto cannot increase school taxes because these are established by the province. Ultimately, this fundamental difference in governance means that urban policy largely depends on the politicians and the ideologies of the political parties at the provincial level.

The notion that political fragmentation facilitates residential choice is deeply rooted in the fields of economic and political geography. In 1956, economic geographer Charles Tiebout hypothesized that the prevalence of many local governments offers residents many choices in selecting the jurisdiction that maximizes their personal utility. Residents will "vote with their feet" by moving freely among local jurisdictions until they find a locality whose package of goods and services matches their personal economic utility. Local governments thus compete for residents by offering quality public services and competitive taxation rates. Of course, Tiebout assumed that residents have access to information about localities and can freely move among a region's jurisdictions.

The legal status of local governments is derived from state constitutions. Localities are subunits and administrative branches of states. They have a dual role. First, local governments are formed to satisfy the demands of local citizens. Second, as administrative units, they implement the state's public policies. In fulfilling these roles, local governments have organized various forms to govern locally. Table 7.3 describes the four institutional arrangements: mayor-council; council-manager; commission; and representative town meeting.

The power of local government is generally stated or implied. Even though the US Constitution never mentions local governments, the Tenth Amendment implies that the state or the people have the power to regulate local governments. The Constitution stipulates the powers of state government. Then states stipulate the powers of local governments in charters, including classified or specific charters and home-rule charters. Home-rule charters typically have more autonomy as jurisdictions than specific or classified charters.

Specifically, *Dillon's Rule* and *home rule* are two legal concepts that stipulate the scope of power for local governments. According to

Table 7.3   Forms of Local Government

Form	Institutional	Geography	Example
Mayor-council	Separation of powers between directly elected mayor and city council. Mayor has executive powers, and council has legislative powers. Mayor (strong or weak) is directly elected to office on a full-time basis and is paid.	Older, larger cities, or very small cities of under twenty-five thousand population. Predominantly in the Mid-Atlantic and Midwest of the United States.	Los Angeles, CA; Houston, TX; Minneapolis, MN
Council-manager	City council oversees the general administration, makes policy, and sets budget. Council hires a city manager to carry out day-to-day administrative operations. The mayor (strong or weak) is chosen from among the council members on a rotating basis.	Predominantly in cities with populations of over ten thousand. Generally in the Southeast and Pacific Coast areas.	Phoenix, AZ; San Diego, CA; Salt Lake City, UT
Commission	Voters elect individual commissioners to a small governing board. Each commissioner is responsible for one specific aspect, such as fire, police, public works, health, or finance. One commissioner is designated as chairperson or mayor and presides over meetings. The commission has both legislative and executive functions.	The oldest form of government in the United States; exists today in only a few cities.	Sunrise, FL; Fairview, TN
Representative town meeting	All citizens can attend and participate in town meeting discussion as a form of direct democracy. Individuals are chosen by the general electorate to represent them in voting. The selectmen are responsible for creating and implementing policy.	Rare form, primarily found in small towns and municipalities in the New England states.	Bowdoin, ME; Lexington, MA

Source: DeSantis, V. S., and T. Renner. 2002. "City Government Structures: An Attempt at Clarification." *State and Local Government Review* 34(2): 95–104.

Dillon's Rule, municipalities have only the powers that are expressly granted to them by the state. The rule grants only powers that are essential and indispensable to the existence and functioning of the locality. Forty states currently permit the use of Dillon's Rule. In contrast, home rule creates local autonomy and limits the degree of state interference in local matters. The scope of power is wide and varies by state. Structural home rule grants power to localities to select the form of gov-

ernment and charter. Functional home rule grants power to localities to exercise local, autonomous self-government. Fiscal home rule grants power to determine revenue sources, to tax, and to borrow monies. Personnel home rule grants power to establish employment rules. Thirty-nine states grant home-rule charters, and eleven states granted limited home-rule charters.

The powers to annex land and incorporate a local government are two of the broadest local powers. State constitutions and statutes set the terms of annexation and incorporation. Incorporation is the process of forming a new city, and annexation is the process of incorporating unincorporated land into a locality, thus growing the territory and authority of an existing city. Expanding the territory of a locality grows the population and tax base and extends public services. Some examples of historic annexation include Boston's annexation of Jamaica Plain, Baltimore's annexation of Roland Park, and Chicago's annexation of Lake, Jefferson, and Hyde Park. While large annexations are rarely achieved today, the incorporation of new jurisdictions is still common. For instance, Lakewood, California, was formed in 1954 to avoid annexation into the City of Long Beach. Previously unincorporated, Lakewood established a contract with Los Angeles County to provide public services, making it the first among many cities to become a "contract city." In this arrangement, localities directly establish a provision of public services and a cost-sharing plan.

In Canada, local governments are notably less fragmented because there is a strong tradition of regional government. There are fewer than four thousand local governments, and of them, some two hundred are various forms of regional governments. Regional districts are found in British Columbia, regional municipalities are found in Nova Scotia, and regional county municipalities are found in Quebec. The regional nature of these governments inhibits the same level of competition among local governments that is common in the United States.

The metropolis is composed of many local, independent jurisdictions. Each maintains some level of autonomy and self-governance, and as a result, local government is fragmented in both spatial and governance terms. The power that states and provinces grant to local governments reinforces the ability of localities to pursue this independence. During the second half of the twentieth century, the impacts of this local independence had a dramatic effect on the city. The rise of the neoliberal city, also known as the entrepreneurial city, is perhaps the most important outcome. The historical roots of the entrepreneurial city date to the 1930s during the Great Depression. Economist John Maynard Keynes argued for government investment in large-scale infrastructure projects such as roads and bridges as well as social welfare spending to improve human capital. Doing so would stimulate the economy and induce the private markets to invest in job creation. From Roosevelt's New Deal through Johnson's Great Society, cities benefited from public investment in housing, roads, parks, schools, jobs, and social welfare.

However, as discussed in chapter 5, the arrival of the 1980s ushered in a new era of public disinvestment in urban America. The loss of manufacturing jobs and the flight of urban residents to the suburbs hurt the urban economies. In particular, big cities were nearly bankrupt as crime, poverty, and a decaying infrastructure took its toll. New York City is a case in point. In 1975, decades of urban decline culminated with financial calamity. The city was faced with a $1.7 billion deficit and nearly declared bankruptcy when President Ford refused to agree to a bailout. Years of fiscal austerity followed; schools and welfare services faced deep cuts. Consequently, fiscally conservative mayors were elected, including Ed Koch, Rudy Giuliani, and Michael Bloomberg.

Cities turned to the market as a source of new resources. In an effort to attract and retain new residents, jobs, and visitors, cities rebuilt their downtowns—hotels, convention centers, stadiums, condominiums, waterfront recreation, and visitor centers. Cities became entrepreneurs for new resources in the market, and they competed for them with other cities. For instance, Boston and Baltimore built waterfront festival marketplaces. Philadelphia rebuilt Center City. Vancouver, Atlanta, and Montreal overhauled their urban landscapes to host the Olympic Games. Thus, cities entered this new era as individual rational economic players in a race for scarce resources. Let us now focus on the responses to the fragmented metropolis: the regionalization of governing structures and processes.

REGIONALISM

From the 1950s until the 1980s, efforts to overcome the fragmented nature of local government grew. The answer was to reduce the number of local governments through the creation of new regional governments. This period of old regionalism, as it was known, sought to merge and consolidate towns, cities, and counties into one regional unit. Then, during the 1990s, a new regionalism movement developed. This represented a political shift that focused less on the governmental institution and more on the process of governance. The goal was to create a political environment through governance that would reap the benefits of regional institutions without the institutional change in political structure. These movements are reviewed in turn.

Perspectives on Metropolitan Government

The institutional organization of metropolitan government has long been a source of debate in the theory and practice of urban politics. In theoretical terms, two geopolitical perspectives have shaped the debate on metropolitan structure. Whereas the organic whole perspective views the metropolitan area as a single system, the interdependent social and economic activities that form the region, the polycentric region perspective views the metropolitan area as multiple smaller systems, the sum of many social and economic activities in the region. In practical terms, a collectivist-rational approach to the organic whole would suggest that the regionalization of these activities would improve the region. But an individualist-rational approach to the polycentric region would suggest that the fragmented nature of the metropolis would improve the region.

The region as an organic whole can be characterized by three waves of decentralization in the twentieth century. From the 1900s until about the 1930s, the first wave of the decentralization of population and economic activity occurred as the urban problems of poor housing and old infrastructure grew commonplace. The political response was to annex land to central cities. From the 1950s until the 1980s, the second wave occurred after World War II as suburban growth boomed. The political response was to differentiate the politics of cities and suburbs as separate jurisdictions with separate issues. Then, beginning in the 1990s, the third wave occurred as cities and economies globalized. The political response was to view cities and suburbs as interdependent jurisdictions with shared economic fates. The urban policy implications called for collectivist responses: (1) reduce the number of actual governments in the region to overcome fragmentation, and (2) increase mandatory coordination and cooperation efforts among local governments to achieve regionalist interests.

In contrast, perspectives on the region as a polycentric metropolitan area can be characterized by the relationship between the market and the prevalence of local governmental units. In any region, the local governments represent the *sum* of their independent jurisdictions and serve to enhance the collective preferences of the citizenry. The polycentric metropolis defers to the market to determine the optimal number of local governments by inducing competition. So the supply of the local government is a function of the demand for public services and goods. To achieve effectiveness and efficiency, lower public cost per resident of desired services results in equilibrium. Such competition would force those ineffective and inefficient local governmental units to either change the provision of public services or reduce their price (e.g., local taxes). The structure of local government is designed to maximize a resident's preferences by enhancing competition among local governments. The urban policy implications called for individualist responses: (1) increase the number of local governments, and (2) maintain a healthy number of local governments with boundaries that are defined by economic, not political, terms.

Approaches to Regionalism

Regionalism is both an institutional and political approach to govern the organic whole of a metropolitan area. Indeed, the metropolitan United States boasts long a history of mergers, annexations, and consolidations of its local governments (box 7.3). This regionalization can generally be thought of as structural regionalism, or "old regionalism," in which the structure of local governmental units is changed. Other approaches to regionalism include coordinating, administrative, and fiscal regionalisms. While these other approaches do not involve structural changes, they seek to emulate the regional goals of structural changes.

Box 7.3 Louisville and Memphis: Merger Mania?

In 2003, the City of Louisville and its surrounding jurisdiction, Jefferson County, merged into a single consolidated jurisdiction. In 2010, after a heated political debate, residents of Shelby County overwhelmingly voted not to merge with the City of Memphis. While the Louisville-Jefferson merger was the largest jurisdiction in thirty years to consolidate, the Memphis-Shelby merger is yet another failed attempt—among dozens—to consolidate local governments. Is there a resurgence of city-county consolidation, or is this case an exception to the norm of the political fragmentation of local government?

The push to merge Louisville and Jefferson County evolved over two decades. Business elites and politicians held that the merger was a policy response to the socioeconomic decline of the city. Public services would be improved because new economies of scale would be achieved. Redistribution of public resources would improve the social and economic status of residents in the city and suburbs. After the merger, Louisville's territory and population soared. Prior to the merger, the city was 60 square miles, and afterward the city grew to 386 square miles. In 2010, the population more than doubled, from 256,231 to 741,096 residents. Similarly, the city's population ranking jumped from sixty-seventh to seventeenth, making Louisville a "Top 20 City" in the United States. The median household income grew from $28,843 to $39,457. Louisville became a new city with a new profile.

In 2009, business and political elites supported a proposal to consolidate Memphis and Shelby County. Drawing on the two prior failed attempts to consolidate in 1962 and 1971, the elites argued that it was imperative to consolidate to save the City of Memphis from prolonged urban decline. The Metropolitan Government Charter Commission and the coalition group Rebuild Government argued that the economies of scale would produce better, more efficient public services. Stronger ethical leadership and a regional voice on economic development matters would also improve not only the city but the region as well. Opposition was strong. The coalition Save Shelby Now represented the opponents of the consolidation proposal. The group argued that suburban Shelby County residents did not want to inherit Memphis's struggling education system, rampant crime, and corrupt bureaucracy. Ultimately, whether or not to consolidate Memphis and Shelby County was brought to a referendum vote in 2010. The results were resounding. It passed in Memphis with 51 percent. Yet 85 percent of suburbanites voted not to consolidate. The jurisdictions did not merge.

Does the Louisville-Jefferson place city-county consolidation back on the urban agenda? Or does the Memphis case suggest that it is otherwise still a difficult policy alternative to implement? While many have argued that local consolidations are politically infeasible, the Louisville merger demonstrates otherwise. Since the Louisville consolidation, other cities such as Buffalo, Cleveland, and Milwaukee took notice and considered consolidation but failed to act. Consolidation produces unintended consequences. Suburbs may no longer be associated with the central cities after consolidation. The political influence can shift from city to suburb. Economies of scale may produce increased efficiencies, but they may also diminish the level and quality of services in poor neighborhoods. Political power also shifts and can create a stronger institutional mayor. These cases effectively illustrate that who governs matters. The "who" may be the mayor and regime of a central city, the suburbs, or the region. The "who" may also be the mayor and regime of a consolidated city-county. Whoever has the power and the voice can determine the outcomes of these initiatives.

Coordinating regionalism brings cities together to foster a spirit of regional cooperation, planning, and service delivery in pertinent policy areas of shared interests. There are approximately 450 regional coordinating organizations in the United States, and they include councils of government, metropolitan planning organizations, and various development districts. The type and frequency of coordinating activities varies significantly by region and can be classified into four common activities. The many local governments of a region might band together to coordinate policy issues that are regional in scope, such as transportation planning, environmental monitoring, land use and zoning, and public services. Ad hoc coordination, as in Austin and Raleigh-Durham, is the most common activity and occurs when multiple jurisdictions plan regionally, without a written agreement. Advisory coordination, as in Denver, occurs when local governments in the region come together to draft a written regional plan across many policy areas; yet there is little, if any, institutional mandate to implement these plans. Supervisory coordination, as in San Diego and Seattle, occurs when written plans are paired with a regional implementation strategy. Last, authoritative coordination, as in Minneapolis and Portland, occurs when a regional body has statutory authority to mandate compliance with regional policies and plans. Regional coordination occurs in many forms, and its ability to implement and enforce regional policies varies widely.

Another approach is administrative regionalism. The rise of many large suburban jurisdictions in sprawling regions, especially the Sun Belt and the West, has created administrative burdens on local governments. New cities that experience rapid population growth over a short period of time often do not have an adequate infrastructure, labor force, or expertise to deliver public services such as water, sewer, trash pickup, or libraries. So these cities sometimes regionalize their administrative service delivery to curb expenses and benefit from economies of scale. Cities might formulate interlocal agreements that stipulate a cooperative arrangement to share services and administrative capacity. Alternatively, regional special districts, such as independent school districts, might be created as autonomous regional units. For example, in the Dallas-Fort Worth Metroplex, there are over one hundred independent school districts, many of which cross municipal boundaries. While some cities find that sharing the activities eases the burden for the provision of public services, others cooperate out of fiscal necessity.

The last approach is fiscal regionalism. Socioeconomic disparities are prevalent in the cities and suburbs of the metropolitan United States. Wealthy municipalities are able to provide high-quality public services at a lower tax rate. Poor municipalities struggle to provide public services at higher tax rates. The metropolitan irony, of course, is that poor residents of poor cities pay more (i.e., relative tax burden) and receive less (i.e., quality public services). Fiscal regionalism attempts to create the capacity or authority to redistribute the benefits from economic growth across the entire region. Because few means exist whereby a local government can share in the region's growth, some regions have adopted a model to level the metropolitan economic development playing field. Regions such as Minneapolis and St. Paul and Dayton rely on regional tax-base revenue sharing to limit socioeconomic disparities. This approach achieves the outcomes of institutional regionalism in a way that does not require merging or consolidating local governments.

The New Regionalism

During the 1990s, a paradigm shift emerged in the thinking on regionalism. Scholars and practitioners shifted attention from the structural change of government institutions to the governance processes of local governments. Whereas regional governmental units act as the institutional policy-making bodies, regional governance focuses on the formal and informal organizing of institutional relationships that constitute the local governing of a metropolitan area. The new regionalism seeks to build cooperation among many local political actors of multiple jurisdictions to bring them together to develop relationships and work on policy issues of shared interest.

One of the most well-known new regionalists is David Rusk. The former mayor of Albuquerque, New Mexico, Rusk became a national expert on regionalism during the 1990s. His theory of relative elasticity holds that central cities that have been able to expand (annex) have experienced more favorable social and economic results than those in which annexation is limited. His book *Cities without Suburbs* puts forth the idea that local government consolidation (e.g., regional government) and regional tax-base sharing should be encouraged and that regulations should be implemented to dramatically limit suburbanization. Rusk has been sought after to apply his principles to individual metropolitan areas around the nation, and his work has given new life to efforts to regionalize governmental cooperation and grow tax bases (box 7.4).

Box 7.4 Minneapolis-St. Paul: Tax-Base Sharing

In 1971, Minnesota's Fiscal Disparities Act called for the implementation of a program to share the value of the commercial-industrial tax base of local jurisdictions with others in the Minneapolis-St. Paul metropolitan area. The rationale for tax-base sharing is an intent to foster a supportive environment in order for new regionalist policies to flourish. It has four specific goals: (1) reduce competition among communities for commercial and industrial properties to add to their tax bases; (2) create a fairer distribution of tax benefits from properties that impact on and are supported by surrounding communities; (3) reduce disparities in tax bases; and (4) promote orderly urban development, regional planning, and smart growth by reducing the impact of fiscal considerations regarding highways, transit facilities, and airports on the location of business and residential growth. The region's implementation is noteworthy because it spans a large territory and generates a large tax base that is shared regionally. While several other jurisdictions (Dayton, Ohio; Hackensack Meadows District, New Jersey; and Rochester, New York) have implemented similar regional tax-base sharing policies, no other region has implemented a program of the scope and scale of the Twin Cities program.

With a regionalist perspective, policy makers view the region as one large, interconnected economy. The program seeks to reduce the negative externalities associated with political fragmentation. It is an innovative policy design to address growing fiscal disparity concerns. The region comprises 172 cities, villages, and townships among eleven counties. Also, there are forty-eight school districts and sixty other taxing authorities. Each municipality is required to contribute a portion of the increase in value from its commercial/industrial (C/I) property to a regional pool. The region's policy makers held that while commercial and industrial development provides needed tax revenue for certain municipalities, these developments are largely funded through regional and state financing. Then, each municipality shares in the increase in property value that occurs in a specific area after a certain date.

In effect, the tax-base sharing redistributes fiscal resources to alleviate the socioeconomic disparities among local jurisdictions in the region.

In practice, each taxing jurisdiction contributes 40 percent of the growth in its C/I property-tax base to a regional pool. In 2003, the region's tax capacity was valued differentially by location: central cities at $185 million; the inner-ring suburbs at $167 million; the developing suburbs at $40 million; and outlying areas at $16 million. Tax capacity refers to the ability of a jurisdiction to raise revenue through taxes based on the ability of its residents and C/I worth. So as the value of the residential and C/I properties increase, the jurisdiction's ability to raise more revenue increases. Tax-base sharing allows the other parts of the region that contributed to the financing to benefit, not only the locality with new development. Funds are then distributed to the regional participants in the pool. The distribution of the pool is based on fiscal capacity, defined as equalized market value per capita. If the locality's fiscal capacity is the same as the regional average, its percentage share of the pool will be the same as its share of the area's population. If the locality's fiscal capacity is above the regional average, its share will be smaller. If the locality's fiscal capacity is below the regional average, its share will be larger.

University of Minnesota law professor Myron Orfield is perhaps the region's and nation's leading advocate for tax-base sharing. He argues that the results are meaningful. During the 2000s, approximately one-third of the region's C/I tax base went into the regional pool. About three-quarters of the region's localities participated in tax-base sharing. Within the region, tax-base disparity (measured by per capita C/I value) was reduced from fifty to one to about twelve to one. While critics argue the tax-base sharing policies are nonstarters in most other regions, there is little doubt that the Twin Cities' policies reduced fiscal disparities.

Rusk's analysis finds that metropolitan health is driven by central-city elasticity, or the ability of a city to expand the territory of its jurisdiction. He classifies these regions into categories of relative elasticity, which is based on the percentage increase in central-city land area expansion from 1950 to 1990 (see table 7.4). Rusk asserts that metropolitan areas with more elastic central cities have higher rates of job creation; higher average incomes; higher population growth; smaller central city-suburb income gaps and smaller concentrations of poverty; and less residential racial segregation than metropolitan areas with less elastic central cities. According to Myron Orfield, author of the influential book *Metropolitics*, says, "David Rusk showed that areas that had created metropolitan governments by consolidation or annexation were less segregated by race and class, more fiscally sound, and economically healthier."

Can suburbs survive without their central cities? Some scholars find that there is a strong interdependency between cities and suburbs. There is a collective, shared fate among cities and suburbs—a regional interest that is larger than any suburb or city. Regional planning promotes economic efficiency, addresses environmental concerns of uncontrolled sprawl, makes regions more

Table 7.4 Elastic Cities and Suburbs

Area/City	City Population Change 1950–1990	Metro New-Home Buyers 1950–1990	City Capture-Contribute Percentage	Examples
Zero elasticity	−247,392	818,853	−30%	New York; Detroit
Low elasticity	67,352	667,340	10%	Chicago; Milwaukee
Medium elasticity	66,170	509,559	13%	Des Moines; Cedar Rapids
High elasticity	241,625	628,985	38%	Kansas City; Indianapolis
Hyperelasticity	229,133	484,703	47%	Las Vegas; Little Rock

Source: Rusk, David. 1995. *Cities without Suburbs.* Washington, DC: Woodrow Wilson Center Press.

competitive globally, and confronts the endemic issue of concentrated poverty. In many regions, particularly in the Rust Belt, regions are fully developed, and annexation and consolidation are effectively not options. Thus, several policy implications are apparent: (1) sprawl should be curtailed through regional land-use planning; (2) concentrations of poverty should be dissipated by ensuring that all suburbs maintain a "fair share" of mixed-use housing; and (3) fiscal disparities among local jurisdictions should be curbed through redistribution. New regionalists look toward various policy examples and best practices to achieve these goals. Urban growth boundaries, such as Portland, Oregon, and Baltimore County, Maryland, regionalize land-use planning to limit suburban development on the metropolitan fringe, which limits sprawl (see figure 7.4). Revenue-sharing programs, like the one in Minneapolis, redistribute property-tax revenue from wealthy to poor jurisdictions. Montgomery County, Maryland's Moderately Priced Dwelling Unit program mandates that 15 percent of the jurisdiction's housing stock remain affordable.

Yet new regionalism is not without its critics. Some argue that politics will trump economics in the quest for new regionalism. There is a long history of the localized nature of self-government, from Thomas Jefferson's views on the agrarian society to Alexis de Tocqueville's local views on democracy. Indeed, the governance of towns is rooted in small communities of local political actors who value local identity, which makes it challenging to cede power or government to another local jurisdiction. They control land use and dictate their own local rules. Because suburbs remain spatially segregated along dimensions of race and class, there is little political support among suburbanites to help cities. The political fragmentation of suburbia reinforces the autonomous nature of local policy and planning practices such as zoning, housing, transit, and services. In the end, the politics of suburban growth and urban decline generally fails to bring together politicians to cooperate on regional policy issues. The political and fiscal costs are prohibitive, and the exclusionary structure of the fragmented metropolis makes it difficult to find common ground. Box 7.5 highlights the political and planning challenges of revitalizing Providence.

In summary, regionalism is an institutional and political framework whereby local governments come together to act in the interest of the region. The contemporary metropolitan area is fragmented and composed of a plethora of jurisdictions, including cities, towns, special districts, and planning organizations. While some theorists argue that

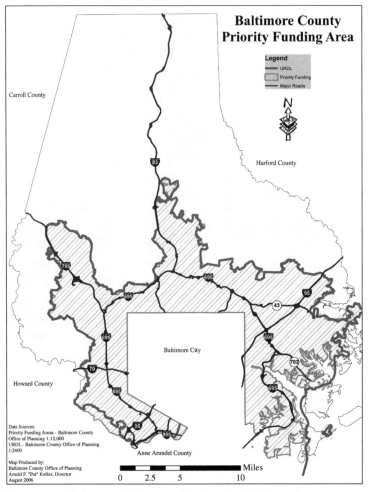

Figure 7.4   Urban-rural demarcation line in Baltimore County, Maryland. *Source:* Baltimore County Office of Planning.

Box 7.5 Providence: The Renaissance City

In 1636, Englishman Roger Williams was the first settler of Providence, Rhode Island. The city has a rich history that is part of the nation's colonial fabric. The colony first flourished as a trading post with local natives and then boomed during the Industrial Revolution. The growth of iron, textile, and cotton mills fueled the city's urban development from 1850 to 1910. During the city's industrial heyday, European immigrants, particularly Irish, Italians, and Portuguese, settled in Providence for its ample employment opportunities in the mills. In 1940, the city's population peaked at 253,000. The postwar suburbanization led to the precipitous decline of Providence, a familiar legacy of many American central cities.

For the next several decades, the deindustrialization of Providence's economy wiped out many middle-class jobs. The population shrank as residents migrated to other cities. Today, Providence is a city of approximately 178,000 residents in a region of 1.6 million. The city is part of the greater Boston-Worcester-Providence metropolitan area of 7.5 million residents. In 2009, after five decades of socioeconomic decline, the city's motto was changed to "The Creative Capital" as a tribute to its successful effort to revitalize the city. One of the symbols of Providence's turnaround was the NBC television series *Providence*. The narrative showed iconic landscapes of a renewed city with tight-knit neighborhoods and a strong sense of community. Through the lens of the show, the nation witnessed the rebirth of an industrial city—a renaissance.

Such a renaissance was not an accident; in fact, it was a deliberate effort that spanned nearly two decades. Local politicians crafted public policies to converge on a window of opportunity to revitalize the city. The city's biggest booster was the mayor, Buddy Cianci, one of the nation's longest-serving big-city mayors. For twenty-one years between 1984 and 2002, the Cianci administration platform focused on renaissance policies including rebuilding public infrastructure; improving city services; attracting and retaining businesses; and improving the quality of life for the city's residents through new economic opportunities and stable neighborhoods. A strong mayor, Cianci led the public-sector effort to implement renaissance policies.

During the 1980s and 1990s, the city's downtown was dramatically transformed through the major projects. The $169 million Capital Center project relocated rivers and railroads, and a highway interchange was constructed that easily connected the city to Interstate 95. Next, two hotels were built and a convention center and arena were erected for nearly $500 million. Then, using land-sales tax rebates and abatements, the mixed-use commercial center, Providence Place, became the city's premier landmark. Figures 7.5 and 7.6

Figure 7.5   The old Dynamo Building, which was one the city's original power plants, was slated for a museum and later condos. It has sat empty for a long time. (Photo by Tom Vicino)

Figure 7.6   Waterplace Park along Providence Harbor. Part of the Providence skyline is seen in the background. High-rise condos and commercial/recreation sites highlight the city's transformation. (Photo by Tom Vicino)

showcase several redevelopment projects in the city. In sum, Cianci's policies yielded over $1.2 billion of public investment in the city.

Scholars of local economic development examine the politics of the policy-making process to explain how and why urban revitalization occurs. In the case of Providence, an urban regime of public- and private-sector elites mobilized quickly to take advantage of new opportunities, and a dedicated policy entrepreneur, Buddy Cianci, maintained the momentum for the renaissance of the city. While the physical results were stunning, the new, shiny buildings and pristine landscapes do not necessarily mean that a renaissance occurred. Indeed, there is ample evidence of the physical renaissance of Providence. Public policies transformed rivers, rails, roads, and buildings—all abandoned—into new spaces. Yet nearly one-quarter of the city's population still lived in poverty, and employment opportunities lagged behind those of other large cities in New England. These dual realities raise important questions as to who benefits from urban revitalization: downtown and its tourists or the residents of poor neighborhoods? Ultimately, it is up to policy makers, planners, and residents to reconcile these dualities.

political fragmentation will enhance choice and efficiency in local government, others argue that it undermines the region's organic whole and collective interests. In either case, the political fragmentation in regions makes it difficult to address economic development, service provision, or democratic voice at the regional level. Old regionalists argue that regional government is the solution. New regionalists argue that cooperation on shared policy issues is more pragmatic. However, support for regionalism is weak. These solutions raise problems of equity and democratic representation. Ultimately, the ability to address regional problems depends on the political feasibility and economic conditions of the region and its local governments.

FUTURE PROSPECTS

The governance of the cities of North America has a long history that dates to the beginning of urban development. Throughout the growth and development of cities, observers of urban politics have asked the question about who governs the city. There is no simple answer to this question. A reflection on the history of urban growth, and later suburban growth, shows that many social and economic forces such as immigration, the rise and fall of manufacturing, sprawl, and the globalization of metropolitan areas shaped not only the governance of cities but also the governance of suburbs and their regions.

At the peak of the growth of big cities in the United States, power was concentrated in the hands of a few leaders of organizations known as political machines. Until the early twentieth century, bosses of these machines consolidated decision making and controlled policy

agendas in the city. Then, progressive reforms weakened the power of the political machine. Until the 1950s, political elites maintained power over the city. Later, urban regimes developed coalitions between the public, private, and nonprofit sectors to govern cities as the cities' economic development grew increasingly important. Thereafter, power was decentralized to the suburbs as people and jobs moved out of the city and into the suburbs. The effects on the metropolis were dramatic. New suburban governments grew annually, and political fragmentation dominated the metropolitan landscape. Some argued this trend was wasteful, irrational, and inefficient while others argued that competition for people and resources was good for the economy. Accordingly, governing the cities and suburbs turned toward a regional focus.

While the Canadian experience is similar to that of the United States, it is distinct in several ways. Canada's two largest cities were governed by political machines, but that power diminished during the early twentieth century as urban reform swept the nation. There are significantly fewer urban residents in Canada, and while they suburbanized in a pattern similar to the US pattern, Canada is still very highly urbanized. Eighty percent of residents live in urban areas. Consequently, cities are fragmented, but they remain significantly less fragmented than their US counterparts. Regional governments are commonplace, which reduces the competition for resources. Yet, in much the same way, politicians and elites have come together as boosters for the entrepreneurial city.

In conclusion, political machines, elites, and regimes governed the city and later, the suburbs. The decline of the central city and the phenomenal growth of suburbia played an important role in refocusing the question of who governs the city to who governs the suburbs and then to who governs the region. Whether it is the city, the suburb, or the region, it is clear that place and scale matter for who governs. The geography of who governs offers a multiplicity of responses based on the urban economy, the structure of governance, the social and cultural dynamics of cities, and the urban environment.

SUGGESTED READINGS

Cohen, A., and E. Taylor. 2000. *American Pharaoh: Mayor Richard J. Daley, His Battle for Chicago and the Nation.* Boston: Little, Brown.

Dahl, R. A. 1961. *Who Governs? Democracy and Power in an American City.* New Haven, CT: Yale University Press.

Dreier, P., J. Mollenkopf, and T. Swanstrom. 2001. *Place Matters: Metropolitics for the Twenty-First Century.* Lawrence: University Press of Kansas.

Leazes, F. J. Jr., and M. T. Motte. 2004. *Providence: The Renaissance City.* Boston: Northeastern University Press.

Miller, D. 2002. *The Regional Governing of Metropolitan America.* Boulder, CO: Westview Press.

O'Connor, T. H. 1997. *The Boston Irish: A Political History.* Boston: Back Bay Books.

Orfield, M. 1997. *Metropolitics: A Regional Agenda for Community and Stability.* Washington, DC: Brookings Institution Press.

Smith, C. F. 1999. *William Donald Schaefer: A Political Biography.* Baltimore: Johns Hopkins University Press.

Stone, C. N. 1989. *Regime Politics: Governing Atlanta, 1946–1988.* Lawrence: University Press of Kansas.

CITIES ON THE WEB

The White House Office of Urban Affairs: http://www.whitehouse.gov/administration/eop/oua.

The United States Conference of Mayors: http://www.usmayors.org/.

The National League of Cities: http://www.nlc.org/.

The Brookings Institution Metropolitan Policy Program: http://www.brookings.edu/metro.aspx.

Governing: http://www.governing.com.

The Next American City: http://americancity.org/.

CITIES AND MAYORS ON FILM

Street Fight: A Film by Marshall Curry. 2005. Magnolia Home Entertainment. *A documentary on Mayor Cory Booker of Newark, New Jersey.*

BUDDY, The Rise and Fall of America's Most Notorious Mayor. 2006. Laurel Hill Films. *A documentary on Mayor Vincent Cianci of Providence, Rhode Island.*

The Nine Lives of Marion Barry. 2009. HBO Films. *A documentary on Mayor Marion Barry of Washington, DC.*

The World That Moses Built. 1988. PBS Masterpiece. *A documentary on master planner Robert Moses of New York City.*

The Times of Harvey Milk. 1984. Telling Pictures Films. *A documentary on board of supervisors member Harvey Milk of San Francisco, California.*

8

Planning and Politics
AMANDA HURON

Cities share two key characteristics: one, they are relatively densely populated, and two, they are home to relatively diverse groups of people. Because in urban areas people of diverse cultures, backgrounds, and ideals must share limited space and resources, cities are often sites of conflict over how land is used and resources are distributed. Struggles over land and resources manifest in conflicts among different groups of residents, between residents and local government, between residents and developers, and in other ways. At root, these struggles are over what the city should look like, how it should function, and what purposes it should serve.

City planning can be understood as a mechanism by which such conflicts may be resolved. Among their many duties, city planners work to design parks, transportation systems, and public spaces; determine appropriate uses for different parcels of land; encourage housing and commercial development in targeted areas; and ensure the city develops as a coherent whole. Planners can operate at different scales: while some may work with particular neighborhoods, others may work along the entire stretch of a city's waterfront or work regionally with planners in neighboring suburban jurisdictions. Depending on the predilections of a city's elected

officials, city planners may be more oriented toward technocratic work, such as writing zoning codes, or toward pursuing social goals, such as increasing equity among disparate populations. The purpose of city planning is to shape cities in the public interest by developing neighborhoods with a variety of residential options rather than in the individual interests of a few people or actors. While "the public interest" may appear to be a neutral concept, it is in fact a highly political idea. City planning, therefore, is an intrinsically political act.

ORIGINS OF THE CITY PLANNING PROFESSION

The creation of the urban planning profession in North America is generally dated to 1909, when the first city planning conference in the United States was held, in Washington, DC. The purpose of the new profession was to bring order to the chaotic cities of the Industrial Revolution. These were cities marked by extremes of wealth and poverty, crowded living quarters, and unsafe work conditions. In New York City, photographer Jacob Riis documented the slum conditions of New York's working poor. He photographed entire

Figure 8.1   *5 Cents a Spot.* Photograph illustrating the cramped living conditions of tenement dwellers in New York City. (Photo by Jacob Riis, 1889)

families living in single rooms and the difficult, crowded conditions of sweatshop labor (see figure 8.1). His photographs spurred a revolt against the terrible conditions—a revolt based on both genuine concern for the poor as well as fear that fires and diseases would also hurt the wealthy, who lived nearby.

In its early phases, city planning was conducted outside the context of city government, which was at that time linked to big machine politics and seen as irredeemably corrupt. Independent citizens' boards hired private planners to make recommendations on urban development; the first one was founded in Hartford, Connecticut, in 1907. But the attempt to remain above the political fray became frustrating for the obvious reason that elected officials had no reason to listen to planners or follow their carefully reasoned advice. In the 1940s, the planning profession began being incorporated into city government, the goal being to become more

politically effective, that is, to get the people who actually had power in the city, like the mayor, to pay attention. Of course, this meant that planning ran the danger of becoming politicized—what the early founders of the profession feared. With planning openly under the jurisdiction of elected officials, it could have more effect—and could also be corrupted. Today, city planning happens both within city agencies overseen by mayors and also in independent commissions that exist outside the electoral process.

Over the course of the twentieth century, planners have tried out several different approaches to their work. For years, the standard approach was that of the comprehensive, rational planner: a trained expert who made decisions about how urban land should be used, without seeking input from the people whose everyday lives would be affected. In the 1960s, citizens and planners alike began criticizing this approach as "top-down" planning.

Rather, they argued, cities would benefit from "bottom-up" planning that sprang directly from the needs and desires of urban dwellers. Lawyer Paul Davidoff developed the concept of "advocacy planning" in order to ensure that multiple voices were heard throughout the planning process. The role of the planner, he argued, should be to act as an advocate for people who were ordinarily ignored by the planning process. In the 1970s, Norman Krumholz, working as a planner in Cleveland, developed the concept of equity planning. Equity planning, the Cleveland City Planning Commission declared, "requires that locally responsible government institutions give priority attention to the goal of promoting a wider range of choices for those Cleveland residents who have few, if any, choices."

Since the mid-1960s, planners have been concerned about the degree to which regular people—"non-experts"—participate in the planning that is performed on their behalf. In her classic 1969 article, "A Ladder of Citizen Participation," Sherry Arnstein roundly criticizes the planning profession for engaging urban residents in exercises of participation that are not, in fact, genuinely participatory. At worst, she argues, planners engage in a pretense of participation in order to manipulate people into approving their ideas. Often, planners select a few token citizen faces to sit on review boards but don't actually listen to what these participants believe their neighborhoods need. It is quite rare, Arnstein notes, for citizens to reach full levels of participation in the planning process: what she calls "citizen control." What Davidoff, Krumholz, Arnstein, and other planners have recognized is that planning is inherently political. The question for planners is how to deal with the political nature of their work.

PLANNING VISIONARIES

One way to understand the evolution of city planning and politics is through examining the ideas of people who have been influential in the realm of city planning from the late nineteenth century through the early twenty-first. While these six do not represent the totality of planning ideas that have been developed in North America, their ideas form the underpinning for many contemporary discussions of city planning. And each person profiled here had a politics—a way of seeing the world—that informed how he or she thought about cities.

Ebenezer Howard: The Garden City

Ebenezer Howard, an Englishman, championed the idea of healthful living for working people. In his 1898 book *Garden Cities of To-morrow*, Howard lays out his vision for garden cities: towns that could provide an alternative to the densely packed, disease-ridden, and unaffordable city of industrial London. For Howard, a garden city would combine the culture and convenience of the city with the calming green of the country. Garden cities would be surrounded by belts of agricultural land, both so that the town could feed itself and to prevent the town from sprawling out beyond its original borders. Howard's sketches of his garden cities prompted excitement throughout England and, ultimately, the world (see figure 8.2). But Howard was not a utopian: he wrote to appeal to investors, whom he needed to convince in order to obtain the capital to purchase the land to found the towns.

Howard is remembered in large part for the physical design of his towns. The idea of

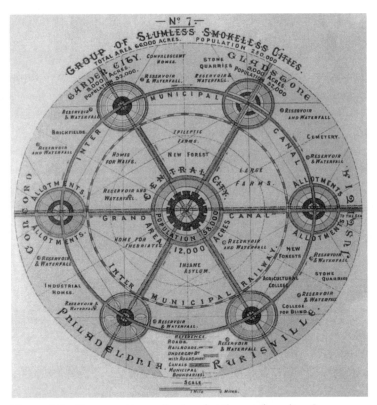

Figure 8.2   Ebenezer Howard's plan for the garden city. *Source:*
Ebenezer Howard, *Garden Cities of To-morrow*, originally published
1898.

warding off sprawl through creating a belt of green around the town and the focus on building a mixed-use community that could meet all of a family's basic consumer and cultural needs have proven prescient. New urbanists today are still drawing on Howard's vision. Yet what was more important to Howard—and what has been mostly lost in how the garden city idea has been taken up—was his social and economic vision for his garden cities. Howard proposed the radical idea that the cities be owned collectively by their residents. As the land rose in value over the years, revenues obtained from higher rents would flow not to individual landlords, as was the case in a city like London, but into a

collective coffer. The townspeople could then put this income toward the development of institutions of culture and social welfare. This, Howard proposed, would solve the problem of ever-increasing housing prices in the city as well as create a self-sustaining town. Howard was expressly concerned with the social inequity engendered in industrial cities like London and thought this problem could be addressed by people working collectively in the garden city. A few garden cities were built in England, Germany, Canada, and the United States (see box 8.1), though they mostly took up Howard's ideas of physical design rather than his accompanying vision for new economic and social structures.

Box 8.1 Greenbelt, Maryland: Community Ownership

In the midst of the Great Depression, the federal government decided to take on the problem of urban slums by constructing a series of "greenbelt" cities across the United States, where people of modest means could enjoy inexpensive housing in a green setting. Though Rexford Guy Tugwell, the director of FDR's Resettlement Administration, initially hoped to build three thousand greenbelt cities, only three were built in the end. Between 1935 and 1937, the Resettlement Administration sponsored the construction of Greenhills, Ohio, outside Cincinnati; Greendale, Wisconsin, outside Milwaukee; and Greenbelt, Maryland, outside Washington, DC. The new towns were based in part on Ebenezer Howard's garden city vision, designed to give working people the tranquility of the countryside while still providing the culture and convenience of the city. Unlike the more sprawling suburbs that came later in the century, the new towns were designed to have coherent economic and cultural centers that were within walking distance of all residents. Greenbelt's Art Deco town center, for example, held a supermarket, movie theater, recreation center, pool, and elementary school; the town was filled with parks and surrounded by a "greenbelt" of over eight thousand acres (see figure 8.3). Planners designed walkways and bike paths to go under major street intersections, separating pedestrian and bikers from cars and reducing the possibility of accidents. This was an eminently walkable place long before "walkability" was even a concept in the planning lexicon.

But what is most interesting about Greenbelt—indeed, what is most interesting about Howard's garden city vision—is less its physical planning than its economic and social basis. Howard's innovation was that his garden cities and the businesses therein should be owned cooperatively by their residents. Cooperative ownership, he argued, would help keep land

Figure 8.3   Greenbelt, Maryland. The town center is characterized by art nouveau architectural style. (Photo by John Rennie Short)

and housing prices from skyrocketing and would keep products affordable. Greenbelt was not cooperatively owned at first—it was developed by a federal agency, and later, ownership of the town was transferred to the Federal Public Housing Authority. But in the early 1950s, when the government put Greenbelt's land up for sale, its members collectively purchased much of the town's housing and land and turned it into a cooperative—thus retroactively coming closer to Howard's original vision. Today, about 20 percent of Greenbelt's housing is still part of the cooperative. Two of its businesses—the supermarket and a café—are still cooperatively owned as well. Because of its unique architectural, social, and economic history, Greenbelt was in 1997 designated a national historic landmark—the first planned community in the nation to receive the distinction.

The garden city movement made hardly a dent in the massive tide of suburban development that washed over the United States later in the twentieth century. Yet the idea of cooperative ownership of towns, in which residents must work together to take care of the place in which they live and play, has adherents. A place like Greenbelt, Maryland, still serves as a model for people interested in living in walkable communities with plenty of green space and the opportunity to work collectively with their neighbors to maintain their communities.

Daniel Burnham: The City Beautiful

"Make no little plans," architect Daniel Burnham is said to have warned, "they have no magic to stir men's blood." Burnham thought big, and he planned big. A stalwart Chicagoan, he came to fame for his design of the 1893 World's Columbian Exposition, also known as the Chicago World's Fair. The fair was planned for the four hundredth anniversary of Columbus's arrival in the New World, and, though its opening was delayed a year due to financial problems, it was meant to serve as an announcement to the world of US ingenuity and power. The fair was a coming-out party of sorts for the city of Chicago and the nation, and it worked. In the six months that the fair was open, it received approximately twelve million individual visitors—just about one-fifth of the entire population of the United States at the time. The fair generated enormous excitement around the country and the world—one woman said she walked all the way from Galveston, Texas, to attend.

Part of what drew the millions of visitors was the fabulous "white city," Burnham's neoclassical design for the multiple buildings that made up the fairgrounds (see figure 8.4). In a city famed for its dirty factories and bloody slaughterhouses, the white city offered a luminescent vision of urban beauty, coolly poised on the edge of Lake Michigan. This was a city quite at odds with most Americans'—and most Chicagoans'—understanding of urban life. The 1893 fair marked the beginning of the "City Beautiful" movement, which insisted that cities did not have to be grimy, soot covered, and disease ridden—they could be clean, thoughtfully designed, and pleasing to live in.

After the success of the fair, Burnham in 1902 went on to create a new plan for Washington, DC. While the capital had originally been laid out a century earlier by Frenchman

Figure 8.4   Crowds gather on July 4, 1893, in the famed white city of the World's Columbian Exposition, Chicago. (Photo courtesy the Brooklyn Museum Archives Goodyear Archival Collection)

Pierre L'Enfant, Burnham's plan extended and enhanced L'Enfant's vision. In Washington, Burnham was able to realize his white city in a more permanent way, with dozens of marble federal buildings that imitated the designs of ancient Greece. Though the plan took many years to realize, the monumental core of Washington, DC, still stands as testament to the City Beautiful movement.

Patrick Geddes: The Regional City

Patrick Geddes was a Scottish biologist, geographer, and town planner who introduced the concept of the "region." As a biologist, he understood the concept of biological evolution and as a sociologist and geographer was attuned to man's interaction with the environment. These influences helped him develop the idea that the city was a series of interlocking relationships between the natural and social environment. Both social and natural processes created the spatial form of cities. He suggested that urban planners ought to begin any plan with a survey of the natural features—the geology, climate, and geography—as well as the economy and social institutions of the city and region. The idea of "survey before plan" may seem obvious today, but one hundred years ago, this was revolutionary thinking. Between 1915 and 1919, Geddes wrote a series of town-planning reports on at least eighteen Indian cities; he also drew up plans for Tel Aviv and Jerusalem. His book *Cities in Evolution* explores the complexity of cities, their morphology and design. In many ways, his work foreshadows the development of environmental planning of the 1970s, which integrates natural and human systems in conjunction with new environmental regulations set forth by the US Environmental Protection Agency (we expand on this more in chapter 13, which discusses the influence of sustainability on urban planning).

Through his writings, exhibitions, and plans for various cities and regions, Geddes influenced the American urban theorist Lewis Mumford. Mumford wrote some twenty books and a thousand articles and reviews, many on urban history and urban culture. One of his most significant was the 1961 *The City in History*. In 1923, Mumford, along with several others, helped to found the Regional Planning Association of America, which advocated limited-scale development and the concept of the region for city planning. Like Geddes, Mumford believed in looking beyond the buildings and streets to see the network of human relationships that are at the core of the city. Although Mumford was not an architect or planner, he became the spokesman for the Regional Planning Association of America. This group lobbied business and government to establish regional cities as a counterpoint to the congestion and chaos of the city. Mumford is still regarded as the leading twentieth-century authority on the history, design, and function of cities.

Le Corbusier: The Radiant City

The Swiss architect known as Le Corbusier (born Charles-Edouard Jeanneret) began working in Europe in the 1920s. Though his early projects were villas for wealthy individuals, he soon took an interest in developing apartment buildings that were made affordable by the use of mass-production techniques and that used industrial design to create, as he put it, "striking, exciting relationships" of architectural form. Corbusier famously thought of his apartment homes as "machines for living." But Corbusier did not want to just erect single buildings. Rather, he was interested in urban form more broadly and in creating urban environments in which space was used efficiently and elegantly. "My own duty and my aim," he wrote, "is to try and raise people out of their misery, away from catastrophe; to provide them with happiness, with a contented existence, with harmony. My own goal is to establish or re-establish harmony between people and their environment."

Corbusier's ideal city was marked by extremely tall, densely populated towers, surrounded by swaths of open green space and connected by megahighways; he referred to his vision as the "radiant city." The radiant city ideal was remarkably influential in mid-century US urban planning. In New York City, Parks Commissioner Robert Moses knocked down thousands of homes to make room for his highways, megablocks of housing, and public parks. In cities across the United States, officials bulldozed neighborhoods designated as "blighted" and erected downtown arenas and massive public housing projects in the name of urban renewal. The story of the Pruitt-Igoe public housing complex in St. Louis is instructive. The massive complex, made up of thirty-three identical buildings of eleven stories each, was built in 1955. It was designed by famed Japanese architect Minoru Yamasaki, who would go on to design the World Trade Center towers in New York; when the complex opened, it was hailed as an architectural masterpiece. But it turned out that the combination of high-rise housing and gross undermaintenance did not create a good environment for living. Over time, the complex became a notoriously hard place to live. In 1972, just seventeen years after its opening, the city of St. Louis demolished Pruitt-Igoe in a series of spectacular explosions (see figure

Figure 8.5 The demolition of the Pruitt-Igoe public housing complex, St. Louis, 1972. *Source:* Wikimedia.

8.5). Pruitt-Igoe became a symbol—almost a cliché—of modern urban planning and the radiant city gone horribly wrong.

Frank Lloyd Wright: The Decentralized City

Frank Lloyd Wright is perhaps the most famous architect the United States has produced. He designed a wide range of buildings over the course of his life and may be best known for his "prairie-style" houses: slung low to the ground, emphasizing horizontal lines, and made of local materials. While a number of these structures were located on urban lots, Wright preferred to place his houses in more rural settings, in which the home could become part of the natural landscape—he referred to his work as "organic architecture." For while Wright was concerned with his individual works of architecture, he was just as concerned with how his buildings interacted with the earth and with how Amer-

icans should dwell on the land more broadly. Indeed, he was very much an urban planner—albeit one who hated cities.

Wright found cities oppressive and inherently undemocratic. Cities, he thought, were unavoidably ruled by "mobocracy." As he wrote, "Even the small town is too large. . . . Ruralism as distinguished from Urbanism is American and truly Democratic." For Wright, the fulfillment of American democracy depended on a Jeffersonian ideal of small, self-sufficient homesteads scattered across the countryside. In opposition to Corbusier's vision of collective living in the city, Wright held up the sanctity of the individual on his own piece of land. Wright used the term "Usonia" to refer to his vision for how Americans should interact with the landscape; within the broader ideal of Usonia, he drew up specific plans for Broadacre City, his idealized American hamlet. Broadacre City would be just four square miles and would house only 1,400 families. There would be at least one acre of space for every person and at least one car for every adult. People could easily whiz about between settlements in their cars along broad highways and through the air by helicopter. Wright began promoting his vision for Broadacre City in 1932 and continued until his death in 1959. Ultimately, the physical form of Broadacre City was an ideal of rural living that served as an inspiration for American suburbia. Homes like the E. H. Pitkin cottage, an island summer cottage in Ontario, and Fallingwater, a house in southwestern Pennsylvania, embodied his vision of integrating architecture into the natural landscape.

Although Wright designed many of his structures for rural or suburban areas, one of his more enduring designs is the Guggenheim Museum in New York City. Drawing inspiration from a nautilus shell, the building encourages visitors to begin at the top floor and work their way through all of the different exhibits by moving down circular ramps (see figure 8.6).

Figure 8.6   Interior of Frank Lloyd Wright's Guggenheim Museum. (Photo by John Rennie Short)

Jane Jacobs: The Organic City

Jane Jacobs was an architectural critic who, in the 1950s, was living in Manhattan's Greenwich Village neighborhood. At a time when much of American popular culture was oriented toward the brand-new, booming, and mostly white suburbs, Jacobs lived in a world firmly enmeshed in the organic fabric of dense and diverse city life. But the city she loved was under attack. In New York City, Robert Moses was busily carrying out Corbusier's vision through rapid-fire construction of highways and enormous housing blocks, which necessitated the destruction of many an older New York neighborhood.

Urban renewal, which coursed through many US and Canadian cities in the 1950s and 1960s, was an attempt to revitalize downtowns on a massive scale. Yet "renewal" often spelled destruction of older neighborhoods that were deemed slums, when in fact they were lively places full of rich social networks and vibrant economies. When Moses began plans for a highway that would slice through her neighborhood of Greenwich Village, Jacobs fought back with writing and activism. The highway was defeated, and in 1961 Jacobs published what became an instant classic, *The Death and Life of Great American Cities.*

The *New York Times Book Review* called her book "perhaps the most influential single work in the history of town planning

. . . a work of literature." In her first sentence, Jacobs tell us: "This book is an attack on current city planning and rebuilding." In her first few pages, she offers damning critiques of Howard, Burnham, Le Corbusier, and the "decentrists," among whom she surely included Wright. None of these men, Jacobs argued, understood how real cities worked. "From beginning to end," she concludes her introduction, "from Howard and Burnham to the latest amendment on urban renewal law, the entire concoction is irrelevant to the workings of cities. Unstudied, unrespected, cities have served as sacrificial victims." Throughout the book, she sought to make plain her observations of the complex workings of urban life and urged respect and support for cities and neighborhoods that grew slowly, organically, and according to the needs of their inhabitants—and to argue against the top-down planning that had come before. Jacobs is most famous for her observations of New York City, but she moved to Toronto in 1968, in part because of her opposition to the United States' involvement in the Vietnam War. In Toronto, she continued her urbanist activism, fighting a proposed expressway, working for improved public housing, and twice being arrested for her efforts. Though Jacobs was certainly no planner—being referred to as one would have horrified her—her vision and analysis has had enormous influence on how people think about cities and urban life.

Richard Florida: The Creative City

In the early years of the twenty-first century, urban planning scholar Richard Florida has captured the imagination of North American city officials with his story of a "creative class" of people whose presence, or lack thereof, can make or break a city's economy. For Florida, cities that thrive in the twenty-first century will be those that can attract members of the creative class: a broadly defined group that works in the loosely defined "knowledge industry" and that values diversity, walkability, and the ineffable "urban experience." Florida believes members of the creative class are drawn to Jacobs's vision of good city life. Creative-class types want diverse urban neighborhoods that feel authentic, not cookie cutter strip malls. They want to be able to walk or bike most places, not be stuck in traffic. They value easy access to rich cultural institutions, recreation opportunities, and shopping. And they value tolerant places; in one of his studies, Florida finds that cities with larger populations of gay people are more likely to attract the creative class.

Florida, who focuses on planning as an economic development tool, turns the traditional idea of urban economic development on its head. He notes that, historically, cities eager to grow their economies spent a lot of time, effort, and tax dollars trying to lure big companies to relocate within their borders. Instead, he argues, urban officials should be working to entice members of the creative class to come live in their cities. If the workers want to live in the city, he claims, the companies will follow. Cities that remake themselves in ways that appeal to members of the creative class, he argues, will be rewarded with economic growth. At a 2008 speech in Calgary, for instance, Florida warned that the city should not rely too much on natural resources but should instead invest in the creativity of its residents.

Florida is not without his critics. Some argue that focusing on attracting young, hip employees at the expense of bringing in big companies will ultimately fail. Others accuse him of promoting policies that would remake cities for young people with disposable income while ignoring the needs of lower-income urban residents: this approach to urban planning, they warn, is a recipe for displacement of the poor. The jury is still out on Florida's theories. But his influence on urban planning and policy trends in twenty-first century North America is undeniable.

ELEMENTS OF PLANNING

City planning can encompass a dizzying array of physical, economic, social, and cultural elements. Some planners are focused more on questions of physical form, while others are more concerned with urban sociality, ecological concerns, and other questions of how urban dwellers experience the city. Four of the fundamental elements of city planning—zoning, transportation, public space, and comprehensive planning—are considered here.

Zoning

Zoning determines how land may be used and has historically been one of the primary functions of urban planning. The first zoning ordinance in the United States was created in New York City in 1916; Canada's first zoning ordinance was passed in 1924 by the town of Point Grey, in British Columbia. While other cities had already passed ordinances restricting certain kinds of land uses, New York's was the first zoning ordinance that regulated land use for every single piece of property within a city. The main argument for the ordinance was to protect property values, with the idea that doing so would be good for the tax base

of the city as a whole. Many jurisdictions followed New York's lead, including the town of Euclid, a suburb of Cleveland. Euclid leaders had instituted zoning because they were worried that Cleveland's industry would begin to spread into their town. Upon passage of their zoning ordinance, the Ambler Realty Co., which owned a large tract of land in Euclid, sued the town. Ambler argued that the town's zoning unconstitutionally prohibited the company from developing its land as it saw fit: that it represented a "taking" of private land. The case went to the Supreme Court. In 1926, the Supreme Court decided in *Village of Euclid, Ohio v. Ambler Realty Co.* that zoning was constitutional and did not constitute a taking from private property owners. Within ten years of the *Euclid* decision, 85 percent of all American cities had zoning ordinances.

Zoning is, in a sense, the rationale for the existence of urban planning. Common sense tells us we shouldn't locate a smoke-spewing factory next to a day-care center; zoning prevents such incompatible land uses from butting up against each other. A cursory look at any zoning map underscores the physical nature of this elemental component of city planning (see figure 8.7). Yet zoning is also an inherently social undertaking. Many suburbs, for example, are zoned to require that houses sit on lots of a certain minimum square footage, thus essentially excluding people who cannot afford a certain lot size from living in the suburb (see box 8.2). In practice, this has often meant exclusion of people by race as well as income. While they may be cloaked in the drab language of law, zoning decisions are in fact highly political. Houston, Texas, doesn't have any zoning at all—an approach which is just as political as micromanaging land use down to the last square inch (see box 8.3).

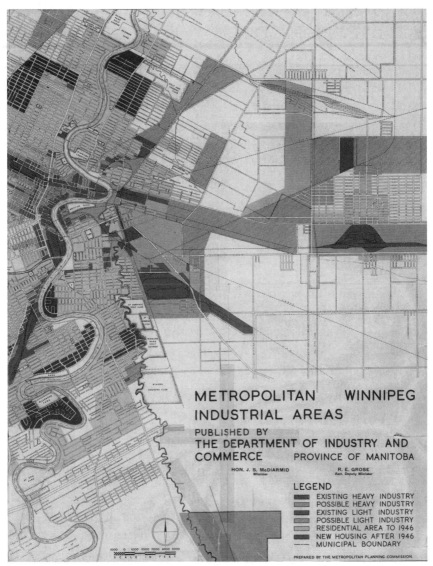

Figure 8.7   Greater Winnipeg proposed zoning regulations district map. Zoning districts include areas designated for industry, agriculture, multiple-family residence, limited commercial activity, and others. *Source:* Image courtesy of University of Manitoba Archives and Special Collections, http://www.flickr.com/photos/manitobamaps/2130426337/sizes/l/in/photostream/.

Box 8.2 Geographic Perspectives on Affordable Housing

Housing affordability has long been a problem in many of the cities of North America. But housing markets tend to be highly local, and rents vary sharply by location. In 2012, the median rent for a two-bedroom apartment in Buffalo, New York, was $887, while in New York City the median rent for the same size home was $3300. Why the geographic disparity? One reason is classic supply and demand: many people want to live in New York City, in part because the city has many jobs, and high demand for housing drives up costs. Buffalo, in contrast, has fewer jobs, much lower housing demand, and therefore much lower housing costs. Yet many of the people who live in New York City do not earn high wages—they may work in the city's service industry or in the public sector. How, then, can they afford to pay the high rent? One way is through affordable housing programs sponsored by their cities—often designed in part by planners.

To understand the question of housing affordability, it's important to be familiar with some key concepts. First, it's important to clarify what the term "affordable" means. Housing is generally considered affordable if a household does not spend more than 30 percent of its gross income on total housing costs, including utilities. Whether or not a given rent level is considered affordable, therefore, depends on the income of the household that occupies it. When city planners say they are developing affordable housing, they mean they are developing housing that will be affordable to people at a certain income level.

Second, therefore, it's crucial to know how planners are defining income levels. Generally, planners target households that earn below a certain percentage of the median family income (MFI) or area median income (AMI) of the metropolitan area in which they are operating. Consider the case of the Bronx, one of the five boroughs that make up New York City. In 2010, the median family income for the New York City metro area, which includes the city's five boroughs and the three wealthy suburban counties of Putnam, Rockland, and Westchester, was $63,200. But median household income for the borough of the Bronx itself was just $34,264. According to the US Department of Housing and Urban Development, households may be considered low income if they earn below 80 percent of the area median income; much affordable housing development is targeted to these "low-income" households. In the New York City metropolitan area, a household is considered low income if its annual income is below $50,560 (or about $4213 a month). Affordable "low-income" housing in the New York City area, therefore, would be housing that costs no more than $1264 a month. But let's return to the Bronx. Median income in the Bronx itself is far lower than that of the whole metropolitan area, and the median monthly earnings of a Bronx household is only $2855. The "affordable" rent of $1264, therefore, while it may be affordable to families in other parts of the metropolitan area, is hardly affordable to most households in the Bronx. There is a spatial mismatch in affordability levels across the metropolitan area.

When city officials and planners promise affordable housing, therefore, it's important to understand exactly what they mean by "affordable." Are they basing affordability calculations on the median family income for the entire metropolitan area or on the median income for just the city in question? Are they targeting households at 80 percent of the median income, or are they trying to serve households who earn much less—for example, only 30 percent of the median? The scales of geography and income at which planners are working determine the degree of housing affordability they create.

Another geographic component of affordable housing, of course, is the question of where such housing should be located. Many cities have poor track records of having built public housing in isolated areas, far from public transit and job opportunities. Today, cities are more aware of the need to build affordable housing in places that are convenient for residents who may rely on public transportation. Some jurisdictions also work to ensure that affordable housing is dispersed throughout different neighborhoods so that the poor are not ghettoized in certain areas. Zoning restrictions can make an even distribution of affordable housing difficult: if a community is zoned for single-family detached homes, it will be difficult to develop affordable housing there, since affordable housing tends to be designed in a more efficient, densely built manner. Through community conversations and action, zoning regulations can be changed to encourage a more equitable distribution of affordable housing development. Ultimately, the geography of affordable housing is shaped by politics.

Transportation

Transportation has always been an important element of urban form. North America's earliest cities were built for walking. Before the invention of omnibuses, streetcars, subways, and automobiles, most urban dwellers commuted to work, ran errands, and pursued leisure on foot. This meant cities had to be relatively small in size and were therefore relatively densely populated, with people of diverse backgrounds and classes living in relatively close proximity. As transportation technology developed, people were able to move longer distances faster, and cities were able to spread out. From the streetcar suburbs of the early twentieth century to the far-flung exurbia of the late part of that century, changing transportation modes have made for a vast expansion of suburban life.

In the early twenty-first century, transportation has become a key element of planning for "smart growth." The continual unfolding of suburban sprawl across the American landscape and the increasing headache of commuting through it has pushed planners to try to do something to encourage people to drive less and live more closely together. Once upon a time, a transportation planner focused on designing good highway interchanges; today, she pushes for increased funding for mass transit, designs dense residential and commercial centers near transit nodes such as subway stations, and maps out bike lanes. In an effort to encourage cycling over driving, several US and Canadian cities have adopted bike-share programs that allow people to rent bikes for quick trips all over town. In Montreal, for example, the Bixi bike-share program, launched in 2009, makes

Box 8.3 Houston: The Politics of Zoning

Houston is well known as the only major city in the United States without zoning. Houston is also the only large US city in which voters have been allowed to directly weigh in on the question of whether their city should be zoned. All three times—in referenda held in 1948, 1962, and 1993—the voters of Houston have rejected the idea. Proponents of zoning argued that it would help keep inappropriate commercial and industrial uses from invading residential areas and that a lack of zoning makes for uncertainty for investors in terms of how land will be developed. They argued more broadly that zoning would protect the health and welfare of Houston's citizens, prevent overcrowding and easing traffic congestion. Opponents argued that zoning would inflate housing prices by limiting the density of housing development and that it could lead to economic and racial segregation. They further argued that zoning represented an unnecessary government infringement on private property rights. The free market, they asserted, would ensure that development took place in ways that were desirable to home buyers and purchasers of commercial real estate. Analysis of Houston's elections on the zoning question reveal that low-income people in older parts of the city tend to oppose zoning, while middle-income people in newer areas tend to support it.

While Houston has no zoning system per se, it is not accurate to portray the city as a Wild West of anarchic land use. The city does have regulations, some of which relate to housing. In 1940, the city enacted a subdivision code, which mandated minimum lot sizes for new development. This meant that until the code was reformed in 1998, it was difficult to build anything other than detached single-family homes. And as in other cities, private homeowners' associations maintain restrictive covenants dictating how land within their borders can be used—covenants that tend to be more restrictive than zoning. Houston also has many land-use regulations that favor driving, including minimum parking requirements that require ample provision of parking spaces for any new construction; mandated minimum setbacks of new construction from the road, which tends to result in buildings fronted by oceans of parking lot; and mandated wide roads and long blocks, which favor driving over walking. Houston is a notoriously sprawling Sun Belt city, hyperreliant on the automobile. Only 5.9 percent of employed adults commute via public transit, and the average Houston household spends an astonishing 20 percent of its income on transportation expenses—higher than any other US city except Dallas. Whether Houston's sprawling auto dependence is the result of government land-use regulations—or lack thereof—is a subject of debate. What is clear from the case of Houston is that the question of zoning brings up larger questions about the role of government and the market in urban land use.

Figure 8.8   Making use of the Bixi bike-share program in Montreal. (Photo by Greg Brown, 2012)

over five thousand bikes available to would-be peddlers (see figure 8.8). Interestingly, the idea for a citywide bike-share program was first proposed by a Dutch anarchist collective called Provo; in 1965, the group authored a plan in which the city of Amsterdam would purchase a platoon of white bicycles that would be distributed across the city for free use by the public.

Another one of Provo's ideas was to ban cars from the Amsterdam city center. A version of this idea, too, has taken hold in some cities. The British government, for example, has instituted "congestion pricing" in London, which requires people to pay in order to drive into the central part of the city in order to cut down on traffic and encourage alternative methods of transportation. Planners pushed for congestion pricing in New York City as well, but the idea was defeated by the New York state legislature, citing the expense to drivers. But the idea may yet take hold in densely populated North American cities. A 2011 survey of Toronto residents, for instance, found public support for instituting congestion pricing in order to fund public transportation.

Public Space

Planners have long been tasked with creating good public spaces. In his iconic 1979 film, *The Social Life of Small Urban Spaces*, sociologist William H. Whyte outlines what a good public space requires. Like Jane Jacobs, Whyte insists that actual observation of public spaces over time reveals a plethora of information about how urban dwellers use space: information that planners should incorporate into their public space design. In his time-lapse photographic observations of New York City's public spaces, he discovers some key points about how people use public spaces—and he clearly delights in his process of discovery.

Whyte devotes a section of his film to the presence of people whom he says are considered "undesirables" in public space: a group that he says is usually made up of "winos" and "derelicts," but that may also, depending on the beholder, include "bag women, people who act strangely in public, 'hippies,' teenagers, older people, street musicians, vendors of all kinds." For Whyte, the problem is not the presence of these people, but how the city and retailers react to them. Since these people are members of the public, should public space be designed with them in mind? Or does their very presence in public space make the space unwelcoming for other members of the public? Questions of who constitutes the "public," for whom public space should be designed, and how it should be used and regulated have roiled planners for years.

Of course, public space is not just plazas, parks, and sidewalks (see figure 8.9); it also includes indoor spaces such as libraries, schools, recreation centers, and other publicly owned

Figure 8.9   Fells Point in Baltimore is a vibrant public square surrounded by restaurants and shops. (Photo by Lisa Benton-Short)

facilities. The needs of a city's population shift over time, and needs for various kinds of public space may shift as well. In some cities, for instance, including Washington, DC, and Kansas City, Missouri, dozens of public schools were closed in the early 2000s (see box 8.4). What happens to these public spaces once their original use is terminated? Can they be put to another kind of public use? For planners, the purview of public space is large.

Box 8.4 Washington, DC: Planning for Reuse of Public Facilities

When a city closes a public school, what should happen to the building? While this is seemingly a question of education policy, it also becomes a question of city planning—one that can be highly politicized. In 2007–2008, Washington, DC, closed twenty-three of its public schools under the tenure of public schools chancellor Michelle Rhee. As of this writing, the city is still trying to figure out how to reuse many of the school buildings. Should they be rented to charter schools? Sold to developers? Reopened as community centers? The now-empty schools sit as a reminder of the close relationship between public space and politics (see figure 8.10).

Public schools, particularly elementary schools, hold a special place in American neighborhood life. Elementary schools are generally sited to serve particular neighborhoods, based on the idea that young children should be able to walk to school. And elementary

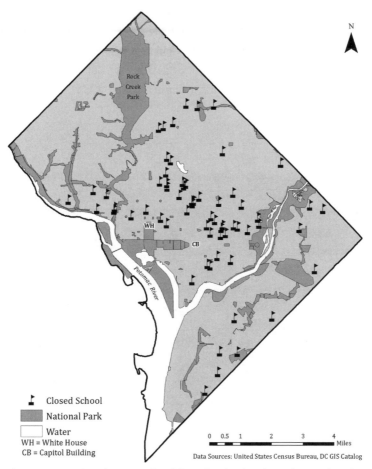

Figure 8.10   Google map of public schools that have been closed in Washington, DC, since 1974. *Source:* Map created by George Washington University Geography Department.

schools often serve other community functions as well, including as polling places and community centers. When a school closes, a neighborhood often loses not just a school, but a center of community life. Demographic shifts in Washington, DC, and shrinking school-age populations in some neighborhoods mean that school closures may make sense. But what happens when the city's young population begins to rise again? And what happens to these school buildings in the meantime? These are questions planners can help address.

The case of DC's closed schools highlights the relationship between physical planning and public services. The Crummell School, for example, is located in DC's Ivy City neighborhood, a relatively isolated and impoverished area. Named for prominent black minister and educator Alexander Crummell, the elementary school was built in 1912 as part of the city's segregated school system; it served the black students of Ivy City. The school did not just educate students; it also served as the home base for many neighborhood initiatives, including the newsletter *Ivy City Voice*, an independent preschool, and an organization that supported the neighborhood's small businesses. When the school was closed in 1977, the neighborhood lost its center. Since its closing, children from Ivy City have had to navigate across major thoroughfares to attend school in an adjacent neighborhood. Ivy City residents have periodically organized to try to reopen their school as a community center. In 2002, they were able to obtain historic landmark status for the school, which ensures that it will note be torn down. But as of this writing, the Crummell School remains vacant and boarded up, a worsening eyesore in a neglected neighborhood (see figure 8.11).

Figure 8.11   The historic Crummell School in the Ivy City neighborhood of Washington, DC. The school was closed in 1977. (Photo by Madeleine McCambridge, 2010)

Comprehensive Planning

The above elements, along with many more, should be accounted for in a city's comprehensive plan. Comprehensive plans are documents that outline a vision for a city's future. Carefully researched, these plans make use of demographic data as well as information about the city's capacity for growth. The state of Oregon defines a comprehensive plan as "a generalized, coordinated land use map and policy statement of the governing body of a local government that interrelates all functional and natural systems and activities relating to the use of lands, including but not limited to sewer and water systems, transportation systems, educational facilities, recreational facilities, and natural resources and air and water quality management programs." One of the most admired comprehensive plans in North America is that of Portland, Oregon, which includes an urban growth boundary—a belt of green surrounding the city to minimize sprawl and maximize access to nature. Though Portland's urban growth boundary has shifted

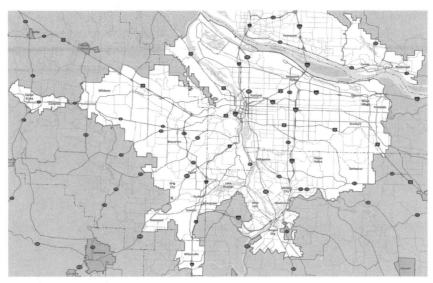

Figure 8.12   The urban growth boundary of Portland, Oregon. Portland is in the center, and the line represents the urban growth boundary as it was instituted in 1979; the boundary has expanded slightly in the intervening years. (Map by Lisa Benton-Short)

slightly over time since its institution in 1979, it has won plaudits for the way it has helped the city relate to its surroundings (see figure 8.12). New York City's *PlaNYC: A Greener, Greater New York*, released in 2007, is another example of a comprehensive plan. It focuses on growing the city by one million people, combating climate change, strengthening the city's economy, and improving the quality of life for everyone in the city.

Comprehensive plans are laudable documents that require years to create. But in order for such plans to be relevant, they must be drafted in such a way that they are open to revision while still retaining their overall vision. In New York City, for instance, planners issue yearly progress reports detailing their successes and challenges in implementing PlaNYC. When the city can't implement a piece of its plan—for instance, when the New York state legislature refused to permit congestion pricing in Manhattan, thus derailing

a key component of the city's transportation planning—the plan must be adjusted accordingly. Comprehensive plans may be visionary documents, but they exist in the messy and apparently irrational world of politics. But politics has its own rationality, and planners must be prepared to understand the politics of their cities if they are to get anything done.

PLANNING AND POLITICS INTO THE FUTURE

Into the next decades, North American urban planners will be dealing with a number of issues that may prove politically difficult.

One question is that of sustainability, a topic we examine in more detail in chapter 13. Planners and city leaders are increasingly interested in creating sustainable cities—cities that are walkable, bike friendly, and energy efficient and that make room for nature. While sustainability may appear to be a cause everyone can agree on, when it comes to making decisions that appear to pit economic development against ecology, decisions can become quite difficult. The failure of congestion pricing in New York City and the difficult and time-consuming process of restoring urban streams are just two examples of the challenges of enacting sustainable urban plans (see box 8.5). For cities like New Orleans that are particularly susceptible to imbalances with natural systems, planning for sustainability is all the more important—and all the more difficult.

Box 8.5 Vancouver: The Right to the City

Over the past decade, the *right to the city* has become a powerful call in both academic and activist circles. The writings of Henri Lefebvre, who coined the phrase in the midst of the urban revolutions of 1968, is the starting point for theoretical discussions of the right to the city. For Lefebvre, the right to the city is the right to not be alienated or marginalized in decision-making processes that frequently revolve around the use of urban space. More broadly, the right to the city is the right to the freedom of habitat and to inhabit—that is, the right to be in a place, and the right to make that place one's own. Lefebvre sees the city as a creative work—an *oeuvre*. The right to the city includes the right to participate in creating that collective work that is the city. Around the United States, Canada, and the world, the idea of the right to the city has been put to work in struggles over the rights of poor people to live in informal settlements, the rights of day laborers to congregate in public to find work, and the rights of the homeless to exist in public, among many other struggles. At the core of the right to the city analysis is the understanding that space—in this case, urban space—does not exist naturally but is socially produced. The city is constantly made and remade by private developers, public planners, and everyday inhabitants. It is this work that both creates the city and provides or denies access to its resources. As geographer David Harvey writes, the right to the city is a collective right to decision making over how to create and distribute the surplus that constitutes cities and that cities generate. This right, then, is to participation in a democratic process.

In Vancouver, the right to the city has been evoked in struggles against gentrification broadly and with regard to the 2010 Winter Olympics specifically. In the lead-up to the 2010 Olympics, questions of how the city should be shaped, and in whose interests, came to the fore. Vancouver is the least affordable global city, with a 2010 median house price of $540,900 but a median household income of only $58,200. The city's Downtown Eastside neighborhood, which has long been known as the poorest postal code in Canada, was adjacent to the official 2010 Olympic Village. Between 2008 and 2010, over 1,500 market-rate units of housing—mostly condominiums—were built in Downtown Eastside; during the same period, over 1,600 affordable units of housing were lost in the area. The housing churn, activists believed, was the result of Olympics-fueled speculation. In response, housing activists set up what they dubbed an "Olympic tent village" in the heart of Downtown Eastside. They took over a parking lot owned by a major developer, set up about 150 tents, and created a twenty-four-hour community space, complete with free meals, a conflict resolution system, and even recycling (see figure 8.13). Pressure brought by the encampment resulted in over forty homeless residents of the tent village securing long-term housing; the village itself served as a reminder that urban space is highly political and that urban dwellers working together can determine how spaces in their city are used.

Figure 8.13   Building the Olympic tent village in Downtown Eastside, Vancouver. (Photo by Angela Wakefield, 2010)

Another question is that of income inequality in cities. Increasingly, many US cities are experiencing growing income equality between the rich and the poor. Issues of inequality rise to the fore in many instances: in public schools, where schools in wealthier neighborhoods, because they receive private donations from parents, may be superior to schools in poor neighborhoods; in city services, where funding for services for low-income families, such as subsidized child care, may be pitted against services that are perceived to cater to higher-income people, such as dog parks; and above all in housing, where increasing gentrification in some city centers threatens to displace lower-income, long-term residents who cannot afford rents bid up by higher-income newcomers. What income inequality means for urban life and how it can be addressed are questions planners will need to take seriously.

A third question is the relationship between planning and heightened security efforts. In the wake of 9/11, cities have tightened their security by adding security cameras, increasing inspection of packages on public transportation, cordoning off buildings that are perceived to be in danger of attack, and other means (see figure 8.14). In cities along the US-Mexico border, urban planners may need to deal with the regulation of border spaces. The relationship between city planning and law enforcement—including both

Figure 8.14   Security in Philadelphia. (Photo by Lisa Benton-Short)

Figure 8.15   The People's Library at the Occupy DC encampment in McPherson Square. (Photo by Elvert Barnes, 2011)

local police and federal forces—is one that planners increasingly will need to confront.

Finally, all these challenges relate to the future of public space. In the fall of 2011, the Occupy Wall Street movement filled US public spaces with protestors. The protests, one *Washington Post* reporter noted, "have done what so many planners, designers and architects strive for but fail to achieve: They have 'activated' the urban core." The protests made downtowns come alive, but in very particular ways. In Washington, DC, and many other cities, the

People's Library in the Occupy encampments played an important role in stimulating discussions (see figure 8.15). As Occupy Wall Street encampments around the country have shown, urban space is political. Planning is an attempt to mediate amid the politics and arrive at a solution that works for the greater common good. The best-laid plains can fail: in a city, people will always disagree. Good planning can help make good cities, but ultimately, the best cities are created collectively by the people who dwell in them together.

Box 8.6 Detroit: Citizen Participation in Remaking a Shrinking City

The city of Detroit is shrinking. Once an industrial powerhouse with well-paying jobs that launched thousands into the middle class, it is now a decaying city, deserted by employers and workers alike. From 1950 to 2010, the city's population plunged from 1.85 million to just over 714,000. Between 1970 and 2000, 161,111 buildings were demolished, and only 9,000 building permits were issued. Today, one-third of the city's enormous land mass is vacant: many parts of central Detroit, overtaken by high grasses, resemble the prairie (see figure 8.16). The unemployment rate is over 20 percent. As the 2012 award-winning documentary film *Detropia* illustrates, the city is going through wrenching times.

The city, working with input from city planners from across the country, has come up with a plan to "rightsize" Detroit. Rightsizing means cutting services to certain parts of the city and concentrating residents in a central area that could be more efficiently connected to city services like sewer lines and trash collection. Other deindustrializing cities are embracing rightsizing policies as well, including Youngstown, Ohio, and cities in the former East Germany.

But the idea of rightsizing has caused tension in Detroit because it would require people to leave their homes and resettle in other neighborhoods. So the city has stopped using the term "rightsizing" and is now insisting it will not use eminent domain to force people to move. As of this writing, it is therefore unclear exactly how the city is going to shrink itself.

In the meantime, people who live in Detroit aren't waiting for the city to come up with a plan. Because there is so much vacant land, there has been real creativity on the part of the people of Detroit in terms of how to use that land. One of the ways people are using the land is for growing food. Indeed, an urban gardening renaissance has begun in Detroit. The Detroit Garden Resource Program began working with eighty community gardens and urban farms in 2004, and as of 2009, it was working with 875: a tenfold increase in five years. The group estimates that today there are 1,500 community gardens and farms in the city. Because there is not a single national chain grocery store in the entire city, these gardens are filling a real, practical need for accessible produce.

Detroit residents are also starting to rethink how to revitalize their economy more broadly. Some Detroiters argue that just as their city once represented the American ideal in terms of enabling working people to achieve middle-class status on a large scale, its residents can today take the lead in terms of thinking through how to reenvision work and the economy writ large. As longtime Detroit activist Grace Lee Boggs writes, "Detroit is a city of Hope rather than a city of Despair. The thousands of vacant lots and abandoned houses provide not only the space to begin anew but also the incentive to create innovative ways of making our living—ways that nurture our productive, cooperative, and caring selves." Detroit may yet be a model for the future of urban America—both in terms of planning and in terms of larger questions of remaking the economy and work.

Figure 8.16   The twenty-first-century Detroit prairie. This intersection is a nine-minute drive from downtown Detroit. (Photo by Amanda Huron, 2011)

SUGGESTED READINGS

Bloom, B., and A. Bromberg, eds. 2004. *Making Their Own Plans/Belltown Paradise*. Chicago: White Walls Press.

Bratt, R. G., M. E. Stone, and C. Hartman, eds. 2006. *A Right to Housing: Foundation for a New Social Agenda*. Philadelphia: Temple University Press.

Fainstein, S. S., and S. Campbell, eds. 2011. *Readings in Planning Theory*. 3rd ed. New York: Wiley-Blackwell.

Friedman, J. 1987. *Planning in the Public Domain: From Knowledge to Action*. Princeton, NJ: Princeton University Press.

Hall, P. 1988. *Cities of Tomorrow*. 3rd ed. Oxford: Blackwell.

Jacobs, J. 1961. *The Death and Life of Great American Cities*. New York: Random House.

Larson, E. 2003. *The Devil in the White City*. New York: Vintage.

Logan, J. R., and H. L. Molotch. 1987. *Urban Fortunes: The Political Economy of Place*. Berkeley: University of California Press.

Medoff, P., and H. Sklar. 1994. *Streets of Hope: The Fall and Rise of an Urban Neighborhood*. Boston: South End Press.

Platt, R. H., R. A. Rowntree, and P. C. Muick, eds. 1994. *The Ecological City: Preserving and Restoring Urban Biodiversity*. Amherst: University of Massachusetts Press.

Thomas, J., and M. Ritzdorf, eds. 1997. *Urban Planning and the African American Community: In the Shadows*. Thousand Oaks, CA: Sage.

CITIES ON THE WEB

Planetizen: The Urban Planning, Design, and Development Network: http://www.planetizen.com/.

Planners Network: The Organization of Progressive Planning: http://www.plannersnetwork.org/.

American Planning Association: http://www.planning.org/.

UCLA Graduate Students Association in the Urban Planning Department publishes a graduate-run journal: http://luskin.ucla.edu/urban-planning/student-organizations/critical-planning.

For a lively discussion about making public spaces more interesting, see the Ted Talk "Liz Diller: A Giant Bubble for Debate": http://www.ted.com/talks/liz_diller_a_giant_bubble_for_debate.html?utm_source=newsletter_weekly_2012-05-02&utm_campaign=newsletter_weekly&utm_medium=email.

In addition, the following films are suggested:

Ewing, H., and R. Grady, dirs. 2012. *Detropia* [film]. New York: Loki Films.

Freidrichs, C., dir. 2011. *The Pruitt-Igoe Myth* [film]. New York: First Run Features.

Whyte, W. H., dir. 1979. *The Social Life of Small Urban Spaces* [film]. New York: Municipal Art Society of New York.

III

URBAN SOCIAL/CULTURAL CHALLENGES

9

Urban Inequities

DEBORAH G. MARTIN

Urban areas are filled with all manner of differences and inequalities. The excitement and bustle of North American cities often showcase the successes of urban processes—large commercial districts; tall, beautiful steel and glass buildings with incredible views; seemingly every contemporary make and model of car on busy streets; billboards advertising the latest television, movies, and fashion; and people of all ages, dressed for work, play, and recreation, moving through busy streets and sidewalks in cars, on foot, on bikes, and in strollers. In smaller cities, there may be fewer people or less variety of activities, but key areas—often downtowns or funky neighborhoods with restored historic homes—highlight the affluence and comfort that urban life offers to many. But urban areas large and small have another side, the side of people struggling in anonymity to feed themselves and their families, people who may work tirelessly in jobs with little opportunity for advancement, or people who have given up on work, who struggle more invisibly with mental demons that plague their days with confusion or with addictions that drive them to seek out drugs or alcohol through any means that they can. We don't usually seek out these other sides of cities; and policy makers and private businesses alike do their best to make them

less visible to us: to hide the seamy side of urban processes that generate so much growth and wealth through capital flows—the buying and selling of goods, services, knowledge, and property—throughout metropolitan areas.

Understanding urban areas in North America means confronting the contrasts between wealth and poverty. Geographers link these physical and social contrasts to the spatiality of these gulfs—the locations of haves and have-nots. While inequality, particularly as measured by income, is not unique to cities, urban areas often offer stark visual contrasts in the landscape that highlight proximate inequality in specific ways. Consider, for example, a view from a pedestrian street in Ottawa, Canada's tourist-oriented Byward Market area (figure 9.1), where different groups of people sit on the sidewalk. A quick visual survey of the street on a nice outdoor day shows some people sitting at a restaurant where they have purchased something to drink. Next to them, in front of the next storefront, is another group of people, sitting in a doorway, with backpacks and sports bags next to them and in front of them along the sidewalk. They are black; the restaurant-goers are white. The juxtaposition of people differentiated by race and possibly class or income demonstrates the inequalities that urban areas produce and

Figure 9.1   City streets—encounters with inequality. Byward
Market area, Ottawa. (Photo by Karen Hill)

contain. Such a scene demands that we consider what produces inequality, how we can "see" it in the landscape, and what it might mean to ask about it. In this chapter, we examine some of the social and economic processes that have historically produced inequality in North American cities and current dimensions of inequality, focusing primarily on race, class, and housing, particularly using social service provision as a case-study framework.

Cities are places where differentiation occurs—where people can specialize in some activities, buying goods or services from other people for those things that they don't do themselves. Such specialization is called the division of labor, because it means that people do specific jobs or activities to economically support themselves, each having different skills and wages. Cities foster economic difference and specialization—innovation, creativity, and the coming together of people with different backgrounds and experiences.

The economic diversity of cities is evident in a variety of ways, from the jobs that people do to land uses and activities. For geographers, identifying difference is about not only the thing or people who differ but the spatial pattern of difference—difference is geographical. The geography of difference, or what we might call the spatial patterns, as well as the things (people, activities, jobs, land uses) that are different, can create inequality. The spatial patterns of difference mean that some groups have more opportunities and resources than others. It is important to understand that while people make choices about where they live and what they do, there are also structural processes—laws and markets, for example—that shape the decisions people can and do make.

In thinking about processes that create and make evident inequality, it is important to differentiate between what is mere difference and what is unequal (and whether inequality is necessarily bad). Cities bring together and host a wide range of differences, from activities to urban denizens themselves—in terms of background, ethnicity, race, culture, class, religion, sexuality, and so on. It is not difference itself that defines inequality but the ways that it is produced and its sociospatial pattern. One kind of difference in North American cities that is a topic of this chapter is segregation, meaning that people of different races or ethnicities may live in different neighborhoods from one another. With voluntary segregation, people choose to live with people who look like them, or worship like them, for example, whereas involuntary segregation means people cannot choose to live wherever they want with any other groups of people. People do not always agree on which inequalities are concerns of social justice—indeed, sometimes inequality just reflects different priorities and traditions or serves as a motivation for creativity and change. Nonetheless, persistent, deep inequalities among people caused by income differences, but also combined with race and ethnicity, are a form of difference that is highly visible in North American cities, and it poses a challenge to the notion that opportunities exist for all people to thrive socially and economically in the United States and Canada.

Geography helps us think about forms of difference in the city, how they happen, and whether they express social, economic, and political inequalities that we should worry about. In both Canada and the United States, equality of opportunity is an important part of national identity and democratic values. Indeed, both countries celebrate difference in their social diversity—Canada as a multicultural mosaic, the United States as a diverse "melting pot" of immigrants. In this chapter,

we confront and examine how geographers understand and connect difference in land use and urban function—difference in economy and value—with social differences such as class, race, and ethnicity, and what sort of inequalities result.

LAND USE AND URBAN FUNCTION

One of the simplest and most overt forms of inequality is differences in land use throughout metropolitan areas. These differences historically existed but were spatially proximate—houses with shops at the front or on the first floor were a staple of eighteenth- and nineteenth-century North American towns and cities. Yet differentiation occurred, both through development of new forms of transportation and the land needed for it and through suburbanization and increasing separation of home and paid work (see box 9.1).

In North American cities, two forms of transportation that have drastically affected the look and organization of land uses are railroads and automobiles, with their associated road networks. These transportation networks need to be near manufacturing and commercial districts and have helped to shape and delineate the geographical patterns of different land uses. They also helped to differentiate forms of work and their locations. Cities such as Calgary, Toronto, Cincinnati, and Chicago, for example, developed extensive stockyards in the early twentieth century, where livestock from ranching lands in the midwestern and western parts of the continent were shipped by rail to be butchered, packaged, and shipped to customers within these cities and other urban centers for wholesale and retail markets and, finally, consumption. In

Box 9.1 Geographical Perspectives on Land Use, Divisions of Labor, and Changing Meanings of Space

North American cities are distinguished in part by their sometimes severe distinctions in land use, which in turn shape expectations about who uses certain urban spaces and when. Some North American urban downtowns are quite empty and quiet after 5:00 p.m. on a weekday, for example, because of the intensity of business uses and dearth of dining, entertainment, or residential land uses. Groups of people in such a downtown late at night could engender scrutiny because of a lack of land uses that would draw them there at that time. Social norms and land-use patterns together foster particular landscape expectations. Indeed, residential segregation has fostered expectations about residents that sometimes have deadly consequences, as when a white resident of a Florida suburb shot an African American teenager walking to his father's house. As in that tragic case, expectations about land use and its users are embedded in our social relations and our imaginaries of place and each other. But these subtly change over time, as do the characteristics of any particular urban location.

Changes in economy and culture produce changes in social norms and physical infrastructure, which help to reshape the city itself. An illustration of such shifts is provided by the urban histories of scholars such as Kate Boyer and Jessica Ellen Sewell, who have investigated how changes in gender divisions in the workplace in the early twentieth century actually helped to transform downtown spaces.

Nineteenth-century North American downtowns had spaces that were delineated for middle- and upper-income women—department stores such as Marshall Field's in Chicago, Macy's in New York, or Hudson's Bay Company in Toronto and Montreal. These establishments created spaces that catered to and made acceptable the downtown leisure of (a certain class of) women. Department stores established grand entrances and salon rooms where women could enter and recharge while shopping downtown. While these spaces provided opportunities and justification for middle- and upper-income women to use downtown spaces *as consumers*, the growth of clerical work in commercial offices, such as corporate headquarters, legitimated the use of downtown spaces for working-class women *as workers*. Conceptualizing women as downtown workers, however, established a different sort and space of interaction between women and men, as women who worked tended to be young and unmarried (because once they married, these women were expected to remain at home, raise children, and care for the household). Some corporations went to great lengths to keep women and men apart as much as possible through the use of separate work entrances and dining facilities. However, in downtowns more generally, businesses and public spaces developed that catered to women workers. These shifts helped to transform social mores around mixed-gender public spaces as twentieth-century cities grew. In studying these changes, scholars such as Boyer and Sewell draw on public and private documents that illustrate predominant social attitudes, such as advertising, personal diaries, and corporate personnel documents, and link these to the physical geographies of North American downtowns and workplaces.

Today, geographers use cases of urban conflict to highlight sociospatial attitudes, whether they be conflicts over "racial profiling" by police or seemingly mundane land-use conflicts. For example, as cities have increasingly zoned for "mixed-use" urban spaces to create twenty-four-hour downtowns and greater urban sustainability, they have at times fostered conflicts between land uses. One such type of conflict is between nighttime dining and entertainment and proximate residential areas. Issues such as parking and late-night noise foster conflicts between residential and entertainment uses when they are closely located in urban areas. In the Buckhead district of Atlanta, Georgia, the proximity of a high-income residential area and a popular district for shopping and late-night dining and dancing fostered an upscale, racially diverse entertainment district in the 1990s and early 2000s. At the same time, however, despite shifting sociospatial norms around race and ethnicity, the clash between residents and business leaders, on the one hand, and the entertainment functions, on the other, made bare the social tension of racial difference. Geographers Katherine Hankins and colleagues trace the dynamics of these tensions through interviews with city leaders and Buckhead business owners and residents and through archival analysis of newspaper coverage that traced the contested spaces of Buckhead and its remaking into a luxury retail district. They argue that race was an unstated (and in some cases, denied) but deeply important social relation shaping the process that eventually razed the dozens of bars and nightclubs in an attempt to "restore" the district to a place of whiteness and wealth. A similar, though less racialized, set of dynamics contributed to the "restoration" of primarily residential zoning to a former entertainment district in Toronto, Ontario, in the 2000s as well. The back-and-forth changes in land use and social relations in cities highlight the continual evolution of urban space and the contestations and inequalities among urban denizens.

the past thirty or so years, many of these lands have been abandoned and redeveloped, signaling the twentieth-century shift from a predominantly industrial urban economy and landscape to one shaped more by land development around consumption: retail and entertainment in particular.

As discussed in chapter 5, economic shifts shaped cultural and social changes, as the manufacturing and industrial jobs requiring little in the way of formal education but offering good pay have declined in number and service-oriented jobs with relatively low wages and benefits have increased. As a result, education—which requires investments by households and government—has become ever more important for economic growth, both at the national and individual level. Families struggling to make ends meet may need the extra paycheck that a teenage child can provide, but such work commitments can interfere with high school and may lead to dropping out or lower achievement levels, which undermines access to college and scholarships to help pay for it. Changes in urban economies, therefore, have unequal outcomes at the household level as well as in the urban economy and landscape overall.

Urban land use is a reflection of, as well as an influence on, the urban economy. A key legal mechanism for guiding the location of various land uses is municipal zoning. Zoning by definition creates an unequal landscape of land use because it defines where various activities are allowed and where they cannot locate. Housing, for example, is designated by planners and enforced through zoning maps for some areas but not others, while downtown cores are preserved for commercial and key transit uses along with some government functions, and industrial districts are placed alongside ports and railroads. Of course, much of planning and zoning attends to patterns set over time, and the separation of land uses was historically important for the establishment of specific functions and areas within cities—such as retail districts where people could shop, manufacturing areas where workers could live near factories, and key transportation arteries to bring people and products to and from cities.

Starting in the first quarter of the twentieth century, formal differentiation of land use through zoning was a way for city governments to establish specific areas for different purposes—residential districts, manufacturing, commercial, transportation, and so on. It made sense for areas that might produce noise and unpleasant odors, for example, to be far from residential areas. In the United States, the Supreme Court decision of 1926 in *Euclid v. Amber Realty Co.*, for the village in Ohio (and the real-estate company) where zoning was challenged, is based on the idea that municipalities have a right to zone as part of their general police powers and charge to maintain public safety. While some property owners have viewed zoning as a restriction on their private property rights, the separation of functions through zoning also ensures predictability of land markets by identifying and protecting land uses in an area. For residential areas, homeowners or developers of land designated for residential uses could be sure that the surrounding neighborhoods would not contain what were perceived to be negative influences on land value. It would be ideal, for example, to purchase a home and know that no one can build a factory or put a racetrack next door. One important element of land value is social differentiation—that is, the ability of an area to seem exclusive. Exclusivity is based on limiting land uses or on limiting access of different people to certain areas. When functions or people are physically separated in space based on social divisions, they are called segregated.

SEGREGATION

Segregation usually refers to the spatial separation of people based on social characteristics, although it can also refer to the separation of functions (such as manufacturing away from commercial districts). It is measured a number of different ways, by looking at spatial dispersion of different groups across a given area (such as a city) or by looking at the relative concentration of particular social groups in space. The index of dissimilarity is one measure that compares the residential dispersion across a physical space of one group within society with that of another group, usually a (more numerically) dominant one. For example, one might examine whether college students are residentially segregated compared with college professors, or Asians compared with whites. Scholars can calculate an index of dissimilarity that compares a random statistical distribution of the population under examination to its actual distribution in urban space. The most common indexes investigate the residential patterns of racial and ethnic groups. Measures of segregation are highly sensitive to overall proportionality of the groups under analysis. In other words, a population that is only 1 percent of a given area will seem highly segregated even if statistically it is widely distributed across a given geographical area, because it is such a

small proportion of the total. In measuring segregation, the size of the areal units will also impact the results; for example, the larger the geographical units, the less a population will seem segregated from another group. Figure 9.2 shows segregation for Detroit, and figure 9.3 highlights Chicago.

Understanding segregation in North American cities requires some examination of how social categories such as race, ethnicity, religion, or class have historically had meaning, and how those meanings have shifted (and continue to shift) until today. In order to make judgments about the significance of segregation, we distinguish between voluntary

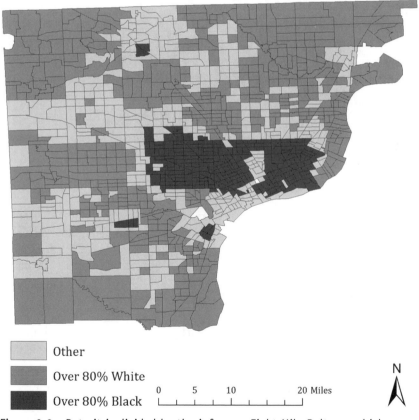

Other

Over 80% White

Over 80% Black

0   5   10   20 Miles

N

Figure 9.2   Detroit is divided by the infamous Eight Mile Beltway, which serves as the clear boundary for the city's black and white populations. *Source:* US Census Bureau.

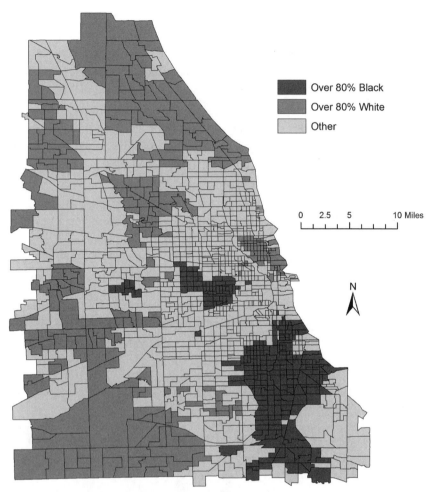

Figure 9.3   The Chicago black ghetto has not disappeared. According to 2010 census figures, the ghetto has stabilized as two large areas on the West and South Side of Chicago. The dark gray marks census tracts that are 80 percent black. The medium gray areas, mainly in the suburbs, are 80 percent white. *Source:* US Census Bureau.

and involuntary segregation. For example, we might see the separation of people by social group as a "natural" and voluntary outcome of the tendency for people to want to live near and interact with like-minded people with similar backgrounds and values. Such a perspective views residential segregation as an interesting spatial expression of social norms, but not as anything pernicious or problematic. In fact, for some social groups, segregation can foster support networks and enable people to find jobs, build businesses, and succeed in a new country by drawing on shared language and values of other immigrants from the same area. Chinatowns in many cities, for example, started out in the 1850s–1900s as the only places where Chinese immigrants could live because of hostility and discrimination from largely white majorities in cities such as Chicago, Vancouver, and San Francisco. Such segregation was involuntary. In the past thirty to forty years, however, these areas close to downtowns with distinct Chinese architecture and thriving businesses became tourist attractions, in some cases because of a shared effort by Chinese business leaders and city officials to improve the areas' infrastructures and market them for tourists. So the negative of discrimination and segregation created an ethnic enclave that both fostered the growth of Chinese businesses and later became vibrant and valued commercial districts within their cities. As illustrated by Chinatowns in North America, segregation has distinct patterns and effects that can change over time.

The difference between an enclave and a ghetto is primarily the degree to which the separation of that ethnic group is a choice by that group or imposed by the host society and the ability of the group to participate in the broader economy outside of the segregated neighborhood. Ghettos historically were enforced by law and today are limited or maintained primarily by severe economic deprivation that keeps the ghettoized population from being able to integrate into other neighborhoods. Whether segregated neighborhoods function as enclaves that offer benefits like social support and cultural expression to their residents depends a great deal on the internal resources of the community and on its reception and linkages with other communities and government. Where some segregated communities, such as those of Chinese immigrants in the twentieth century, fostered business growth and social support, others, such as poor, predominantly black ghettos in cities like Chicago, Detroit, or East St. Louis, embody the idea that separation fosters isolation and decline. The significance of segregation lies not simply

in the fact of a geographical pattern but in the social impacts of that separation. Measuring segregation is not enough, therefore, if we want to understand how it affects people and the cities in which they live. If, for example, blacks are highly residentially segregated in a given city, and schools are neighborhood based, it means that black and white children will be unlikely to encounter each other in the same schools. Furthermore, if such a racial pattern is overlaid by an economic segregation, in which schools in some areas—white neighborhoods—are much better funded and have better educational outcomes, then segregation has an impact beyond mere social separation. Its impact fosters an achievement gap that is unequal because it is the product of the residential segregation.

Suburbanization of North American cities is one force that, in some cases, fosters and exacerbates race and class inequality in urban areas. In the twentieth century, the advent of internal combustion engines changed rural as well as urban work, which helped to solidify urban-oriented industrial economies as farm labor decreased while urban-based factory work increased. Subsequently, in the second half of the century, suburbanization of the middle class expanded to more working-class residents, enabling them to use cars and new roadways to spread ever farther from workplaces. At the same time, however, the relatively new forces of zoning were deployed in ways designed to "protect" suburban residential areas from difference, be it due to social cleavages or land-use variation. In the United States, protective "covenants" ensured that homeowners in some exclusive areas were barred from selling their homes to anyone except existing (often white, middle-class, and Protestant) social groups of that area. Slowly, these racial covenants were overturned by courts.

Racial segregation in residential areas, within urban city centers and across metropolitan areas, has been to some degree a feature in US and Canadian cities for much of the second half of the twentieth century. In the United States, segregation declined in the 1990s and 2000s, but segregation of visible minorities actually increased in many Canadian cities. Because of differences in census data between the two countries, the pattern is much more explicit and known in US cities than in Canadian cities. Cities in the United States are generally highly segregated by race, even when income is taken into account. For example, a 2000 study by Joe Darden and Sameh Kamel shows that blacks and whites, even of the same income categories, are generally segregated from each other. Since 1990, however, segregation of all groups has declined—that is, with increasing residential mobility, blacks, Latinos, and Asians now live in more diverse neighborhoods, although whites and blacks are still unlikely to live in the same neighborhoods. Indeed, the most affluent blacks in the United States are more likely to live in poorer neighborhoods than the most affluent whites. While it is relatively easy to see that residential segregation occurs, it is harder to judge its significance in and of itself. Patterns of residential racial segregation coexist with other measures of racialized inequality—that is, inequality that is coincident with, and intertwined in, the category of ethnic background and/or skin color. In particular, educational achievement, overall average household wealth, and percentage of a given population in poverty all vary in North America by race (see figure 9.4), and, as measured through analyses of US Census data, all are worse on average for black households than for white households (with Asian households closer to the levels of white households and Latino households generally lower than Asian but higher than black households). These average trends are overall trends with lots of variation by region and specific household type. However, the very notion of specific racially identifiable households is somewhat problematic as far as generalizations, especially because the national censuses in both countries now recognize "multiple" racial or ancestry categories for individuals.

Segregation's Consequences

For North American cities, despite the problems with measuring or defining what race means, we can recognize a range of types of segregation—by land use, economic activity, and household residential characteristics—and examine what sort of differences coincide, and question whether these inequalities matter for sociospatial outcomes. We might ask whether poverty is concentrated spatially, and if so, the related social and landscape effects. Concentrated poverty can be visibly evident in commercial streets with few retail outlets, neglected potholes, trash blowing in the streets, graffiti on buildings, and residential buildings with peeling paint, sagging stairs, and boarded windows. It is also evident socially in schools with high numbers of economically disadvantaged children who arrive at school hungry (and may, thankfully, be fed via government free and reduced-price breakfast and lunch programs), who often have poor educational outcomes, and who subsequently have few job prospects. For example, in heavily segregated metropolitan Detroit, Michigan, vast tracks of abandoned

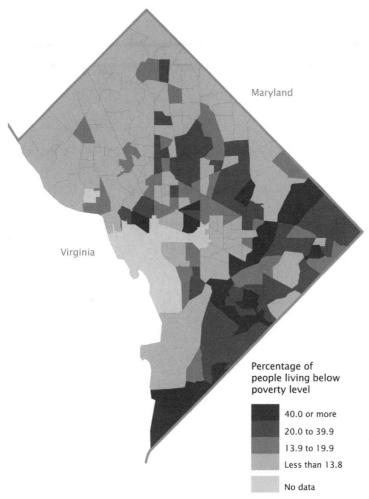

Figure 9.4   This map of poverty in Washington, DC, is strongly correlated with race. In the southeast of the city, where poverty is highest, the population averages more than 90 percent black. *Source:* US Census Bureau.

land typify the city landscape. The school system lacks resources and, as a result of population decline, is underenrolled. Meanwhile, neighboring suburbs such as Grosse Pointe, Michigan, have long boasted some of the best schools in the state. These patterns are outcomes, but also underlying causes, of long-standing racial segregation in the Detroit area. As geographer and legal scholar David Delaney has pointed out, the legal

challenges to school segregation in Detroit in the early 1970s achieved a resolution that stopped at the city's boundaries. What that meant was that Detroit had to integrate its racially segregated schools, but its surrounding suburbs were excluded from the required busing remedy. Yet the suburbs were growing and were increasingly white. As Detroit's infrastructure and tax base declined in the face of rising international competition to the US car industry in the 1970s, population fell as "white flight" occurred with middle- and upper-income and predominantly white families settling in suburban areas. Partly as a result, the city of Detroit by 2000 had a population that was over 80 percent black. School segregation became an issue of a black city district and primarily white subur- ban district, and the two systems remained completely separate.

The fact of a "majority-minority" city is not unusual in the United States (although less common in Canada) and points to the complexities of difference and inequality. (In the United States, "majority-minority" usu- ally refers to cities with a majority black population; in Canada, such a city does not exist, but Toronto, Ontario, has almost half its population designated as "visible minority," and there are several suburban municipalities, including Markham and Brampton in the Toronto region, that have minority-majority populations.) There are several reasons for this difference between US and Canadian cit- ies. First, large municipalities in Canada dilute the effect of racial concentration, and second, racial concentration (through immigration) in Canada's cities is very recent. Atlanta, Geor- gia, with over 50 percent of its population African American, is a majority-minority city, but it also enjoys a reputation as one of the economic powerhouses of the United States, with vibrant financial, consumer services, manufacturing, and transportation industries (Equifax, CNN, Coca-Cola, and Delta Air- lines all have their headquarters there; by contrast, Detroit's one major headquartered company is General Motors). Nonetheless, as in many cities in North America, schools are a source of tension that highlights the underlying segregation and inequality of race and class. In some cities, the problems and challenges of schools have been addressed in part by activist parents, some of whom have helped to spur the charter school movement (see box 9.2).

Box 9.2 Atlanta, Georgia, and the Challenges of Urban Schools

The city of Atlanta, Georgia, has over four hundred thousand people, more than 50 percent black, in a metropolitan region that is home to more than five million people. Atlanta is a sprawling city, with twenty counties in its census-defined metropolitan area. The city is a major business capital, headquarters to companies ranging from retail and manufacturing giants to telecommunications and power industries, including Coca-Cola, Home Depot, Delta Airlines, Southern Company, CNN, and SunTrust Banks. Like the United States as a whole, it has a painful and significant racial history (including having much of the city burned by Northern troops during the Civil War). Atlanta was formally and informally segregated along a north-south, white-black "color line" up until the desegregation orders of federal courts that started in the 1950s in schools and extended in the 1960s to housing and labor markets. Desegregation of schools coincided with housing and social forces that fostered significant "white flight" from the city to the suburbs. In some parts of high-income Atlanta such as northern Buckhead neighborhood, rather than move to the suburbs, white families increasingly sent their children to private schools. Many public schools became concentrated with poor children, especially after housing antidiscrimination law enabled middle- and upper-income black families to suburbanize as well.

By the early 2000s, Atlanta's black and poor children were disproportionately represented in the public school system: in 2012, 78 percent of all students were African American, and almost 75 percent of all students qualified for the federal free and reduced-price lunch program. This profile of the public schools does not match that of the city overall, however. Along with Atlanta's extensive sprawl has been a great deal of urban neighborhood investment, and Atlanta is home to several high-income, diverse or majority white neighborhoods. Its historic housing stock, paired with investments in a public transportation system that includes light rail and urban renewal along former industrial rail corridors, have encouraged middle-class settlement in several neighborhoods in the northern, northeastern, and eastern quadrants of the city in particular. This gentrification has been paired with an activist sensibility on the part of many middle-class parents in the school system. As a result, the quality and characteristics of schools vary significantly by local neighborhood geography. As detailed in research by Elizabeth Henry and Katherine Hankins, some white families worked to create a culture of white investment in the neighborhoods and schools. Activism around neighborhood identity and resistance to highway construction fostered a network of parents who remained engaged with the public school system and campaigned for their neighbors—some of them gentrifiers in the 1980s and 1990s—to use the public school system. With the growth of alternative "charter" schools, some of these neighborhood activists found a new direction for their civic engagement, that of founding and supporting publicly funded schools that operate outside of the usual public school regulations and that could be geographically targeted to serve certain neighborhoods. The resulting pattern is one common in many American cities, with a small number of public schools highly regarded and successful while disproportionately white and middle or upper income, and a larger number of schools struggling to educate poor and largely minority children.

HOUSING

The topic of schools and residential segregation highlights the important role of housing in urban areas as the site for urban social service delivery—especially and most frequently schools and parks, but also police, firefighters, and garbage collection. Housing is a significant category of land use, one that, because of the urban services that support it, tends to cost more in city services than it produces in tax revenue. The stereotype of North American cities is to contrast a socially and economically diverse urban central city with socially homogenous residential suburban towns. In the North America of the twentieth century, such an image does not match reality. Racially and ethnically diverse suburban residential areas coexist along with exclusive, predominantly white urban enclaves. Suburbs are also home to many corporate headquarters and back offices as well as retail malls.

North American suburban areas are perhaps more likely than some central cities to be the "gateway" residential neighborhoods for new immigrants, and high-cost, high-amenity neighborhoods exist in downtowns as well as in secluded suburbs. North American cities overall share many commonalities in housing, including a mix of denser housing, such as apartment (rental) and condominium (owner-occupied) buildings, as well as areas with single-family homes with a range of lot sizes. These housing types exist in central cities as well as suburbs, although the characteristics of apartment blocks in downtown areas vary significantly from those in suburban locations. Certainly, the amount of density as compared to houses with yards varies significantly from city to city, depending on the particular historical eras of city growth, local land-use regulations, and demographic trends. In New York City or Toronto, for example, many people live in high-rises, rely on public transportation, and experience urban life very much in terms of a built environment. Yet in other areas, such as Chicago, Calgary, or Phoenix, the built environment is quite low-rise outside of the central business district, and people at a wide range of income levels live in single-family homes or duplexes with small yards. Some people live in areas that are truly accessible only by car, and the landscape is dominated by grass with some trees—how large they are depends on how old the houses are—and there may be sidewalks, but they curve with the streets and may not go anywhere outside of the housing development. The presence of a variety of housing types in most metropolitan areas does not mean that everyone has equal choices in housing. Housing in most places is structured as an individual consumer decision, based on personal preferences and knowledge, economic resources, and market factors such as supply of housing. The "market" factors are shaped by the political and economic processes that foster certain kinds of residential development—so what people choose as far as housing is shaped (and constrained) by the landscape of offerings.

For much of the twentieth century, shifts in transportation and manufacturing technologies, as well as government policies, helped to transform North American cities by land use. The United States and Canada have each had different government approaches to provision of housing, especially for those in poverty, which has shaped varying urban landscapes in each country. Housing is one sector where these changes fostered dramatic shifts in how people live and get around in their cities. Although suburbanization was already occurring in the second half of the nineteenth century, it was the development of transportation systems in North America, particularly streetcars, that enabled working classes as well as middle classes to move to geographically dispersed and less dense areas outside of the central cities and core manufacturing sites. Working-class residential suburbs developed in proximity to suburban factory locations. Cities grew even more dispersed and geographically extensive with the development of automobiles and the concomitant rise in government-funded road and highway construction (see box 9.3).

Government Policies and Public Housing

Although these patterns affected cities in both countries, the degree of suburbanization, single-use zoning, and highway construction over public transportation investments differed significantly between them. As introduced in chapter 5, in the United States, significant federal investment in the interstate highway system, in addition to post–World War II investments in education

Box 9.3 Boston, Massachusetts: Urban Growth and Change

Boston, Massachusetts, has been a center of US economy and politics since the colonial era. Along with cities like Charleston, South Carolina, Savannah, Georgia, and Philadelphia, Pennsylvania, its contemporary identity lies in part in its role in the history of the United States from colonialism and especially through independence. Geographically, the city has a dense, historic urban core that, despite changes over four centuries, maintains strong retail, commercial, and residential functions.

As a colonial city, Boston experienced waves of migration as different groups of immigrants arrived and settled there. In the nineteenth century, Boston was an important site for immigrants from Ireland and Italy, creating a social divide between the city's Protestant elites and Catholic newcomers—the latter of whom eventually also become prominent in city and national politics, as with the Kennedy family. The city grew geographically as rail transportation, subways, and highways helped foster expansion, despite its core density and location on the Massachusetts Bay. Much of the contemporary city is a mix of formerly rail suburbs that were annexed by Boston, plus a more auto-oriented set of independent town suburbs beyond. Its metropolitan footprint today extends from New Hampshire to Rhode Island.

Within the city limits, former towns maintain their distinct monikers and identities in neighborhoods such as Mattapan, Dorchester, and Roxbury. Today these neighborhoods are predominantly minority and poorer than the city as a whole. They experienced depopulation of white residents ("white flight") in the 1960s and 1970s caused in part by (sometimes violent) opposition to busing in the mid-1970s to desegregate the public school system. Nonetheless, unlike some other US cities such as Atlanta, Detroit, Chicago, or Cleveland, which also struggled with school desegregation, Boston remains, according to US 2010 Census data, a majority (54 percent) white city, with less than 25 percent black, and with significant percentages of both Asian (over 8 percent) and Latino (over 17 percent) residents. Indeed, some of the city's investments in magnet and so-called testing schools, where students qualify for admission based on achievement tests, have helped to produce some extremely high-quality public schools.

Boston's contemporary role in the twenty-first-century North American political economy includes being a base for higher education (Boston University, Boston College, Harvard, Massachusetts Institute of Technology, Brandeis University, and Wellesley College are just some of the colleges or universities based in the city or one of its suburbs); financial and insurance industry giants (such as Bain Capital, Fidelity Investments, and Liberty Mutual Insurance); and manufacturers such as New Balance and Bose. The city itself has over six hundred thousand people, but it is the metropolitan area with more than four million people in 2010 that houses much of the economic activity; Boston's Route 128 corridor, later expanded and overlaid with Interstate 93 and then replicated farther west with a second "ring road" in Interstate 495,was one of the first to develop into an economic innovation corridor, with pioneering high-technology industries such as Polaroid, Wang Laboratories, Digital Equipment Corporation, and Raytheon. At the same time, downtown areas, such as Boylston Street in figure 9.5, attract many affluent residents and tourists for shopping and dining.

Figure 9.5   This upscale neighborhood on Boylston Street is in Boston's historic urban core and has maintained strong retail, commercial, and residential functions. (Photo by Lisa Benton-Short)

and housing for veterans, accelerated the development of suburban residential areas for families from working, through middle, to upper incomes. The federal government also subsidized the mortgage market through the development of a real-estate appraisal system and a tax structure that allowed for mortgage interest deduction, helping to fuel suburban residential development and, ultimately, sprawl. Housing for the lowest-income families was provided as part of urban renewal, which resulted in the razing of entire blocks of older urban residential and mixed-use buildings and replacing them with "public housing." The predominant image of public housing in the United States is a large complex of modern, inner-city apartment blocks, surrounded by walking paths, empty space, and some surface parking. In cities throughout the United States, distinct areas

with large apartment buildings and vast, empty land—originally envisioned as open and inviting green space interspersed with benches and walkways—became new urban inner-city ghettos, where poor and eventually largely minority residents lived. From small cities such as East St. Louis, to Chicago, Atlanta, or Boston, a landscape of what William Julius Wilson dubbed the "urban underclass" was unintentionally produced, leaving poor populations largely separated from growing areas of urban service delivery and jobs. However, public housing also includes low-rise townhomes and sometimes single-family homes. Indeed, since the 1980s, many families have used federal vouchers to rent apartments in the private market, from urban to suburban locations.

Canadian cities, by contrast, better supported public transportation and develop-

Figure 9.6   Regent Park housing project in Toronto. *Source:* Google Earth.

ment policies that for much of the second half of the twentieth century encouraged mixed-use and mixed-income development. This is not to claim that Canadian cities are far less segregated. In addition, Canadian cities remain very automobile dependent, and while some cities do have good public transportation, spending on roads still far outweighs that spent on public transit. Canada, too, funded social housing for the poorest of the poor. Investments in urban public transportation helped cities like Montreal and Toronto maintain vibrant middle- and upper-income urban neighborhoods, however, and some of the larger social housing complexes were built in suburbs rather than inner-city areas. Despite these efforts, urban development in Canada is still sprawled and segregated. Toronto, for example, had areas of social housing, where poverty was concentrated and associated social problems such as youth violence occurred. Toronto's Regent Park social housing complex resembled American complexes like Cabrini-Green in Chicago, although it was not as physically separated from the diverse urban uses surrounding it (see fig-

ures 9.6 and 9.7). It, too, is a large complex of buildings with apartment units, featuring empty "green" space, parking lots, and pathways. Both Cabrini-Green in Chicago and Regent Park in Toronto are located in the central city, relatively close to public transit and downtown businesses and services. Although for many years both were primarily very poor and stigmatized as a result, today both areas have gentrified somewhat. In the late 1990s, planners and policy makers in both Chicago and Toronto recognized the locational value of these respective public housing complexes. Both have since been the target of redevelopment—most of the large apartment blocks in Chicago's Cabrini-Green complex were torn down in the late 1990s in favor of the development of retail services (including a large supermarket) and, echoing the original housing built for returning World War II veterans in the area, lower-rise and lower-density townhomes with a mix of household incomes (some on public assistance for housing, some not). In the case of Toronto, complexes like Regent Park are integrated with mixed income levels due to market forces. Although some

Figure 9.7   A view of Regent Park housing in Toronto. Wikimedia

attempts were made to create policies that require new developments to include social housing, these have failed to be enacted.

In both countries, more so than in western Europe or East Asia, housing is predominantly a market good—less than 5 percent of households in either the United States or Canada live in public or social housing. Direct government involvement in public or social housing is on the wane as responsibility for affordable housing falls increasingly on municipalities rather than states or provinces or on the federal governments. Developments in urban housing for much of the post–World War II era were based on a largely heterosexual middle-class "life-cycle" model that anticipated most families with young children would live in suburban single-family homes, and then young people would move to apartments in downtown areas as they established careers and sought a cosmopolitan lifestyle with access to bars, restaurants, and entertainment. Then, when

they married and started to have children, they would move to houses in the suburbs or in more residential city neighborhoods. Finally, older residents were expected to seek housing in central-city apartments with amenities such as access to health services and restaurants and cultural entertainment. However, social and demographic changes during the same time frame meant that, by the 1970s, households did not necessarily resemble or seek the same characteristics as the model suggested. As of 2011, single-person households outnumbered married-couple households in both the United States and Canada (see box 9.4). Increasingly, these individuals are just as likely to seek to purchase a home in a suburban location as to live in a central-city location. Costs are often cheaper for suburban housing, and although central cities typically offer greater cultural and entertainment offerings, these may be less appealing than the opportunity to build equity as a homeowner.

Box 9.4 Toronto, Ontario: Urban Growth and Postindustrial Renewal

As Canada's largest city, with over 2.5 million people, Toronto is a center for immigrants to Canada, telecommunications industries, manufacturing, and cultural institutions. The history of its Lake Ontario waterfront is a nearly century-long study of first government-led followed by private redevelopment that transformed primarily industrial and rail lands into a highly developed entertainment, tourism, and residential landscape. The city was founded as a fort (Fort York) on the shores of Lake Ontario, and it grew both along the lake and northward (coincidentally, also uphill) from there.

As the growth of Canada's economy and political identity was based in part on the development of federal rail lines linking East and West, so, too, Toronto's industrial development was based on extensive railroad lines going into the city along the shores of Lake Ontario, connecting Toronto with points to the east and west of the country. (Indeed, many North American cities, and certainly all those located along waterways, had the core of their industrial activities colocate, with railroads, along those waterfronts as well.) Through these rail and then highway linkages (the Queen Elizabeth Way also traversed the city parallel to the rail lines along the lake), Toronto was cemented in the industrial era as the center of Canada's manufacturing economy, from meatpacking to automobile construction. The geography of this legacy meant that the city's major environmental amenity, the shores of Lake Ontario, were inaccessible to most residents from the second half of the nineteenth century through much of the twentieth century because of the intense transport and industrial land uses there.

Starting in the late 1960s, various levels of government, from the provincial level through Crown corporate entity Canadian National Railway, sought to redevelop parts of the waterfront. The Ontario Place marina and recreational site was created on islands adjacent to the Royal Agricultural and Canadian National Exhibition Fairgrounds, and in 1976 the telecommunications CN Tower was completed. The Toronto Argonauts football team and expansion National Baseball League Blue Jays played in the Exhibition Stadium in the 1970s and 1980s. Much of the lands adjacent to these attractions remained part of the CN rail lines, the highway, and associated industries. In the 1980s, more of Toronto's waterfront was opened up to the public, such as through the private Olympia and York development of the Queen's Quay terminal on reclaimed (privatized) CN lands on the waterfront due south of the downtown. In the 1990s, much of the remaining CN nonactive rail lands were sold to developers, and high-rise condominium housing was developed along a significant portion of the remaining waterfront, transforming the skyline of the city. Today the waterfront is dominated by high-income residents. Research by David Hulchanski suggests that the city of Toronto is so increasingly divided by income and socioeconomic status that it is more accurate to speak of three geographically distinct cities. Hulchanski studied changes in income from 1970 through 2005 and found that city number one is mainly white and has seen incomes increase significantly (with many living in the waterfront area and in the center of town); city number two is characterized as middle-income residents whose incomes have decreased, and city number three is characterized as areas of poverty, single-parent families, and areas with high levels of foreign-born residents who experienced a decrease of incomes by more than 20 percent. The transition of land from industrial and railroad use to private commercial and residential functions is an example of how urban infrastructure and land tenure changes over time, significantly altering urban space and land ownership. However, it is important to remember that redevelopment might appear to benefit the general public but can also reinforce or exacerbate patterns of inequality and segregation.

Since the economic crisis of the housing market in 2008, homeownership is particularly unevenly distributed geographically and socially. Before the early 2000s, homeownership rates in the United States were about 65 percent of the total population, but during the George W. Bush administration's push for an "ownership society," the number of homeowners nationally increased to over 67 percent of the overall population. Homeownership was expanded to poor and minority urban residents, but often not at the most competitive loan rates. Elvin Wyly and colleagues have found that even when accounting for differences in income and assets, minorities were explicitly targeted by subprime lenders, which often meant that they paid more in interest and closing costs than their white counterparts with the same income. When the crisis hit and values fell, some people stopped paying their mortgages and let the banks take over—especially property owners who bought housing in order to rent it out. As a result, in these neighborhoods, abandoned properties contributed to the overall sense of economic decline. Foreclosed properties tend to fall into disrepair and sometimes are targets for thieves seeking, for example, valuable copper that may be in the home's wiring and/or pipes. People sometimes use the houses as a place

to sleep or take drugs or simply for graffiti. All of these activities shape a landscape that looks decayed and uncared-for, compounding the struggles for the residents and businesses of such neighborhoods. The foreclosure crisis is not simply one of core urban areas, however; it also has devastated some suburban areas (as chapter 11 details). In some parts of Florida, for example, in Lee County outside of Fort Myers, empty houses from the foreclosure crisis proliferate the landscape, creating a dearth of community and fostering an unkempt atmosphere, further depressing home values for the remaining residents. Urban inequalities, therefore, have a sometimes unexpected pattern to them. The foreclosure crisis in particular highlighted the degree to which racial minorities experience uneven and unequal access to financial resources such as mortgages, but it also exposed the degree to which many households, regardless of income or race, were living on increasing and unsustainable levels of debt, encouraged by lending practices of banks.

HOMELESSNESS

One highly visible failure of housing markets is in providing for individuals who lack

Figure 9.8   A man pushes his belongings and a collection of cans for resale to a recycler on a New York City street. (Photo by John Rennie Short)

housing entirely. Homelessness is a problem in both the United States and Canada, and it is most visible in urban areas (see figures 9.8 and 9.9). Cities large and small face problems of individuals who sleep in parks or by rail lands and under bridges (some of these being relatively hidden from public view and police attention) and spend daylight hours in public spaces such as the sidewalk, park benches, libraries, and city hall plazas. The reasons that people are homeless are complex; they usually involve a combination of a lack of resources at the individual and government level, including poverty, mental illness, substance abuse, and sometimes a precipitating family crisis. The "typical" or perhaps stereotypical homeless person faces mental illness and substance abuse and would rather be alone on the street—or with a community of street people—than accept help, and conditions, from others. As found by sociologist Mitchell Duneier, this seemingly individual choice sits in a context of insufficient access to or provision of affordable housing and mental health support on the part of government. Families, too, end up homeless, including parents with children. The stages to homelessness often start with mounting bills at home

(rented or owned), leading to eviction or foreclosure, sometimes days or even months sharing housing with relatives or friends, until at last other people's hospitality runs out and the individual or family has no place to go. At that point, some people end up on the street, while others find assistance from public and private nonprofit agencies who manage shelters. The social safety net of shelters, when it works as planned, provides a safe place for people to sleep and also to receive training and assistance for finding and keeping a job, managing finances, and treating underlying health issues (mental or otherwise). Such "wraparound" services are expensive and hard to maintain, but without them, shelter living is at best a temporary roof rather than a hand up to self-reliance.

Figure 9.9   Panhandler on the streets of Ottawa. (Photo by Karen Hill)

Since the mid-1990s, social service agencies have increasingly turned to a "housing first" model of sheltering homeless people, which means that rather than provide temporary shelter, individuals without housing are immediately placed into longer-term housing with accompanying services. This model is a drastic shift from emergency shelters, which provide overnight accommodation and meals but little else to address the daytime or long-term needs of the chronically homeless. Simply sheltering people, while meeting emergency needs, does not address longer-term issues of adequate and affordable housing. Shelters do not always provide long-term mental health services, medical services, and other types of ongoing care. The housing first model seeks to take care of housing first (hence the name), with self-reliance coming later. In some cases, individuals may need long-term services. In the full housing first model, these services are built into the program.

These two forms of social service for the homeless have quite different impacts on the landscape. Typically, emergency-style (overnight) shelters have had central-city locations to be accessible to the populations seeking them. These clients include considerable diversity—women and men, individuals suffering from mental illness, and those with substance abuse problems (these categories are not mutually exclusive), some of whom may be long-term homeless while others face simply a temporary setback. These shelters can be large and, because of their function, can be a site nearby which some homeless people congregate during the daytime hours (because they have no place else to go, because these shelters are often in central locations, and because it is where their community is). By contrast, many housing first facilities oper-

ate on a small-scale group home or apartment unit model. This housing is generally less visible in the landscape. With the presence of wraparound services, individuals in housing first facilities often can stay at the housing during daytime hours rather than being out on the street. In addition, during the day, they have regular responsibilities or check-ins with support staff to ensure that they have access to job training, mental health, or other life skills counseling, as needed.

By contrast, the proximity of overnight-only shelters to other urban services, such as government agencies, major transportation hubs such as train or bus stations, and private businesses, can foster tense on-street interactions with individuals going to jobs or patronizing businesses in the same area. People on the streets or sidewalks on their way to stores or work can feel uncomfortable when passing or seeing other individuals who clearly have little to no access to adequate clothing, showers, and food. In turn, homeless individuals might panhandle or verbally call out and harass other people on the street (see box 9.5). Figure 9.10 illustrates how the city of Ottawa has created an alternative to panhandling. These sidewalk confrontations are the front lines of urban inequalities; they are impossible to ignore. For people who have housing, they are an unpleasant reminder that some people do not have, for whatever reasons, the same daily comforts. Many people are distressed by this inequality, but responses are mixed as to how they feel or what they think should be done about it. For some, it is easiest to assume that homelessness is caused by individual failures—inability to hold a job, keep off drugs or alcohol, or make "good" choices. For others, it is a reminder that, were it not for whatever help they had to get an

Box 9.5 Worcester, Massachusetts: Problems of Homelessness and Panhandling

As a smaller North American city (with fewer than two hundred thousand people), Worcester may not be the obvious type of place to struggle with issues of panhandling and homelessness. Yet small cities are not immune to problems of inequality and poverty. With a formerly robust industrial and manufacturing economy, Worcester today offers a mix of industrial and service employers as well as biotech, medical, and higher education fields. It is home to the University of Massachusetts Medical School, a campus of the Massachusetts College of Pharmacy and Health Sciences, and numerous additional colleges and universities. As New England's second-largest city (after Boston), it is also a key location for social services in Massachusetts. Until 2009, it had long been home to one of Massachusetts's only two so-called wet emergency shelters, where homeless individuals could find a bed regardless of their sobriety status. Instead of emergency shelter, the city and its partner social service agencies reconfigured their shelter system to emphasize wraparound housing assistance and services using the housing first model, with a goal to reduce overall homelessness. While the strategy has helped to improve and coordinate homeless assistance, it has not reduced panhandling in the city. Up until recently, panhandling occurred at some of the busiest intersections across the city, with individuals regardless of weather holding signs asking for money, explaining that the sign holder is, variously, a war veteran, looking for work, hungry, and so on. The visibility of the phenomenon over time prompted the city council to enact a law in 2013 to limit panhandling at major intersections by banning solicitation of anyone in a vehicle. The public discussion of the issue by city councilors focused on public safety, as panhandlers would sometimes walk into traffic in order to collect change or bills from car occupants.

The degree to which the concerns about panhandling were primarily about public safety, however, is in question when Worcester's so-called tag days are taken into account. Until the practice was banned in 2013 along with panhandling, it was routine at certain times of the year in Worcester for the staff, volunteers, and young participants in Worcester's youth clubs, especially sports leagues, to take to the streets on a weekend day to collect money in large buckets to raise funds for their organizations. In practice, these tag days were similar to panhandling: participants held signs asking for money, and people stood on street corners, ready to walk up to cars where occupants offered money out their windows. The only difference was that the people involved in tag days looked like they were wearing clean clothes and had access to hot showers and breakfast, whereas many of the more day-to-day panhandlers did not. But when the city council engaged in discussions about the need to restrict panhandling, as it did in the summer of 2012, it became clear that in order to pass a law, they would have to also ban tag days or face claims of targeting one group for free-speech limits. The debates over panhandling in Worcester highlight the discomforts that many people feel about visible poverty and the contradictions that ensue when they seek to make it harder for people with minimal resources to be visible in the public landscape.

Figure 9.10   A kindness meter in Ottawa. This former parking meter has been repurposed to allow people to donate money to charity rather than giving it directly to panhandlers. Kindness meters are painted a bright red, and people can insert coins to "donate" directly to services for the homeless. The purpose is to prevent panhandlers from spending money on alcohol or drugs. *Source:* Wikimedia.

education and/or a job, sometimes the help of a friend or parents to pay a bill, or their own strong mental resilience, they, too, might be on the edge. The problem of homelessness is certainly compounded for many by mental illness and the distressing side-effects of drugs and unreliability of treatment to keep mental demons away.

The emergency shelter model does not usually serve families or couples; sleeping accommodations are tailored to individuals, and men and women are usually separated (figure 9.11). Some do have family accommodations, especially in cases involving children; families are placed in separate shelters or in hotels at the expense of the state agency in charge of family well-being. In Massachusetts, for example, homeless families are housed in family shelters when spots are available, but when demand is higher than supply, the state pays for them to stay in hotels rather than be in overnight shelters. However, that means that these families do not have access to kitchens or other appropriate settings where, for example, school-age children can complete homework. Regardless of household status, some individuals or families choose to sleep outside (or in their cars) rather than in shelters, despite the obvious safety issues of being outdoors, as a means to exert some control and choice over their own situation. An excellent illustration of the choices and community networks of support that develop among homeless individuals is provided in sociologist Mitchell Duneier's book *Sidewalk*.

Different cities and their states and provinces have different particular approaches to addressing issues of homelessness, and some have more aggressive policing to limit how visible homelessness is to the casual observer. Some people who spend much of their day on the streets of some cities may in fact have housing at night, while others who appear well sheltered may have quite contingent and unstable nighttime shelter. Homelessness may be an obvious and extreme form of inequality, but sharp observers of urban North America can see a wide range

Figure 9.11   Emergency shelter and empty street space in Worcester, Massachusetts. (Photo by Alex Scherr)

of social differences in people and everyday urban landscapes. Less clear are the social networks and policies that address it. These are an issue of urban governance, as described in previous chapters.

The topic of urban inequality highlights the fact that the cities of North America offer a wide range of visual and experiential contrasts. Differences in land use, zoning and regulation, economic function, and neighborhood identity are evident in the social separations of class and race or ethnicity. Difference is a hallmark of cities; they bring together economic and social diversity. Yet difference in social extremes can be the basis of urban inequalities that are rooted in historical legacies of segregation and that can be maintained through uneven resource delivery, as with urban schooling. Where inequalities persist across race, ethnicity, and class, social fragmentation and divide can result. Cities do not create social inequality, but the economic processes that shape urban places foster unevenness of all sorts. Urban life can magnify inequalities through proximity, as when people of vast income difference encounter one another on the streets. Such visual encounters, which sometimes develop into interaction, offer a means for society to confront our socioeconomic unevenness.

SUGGESTED READINGS

Anderson, K. J. 1991. *Vancouver's Chinatown: Racial Discourse in Canada 1875–1980*. Montreal: McGill-Queen's University Press.

Boyer, K. 2003. "'Neither Forget nor Remember Your Sex': Sexual Politics in the Early Twentieth-Century Canadian Office." *Journal of Historical Geography* 29(2): 212–29.

Briggs, X., S. J. Popkin, and J. Goering. 2010. *Moving to Opportunity: The Story of an American Experiment to Fight Ghetto Poverty*. New York: Oxford University Press.

Darden, J. T., and S. M. Kamel. 2000. "Black Residential Segregation in the City and Suburbs of Detroit: Does Socioeconomic Status Matter?" *Journal of Urban Affairs* 22: 1–13. doi:10.1111/0735-2166.00036.

Desfor, G., and J. Laidley. 2011. *Reshaping Toronto's Waterfront*. Toronto: University of Toronto Press.

Duneier, M. 1999. *Sidewalk*. New York: Farrar, Straus and Giroux.

Hankins, K., R. Cochran, and K. Derickson. 2012. "Making Space, Making Race: Constituting White Privilege in Buckhead, Atlanta." *Social & Cultural Geography* 13(4): 379–97.

Henry, E. E., and K. Hankins. 2012. "Halting White Flight: Parent Activism and the (Re)shaping of Atlanta's 'Circuits of Schooling,' 1973–2009." *Journal of Urban History* 38(3): 532–52.

Jackson, K. T. 1985. *Crabgrass Frontier: The Suburbanization of the United States*. New York: Oxford University Press.

Logan, J. 2011. "Separate and Unequal: The Neighborhood Gap for Blacks, Hispanics and Asians in Metropolitan America." US2010 Project, Brown University, August 2, 2011. Available online at http://www.s4.brown.edu/us2010/Data/Report/report0727.pdf. Last accessed July 24, 2012.

Sewell, J. E. 2011. *Women and the Everyday City: Public Space in San Francisco, 1890–1915*. Minneapolis: University of Minnesota Press.

Wilson, W. J. 1987. *The Truly Disadvantaged: The Inner City, the Underclass, and Public Policy*. Chicago: University of Chicago Press.

Wyly, E., M. Moos, and E. Kabahizi. 2009. "Cartographies of Race and Class: Mapping the Class-Monopoly Rents of American Subprime Mortgage Capital." *International Journal of Urban and Regional Research* 3(2): 332–54.

CITIES ON THE WEB

For more about homelessness:

The State of Homelessness: endhomelessness.org. *The alliance releases new data on homelessness by state and city.*

Homelessness—HUD: www.hud.gov/homeless/. *Research, fact sheets, links to government and private organizations and other resources.*

National Coalition for the Homeless: www.nationalhomeless.org/. *National advocacy organization working to end homelessness. Provides information on homelessness and related issues.*

For more about poverty:

US Census Bureau Poverty Main: http://www.census.gov/hhes/www/poverty/poverty.html. *On poverty in the United States.*

CCSD Facts & Stats Fact Sheets on Economic Security: http://www.ccsd.ca/factsheets/economic_security/poverty/index.htm. *On poverty in Canada.*

For more about segregation:

US Census Bureau Housing Patterns: http://www.census.gov/hhes/www/housing/housing_patterns/pdftoc.html. *Data about segregation and housing in the United States.*

City Stats: http://citystats.uvic.ca. *For information on measures of segregation in Canadian cities.*

10

Urban Demographics and Identities
NATHANIEL M. LEWIS

Like most sections of this book, this chapter would look much different if it had been written fifty years ago. In 1963, the demographic and economic profiles of most US and Canadian cities reflected a postwar baby boom and a dominant North American manufacturing sector. They reflected what appeared to be a future of growth and security for most citizens, anchored by national governments investing heavily in public education, housing, and infrastructure development. Identity, while it had always been a complicated concept in reality, was often cast as something based on unproblematic categories of race and ethnicity. Early studies in geography and sociology on immigrant and ethnic groups, such as the Polish and the Italians, tended to frame them as uniform populations from one country (and one culture) that needed to be assimilated by a new, "host" country and culture. By 1963, reflecting a turn to quantitative models and a "regional science" approach in the study of cities, population (including immigration) was just one of the many inputs or outputs that contributed to the growth or decline of North America's now burgeoning industrial city-regions. Although many cities had Chinatowns, Little Italies, and Greektowns that expressed ethnic identities spatially, the identities *of cities* themselves had become just

as important in the mid-twentieth century. Industrial proficiency became a point of pride for many cities, reflected in nicknames like Motor City (Detroit, Michigan), Steeltown (Pittsburgh, Pennsylvania, and Hamilton, Ontario), and—a few years later—Silicon Valley (San Jose, California).

Fifty years later, the population and social geographies of North American cities and our approaches to studying them have changed considerably. Many of the same baby boomers that were children or teens in 1963 are now approaching or have reached retirement age, and the fertility rate (number of children born per woman of reproductive age), well above 3.0 in the 1960s, has in many regions fallen below the 2.1 replacement rate needed to keep the population stable. Consequently, the immigrants once seen mostly as cogs in the wheel of economic and industrial growth are now the primary source of population growth in many cities and the dominant employees in many sectors. With the removal of restrictive immigration quotas in the mid-1960s and ongoing improvements in global transportation and communications since then, immigrants to the United States and Canada come from increasingly diverse backgrounds. And far from mid-century conceptions of immigrants as factory workers and ghetto residents, present-day newcomers are bringing the type of financial capital and technological know-how that has the power to transform North American cities in novel ways. In economies that have become more global than national, US and Canadian cities have become the flashpoints for flows of goods, knowledge, and people, new development approaches, and new, hybrid forms of identity.

Approaches to geography have kept up with these changes. Critical approaches to urban, social, and economic geography have acknowledged that globalization has done more than simply make cities and their residents more global or transnational. It has also contributed to conditions of insecurity and marginalization that disproportionately affect the poor, the foreign born, and the racialized. At the same time, advances in feminist geography have demonstrated that identities such as male and female—as well as white, black, gay, straight, and others—not only create very different experiences of the city but are themselves *constructed* through the discourses and narratives of the media, urban institutions, and day-to-day social interactions.

Drawing from these recent urban transformations and the geographic approaches that have sought to capture them, this chapter highlights the *variations* in demographics and identities that have emerged between and within cities despite growing transnational linkages, broadly cosmopolitan identities, and increasingly uniform approaches to urban development. The following sections show that the imperatives of urban growth and capital accumulation continue to inform attitudes about immigration, urban development, and social and ethnic difference, but in the context of economies that are more volatile and fragmented than they were in 1963. They also reveal that identities are not just categories of cities or residents but things that are actively shaped, employed, and inscribed in processes of urban development. In fact, the identities of city dwellers and cities themselves are mutually constituted; that is, they inform each other.

DEMOGRAPHIC TRANSITIONS

North America is entering a new phase of what social scientists call the demographic transition. In this multistage process, countries shift from high birthrates and high death rates (stage 1) to high birthrates and decreasing death rates (stage 2), to decreasing birthrates and death rates (stage 3), and finally low birthrates and death rates (stage 4). These changes arise from both economic changes, such as the transition from labor-heavy, taxing agricultural economies to more streamlined industrial economies, and social changes, such as the increasing availability of health care and birth control. Stage 5, where deaths *exceed* births, was long considered a hypothetical stage in the demographic transition but is now becoming a reality in many parts of North America. In 2011, the first wave of baby boomers (those born between 1946 and 1964) reached age sixty-five, the age commonly used to define the boundary between working age (twenty-five through sixty-four) and elderly. The relative size of the elderly population will increase substantially in the next two decades. In the United States, for example, the number of elderly citizens per one thousand working-age adults, generally known as the dependency ratio, will increase from 246 to 411 between 2010 and 2030 (a 64 percent increase).

While demographic attributes are often described in the context of countries (e.g., *national* fertility rate), the effects of population aging are experienced differently in various regions and cities (see figure 10.1). In some places, the decline may be softened slightly. In California, which is geographically close to immigrant source countries such as Mexico and

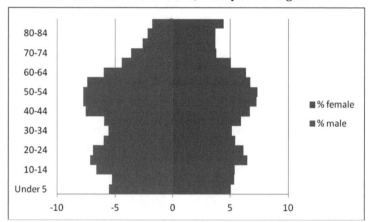

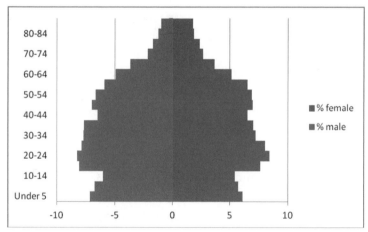

Figure 10.1   Population pyramids for Scranton–Wilkes-Barre and Durham-Chapel Hill regions, 2010. While demographic change is often described in terms of countries, there is considerable variation in what cities and regions within countries experience. In the Rust Belt region of Scranton–Wilkes-Barre, the largest part of the population is approaching retirement. In the Sun Belt technopole of Durham-Chapel Hill, which successfully retains a large proportion of its university graduates, the largest part of the population is university age or working age. *Source:* Nathaniel Lewis, using US Census Bureau, *American Community Survey, 2010 3-Year Estimates*.

anchored by the immigrant gateways of Los Angeles and San Francisco, the dependency ratio will increase only from 214 to 350 (61 percent increase). In other locales, however, the effect may be far worse. In Quebec, for example, many abandoned the Roman Catholic Church and traditional family structures in the 1960s and now frequently opt for common-law relationships instead. Consequently, the provincial fertility rate—the number of children per woman of childbearing age—has stayed below 1.5, and Quebec's population decline is pronounced in many areas outside of Montreal. In cities throughout the Northeast, Midwest, and Great Plains regions, such as Providence, Rhode Island, Cleveland, Ohio, and Winnipeg, Manitoba, transitions away from heavy manufacturing and agricultural industries (e.g., food processing) have generated out-migration, making the maintenance of stable populations even more difficult.

Imminent population decline has implications for many aspects of life in North American cities, ranging from job markets to the sustainability of health and social security programs. Box 10.1 highlights such demographic changes in Chicago. In places becoming increasingly top-heavy with elderly residents, there may not be enough working-age people to replace the jobs left behind by retirees or to provide the social and medical services they may need. Housing is perhaps the most pressing and visible challenge for North America's aging cities (see figure 10.2). In addition to the economically driven housing bubble referenced in the previous chapter, a larger "generational" housing bubble will occur during the next two decades. The future of most urban housing markets, however, depends on the willingness of young buyers to enter the market. Unfortunately, the retirement of the large boomer generation and a slowly growing younger population means that in most places there will be far more buyers than sellers, with the possible exception of retirement communities like those in Arizona and on Vancouver Island, British Columbia. In addition, the current postbubble recession means that unfavorable lending and financing terms may discourage young buyers from entering the market. The consequences will involve decreasing home values and, possibly, declining equity and retirement savings among middle-class boomers.

Box 10.1. Chicago: Second City or City in Decline?

For the first time in its recorded population history, Chicago reported a loss in 2010: census figures showed the population of the city had shrunk by about two hundred thousand residents (a 5 percent decrease) since 2000, dropping from 2.9 million to 2.7 million residents. To some extent, the shift could be attributed to the same economic shifts affecting other manufacturing-heavy cities such as Detroit, Cleveland, and Pittsburgh. Manufacturing makes up about 10 percent of the economy of Chicago's metropolitan area, compared with about 7–8 percent in the quickly growing Sun Belt tech poles, such as Phoenix, Atlanta, and Durham-Chapel Hill in North Carolina. The population decline, however, was not spatially uniform. Between 2000 and 2010, census tracts in the downtown core and the "collar counties" to the city's north, west, and south continued to grow (allowing the larger metropolitan area to grow by 3 percent), while the noncore neighborhoods and inner suburbs of Chicago recorded losses.

On one hand, these trends reflect a commonsense logic that residents are continuing to seek out better schools and job opportunities and more affordable housing in far-flung suburbs because downtown areas are more dangerous and more expensive. On the other hand, they can also be attributed to the disparate mobility patterns of racial groups living in different portions of the city. Among Chicago's white population, which decreased slightly, the trend was mixed: young, white professionals moved into the Loop and other downtown neighborhoods. Many of these areas had been redeveloped as part of Chicago's efforts to remain the United States' "Second City" and become an emerging global city, which included a bid for the 2016 Olympic Games. Meanwhile, the aging white residents in out-of-center Slavic neighborhoods (e.g., Archer Heights) on the west side of the city moved elsewhere, sometimes to retirement or care communities in suburbs or other counties and states.

The Hispanic population of Chicago, which had increased by 11 percent between 1990 and 2000, grew by only 4 percent in the next ten years. Recent and second-generation immigrants entering the middle class moved to the suburbs, though most still worked mostly in low-order service professions. Meanwhile, some new immigrants skipped over Latino "gateway" neighborhoods such as Little Village and moved directly to the suburbs. The most striking story, however, was a 17 percent decline in the black population, which defies any singular explanation. Increases in the black population of far-flung DuPage County suggested a flight to the suburbs, while other sources suggested that some had migrated to southern cities with growing black populations such as Charlotte and Houston—a reversal of the northward black migration of the early twentieth century. The decline, however, may have been more "push" than "pull." African American South Side neighborhoods such as Englewood faced continued disinvestment by the municipal government, poor-quality schools, high crime, and home foreclosures during the 2000s. The Chicago Housing Authority's Plan for Transformation, for example, closed many of the city's high-rise public housing projects without quickly developing the low-rise, mixed-use alternatives it had proposed.

IMMIGRATION TRENDS

Patterns of immigration in North America today are far different from those of the 1960s. In the later part of the decade, the US Immigration Nationality Act (1965) and revisions to Canada's Immigration Act (1967–1968) removed quotas on immigration from countries in the developing world. Although the origins of immigrants were now different than they had been in the first part of the century, most continued to fit the profile of the industrial-era immigrant (i.e., low income and low skilled) and tended to gravitate toward ethnic gateway neighborhoods such as New York's Washington Heights (Puerto Ricans), Miami's Little Havana (Cubans), and Los Angeles's Koreatown (Koreans), sometimes settling in areas previously occupied by a different ethnic group (e.g., the replacement of Czechs with Mexicans in Chicago's Pilsen). During the 1970s, 1980s, and even the 1990s,

Figure 10.2   Houses under construction, Fort McMurray, Alberta. (Photo by Nathaniel Lewis)

there was still little evidence to contest the early twentieth-century conceptions of urban immigration as a process in which neighborhoods were "invaded" by one group and then "succeeded" by another.

In the twenty-first century, however, it is clear that immigrants' destinations and their patterns of settlement have changed considerably. Traditional immigrant ports of entry (e.g., New York) and the ethnic enclaves within them have been replaced by a range of dynamic gateway cities, ranging from Montreal, Quebec, to Washington, DC. These cities range from huge metropoles to midsize cities, may be coastal or interior, and are "hyperdiverse," comprising multiple ethnic groups—often within the same neighborhood or suburb. There are several explanations for these shifts. First, socioeconomic conditions in both North American cities and many sending countries have changed considerably. Education levels in many Asian and Latin American countries have improved,

meaning that many new immigrants have the potential to contribute to growing sectors such as health, technology, and business—a shift that Canada has acknowledged by using a skills-based evaluation of applications for immigration. Consequently, immigrants are less frequently bounded by the institutions of the factory and the enclave that defined imaginaries of immigration in the early North American city. Smaller cities such as Atlanta, Charlotte, Kansas City, and Winnipeg, as well as cities in border regions, have gained a foothold in this postindustrial economy, which has created both new trade and business linkages with other countries and a growing demand for workers in these places. Newcomers are no longer just long-term industrial labor; they may also be temporary workers or corporate recruits.

Second, patterns of immigrant settlement within cities have become more varied, and immigrant neighborhoods have become more diverse. With increasing unevenness in the

Box 10.2. Washington, DC:
From Black-and-White City to Rainbow Region

Washington, DC, while renowned for its planned monuments, museums, and plazas, has long been—at its core—a prototypical US East Coast city bifurcated by class and race. The white and African American populations of DC have traditionally been divided by the north-south thoroughfare of Sixteenth Street, with blacks on the east and whites on the west. That line, however, has both (1) shifted eastward as parts of the downtown core are redeveloped and (2) become much fuzzier as traditionally white or black neighborhoods have become multiethnic immigrant neighborhoods. In the 1970s and 1980s, the city was home to about 120,000 foreign born, or 2.5 percent of the population. In the past thirty years, however, the immigrant population of DC has quintupled, and there are now more than one million immigrants in the metropolitan region. In most immigrant gateway cities, settlement patterns have been explained through a spatial assimilation model, in which immigrant groups first settle in an ethnically concentrated inner-city area and—over time—disperse into other areas as their incomes and education levels increase. In addition, immigrant settlement in most cities has been dominated by one or two groups, such as Cubans in Miami, Irish and Italians in Boston, and Mexicans in San Antonio (see figure 10.3). The recent experience of Washington, DC, contradicts both of these trends. New immigrants coming from Latin America (El Salvador and Bolivia), Asia (Korea, India, and Vietnam), and the Middle East and Africa (Iran and Ethiopia) have settled in a wide range of both inner-city and suburban neighborhoods—ranging from Adams Morgan at the center of Washington, DC, to Fairfax, Virginia, twenty miles to the west.

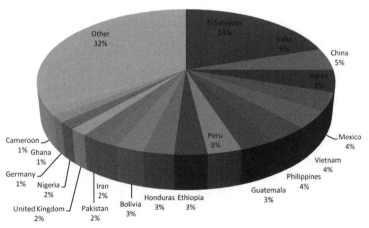

Figure 10.3   Not a traditional immigrant gateway, the Washington, DC, metropolitan area's immigrant population has exploded during the past thirty years and includes groups from every continent.
Source: Nathaniel Lewis using US Census Bureau, *American Community Survey, 2010.*

There are, however, significant differences in settlement patterns among ethnic groups. The most dispersed groups, Indians and Chinese, tend to be located in suburban Virginia and—having often arrived with high-level technical degrees—make up a large portion of the area's "natural sciences" sector that now comprises over 25 percent immigrant workers and is blossoming in out-of-center tech poles such as Herndon and Fairfax in Virginia. Other groups, such as Ethiopians, have settled in the suburbs as well as center-city areas such as Adams Morgan/Mount Pleasant/U Street. This patchwork neighborhood is a particularly interesting example of DC's multiethnic character. Until the 1950s, U Street was DC's answer to Harlem, New York, a vibrant center of African American arts and culture. The area declined quickly, however, following riots after Martin Luther King Jr.'s assassination in 1968. It has since been revitalized by Ethiopians, Salvadorans, Vietnamese (who are concentrated almost exclusively in this neighborhood), and, increasingly, young white professionals. As Adams Morgan/Mount Pleasant/U Street becomes more popular, however, housing prices have become high enough to put the neighborhood out of reach for many of the city's newest immigrants (see figure 10.4).

Alongside Washington, DC's transition from black and white to multiethnic has been a related transition in the identity of the city—from sleepy "government town" to leader in the postindustrial economy. One of the reasons that Washington, DC, had never become established as an immigrant gateway was the absence of a large industrial sector like those in Detroit, Cleveland, Chicago, Toronto, Montreal, and other traditional gateways. Incidentally, DC's now-booming economy, anchored by the US federal government, may be creating

Figure 10.4   Ninth Street NW in Washington, DC, once the heart of the large African American community, has become one of several "Little Ethiopias" in the district. (Photo by Nathaniel Lewis)

a higher demand for labor. Census 2010 data revealed that for the first time, Washington, DC, surpassed San Jose (the other US city profiled in this chapter) to become the city-region with the highest median household income ($84,523). The rising income level has been galvanized by the influx of law and lobbying firms with an interest in the country's increasingly fast-paced health-care and financial regulation reforms. DC is also home to an ever-growing snowball of contractors that serve the city's large "public economy," character-ized by out-of-center agency compounds such as the Central Intelligence Agency (Langley, Virginia) and the National Institutes of Health (Bethesda, Maryland). This number-one rank-ing, however, masks deep disparities. About 11 percent of the population (mostly African Americans) qualifies as "very poor" (household income of $5,000). In addition, the city's new immigrants do not figure prominently in the sectors for which Washington, DC, is best known (and which pay the most), including law, social science, government, and policy making. While Washington, DC, has become an immigrant city, newcomers are not typically found in the offices of Capitol Hill.

The increasing size and diversity of the DC area's immigrant population, however, has not eliminated long-standing black-white cleavages or prevented new tensions between existing communities and new immigrants. The most recent mayoral election, for example, showed that African American and white residents voted along racial lines: Whites generally voted for losing candidate Adrian Fenty, who promised strict reforms for low-performing public schools and the provision of city services. Meanwhile, Vincent Gray—who garnered most of the African American vote, promised greater sensitivity to the welfare of low-income blacks in poor, peripheral neighborhoods east of downtown, such as Anacostia and Congress Heights. Interestingly, some new immigrant communities have generally avoided partici-pation in "mainstream" community politics or events, demonstrating that spatial dispersal does not always create social assimilation. In Annandale, Virginia, Korean immigrants have tended to patronize Korean supermarkets, restaurants, and shopping centers, many of them marked only in Korean-language signage. Recent efforts by the local business association to get Korean businesses to make their presence "official" by participating in the town's redevelopment and marketing plans have gone generally unsupported or unnoticed by the Korean community. The Washington, DC, case thus makes clear that more diffuse patterns of immigrant settlement do not always transform interethnic relationships or the tensions that might accompany them.

housing stock and pricing in downtown cores, multiple groups may simultaneously settle in the neighborhoods that are the most cost effective. Brooklyn's Sunset Park, for example, has transitioned from a mostly Norwegian American enclave (pre-1960s), to a mostly Hispanic one (1990s), to a dynamic ethno-scape including Chinese, Indians, Mexicans, Indians, Filipinos, and Bangladeshis in the 2000s. Immigrants groups now also tend to be more dispersed within cities. In a phe-nomenon that geographer Wilbur Zelinsky referred to as "heterolocalism," dispersed im-migrant groups in gateway cities rely on the ties created at sports games and community centers rather than the consistent, day-to-day interaction of an ethnic enclave. Immigrants who come as professionals with financial capital (or who can leverage loans from home or through communal rotating savings funds) may choose to settle away from traditional ethnic enclaves to start a business or to access better-quality housing and schools. This growing diversity of locational choices among immigrants has led to what geographer Wei Li calls "ethnoburbs," which are clusters of immigrants living in suburban residential and business districts. One example is the Chinese community of San Gabriel, California. Since the 1960s, many upwardly mobile Chinese moved out of Los Angeles's Chinatown and adjacent inner-city neighborhoods and into the burgeoning suburbs. While some of these newly suburban Chinese families dispersed spatially, others settled in high-concentration clusters such as the one in San Gabriel, creating ethnically distinct economic and social formations well outside the city center. Li notes, however, that ethnoburbs are typically *multiethnic* communities in which one ethnic minority group constitutes a significant proportion of the population but not necessarily the majority. In this way, ethnoburbs may include several different immigrant and ethnic communities working and living side by side.

Many have argued that the increasing diversity and diffusion of immigrant settlement in North American cities has led to hybrid forms of identity that transcend the traditional boundaries of segregation and ethnic politics. In his book *Creating Diversity Capital*, Blair Ruble argues that the growth of immigration in ethnically and racially bifurcated cities such as Montreal (French Cana-

dian/Anglo Canadian) and Washington, DC (black/white) has allayed some of the tensions between opposing groups and allowed for forms of cultural hybridity, for example, the crowning of a bilingual, West Indian queen in Montreal's St. Patrick's Day parade. Neighborhoods where large numbers of mixed-race households are present also tend to be more diverse and less segregated.

The increasing heterogeneity of immigrant and ethno-racial settlement patterns, however, cannot mask the persistent disparities and inequalities among the experiences of different groups or between those of "new" groups and the white, Euro-American (or Euro-Canadian) "mainstream." Geographers Mark Ellis and Richard Wright find that only mixed-race households appear to be attracted unequivocally to diverse neighborhoods, whereas black and white households tend to seek out a multiethnic or multiracial neighborhood *only* when the majority population is something other than their own race. White households, for example, would be more likely to gravitate to a multiethnic neighborhood with a black majority rather than one that was almost completely black, but less likely to go a multiethnic neighborhood with a white majority than one that was mostly white. Moreover, black and white households remain highly segregated at the neighborhood level. Black immigrant households are among the most segregated. Dominicans in New York, Haitians in Montreal, and Jamaicans in Toronto tend to remain in specific enclaves with lower-quality housing and occupy the least-skilled and lowest-paying employment positions.

The clear persistence of ethno-racial segregation and the vastly different experiences of specific groups indicates that few, if any,

North American cities have attained some kind of postethnic, postracial nirvana. In fact, debates over immigration and identity in North American cities have become even more heated during the past two decades. The United States and Canada, however, have very different approaches to immigration policy. In the United States, immigrants are typically admitted based on claims of family reunification and are tacitly expected to take on an "American" civic identity. Canada adopted a skills-based immigration regime in 1968 with changes to the immigration act and officially adopted a policy of multiculturalism in 1971, since positioning itself as a cultural "mosaic" in contrast to the "melting pot" of the United States (see figure 10.5). As a smaller country that has recently recorded fertility rates lower than those of the United States, Canadian policy has typically framed immigration as integral to its economic future. In the United States, the debate over the value of immigration has been more polarized, with the anti-immigration side typically adopting either economic arguments ("Immigrants take US jobs") or sociocultural arguments ("Immigrants are not speaking English or becoming 'American'") to support their claims. Interestingly, several Canadian provinces and US municipalities are now also creating policies or agreements in an attempt to shape their immigration destiny (see box 10.3).

In general, economic arguments against immigration are difficult to sustain. In most cities, immigration tends to increase average rents, support firms, and boost the overall economy, resulting in constant or increasing incomes. In high-immigration cities where immigrants keep the population stable and invest in otherwise decaying neighborhoods,

wages among lower-skilled workers tend to be higher than those in low-immigration areas, even though there are slightly greater wage disparities between low- and medium-skilled workers. The argument that immigrants create social fragmentation retains more popularity because while it is difficult to prove, it appeals to emotion rather than economic rationality.

Some critics have argued that both the economic and social arguments against immigration are really about immigrants' children—the "second generation." It is true that the children of immigrants create an aggregate economic burden since they use the same public services (e.g., schools) as other children but their parents, on average, have lower incomes and therefore pay lower taxes. Similarly, it is the second generation—not new immigrants—that have contributed most heavily to *visible* ethno-racial change in many regions of North America during the past several decades. Yet the debates that these changes have triggered—and which are often initiated by older-generation Americans and Canadians—have typically targeted new immigrants, relying on a "Peter Pan" conception of immigrants that fails to acknowledge their upward mobility over time. An interesting paradox has thus emerged: the baby boomers are the most likely to oppose immigration, yet the demographic and economic gaps they are leaving behind are precisely why immigrants and their children are becoming so necessary. It may be time, then, for some older US residents to look past their conceptions of identity and belonging to attract and invest in the first- and second-generation immigrants, who will sustain the future of North American cities.

**Recent Immigrant (1965-1971) Percentage of the Population
by Census Tracts, Toronto CMA, 1971**

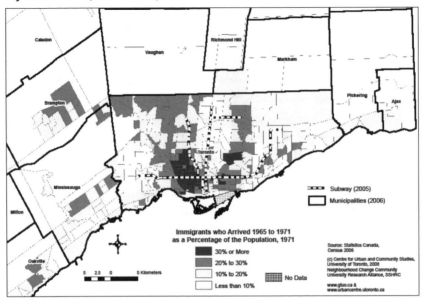

**Recent Immigrant (2001-2006) Percentage of the Population
by Census Tracts, Toronto CMA, 2006**

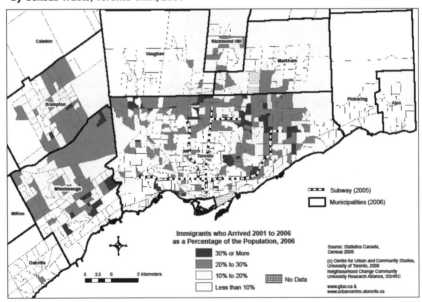

Figure 10.5   Distribution of recent immigrants in Toronto, 1965–1971 and
2001–2006. Contrary to early theories that predicted immigrants would
typically settle in inner-city ethnic enclaves, newcomers to Toronto and many
other North American cities are settling in the inner and outer suburbs, in
both "ethnoburbs" and more mixed neighbourhoods. *Source:* Courtesy of
Robert A. Murdie, "Diversity and Concentration in Canadian Immigration:
Trends in Toronto, Montréal and Vancouver, 1971–2006" (Research Bulletin
42, Centre for Urban and Community Studies [Cities Centre], University of
Toronto, 2008), 8. Available at http://www.urbancentre.utoronto.ca/pdfs/
researchbulletins/CUCSRB42-Murdie-Cdn-Immigration3-2008.pdf.

Box 10.3 Geographic Perspectives on Regionalizing and Localizing Immigration Policy

Immigration policy, long considered the domain of the US and Canadian nation-states, is scaling downward to regional and local jurisdictions, which may feel the effects of immigration more strongly than the nation-state as a whole. Some individual states and cities are now leveraging or attempting to leverage policies that will mold immigrant flows to their own needs and identities. In Canada, the new policies have been largely provincial and pro-immigration. In the United States, their ordinances have been county-based or municipal and have been more mixed in stance. There have been exceptions, however, in both countries: in 1994, the state of California passed Proposition 187 (overturned by the Supreme Court) to mandate citizenship screening and expel illegal immigrants. In 2007, the town of Herouxville in Quebec passed several ordinances defining unsuitable practices for potential new immigrants, even though the town had no immigrants at the time.

In Canada, immigration policy has typically been regionalized through provincial nominee programs (PNPs), which are federally sanctioned programs that devolve immigrant attraction, selection, settlement, and integration responsibilities to provincial governments. The first PNPs, which relaxed language requirements for new immigrants and allowed individual employers to make nominations, were instituted in the early 2000s. They were intended to incentivize immigration to economically and demographically declining regions (e.g., the Prairie and Maritime provinces) rather than the "MTV" cities (Montreal, Toronto, Vancouver) that account for 80 percent of immigration to Canada. Although empirical research on these programs is still limited, a few studies find that PNPs—while meeting economic and demographic imperatives—often have unintended consequences for immigrants and the communities they settle in. Studies on both Manitoba and Nova Scotia have found that nominees may receive misinformation about the finicky labor and business markets in these regions. In addition, because nominees are encouraged to settle outside of large urban centers, they may end up in small communities not fully prepared to meet their integration needs (e.g., language training) or provide sufficient housing and medical care.

In the United States, hundreds of municipalities and counties have proposed or implemented local immigration policies ranging from "sanctuary" policies (e.g., accepting Mexican consular cards as identification) to those aimed at apprehending undocumented immigrants (e.g., checking the immigration status of anyone arrested). These local initiatives have existed since the 1980s but grew in number to move the border "inward" following 9/11. Pro-immigration ordinances are clustered in the West and in central cities (areas with traditionally high levels of immigration) while anti-immigration measures are clustered in the South, rural areas, and suburbs—areas generally experiencing accelerating immigration. The Northeastern urban corridor is an especially interesting area. Some regions, such as the Washington, DC, metropolitan area, include both sanctuary policies (Takoma Park, Maryland)

and exclusionary policies (Manassas Park and Herndon, Virginia) that play on different conceptions of identity. Takoma Park sees community health and cooperation as important, whereas the Virginian policies invoke a legalized, *American* identity as most important. Demographics may also play a role: the clustering of anti-immigration ordinances in northeastern Pennsylvania may reflect the dominance of older-generation communities that—while not experiencing much immigration—feel that limiting immigration will maintain what they see as their hard-earned stake in the American Dream.

Sources: Walker, Kyle E., and Helga Leitner. 2011. "The Variegated Landscape of Local Immigration Policies in the US." *Urban Geography* 32(2): 156–78; Lewis, Nathaniel M. 2010. "A Decade Later: Assessing Successes and Challenges in Manitoba's Provincial Immigrant Nominee Program." *Canadian Public Policy* 36(2): 241–64.

TRANSNATIONAL CITIES AND IDENTITIES

The increasing density of connections between immigrants, their countries of origin, and the North American gateway cities they settle in has led to the emergence of cross-border practices and identities typically referred to as "transnational." Cities, eager to capitalize on the cachet and dynamism of an international population have also branded themselves as transnational or "global." To some extent, transnationalism has influenced macroeconomic changes, such as the increasing dominance of transnational corporations (TNCs) in the global economy. New York, Los Angeles, Chicago, and Toronto—ranked second, third, fourth, and twenty-second, respectively, in the world rankings of metropolitan-area gross domestic product (GDP)—are home to branches of TNCs such as Verizon (telecommunications), Disney (entertainment), Boeing (hi-tech manufacturing), and Toronto Dominion Canada Trust (finance). At a more human level, transnational practices might include working and living in both New York and London, sending a portion of one's nursing salary from Winnipeg to family in Manila, or creating an activist organization in Toronto in order to influence politics in Sri Lanka.

Transnationalism has often been celebrated as a set of productive international linkages that facilitates innovation and allows people to live beyond the legal regimes or cultural conventions of any one country. Certain case studies bear out this more celebratory perspective. Berkeley political scientist AnnaLee Saxenian has documented the role of transnational immigrants in the economic growth and development of the San Jose-Santa Clara metropolitan area of California, commonly known as Silicon Valley. She argues that the Indian, Chinese, and Israeli professionals who were educated in the engineering and computer science programs of local institutions like Stanford University—and who stayed in the area to work—were central in the establishment of Silicon Valley as the preeminent high-tech cluster in North America. These newcomers, which Saxenian calls "argonauts" (i.e., adventurers), have created a form of global ethnic entrepreneurship through San Jose–area ethnic organizations, such as the Chinese Institute of Engineers and the Silicon Valley Indian Professionals Association. Through these organizations, new immigrants find both a social network as they adapt to life in Silicon Valley as well as a forum for knowledge sharing and a trusted source of potential start-up partners or new investors. But as some of these immigrants return to India, China, Israel, and other countries—sometimes to start new companies with partners found in Silicon Valley—new flows of people and ideas are emerging. Saxenian calls this "brain circulation," as opposed to a one-way "brain drain." Return immigrants have now created their own start-up firms in Bangalore (India), Tel Aviv-Haifa (Israel), and other emerging technology centers abroad, adapting North American products (e.g., smartphones) to meet the technological and financial parameters of other countries. In addition, centers like Bangalore are now creating new technologies of their own and attracting venture capitalists from the Silicon Valley Bank.

Many cities have tried to parlay the diversity of their populations into identities as "global cities" or "cosmopolitan cities." In 1998, Toronto—known for its "hyperdiverse" population including 44 percent foreign-born residents from South and East Asia, Latin America, and the Caribbean—adopted the motto "Our Diversity, Our Strength." The mere presence of transnational immigrants, however, does not imply that their skills or cultural contributions are valued equally to those of native-born Canadians. Only about one-third of immigrants in Toronto are working in jobs at the same skill level of the jobs they left behind. Despite the emphasis on skills-based selection in the Canadian immigration regime, many immigrants find that their existing credentials as doctors, nurses, engineers, or professors are deemed insuffi-

cient to work in those positions in Canada, resulting in a blockage of knowledge transfer, or "brain waste." Instead, immigrants, and especially women immigrants, are often relegated to jobs that are the lowest skilled and in the most volatile sectors, such as manufacturing and food processing.

Noting these kinds of inconsistencies, many scholars have observed that there is nothing inherently transcendent or transgressive about transnationalism; in fact, it may reflect or even perpetuate existing gender and cultural biases. The celebrated immigrant entrepreneurs of Silicon Valley, for example, are mostly men. Feminist geographers have observed that these cases of transnational success are perhaps less common for women, whose mobility may be limited or whose work may be devalued. Immigrant women engaged in child or elder care, for example, may not have the income or flexible schedule necessary to travel back and forth between countries, yet they typically send a large portion of their income to family at home. Women have also suffered disproportionately from some of the ugliest forms of the transnational economy, including the sex worker trade and employee abuse in US-managed *maquiladoras* (i.e., factories) along the Mexican border. Immigrants in most cities also tend not to reach the highest positions in their profession, even when they are working within their desired field. Even in Silicon Valley, few of the Chinese and Indian engineers ever reach positions in upper management. In addition, when immigrants have enough financial capital and social cohesion to transform cities in visible ways, conflicts based on discourses of race and otherness may begin to override the cachet of a "global city" moniker (see box 10.4).

Box 10.4 Vancouver's Transnational Anxieties

Vancouver, the capital of the Canadian province of British Columbia, has long been a gateway for new immigrants, particularly from East Asia and especially China. The Chinese represent the largest immigrant group in Vancouver but are joined by large numbers of Indians, Filipinos, and older groups such as British, Italians, and Portuguese, making Vancouver Canada's second-most diverse city after Toronto. Immigrants from China, however, have one of the longest histories in the city and have received the most attention in citywide debates and discourses over identity. Early Chinese immigrants, many of whom came to work on the Canadian Pacific Railway in the mid-1800s, represented one of the first visible ethnic communities in downtown Vancouver. As Kay Anderson has discussed in her book *Vancouver's Chinatown*, the propagation of "Chinatown" as an idea was as much an effort on the part of the city to keep the Chinese "other" within a delineated geographic space as it was a creation of the Chinese community itself.

Yet the use of racial discourse in the Vancouver media is not an artifact of the past; in fact, it intensified following the upsurge of immigrants from Hong Kong in the 1980s and 1990s, who had moved in anticipation of the return of Hong Kong (a British colony) to China in 1997. In the Vancouver suburb of Richmond, the percentage of people claiming Chinese ancestry increased from 8 percent in 1986 to 45 percent in 2006. In addition, the total percentage of immigrants (about half from Hong Kong or China) increased from 31 percent in 1986 to 65 percent as of 2006, with the annual inflow doubling between 1980 and 1994. At various moments, the surge of immigration has created a "moral panic" in the Vancouver media over both the city's identity and Canadian identity at large. Some claimed that, ironically, the once-colonized citizens of Hong Kong were becoming the colonizers of British Columbia. The 1990s became a flashpoint for anti-Asian discourse in Vancouver, in which several tactics were employed to illustrate the "problem" of Asian immigration. Some articles claimed that Chinese immigrants were fishing illegally in Stanley Park; others claimed that the Asian domination of Richmond was creating a "white flight" to south-of-center exurbs like Tsawassen, and yet others claimed that new Chinese shopping malls were creating a type of "cultural ghettoization" out of line with Canada's multiculturalism. Perhaps the chief vehicle for the creation of moral panic was the claim that wealthy Hong Kong immigrants were building contemporary-style "monster homes" in neighborhoods like Shaughnessy, which had previously been dominated by typically "Anglo" Tudor-style homes. Non-Chinese saw the term "monster" as a reference to the size of the home; Chinese immigrants took it as an unfair, racist derision of homeowners who had simply wanted houses large enough to accommodate multigenerational families.

The climate has changed considerably in the past decade. The acute panic seems to have subsided, and derogatory terms such as "Hongcouver" are less common than they were in the 1990s. The Asian population of Vancouver is also spatially integrated compared to cities such as Los Angeles and Toronto. The influx of Hong Kong property developers and real-estate speculators has transformed many areas of downtown Vancouver (e.g., Yaletown) from low-density zones to collections of glass-and-steel skyscrapers housing both condos and corporations (see figure 10.6). In addition, the so-called super student children of Chinese immigrants are said to have raised the quality of local schools and universities. At the same time, immigrants continue to be blamed for driving up the cost of rent and the competitiveness of schools. Perhaps a more pressing issue, however, is the growing reverse brain drain from Vancouver back to cities such as Hong Kong, Beijing, and Singapore. Chinese businesspeople, who often find themselves unable to reach the CEO level in Vancouver despite equal levels of education and business success (signaling the persistence of a race-based glass ceiling), return to Asian cities where the economy is booming and opportunities abound. Consequently, families in which one or both parents were previously leading "argonaut" lives between Asia and Canada have chosen to firmly ground themselves on the other side of the Pacific.

Figure 10.6   The glass and steel skyscraper developments that began to grace Vancouver's skyline in the 1980s were funded largely by transnational capital from Hong Kong. (Photo by John Paul Catungal)

FROM COSMOPOLITAN
TO CREATIVE

Creative class theory has arguably become the most dominant trend in urban development during the past decade. As shown in chapter 2, economic geographer Richard Florida introduced this idea in his 2002 book *Rise of the Creative Class*. Creative class theory riffed on the changes that were happening in North American cities at the time (e.g., the shift to knowledge-based industries such as biomedical technology and software engineering) by demonstrating that the most successful cities were those that could attract the so-called creative class. A variant of the cosmopolitan global elite described above, the creative class comprises a highly educated population that works in "creative" industries such as arts, education, management, engineering, and de-

sign and that is ostensibly attracted to cities possessing the "three t's:" technology, talent, and tolerance. While the persuasiveness of the theory is evident in hundreds of urban policy plans, such as Toronto's Culture Plan for the Creative City and the Michigan Cool Cities Program, it has been critiqued as an overly simplistic theory that simply grafts the appealing ideas of arts, creativity, and bohemia onto what are otherwise basic economic development ideas (e.g., the importance of human capital and the high-tech firm). For cities unable to attract the next silicon start-up or major design firm, however, the idea of just building a creative identity becomes more attractive. Consequently, many cities have spent millions of dollars on streetscape plans, loft development, large-scale arts and entertainment venues, and marketing campaigns in order to produce a creative image (see figure 10.7).

Figure 10.7   In a few North American cities, art and design have become tools for redevelopment and even reindustrialization of declining areas. In Montreal's Mile End, several boutiques have opened, and street banners advertise a local television program, *Mode Montreal TV*, that focuses on local fashion and design. (Photo by Norma Rantisi)

Based on the way in which "creative cities" are now ranked, tabled, and indexed, even small cities may feel pressured to compete with the Torontos and San Franciscos of the continent, even when their real advantages may lie elsewhere (see box 10.5).

Box 10.5 Halifax: Making the Small City Competitive

While immigration, gentrification, and debates over identity are not limited to large cities, they tend to dominate the study of these topics. Consequently, small cities often find themselves without a strong body of research to guide their planning and development strategies, sometimes opting to mimic the big-city strategies to become "competitive" and "global." One such city encountering these challenges is Halifax, Nova Scotia (population 403,188 in the regional municipality), the provincial capital located on the east-coast periphery of Canada. Left out of the urban discourses dominated by the "MTV" cities of Montreal, Toronto, and Vancouver, the development of Halifax has followed a different trajectory characterized by slower growth, relative cultural homogeneity, and the domination of a few key economic sectors. During the past several decades, the city has carefully toed the line between maintaining its own identity and mimicking its neighbors to the west.

Established by the British in 1749, Halifax has always been a center for both the military and higher education, anchored by a naval base and five universities. Despite development setbacks such as the 1911 Halifax Explosion, in which an exploding cargo ship in the harbor destroyed much of the city's north end, Halifax pressed on and eventually created a city master plan for growth in the early 1940s. The plan would form the foundation of typical mid-century urban renewal strategies that would later be heavily criticized. In the late 1960s, for example, the city government demolished Africville—an African Canadian community at the northern tip of Halifax—in order to build a highway interchange and enlarge the port. The 1970s marked a turn in which residents began organizing to publicly protest new building projects, usually on the premise that they would compromise the preservation of heritage buildings and the historic character of the city.

By the 1990s, however, the city had turned its eye to growth again, and the Greater Halifax Partnership (a development association) adopted the brand of "smart city" to reflect the city's status as having the highest proportion of university-educated residents in Canada at the time. The thought was that playing up education would attract new firms and other talented workers. The realities of working in sectors such as health care, policy, and research in Halifax, however, are somewhat more difficult. National funding outlets and potential clients tend to employ the same logic of a "place effect" or "competitive effect" that has allowed San Jose to emerge as an undisputed leader in the high-tech field: being the best requires being located where that industry is most concentrated and innovation is most likely to occur. Biomedical researchers, for example, are likely to leave Halifax for Montreal or Toronto in order to gain better funding, employment, or opportunities to build their reputation.

Having acknowledged the disadvantages of its position in Canada's urban hierarchy, Halifax has increasingly turned to strategies to grow itself from the bottom up. For example, the municipal government has adopted a city immigration plan to provide incentives for entrepreneurs and professionals, and Halifax is positioned as the target city for the Nova Scotia Provincial Nominee Program. Interestingly, about a third of immigrants to Halifax come from the United Kingdom and the United States, while most immigrants in other Canadian cities are coming from Asia, a discrepancy based on higher barriers to integration and expectations of cultural assimilation in a mostly Anglo province. Increasingly, Halifax is turning to creative city strategies, a trend marked by visits from creative city gurus Richard Florida in 2004 and Charles Landry in 2009. One strategy is to foster the "artistic dividend" (i.e., buzz and cultural cachet) imparted by Halifax's vibrant music scene—a sector bolstered by low-rent practice and performing spaces and an overall low cost of living.

Yet Halifax seems to be conflating the vibrancy of actual creative sectors with creating a "creative-looking" city, marked by loft living, the installation of arts and entertainment venues, and the expansion and intensification of downtown residential zones. In 2009, the city introduced a streamlined development process in which building proposals are approved solely based on adherence to city codes and design guidelines rather than public consultation. Incidentally, Haligonians typically name the city's natural assets, ease of transportation, and laid-back, low-cost living as its most attractive attributes. In an effort to be competitive, it appears that Halifax could risk destroying the advantages it already possesses—advantages that may become even more important in a declining economy and the quest for a greener, more sustainable future in North America.

Globalization has not only informed urban development trends like the creative class but actually fostered the diffusion of development strategies from place to place. Although the diffusion of these "fast policies" is global, their execution is highly local, usually at the neighborhood scale. Two relatively new identity creation strategies are urban villages and business improvement districts. The urban village concept was popularized in the United Kingdom in the late 1990s and typically earmarks a delineated area for medium-density development, pedestrian-friendly measures, and mixed-use zoning rather than the single-use zoning that had spurred the development of industrial parks and suburbs in the 1950s and 1960s. While these measures seem appealing, many geographers have questioned whether developing self-contained villages or "urban campuses" within cities is realistic or sustainable. In their study of Liberty Village in Toronto, geographers John Paul Catungal and Deborah Leslie found that the creation of the village involved two types of displacement: (1) the displacement of an increasingly gentrified, securitized neighborhood from the broader urban network and (2) the displacement of groups (e.g., artists unable to afford redeveloped studio space) who fail to align with the new vision for the neighborhood. Ironically, Liberty Village continues to use art and creativity as key elements of its marketing scheme (see figure 10.8).

Figure 10.8   Business improvement areas, which brand themselves through distinctive signage, aim to repopulate downtown neighborhoods by cleaning and beautifying streets and working with developers to create new residential spaces. (Photo by John Paul Catungal)

The business improvement district (BID), developed in both Canada and the United States in the early 1970s, is a quasi-governmental association in which businesses and property owners within a delineated area pay a surtax for collective, privately provided services such as street cleaning, trash pickup, beautification, business recruitment, and security/police protection. Generally, an executive board of the dominant business and property owners makes decisions about which services to use and how to change the look and feel of the neighborhood. In Toronto, a scaled-down business improvement area (BIA) format often includes residents on executive boards, which could actually deepen local democracy. In Washington, DC, in contrast, large, corporatized BIDs created during a period of dysfunctional urban governance in the early 2000s have taken it upon themselves to fully redesign many postindustrial areas for the upwardly mobile buyer. Some have even taken over public, city-provided services, even hiring off-duty DC police officers as private security guards to patrol areas that are still "in transition."

The central thread of all of these strategies is their emphasis on property speculation and development. For cities seeking to develop their deindustrialized cores or create new identities for themselves, urban villages, BIDs, and zoning changes offer low-cost ways to encourage redevelopment. They do not, however, provide comprehensive plans that consider the broader range of affected residents, including displaced low-income and working-class families. Consequently, it is quickly becoming property developers (e.g., condominium and real-estate companies), not cities themselves, that are circumscribing the identities of neighborhoods—and to some extent, the identities of people living in them. This shift has mixed consequences for different groups of urban residents. For women, condominium development might "liberate" single-income women by making downtown living affordable. It might also employ gender stereotypes for marketing purposes (see box 10.6). For gay men and lesbians, newer, more accelerated versions of development and gentrification may be shifting the "out and proud" visibilities and identities they once helped to establish (see box 10.7).

Box 10.6 Geographic Perspectives on Gender and Gentrification

The Toronto housing market, boosted by high immigration and a large market of young buyers, has entered an unprecedented era of new-build development in the downtown core, with over one hundred thousand condominium units completed in the past ten years. Increasingly, women are both the buyers of these new properties and the targets of real-estate marketing campaigns that employ different notions of women's identities (see figure 10.9). Female one-person households are the largest group of condominium owners in Toronto, and women are featured in the vast majority of advertisements in publications such as *Condo Weekly*.

One on hand, the trend toward women purchasing condos in Toronto has been celebrated as a new phase of liberation, in which women have joined the institution of home ownership in Canada. Typically incentivized through lending practices that favor young buyers, home ownership has long been cast as a step toward becoming a responsible, morally upstanding Canadian citizen. In one way, this is increasingly true: many women, especially in single-

Figure 10.9   In Toronto, the female form and "sexy" marketing are aimed at attracting the growing numbers of single women interested in condo ownership. (Photo by Leslie Kern)

income households, see the purchase of property as a means to financial security or capital accumulation in an increasingly volatile economy. A condominium may also be more affordable than a house for a single woman eschewing some of the pressure to be in a dual-income partnership before purchasing property. The ads that market condos to women echo these ideas, employing images of the liberated, creative, independent woman, much like those in the popular HBO show *Sex and the City*—for example, a woman enjoying nightlife with her female friends, working on an artistic endeavor, or holding a meeting at a coffeehouse.

At the same time, the condominium market also capitalizes on long-standing gender divisions in cities. First, real-estate agents often market certain buildings to women on the basis of security or "peace of mind" features, such as twenty-four-hour concierge, key-card entry, security cameras, and gated underground parking. In this way, developers prey upon preexisting, gendered expectations about fear in the city, especially in newly gentrifying peripheral areas. Because women have been taught to "feel fear," they may be more likely to purchase properties in these more expensive buildings. Second, the extent to which condo ownership actually facilitates women's inclusion in public life may be quite narrow. First, the securitized, multiple-amenity condo may facilitate community *within* the building rather than interaction with the surrounding city. Gyms, patios, on-site coffee shops, barbecue pits, and the other quasi-public areas of the condo building may become women's central social spaces while they carefully pick and choose where and when to engage with the city around them. Moreover, these types of buildings are geared toward a specific type of female consumer, one who can both afford to purchase the condo and use the revitalized downtown core as she sees fit, while less privileged women (e.g., poor, single mothers) may be displaced into the decaying inner suburbs. Third and finally, women—despite becoming a target market for new-build gentrification—are less frequently involved in the organization of gentrification and development processes. Real-estate developers, property owners, and the executive boards of the business improvement areas managing the neighborhoods where these condos are located tend to be mostly male. These men are therefore articulating the supposed needs and demands of the female market and deciding on the best uses for the downtown core.

Source: Kern, Leslie. 2010. "Selling the Scary City." *Social & Cultural Geography* 11(3): 209–30.

It seems that in 2013, North American cities are reaching a turning point. The population boom in full force fifty years ago is on the verge of becoming a population bust with severe consequences for urban housing markets, economies, and livelihoods. The increasingly diverse streams of immigration, enabled by the reforms initiated shortly after the end of the baby boom, represent a potential buffer for this bust. At the same time, the North American stance on immigration is ambiguous and geographically variable. Identity seems to be at the center of this debate. Immigrants are no longer ghettoized, low-skilled providers of manual labor; in fact, newcomers and their children are creating identities as

Box 10.7 Geographic Perspectives on Gay Villages

In the context of changing laws (e.g., gay marriage) and urban processes such as gentrification, the identities of people who are lesbian, gay, bisexual, transgendered, and queer (LGBTQ)—sometimes shortened to "queer"—have also become more complex and contested. Although scholars have given increasing attention to queer communities in rural areas and queer domestic lives, the city remains the geographic focal point of queer studies. According to many, the centrality of the city in queer cultures is historically rooted in the rural-to-urban migrations of the Industrial Revolution, during which single men and women were freed from nuclear family structures. Early gay and lesbian life in cities centered on unmarked bars and lounges, private parties, and informal public meeting places. More recently, however, the expression of nonnormative sexual identities in cities has come to be associated with the gay village.

Early gay villages reflected a "territorialization" strategy in which queer people—usually gay men—bought up businesses and residential property in peripheral neighborhoods in an effort to demonstrate the visibility and upward mobility that they felt were integral to making claims for equal rights. Figure 10.10 reflects a "traditional" space of the LGBTQ community. Some claim that this "territorialization" stage, which occurred in many landmark villages (e.g., the Castro in San Francisco, Church Street in Toronto) during the 1970s and 1980s, was just a preliminary phase in the "evolution" of gay villages. The evolution model suggested that gay villages would become more mainstream as their commercial districts became attractive to heterosexual residents and the growing acceptance of queer people rendered the village less necessary. The past decade has, in fact, been a particularly formative time for the advancement of gay and lesbian rights in North America. In 2005, Canada legalized gay marriage at the federal level, and—as of 2013—eight US states had followed the same path. The US military also repealed its "Don't Ask, Don't Tell" policy in 2011, and a year later, the US Supreme Court judged California's Proposition 8 (a state referendum banning same-sex marriage) to be unconstitutional.

Yet the implications of these changes for LGBTQ identities, and for gay villages specifically, seem far from uniform. In cities such as Montreal and Chicago, gay villages have

Figure 10.10   While the Internet has in some ways expanded the networks and linkages among LGBTQ communities in North American cities, some observe that the "traditional" spaces of the bookstore and the bar are now becoming endangered. (Photo by Petra Doan)

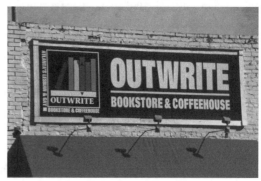

been heavily branded and marketed by business associations and municipal governments. Here, they have evolved into established commercial districts but have also been criticized as "boys towns" (Chicago's village is actually named "Boys Town") that exclude lesbians and the broader array of queer identities. They have also been criticized as areas that crassly commodify sexual identity for the consumption of cosmopolitan heterosexual consumers while offering few venues or outlets for queer people who lack high disposable incomes or whose cultural identities fall outside of the Euro-American mainstream. In a few cases, gay villages may be stripped of their "gay" identity by municipal governments trying to remarket the area to the upwardly mobile heterosexual mainstream. Urban planner Petra Doan finds that Atlanta has purposefully "de-gayed" the neighborhood of Midtown through rent increases, property speculation, closures of bars, and denials of applications for LGBTQ events.

In Canada, where gay rights are both more established (homosexuality was decriminalized in 1968, as opposed to 2003 in the United States), "the village" has become a hot topic in the gay media of many cities. Geographer Catherine Nash notes that recent articles have proclaimed the Church-Wellesley gay village to be passé and undesirable to the queer community. Invoking the idea of the "post-mo," these articles have launched a two-sided dismissal of the village. On one side, they claim that the village has become too commercialized and therefore exclusive, in turn increasing the popularity of "alternative" queer venues in the west-of-center Parkdale neighborhood. They also suggest that because safe space is no longer needed in a new era of full gay rights, the idea of a gay village has become irrelevant altogether. Two hundred miles away, in the national capital of Ottawa, a very different story has emerged. In a city more known for its Cold War–era expulsions of gay men from the civil service than for a highly visible queer community, the mayor and the municipal government designated a six-block section of Bank Street as the official gay village in late 2011. Given its location in a medium-density commercial zone with only a few gay establishments—and its designation at a time when most gay and lesbian rights have been attained in Canada—it is doubtful that territorial visibility or commercialization are the aims of this village. In contrast, the city, prompted by a long campaign by local activists, has finally decided to create a symbolic home for the queer community in a city that has not always been welcoming to it.

Sources: Nash, Catherine J. 2013. "The Age of the 'Post-Mo'? Toronto's Gay Village and a New Generation." *Geoforum*, December 22, 2012. Available at http://dx.doi.org/10.1016/j.geoforum.2012.11.023; Lewis, Nathaniel M. 2013. "Ottawa's Le/The Village: The Creation of a 'Gaybourhood' amidst the Death of the Village." *Geoforum*, February 15, 2013. Available at http://dx.doi.org/10.1016/j.geoforum.2013.01.004.

revitalizers, innovators, and businesspeople. Yet the identities that older Americans and Canadians ascribe to this group sometimes remain stuck in the past, positioning immigrants and their children as perpetual "others." Identity, now more than ever, is also taking center stage in urban development projects geared to creating identities for cities and fulfilling the imagined identities of their would-be residents. Even as North American cities strive to grow into megaregions and become more linked with other countries, the effects of the strategies they use are often felt at the level of the neighborhood. In their efforts to be global and cosmopolitan, cities and private actors such as property developers are targeting the neighborhoods with the potential to become homes for a well-educated but fickle global elite seeking out the next cool, creative hot spot. The result is a set of increasingly fragmented cities in which redeveloped "villages" and decaying, sometimes abandoned neighborhoods exist side by side. Nor has globalization morphed together the identities of urban dwellers. Far from adopting some kind of cosmopolitan mega-identity, women, immigrants, racial minorities, and gay men and lesbians continue to experience urban change in vastly different ways and to shape or contest their identities accordingly. There is little doubt that the next fifty years of urban change will be equally transformative

for these two volatile, sensitive, and fascinating topics of study.

SUGGESTED READINGS

Doan, P. 2011. *Queerying Planning: Challenging Heteronormative Assumption and Reframing Planning Practice*. Farnham, England: Ashgate.

Fincher, R., and J. M. Jacobs, eds. 1998. *Cities of Difference*. New York: Guilford Press.

Kern, L. 2010. *Sex and the Revitalized City: Gender, Condominium Development, and Urban Citizenship*. Vancouver: University of British Columbia Press.

Li, W. 2009. *Ethnoburb: The New Ethnic Community in Urban America*. Honolulu: University of Hawaii Press.

Myers, D. 2007. *Immigrants and Boomers: Forging a New Social Contract for the Future of America*. New York: Russell Sage.

Price, M., and L. Benton-Short, eds. 2008. *Migrants to the Metropolis: The Rise of Immigrant Gateway Cities*. Syracuse: Syracuse University Press.

Saxenian, A. 2006. *The New Argonauts: Regional Advantage in a Global Economy*. Cambridge, MA: Harvard University Press.

Teixera, C., W. Li, and A. Kobayashi, eds. 2012. *Immigrant Geographies of North American Cities*. Don Mills, ON: Oxford University Press Canada.

Zelinsky, W. 2001. *The Enigma of Ethnicity: Another American Dilemma*. Iowa City: University of Iowa Press.

11

Suburban Challenges
BERNADETTE HANLON

In recent decades, suburbs of North America have become sites of immense change. One element of change that has received a lot of media and scholarly attention is the recent rise in suburban poverty. The year 1999 marked the date when large US cities and their suburbs had nearly equal numbers of poor people, but, as Brookings Institution scholars Alan Berube and Elizabeth Kneebone indicate, by 2005, the suburban poor outnumbered the city poor by about one million. In the advent of the 2008 Great Recession, suburban poverty has risen dramatically. According to a recent study by the Brookings Institution, between 2000 and 2008, the poor population of the suburbs of large US metropolitan areas grew by 25 percent, five times more rapidly than the urban poor. As the census figures rolled in, the situation grew worse. As the Brookings study shows, from 2000 to 2010, the number of poor individuals in major-metro suburbs of the United States grew by 53 percent (5.3 million people), compared with 23 percent in cities. In 2010, a total of forty-six million Americans were estimated to live under the poverty line, and some 15.4 million of them lived in the suburbs.

Suburbs have no doubt been hit hard by the recent economic crisis, but it is important to point out that some suburbs have long been suffering from the problem of socioeconomic decline. Suburban decline and poverty is not just a recent problem but has actually been a growing concern since the 1980s. Certainly, unemployment has plagued some suburbanites in recent years, and many suburbs have witnessed foreclosure abandonment in the wake of the housing market crash. However, it is important to point out that certain suburbs have slowly been deserted by decades of disinvestment.

In some cases, the extent of decline among these suburbs is extreme, leading to the emergence of what has been referred to as "suburbs in crisis." Over the past few decades, these suburbs have experienced significant population loss, a large drop in income, and a substantial increase in poverty relative to neighboring suburbs in the same metropolitan area. From 1980 to 2000, a large number of suburbs declined to such an extent that they now closely resemble poor inner-city neighborhoods. These are suburbs with high numbers of poor residents. Minority populations, either African American, Hispanic, immigrants, or all of the above, live in these crisis suburbs. They are typically inner suburbs, although there are some on the metropolitan fringe. Many were once working-class communities where residents had stable jobs with local manufacturing companies which have since left or now manufacture their products without the need for a large workforce. Suburbs in crisis are aging both in terms of people and infrastructure, and they do not generate enough tax revenue to encourage any redevelopment or upgrading of their physical environment. This suburban stress, coined by scholars as part of a "suburban gothic," occurs particularly in older suburbs that face the serious challenges of an aging housing stock, a declining tax base, and significant economic decline.

For over a generation, both scholarly and popular discussions of poverty and economic insecurity in North America were dominated by an inner-city bias. The unstated assumption was that cities were places with problems, to be contrasted with suburbs, the primary sites of success and destinations of opportunity signified by economic growth and prosperity. This supposition has changed. Suburbia, long considered the axis of success, is showing serious signs of vulnerability. There are now numerous challenges confronting North American suburbs. These include socioeconomic decline, a continuing concern about the problem of sprawl, the need for redevelopment, particularly among aging and abandoned suburbs, and the call for social integration in what is now a highly varied and changing landscape.

CHALLENGES AND THE GOVERNANCE STRUCTURE

Metropolitan areas in North America are highly politically fragmented with many suburban and city municipalities, school districts, and townships. Suburbs are governmentally independent political units that can employ

the powers of the state to distinguish them from the city. They can also use these powers to distinguish themselves from one another and attract some and discourage others from entering their jurisdictional boundaries. Suburban municipalities make their own land-use planning decisions, implement their our housing codes, raise their own taxes to support schools and maintain and update local infrastructure, and deliver services such as garbage collection, a police force, and water and sewer utilities. Suburbs can therefore vary in terms of laws, codes, and service provision. The result is a choppy political landscape.

Public governance is only one aspect of the metropolitan political structure. In recent decades, there has been a proliferation of private suburban neighborhoods. These typically comprise single-family housing or condominiums managed by homeowners associations (HOA). These associations enforce regulations and deliver local civic goods and services using fees collected from each resident member (figure 11.1). Residents of these communities literally separate themselves from everyone else, setting their own rules for living there. This, some argue, has led to a problem of "civic succession," where residents in private communities, particularly those that are gated, wall themselves off from the rest of society and avoid taking responsibility for the plight of other citizens. According to the research on gated communities, residents move into these areas for a number of reasons, including a fear of crime, a desire for security and limited contact with strangers, maintenance of property values, and spatial insulation from those who are different from them. Middle- and upper-income residents in particular want to associate with people of a similar class and secure their position

Figure 11.1   A gated retirement suburb in Orange County, California. The development, Palmira, is restricted to residents over the age of fifty-five. (Photo by Lisa Benton-Short)

in society. The spread of private communities in the suburbs ultimately encourages the spatial segregation of classes and ethno-racial groups. Private communities, privatopias, and fortressed cities are symptomatic spatial products of fear and segregation from "the other."

In addition to the problem of spatial segregation, there are also more practical concerns. Evan McKenzie, in his 2011 book *Beyond Privatopia*, points out that as private suburbs continue to age, it is likely that these residential communities will become an increasing burden on local and state governments. HOAs are largely run on a volunteer basis, and there are many examples of financial mismanagement among these organizations, resulting in an inability to fund repairs or manage physical facilities. Financial problems have increased with the foreclosure crisis and the recent real-estate debacle. In addition, there are many examples of legal wrangling over zealous rules and regulations. McKenzie effectively makes the case that there is under way "institutional convergence," where the distinction between public and private governance of residential development has blurred. The privatization of public services may initially relieve the local and state government of the economic

burden of new suburban development. This is, in part, why they are so popular. But as private communities age and suffer management issues, state and local governments are forced to step in to fix the private roads, handle mosquito-infested detention ponds, and manage dilapidated common spaces.

Despite these issues, the privatization of suburbia is likely to continue. Local governments are increasingly adopting a more corporate business approach to governance. Residents of various communities are like consumers, charged fees for services that were at one time provided for by local taxes. In the future, it may be that suburban governments will have to provide the plethora of regulations characteristic of private communities. Local governments are already installing security cameras in different locations and introducing new codes and regulations to prevent certain types of activities. In this era of neoliberalism, there is a strong trend toward privatization, reflected in an increased proliferation of private suburban communities and a corporate model of public governance. This shift means poor suburbanites will be left without when unable to pay for services; residential spaces and related activities will be managed and regulated by private law as much as by the political process; and challenges of segregation, decline, sprawl, and creation of a sustainable suburbia will become increasingly more difficult in a fragmented political landscape

SUBURBAN FORMS AND THEIR CHALLENGES

Most North Americans now live in suburbs. Both Canada and the United States have been truly suburban nations since the 1960s. Long the symbolic bastion of white, middle-class life, suburbia in both countries has been molded by a diverse population. It is now well recognized that North American suburbs vary by race, ethnicity, age, and other characteristics. In recent years, the numbers of blacks, immigrants, and different ethnicities living in the suburbs has grown; the suburban population has aged; and there is growing variation in the types of households residing in suburbs, from single-person, gay, or single-parent households to the more traditional, two-person family with children. The traditional model of white middle-class suburbia no longer holds true.

At the same time, the physical environment of suburbs has evolved to include different residential, commercial, and industrial configurations. Many suburbs have grown to such an extent that they span larger areas and include bigger employment centers than many central cities. The expansive decentralization of urban functions has created simultaneously distinct and nebulous settlement forms such as exurbs, edge cities, and edgeless cities whose boundaries and location are difficult to define, especially in relation to the traditional core/periphery model of urbanization. These new forms of suburban development indicate, for some, a new era of postsuburbia where the region has been literally "turned inside out." These newer suburban developments function like cities, but they do not take on the same form as cities. They are expansive, sprawling developments that possess no recognizable center or peripheries. Consuming many square miles of space, they lack large, traditional downtown areas, are not very pedestrian friendly, and are perceived as socially and culturally hollow places.

Today there are many different suburban forms with different characteristics and, as such, different problems (see box 11.1). Some older suburbs have morphed, and the newer postsuburban settlements have emerged to create a complex pattern of metropolitan development in North America.

Box 11.1 Geographic Perspectives on Suburbs

It is a challenge to define suburbs and even more of a challenge to geographically designate different types of suburbs such as inner-ring suburbs, edge cities, edgeless cities, and exurbs. In recognition of the need for definitions, Martin Turcotte, researcher with Statistics Canada, the central statistics office for Canada, produced a document in 2008 titled *The City/Suburb Contrast: How Can We Measure It?* In this report, he offers a number of possible approaches to delineate suburban and urban geography. One approach is the use of municipal boundaries.

North American suburbs and cities have their own distinct administrative and political boundaries. The city is defined as the core or central municipality, separate from peripheral municipalities and towns within the same metropolitan area. However, as Turcotte points out, there are some disadvantages to using municipal boundaries for delineating suburbs. This definition does not consider form or population size, for instance. There are certainly traditional suburbs *within* the central city that would have to be ignored if one uses the municipal boundary definition. For instance, Roland Park would not count because this traditional suburb lies inside the city of Baltimore. At the same time, some periphery municipalities have very large populations and function much like central cities. For instance, Arlington, a municipality outside the central city of Dallas, has a population greater than 365,000, hardly reflective of what might be considered suburban in a traditional sense. In fact, the population size of Arlington is greater than that of the city of Cincinnati. Another example of a "suburban city" is Mississauga, outside of Toronto. With seven hundred thousand people, Mississauga is the sixth-largest city in Canada, but it is located right next to Toronto. Some might describe this as an edge city, since it was built on greenfield land in the 1960s and does have office and retail space. But Mississauga was built mainly to house the institutional functions of city hall and is the center of a very large municipality. Mississauga is not the stereotype of a suburb but rather fits the model of a large postwar suburban-like city even better than Arlington.

As Turcotte suggests, the metropolis is becoming increasingly more complex with the evolution of different types of neighborhoods that do not fit a traditional model of core cities and peripheral suburbs. On the one hand, some neighborhoods close to the downtown area of cities mimic postwar suburbs in form. On the other hand, peripheral areas are extremely dense, contain a variety of land uses, and function more like cities. How, then, do we decide what is truly "suburban" in a so-called postsuburban era?

Gathering statistics on suburban municipalities remains important for decision makers. Policy makers are interested in determining how their jurisdiction is doing relative to other jurisdictions. The same is true of jurisdictional residents. Data must be meaningful to politicians, metropolitan residents, nongovernmental organizations, and local decision makers. The North American census agencies collect data at the municipal level. The main advantages to using the municipal boundary to delineate a suburb are twofold: first, it is simple, and second, the analytical results are applicable to policy and planning. Are municipal boundaries the best we can expect right now? Unfortunately, there is no agreement yet over how or whether we ought to collect data for different types of suburban form; and despite our recognition that the metropolis is far more complicated than the traditional city/suburb dichotomy, we maneuver through a fragmented policy landscape, where funding decisions, land-use planning, taxation, and comparison occur at the local municipal level of geography.

Source: Turcotte, M. 2008. "The City/Suburbs Contrast: How Can We Measure It?" *Canadian Social Trends*. Statistics Canada, catalogue no. 11-008, Winter, 2–20.

Early Elite Suburbs

A number of urban historians have written about the historical development of suburbs in the United States. Probably the most renowned example is Kenneth Jackson. His landmark book, *Crabgrass Frontier*, chronicles US suburbanization from the early romantic enclaves of the nineteenth century right up to the more contemporary suburbs of the 1980s. The Canadian equivalent of Jackson's classic is Richard Harris's 2004 *Creeping Conformity*, a book that examines the history of Canada's suburbs from 1900 to 1960. In this book, Harris emphasizes how the first suburbs of Canada were largely self-built, created by and for working-class families. The result was a mix of housing styles and neighborhood types for working families around Canada's larger cities, right up until the middle of the twentieth century. In the United States, the first suburbs were similarly quite diverse. Some were working-class, self-built suburbs like those in neighboring Canada; others were primarily African American or immigrant enclaves; many were built for the elite of society.

It was these wealthy, elite suburbs that set the stage for what would later become a much more middle-class way of life. The early elite suburbs of the nineteenth century—"bourgeois utopias"—are even today branded by a particular style, largely influenced by landscapes inspired by such designers as Frederick Law Olmsted and Andrew Jackson Downing, and homes informed by the great works of architects such as Frank Lloyd Wright, the Green brothers, Alexander Jackson Davis, and many others. Examples of early well-to-do suburbs include Riverside in Illinois and Llewellyn Park in New Jersey, and then, of course, there are city neighborhoods, such as Roland Park in Baltimore and Beacon Hill in Boston, that were suburbs before being annexed by their respective cities.

Early elite suburbs have been described by Robert Fogelson as "bourgeois nightmares" rather than "bourgeois utopias." Many early wealthy suburbs used restrictive covenants forbidding owners to sell or lease their property to members of certain racial, ethnic, or religious groups, keeping certain groups out. For instance, at one time, there were deed restrictions in Roland Park in Baltimore that excluded African Americans from purchasing homes there. As a result, Roland Park remained a wealthy, white enclave. Other restrictions, such as maintaining certain architectural styles or certain types of housing, had similar effects. For instance, in 1950, Scarsdale, a wealthy older suburb outside New York City, established a building ordinance preventing repetition in the height and width of houses to preclude the development of any tract-style housing indicative of the postwar period. Scarsdale prevented the influx of working-class families into small, similarly built postwar homes. The early wealthy suburbs used their local power to exclude certain populations and maintain a specific social status. Built over a hundred years ago, these earliest suburbs are still today some of the wealthiest places in North America, and, despite their age, there have been few signs of socioeconomic decline in these suburban neighborhoods. Table 11.1 describes the characteristics of different suburban forms since the emergence of the early elite suburbs.

Notwithstanding their wealth and power, however, early elite suburbs are not without their challenges. Examples of typical issues facing old, wealthy suburbs are probably best illustrated by an examination of Upper Arlington in Ohio (see box 11.2).

Table 11.1   **Characteristics of Different Suburban Forms**

Period	Form (s)	Characteristics	Examples
1850 to 1920	Early elite suburbs	Wealthy, intricate landscape design, architectural appeal, historic main street	Llewellyn Park, NJ
	Industrial suburbs	Working class, heavy industry	Essex, MD
1945 to 1960	Postwar suburbs	Middle-class, lower-middle-class; some postwar suburbs have been upgraded; others have experienced socioeconomic decline	Levittown, NY Don Mills, Canada
1980s	Exurbs	McMansion-style developments; fringe communities; very low density	Carroll County, MD
1990s	Edge city Edgeless city	Office and retail development in the periphery; in the case of edgeless cities, development is scattered; for edge cities, development is clustered	Tyson's Corner, VA Mississauga, Canada
2000s	Abandoned exurb	Large abandoned housing development; mostly in the South and West	Laveen, Arizona

Box 11.2 Upper Arlington, Ohio

Upper Arlington is an old suburb located in the Columbus metropolitan area. The relics of elite suburbanization are still found in the old historic part of the suburb, mostly in the form of large mansions and older public buildings of the early twentieth century (figure 11.2). Landlocked by the city of Columbus, Upper Arlington is a separate municipality with its own local government services, tax structure, school district, zoning ordinances, and land-use planning (figure 11.3). Incorporated in 1918, this suburb has evolved over the years to become one of the wealthiest in the Columbus region.

Figure 11.2   House in Upper Arlington, an elite suburb outside Columbus, Ohio. (Photo by Bernadette Hanlon)

Figure 11.3   The elite suburb of Upper Arlington is located just outside Columbus, Ohio. *Source:* Google Maps.

Upper Arlington, like many suburbs of its age, has old sewer pipes, old stormwater systems, old roads, and old housing, all requiring maintenance and upgrading. Local planners and policy makers are concerned about the aging infrastructure and how to fund its redevelopment. At this time, the overwhelming majority of the funding from taxes in Upper Arlington is directed to maintain and enhance the public school system. The Upper Arlington school district is one of the best in the Columbus area. According to local planners, 90 percent of local taxes are used for school funding. There is little tax revenue left for infrastructure redevelopment. This problem has been further exacerbated by the expected loss of $600,000 from the state in 2012 because of the economic crisis affecting Ohio.

Planners in Upper Arlington have been trying to encourage commercial development and attract businesses to improve the suburb's tax base. This has created a lot of tension. Many homeowners of Upper Arlington wish to keep their community largely residential, and there are constant battles over any plans for economic development. For instance, in a recent resolution by Upper Arlington's city council to uphold the planning and zoning board's decision to allow development of the suburb's first hotel, there was outcry from many residents in the community. Meanwhile, the plan is to use the hotel taxes to offset the expected loss of state funding, and, in the minds of local planners, the entire hotel project and other such commercial development will provide the funds necessary to maintain an aging infrastructure. Despite Upper Arlington's wealth, this suburb, like other similar early wealthy suburbs, faces some challenges in this regard. Yet there are different views on tax revenue utilization and land-use planning, especially given the suburb's identity as a purely residential community. Remaining exclusive and largely residential is a difficult task for older suburbs in need of redevelopment and infrastructure updating. Their future as purely residential communities is rather uncertain.

Industrial Suburbs

Other early suburbs are industrial in nature, as chapter 3 briefly discussed. Robert Lewis, in his edited volume, *Manufacturing Suburbs*, documents the migration of heavy industry between 1850 and 1950 to the near suburbs of cities as diverse as Montreal, Baltimore, San Francisco, Pittsburgh, Toronto, Detroit, and Chicago. Lewis explodes the myth of the traditional zonal pattern of development that assumed industry was based only in the central business district of cities. The chapters in his book reveal how the early industrialization of suburbs impacted the social geography of entire metropolitan areas. Workers were pulled from cities into the factory districts, steel mills, railway yards, and metal shops located in the suburbs.

Beginning about the 1970s, these early industrial suburbs, like older industrial cities, were slowly left behind as the economy shifted away from heavy manufacturing in certain locations. Industrial suburbs have since ex-perienced serious socioeconomic decline, and the landscape of these communities are now scattered with contaminated, vacant, and underutilized industrial properties, relics of the manufacturing past. These suburbs once housed the large workforces of such companies such as US Steel, the Consolidated Coal Company, General Electric, and Ford Motor Company (box 11.3). Now they feature prominently as suburbs in crisis. Like many older industrial cities, these suburbs have lost jobs and population, and socioeconomic decline has been extreme.

A major challenge is to develop adequate policies and plans for the revitalization of old industrial suburbs across North America. This is difficult given the suburban political landscape. Many old industrial suburbs are fiscally stressed communities. Because of inadequate tax capacity, these suburbs find it extremely challenging to redevelop old industrial sites, encourage new industry, and revamp existing infrastructure. Housing in industrial suburbs

Box 11.3 Essex, Maryland

An example of an old industrial suburb is Essex, outside Baltimore in Maryland. Located along the waterfront, this suburb has a long history of aerospace and aircraft production. The aircraft and aerospace manufacturer Glenn L. Martin Company located there in 1929, drawing thousands of workers from around Maryland and other parts of the United States. Gaining government contracts to build airplanes, Glenn L. Martin Company employed some fifty-three thousand workers during its heyday of production right around World War II. After the war, the company had to downsize, but residents found other jobs with a nearby steel manufacturer. The suburb of Essex once had a strong industrial base that supported the local economy. Figure 11.4 shows the typical modest, working-class house in Essex.

Beginning about the 1970s, decline in Essex began as industry slowly began to disappear. About 30 percent of the workforce of Essex was employed in manufacturing in 1980; this declined to 14 percent by 2000 and to about 8 percent by 2009. The loss of manufacturing jobs, the construction of shopping malls in suburbs a little farther out, and contamination from local sewer plants in the area each negatively impacted the economy, society, and image of Essex. Income decline and increased poverty occurred. In 1970, the median household income of Essex was about $54,000 but dropped to an estimated $49,700 by 2009. In addition, poverty rates increased dramatically, from 6 percent in 1970 to almost 16 percent by 2009.

Figure 11.4   Typical housing in the struggling suburb of Essex. (Photo by Bernadette Hanlon)

Much of the housing stock in Essex was built during the 1940s and 1950s. In fact, two-thirds of all housing in the suburb was built before the end of the 1960s, some in the form of garden apartment complexes that once housed the Glenn L. Martin Company workers. As decline occurred in Essex, these apartment complexes were increasingly neglected. They became subsidized housing for low-income residents. In efforts to revitalize Essex in the early 2000s, the local county government razed a number of these complexes, displacing tenants. Built in their place were neotraditional town center–style developments. For instance, in 2002 the 1,140 unit Riverdale Village complex was demolished and eventually replaced with the Waterview Town Center, a $45 million project featuring 175 single-family housing units, linked with sidewalks and bikeways to the 96,000-square-foot commercial center that includes a supermarket, a bank, and other retailers. In another similar project, a postwar apartment complex was replaced with a new $60 million development of 262 new housing units with 86 single-family homes and 176 condominiums, a swimming pool, a restaurant, and a private marina. In both projects, the revitalization efforts aimed to take advantage of the waterfront location. Built with a vague notion that they included "affordable housing" units, the property values of these waterfront developments soared during the housing market boom.

At this time, there was a great deal of tension around water redevelopment both in Baltimore proper and the surrounding industrial suburbs. At issue in Essex and neighboring suburb Middle River was the 2000 Senate Bill 509, a measure allowing condemnation and seizure via eminent domain of older apartment complexes and waterfront properties in Baltimore County, the jurisdiction where Essex is located. Some properties were seized and sold to private developers, and in these cases low-income residents in older apartment complexes, modest homeowners, and small businesses along the water were displaced for high-end residential development, restaurants, and private marinas. As in many older inner-city neighborhoods, gentrification took place via similar processes of disinvestment and reinvestment in neighborhoods of the industrial suburb of Essex.

is typically small, built in a "cookie-cutter" style by the company for its workers. This, of course, was done at a time when the company was booming. Like the case of postwar suburbs, the houses in industrial suburbs are now outdated, yet there is a lack of local tax revenue to support any housing redevelopment. Like classic Rust Belt cities, Rust Belt suburbs face the enormous challenges of a shrinking population and tax base, a lack of employment opportunities, and a contaminated and abandoned landscape.

Postwar Suburbs

The steady suburbanization of people and jobs continued most dramatically after World War II. In both Canada and the United States, beginning about 1945, suburbs became much more widespread and accessible for working- and middle-class families. This occurred for a number of reasons. First, there was the growing prosperity among the working classes. Many blue-collar jobs were unionized and paid well, providing the working class with an opportunity to strive for a middle-class lifestyle. Second, new directions in government housing policy were critical. In the case of Canada, the Canadian Mortgage and Housing Corporation (CMHC), created in 1945 and acting as mortgage lender and guarantor of mortgage loans, made home loans widespread safe investments accessible to more and more families. Similar to the Federal Housing Administration (FHA) in the United States, CMHC, by acting as mortgage guarantor, reduced financial risk, helped lower interest rates, and offered borrowers the chance to obtain mortgages with minimal down payments and long payback periods stretched over thirty years. The result was that middle- and working-class families could now afford to buy a home, typically a new home in the suburbs.

In Canada, corporate developers and builders were given access to lines of credit necessary to build in compliance with new high-cost construction standards set by CMHC policy. The availability of capital for both borrowers and large-scale builders and developers encouraged rapid expansion, and new production techniques encouraged the development of standardized single-family housing. The result was the evolution of the classic postwar suburb. Richard Harris refers to them as "corporate suburbs," places with widespread tract-style and homogenous residential developments. He laments how this corporate suburban housing displaced the more diverse owner-built houses of earlier times. This period of suburban history was criticized by some as a breeding ground for conformity and materialism and lauded by others as the embodiment of the middle-class American Dream of upward mobility.

Box 11.4 Don Mills, Canada

Don Mills is a planned community of Toronto built between 1952 and 1965. In his book *Creeping Conformity*, Richard Harris describes Don Mills as the first postwar example of the new suburban type: "the fully planned corporate suburb." It was financed for development by businessman E. P. Taylor. In 1947, Taylor had purchased land about seven miles from Toronto in the township of North York and sometime later, with his executive assistant, Carl Fraser, began to consider the idea of developing a new town. In 1952, he hired Fraser's son-in-law and urban planner Macklin Hancock to design it.

Four elements of the design of Don Mills were unique to suburban development in Canada at the time. The first was the neighborhood principle where the planned suburb was to comprise individual neighborhoods, linked to a town center where the high school, library, and shopping center were located. The second was a separation between vehicular and pedestrian traffic. Pedestrian walkways were lined throughout the community, but the road system was built in such a way as to discourage traffic on local streets. The third was the emphasis on planned green space. Natural topographic features were maintained, and streets were designed to incorporate and maintain natural features such as ravines and mature trees (see figure 11.5). Fourth, Don Mills was not designed to be a commuter suburb; rather, it was to have its own industry and employment for local residents. The attempt was made to build housing that was affordable for local workers. Fifth, the architectural design of the housing

Figure 11.5   Google Earth image of the greenways in the suburb of Don Mills. *Source:* Google Earth.

and other buildings was to be high in quality. As these elements suggest, the design of Don Mills was heavily influenced by the garden city movement.

The Don Mills model of suburban development was very influential in Canada. Other planned communities such as Erin Mills, Scarborough, and Bramalea in the Toronto area owe their roots to the Don Mills prototype. Here a single developer acquires land, builds a cluster of different types of housing with shopping areas, schools, and other civic buildings, and provides separate areas for industry and office development. This self-contained, large-scale model of suburban development was unheard of in Canada prior to the 1950s. Compare Levittown in Long Island, New York, to Don Mills in Toronto, and you can see some similarities and differences in the form of North American postwar suburbanization. Both suburbs were corporate in nature, with Levittown built on a 1,200-acre potato farm by large-scale developer Abraham Levitt and his two sons, Alfred and William. Levittown was a showcase of mass housing production techniques, with some 17,400 houses built with little thought about varying their style or design. In contrast, Don Mills had a more inclusive model of different housing styles and prices, better integrated open space, and a more self-contained land-use structure. Don Mills was, in a sense, Toronto's first edge city.

The leftovers of the postwar suburban boom are the small ranch-style and Cape Cod homes, often less than 1,200 square feet, that remain scattered throughout inner-ring suburbs close to North American cities. In some inner-ring suburbs, the postwar housing has remained unchanged. There has been little reinvestment in the housing stock. These postwar suburbs have begun to experience decline, becoming the latest devalorized urban form (see figure 11.6). In fact, according to recent studies, postwar suburbs with housing built between 1945 and 1960 are more likely to be declining than other older suburbs in the United States. In the case of Canada, the postwar suburbs of Toronto are also experiencing decline, where, according to a recent work by geographers at the University of Toronto, poverty is concentrated and highly racialized. High rates of poverty among people of color are similarly a common feature of declining US inner suburbs.

Scholars William Lucy and David Phillips in their 2006 book *Tomorrow's Cities, Tomorrow's Suburbs* emphasize the importance of the housing stock in the decline of suburbs.

Figure 11.6   The devalorized housing stock of older suburbs, Dundalk, Maryland. (Photo by Bernadette Hanlon)

They discuss the problems associated with adapting the smaller postwar houses to the current desire for large houses. They suggest that there are financing obstacles and zoning regulations and that building codes can make it difficult to adapt the housing structures. However, in some suburbs, these postwar homes have been expanded, a process referred to as mansionization or McMansion infill. New floors have been added, new rooms built on both sides of the original structure. The expansion of postwar homes has occurred in suburbs located in economically vibrant regions and close to strong employment centers. Suburbs such as Pasadena, near Los Angeles, Pimmit Hills, outside Washington, DC, and Levittown in Long Island, New York, are just a few examples where older postwar homes have been expanded or replaced with much larger homes. In fact, these postwar suburbs are not necessarily in decline.

The process of mansionization, or McMansion infill, has created some tension. There are typically issues of incompatibility between the large McMansion-style houses and the remaining smaller homes within a neighborhood (figure 11.7). The teardown or expansion of housing is said to result in a loss of historic character. At the same time, some suburban residents see any interference in the teardown and rebuild process as an infringement on property rights. Conflict can result. According to a recent study of the mansionization process, two-thirds of jurisdictions within fifty large regions reported some form of McMansion infill, and some have implemented regulations to control the phenomenon. The most common regulatory code used is a limit on building height as a way to control oversized houses. However, suburban officials also have mixed feelings on the issue.

Figure 11.7   Mansionization in the Washington, DC, suburbs, Arlington, Virginia. (Photo by Bernadette Hanlon)

Although McMansion infill can negatively impact the character of a neighborhood, local governments recognize the potential benefits in the form of increased property values and, thus, increased tax revenue.

More importantly, however, is the potential impact of McMansion infill on the social configuration of the entire metropolis. In many cases, the teardown process is taking place in some modest-income neighborhoods in the inner ring, leading to a form of suburban gentrification, a process scholar Suzanne Lanyi Charles suggests is occurring in the more modest suburbs of Chicago. McMansion infill has the potential to change the socioeconomic composition of suburban neighborhoods in ways that classical gentrification has changed central-city neighborhoods. Modest-income families may be "priced out" of their suburbs as property values rise because of the redevelopment process. This is a potential challenge facing postwar suburbs with a desirable location but inadequate housing stock.

Certainly, retrofitting suburbia has become more pressing as out-of-date suburbs decline.

In fact, redevelopment of existing communities is an accelerating trend, in part because of downtown population and housing growth, a renewed interest in urbanity, and the implementation of more sustainable planning practices. However, when considering the mansionization process as a form of suburban redevelopment, it is, in some respects, the opposite of sustainability because it introduces lower densities and negatively impacts more modest-income suburbanites.

Exurbs

After the postwar period, suburban growth continued, moving farther and farther out beyond the city and increasingly at lower and lower densities. By the 1980s, the exurbs had emerged. There is no unanimously accepted definition of the exurbs, but there have been a number of attempts to delineate this form of suburban development. For example, some scholars have described exurbs as those counties that extend out sixty to seventy miles from the circumferential highways of a metropolitan area. They are low-density counties that have been added to the metropolitan area since 1960 or are adjacent, nonmetropolitan counties. Based on most definitions, exurbia is low-density development located in more rural areas, and residents who live in the exurbs have long commute times to employment centers or core areas within a metropolitan area. A 2006 report by the Brookings Institution identified exurbs as places where at least 20 percent of their workers commute to jobs in an urbanized area.

Exurbs largely comprise oversized Mc-Mansion-style development far from the urban core, key characteristics of urban sprawl. While there are different definitions of sprawl, well-recognized features include: low-density development; rigidly separated land uses; a lack of vibrant urban centers; a heavy reliance on the automobile; uniformity of housing; and poor street design and walkability. The exurbs represent the extreme of quintessential American sprawl.

The long-lasting effect of sprawl is a major challenge confronting urban planners, policy makers, and metropolitan residents in North America. Of particular concern are the impacts on the natural environment. Environmental problems resulting from sprawling development include increased air pollution, higher energy consumption, loss of open space, farmland, and species habitat, shifts in patterns of local and regional species diversity, stormwater runoff impacting stream ecosystems and water quality, and increased risk of flooding (figures 11.8 and 11.9).

One overlooked area of concern is the increased utilization of on-site septic systems as a result of sprawling residential development. Exurban development goes hand in hand with the proliferation of private septic systems. Being far away from the public sewer systems, exurbs must rely on private systems for waste disposal. The installation of a septic system requires a big enough lot size to provide adequate drainage for the effective treatment and disposal of waste. These systems also need to be a safe distance from any nearby residential groundwater wells. The result is sprawling and scattered large-lot developments untied

Figure 11.8   Building suburban homes often requires the conversion of open space or forested areas. (Photo by John Rennie Short)

Figure 11.9   The construction of suburban divisions creates more impervious surfaces (such as roads and roofs), with less vegetation to absorb storm runoff. (Photo by John Rennie Short)

to any traditional public sewer service area—evidence of the "splintering" of infrastructure and service provision that goes hand in hand with postsuburban development forms.

These septic systems can create nitrogen pollution in nearby streams and rivers, mostly as a result of septic system clustering and a lack of septic system maintenance and repair. For example, a study of the wastewater infrastructure in the Baltimore region found that, specifically in exurban counties, the density of septic systems is typically at or above what is considered high risk for groundwater contamination by the EPA. Also, septic systems begin to fail as they get older, typically after about twelve years. As the exurbs age, septic system failure will become a real problem.

In Maryland's State of the State address in January 2011, Governor Martin O'Malley announced plans for a ban on the use of septic systems for new residential subdivisions with five or more houses. Governor O'Malley cited

these systems as a major source of pollution of the Chesapeake Bay. He stated that "there is one area of reducing pollution where so far we have totally failed, and in fact it has gotten much worse . . . and that is pollution from the proliferation of new septic systems—systems which by their very design are intended to leak sewage into our bay and water tables." Shortly after the State of the State address, O'Malley put forward a legislative bill to implement the proposed ban on septic systems. However, developers and local legislators in many rural and exurban counties protested vigorously, and O'Malley was forced to withdraw the bill. Rural legislators and the housing industry felt Governor O'Malley's plan would effectively prohibit what they considered much-needed development in exurban counties on the metropolitan edge. The desire for endless growth by local government and the lobbying power of the real-estate industry often trumps any concern for the natural environment.

Edge and Edgeless Cities

The term "edge city" was popularized and defined by Joel Garreau in his 1991 book, *Edge City: Life on the New Frontier*. Garreau suggests that an edge city (1) has five million square feet of leasable office space; (2) has six hundred thousand square feet of leasable retail space; (3) has more jobs than people; and (4) is considered by most people to be one place. Edge cities began to emerge in the 1970s and 1980s. Probably the most important feature of these places is the clustering of office space.

Before Garreau, the urban geographer Peter O. Muller wrote about "the outer city," focusing on the expansion of economic activities in the suburbs. He identified four types of outer cities. The first type included places with large-scale shopping malls. Muller then identified high-tech parks, including the classic edge city, Tyson's Corner. The third type Muller described as corporate campuses, the location of office space for large corporations. Finally, the outer city included "mini cities" comprising office space and hotels. Muller's observations demonstrated an amplified decentralization of economic activity into the suburbs beginning about the 1960s. Muller's work was part of a larger body of work at the time on the urbanization of the suburbs. Since this time period, suburbia has continued to become a place of self-generating economic growth, developing functions previously reserved for the central business districts located in the city. Such research demonstrates the way economic decentralization continued in the 1980s and 1990s, specifically in the form of large-scale office space, the primary working environment for the new information age. Examples include Tyson's Corner and King of Prussia in the United States.

The emergence of edge cities coincides, too, with the emergence of what has been referred to as edgeless cities. In their 2003 book, *Edgeless Cities*, Robert Lang and Jennifer LeFurgy reflect on Garreau's edge city work and offer an alternative description of office and retail development in the suburbs. In an empirical investigation of 2.6 billion square feet of office space in twenty-six thousand buildings in thirteen regions, they identify a new metropolitan form of edgeless cities. They define an edgeless city as a highly dispersed office cluster, lacking clear boundaries and containing less than five million square feet of office space (as compared to Garreau's edge city, which has fixed borders and contains at least five million square feet). Examining different metropolitan areas, they suggest that office space is more dispersed in some regions than in others. Two edgeless regions include Miami and Philadelphia. They stand in contrast to regions such as New York and Chicago, where office development is more centered in the core.

As mentioned earlier, recent scholars suggest that the emergence of exurbs, edge cities, and edgeless cities signal our entrance into a postsuburban era. These postsuburban forms are spaces difficult to define geographically. They are without boundary and sprawl in ways that do not fit the traditional monocentric city-region. Edgeless cities are dispersed, low-density forms of development; they are not mixed use, pedestrian friendly, or accessible by transit, and they cannot be remade into traditional downtowns.

Both edge and edgeless cities pose serious challenges if we want to create more sustainable forms of suburban development. As sprawling areas of office development, they raise similar concerns about the impact on natural environment as other forms of sprawl.

They also call into question issues of social and economic sustainability as this pattern of development largely favors strip or big-box retail along arterial roads or freeways, disregarding small, more localized businesses. Planning for more sustainable suburbs focuses on building community in the metropolis. But in edge and edgeless cities, there is no traditional downtown area; few, if any, walkable neighborhoods; no public transit for the few residents; and little in the way of living options to support a variety and mix of social groups. Given these widespread realities, it is difficult to imagine how we might reinvent a more sustainable suburb. However, some scholars have begun to challenge the idea that suburban living necessitates environmentally destructive consequences. They point out that local governments have often proved to be the catalyst and organizing entities for sustainability efforts. Indeed, as more and more US and Canadian cities undertake comprehensive sustainability plans (see chapter 14), they must integrate these plans with the counties where their suburban populations reside. There is

some promise. Suburbs have the potential to capture tremendous amounts of carbon, and their low-density housing offers opportunities for suburban forests. In addition, suburban areas have space for agricultural programs, as the rapid growth in community-sponsored agriculture attests. Finally, new suburbs, if planned right, can take advantage of the latest green technology and design concepts.

Abandoned Exurbs

Data released by the US Census Bureau in 2012 found that for the first time in two decades, the annual growth rate of cities and their adjacent suburbs surpassed that of the exurbs. Between 2010 and 2012, cities and older suburbs increased annually by 0.8 percent, compared with only 0.4 percent in the exurbs. Rising gasoline prices, changing demographics, foreclosures, tightening credit for housing construction, and changes in demand are likely contributors to the creation of the abandoned exurb (figure 11.10; see box 11.5). Abandonment of the exurbs may not be

Figure 11.10   Abandoned subdivision in the wake of the housing market slowdown. The developer stopped building with the crisis, as evidenced by the empty concrete housing pads. *Source:* Google Earth image of exurban development near Adelanto, California.

Box 11.5 Laveen, Arizona

In his book *Sunburnt Cities*, Justin Hollander describes the impact of the recent foreclosure crisis on the outer suburb of Laveen in the Phoenix metropolitan area. He states that county data collected from January 2006 and September 2008 listed 688 foreclosures in the Laveen community, the twelfth-highest in the county of Maricopa, where the suburb is located.

Laveen experienced an explosion in housing construction in the early 2000s. About 80 percent of residences in this suburb were built between 1999 and 2005. Hollander found that between 2006 and 2009, the number of housing units almost doubled from 5,499 to 10,535. Construction may not have stopped, but certainly, few were buying in these new developments. As part of his study, he visited Laveen and observed that about 25 to 30 percent of the housing units in the community were empty. Supplementing his observations with data from the US Postal Service, he found that the majority of the hundreds of homes that were empty had never been occupied. The housing market had collapsed and left empty homes in its wake. Laveen is a classic case where rapid new building and growth during the housing market boom was followed by dramatic price decline, abandonment, and foreclosure during the housing market bust.

Source: Hollander, J. B. 2011. *Sunburnt Cities: The Great Recession, Depopulation and Urban Planning in the American Sunbelt*. London: Routledge.

---

just an episodic event but rather the sign of a trend toward recentralization that may likely continue in the future.

In a *New York Times* editorial on November 25, 2011, Christopher Leinberger, Visiting Fellow at the Brookings Institution and president of Locus, a coalition of real-estate developers and investors, announced "the death of the fringe suburb." According to Leinberger, the baby boomers, those born between 1946 and 1964, and the millennials, those born between 1979 and 1996, are dominant populations who are demanding urban, walkable neighborhoods and suburban town centers. The driving-intensive and low-density exurbs are falling out of favor, and, Leinberger predicts, future demand will continue to drop precipitously in metropolitan fringe areas. In the meantime, reinvestment in city neighborhoods and inner suburbs

will continue, and these places will be the key to economic recovery.

While somewhat dramatic, Leinberger's argument is supported by some recent studies of demography and housing in the suburbs. Scholar William H. Lucy in his 2010 book, *Foreclosing the Dream*, uses lots of data on foreclosures to depict the foreclosure crisis as mostly a suburban event, concentrated in particular in the metropolitan fringe areas of Florida, Southern California, Nevada, and Arizona. Figure 11.11 shows an abandoned house in the Maryland suburbs. According to Lucy, the exurbs of the Sun Belt, as places with lots of new mortgages, suffered tremendously when the foreclosure crisis began. Lucy calls the exurban area the "Ring of Death."

Many of the exurbs of the Sun Belt, in the wake of the housing market crash, did shrink.

Figure 11.11   Vultures sun themselves on the front lawn of an abandoned house in the Maryland suburbs. (Photo by Lisa Benton-Short)

States such as Florida, Nevada, and California, epicenters of the housing market boom, witnessed unprecedented out-migration of residents during the housing market crash, and much of this abandonment took place in what were once rapidly growing suburbs. In an analysis by Justin Hollander of US Sun Belt suburbs such as Laveen, Sunnyslope, and Maryvale in Arizona, and Pine Hills in Orlando, many had abandoned empty housing units, some just newly built. These places were often the same places that experienced the effects of the subprime housing crisis.

But the mortgage foreclosure crisis is only part of the story. There is another important movement taking place that is profoundly altering patterns of growth in the metropolis: demographic change. Many scholars and urbanists suggest that there will be a surplus of single-family housing in the exurbs, and future demand, driven by the aging baby boomers and the youthful millennials, will be for city living. Combined with this demographic change is a shift in thinking in which people want to live closer to the core. This will mean the redevelopment of urban areas.

While infill development is difficult, cities and inner-ring suburbs should recognize the potential and encourage reinvestment in local housing. Certainly, depopulation of fringe areas is a feature of the crisis in the suburban real-estate economy, but evidence suggests that the more recent shift inward is likely to continue in the future.

CONCLUSIONS

Steady suburbanization of people and jobs, which began largely in the early twentieth century, became more significant in the postwar period and then morphed to include exurban growth, the evolution of edge and edgeless cities on fringes of the metropolis, and, as fallout from the Great Recession and the housing market crash, the abandoned exurb. The result is a variety of suburban forms and increasing complexity of the North American metropolis.

Within the suburban landscape are constant cycles of investment, disinvestment, and reinvestment, where each respective cycle is manifested as suburban sprawl, decline, and redevelopment. These processes produce and impact different suburbs at different times. The challenges of sprawl are more relevant in the exurban areas. The postsuburban settlements of edge cities, exurbs, and edgeless cities pose similar concerns for environmental sustainability.

In some suburbs, there is the problem of suburban decline, and long-term disinvestment has led to the evolution of suburbs in crisis. These suburbs include the older industrial suburbs that, similar to older industrial cities, have suffered the consequences of manufacturing decline. There are also challenges associated with suburban reinvestment. For example, mansionization is creating tension in some postwar and older communities. In some cases, it is leading to suburban gentrification. Redevelopment of older suburbs is necessary in order to maintain a vibrant suburbia, and certainly retrofitting sprawling edge and edgeless cities can help create more sustainable suburban forms. However, the challenge of redevelopment is to redevelop without displacing poor and modest-income suburbanites. Concern for environmental sustainability has encouraged the interest in redeveloping suburbs in ways that create a more walkable "town center," but this redevelopment should not be at the expense of disadvantaged suburban residents.

SUGGESTED READINGS

Beauregard, R. A. 2006. *When America Became Suburban*. Minneapolis: University of Minnesota Press.

Fogelson, R. M. 2005. *Bourgeois Nightmares: Suburbia, 1870–1930*. New Haven: Yale University Press.

Hanlon, B. 2009. *Once the American Dream: Inner-Ring Suburbs in the Metropolitan United States*. Philadelphia: Temple University Press.

Hanlon, B., J. Short, and T. Vicino. 2010. *Cities and Suburbs: New Metropolitan Realities in the U.S.* London: Routledge.

Harris, R. 2004. *Creeping Conformity: How Canada Became Suburban, 1900–1960*. Toronto: Toronto University Press.

Hayden, D. 2003. *Building Suburbia: Green Fields and Urban Growth, 1820–2000*. New York: Pantheon.

Hollander, J. B. 2011. *Sunburnt Cities: The Great Recession, Depopulation and Urban Planning in the American Sunbelt*. London: Routledge.

Kruse, K. M., and T. J. Sugrue, eds. 2006. *The New Suburban History*. Chicago: University of Chicago Press.

Lang, R., and J. LeFurgy. 2007. *Boomburbs: The Rise of America's Accidental Cities*. Washington, DC: Brookings Institution Press.

Low, S. 2004. *Behind the Gates: Life, Security, and the Pursuit of Happiness in Fortress America*. London: Routledge.

Lucy, W. H., and D. L. Philips. 2006. *Tomorrow's Cities, Tomorrow's Suburbs*. Chicago: APA Planners Press.

McKenzie, E. 2011. *Beyond Privatopia: Rethinking Private Government*. Washington, DC: Urban Institute Press.

Nicolaides, B., and A. Wiese, eds. 2006. *The Suburb Reader*. London: Routledge.

Phelps, N., and F. Wu, eds. 2011. *International Perspectives on Suburbanization: A Postsuburban World?* New York: Palgrave Macmillan.

Saunders, W. S., ed. 2005. *Sprawl and Suburbia*. Minneapolis: University of Minnesota Press.

Teaford, J. 2007. *The American Suburb: The Basics*. London: Routledge.

———. 1997. *Postsuburbia. Government and Politics in the Edge Cities*. Baltimore: Johns Hopkins University Press.

SUBURBS ON THE WEB

There are a number of interesting sources on the Internet for students, faculty, and the community who are interested in learning more about North American suburbs. The following are some examples:

The Suburbs Project is a research project focused on the study of theory of suburban development and planning in the Canadian context. The website for this project is: http://suburbs.planning.dal.ca/index.html.

Retrofitting Suburbia, by Ellen Dunham-Jones and June Williamson, is a good resource for those interested in the redevelopment of suburbs. The website associated with this book offers information on different lectures, reports, and highlights on different retrofit projects: http://www .facebook.com/pages/Retrofitting-Suburbia/ 29939207705.

The National Center for Suburban Studies at Hofstra University has an excellent website that provides information on upcoming suburban conferences and reports from various studies about US suburbs as well as those in the New York area: http://www.hofstra.edu/Academics/ CSS/index.html.

The Pennsylvania Historical and Museum Commission provides information and resources related to the history of suburbanization in the United States and in Pennsylvania in particular: http://pa.gov/portal/server.pt/community/ pennsylvania_suburbs/5864.

IV

THE URBAN ENVIRONMENT

12

Cities and Pollution[1]

LISA BENTON-SHORT AND CHRISTOPHER DESOUSA

Urban studies textbooks have long ignored the physical nature of cities; instead, the emphasis was on the social, political, and economic rather than the ecological. Yet cities are ecological systems, predicated on the physical world as mediated through the complex prism of social and economic power. In recent years, there has been a renewal of interest in the city as an ecological system with emphasis on the complex relationships between environmental issues and urban concerns and between social networks and ecosystem flows. The city is an integral part of nature, and nature is intimately interwoven into the social life of cities.

Cities have an impact on the environment. For example, the ecological footprint is defined as the amount of land required to meet the resource needs of a city and absorb its waste. Cities in North America, with their heavy energy usage and large waste consumption, have a larger and heavier footprint than most other cities.

There has been an ever-growing awareness over the past half-century that the natural environment cannot possibly continue to sustain the impact of, and provide the resources to maintain, the level of economic activity and material consumption that modern, industrialized societies demand. The most recent version of the World Wildlife Fund's popular *Living Planet Report* noted that if humans continue to act as they do, two earths will be required to sustain our activity by 2030. The fundamental problem seems to be that city dwellers have lost their sense of interdependence with the natural world and thus are probably not cognizant of the full impact that their wasteful lifestyles are wreaking on the planet's delicate ecosystems. Some argue that our only hope for salvation is to properly plan dense urban environments that are able to better manage pollution and optimize resource consumption, all while providing opportunities to reconnect with the natural world. This chapter examines four key forms of urban pollution: land (brownfields), water, air, and climate. We describe how these problems came about, how they manifest themselves in cities, and how policy makers and planners are seeking to address them.

LAND POLLUTION: BROWNFIELDS

Cities pollute the land in numerous ways—from solid waste (garbage) disposal in land-

1. Most of this chapter comes from chapters 11, 12, and 13 in Lisa Benton-Short and John Rennie Short, *Cities and Nature*, 2nd ed. (New York: Routledge, 2013).

fills, to the contamination of soils in industrial and commercial areas. Smokestacks belching pollution into the sky and water churning through mills provided positive signs that factories were prosperous. As previously discussed, one of the most problematic developments in industrialized cities throughout North America has been the steady decline of industry and the exodus of manufacturing firms from central cities since World War II. Although deindustrialization and the closure of polluting factories appears to have left many North American cities cleaner, the derelict structures and polluted landscapes left behind from centuries of manufacturing continue to scar the urban landscape. Commonly referred to as "brownfields," not only are these polluted properties potentially hazardous to human health and the environment, but they also hinder the social and economic vitality of neighborhoods by adding to depressed real-estate markets, increased crime rates, and a sense of community despair.

Public awareness of this form of pollution came to the fore in the late 1970s and early 1980s when disasters such as Love Canal in the United States and the Sydney Tar Ponds in Canada received widespread media coverage. The fact that toxic wastes were discovered in residential neighborhoods in Love Canal brought to people's attention the grave risks to human health and to the environment that such sites pose, leading them to be known anecdotally, yet significantly, as "toxic time bombs." The Love Canal incident marked the first time in US history that federal emergency financial aid was approved for something other than a natural disaster. These events also launched a concerted effort by governments in North America (and Europe) to regulate the problem.

To get a sense of the scale of the problem and develop policies for managing it, a clear and unambiguous definition of the term "brownfields" is important. While the need for this would seem logical enough, the term has actually gone through a number of modifications as our attitude toward the issue has evolved. The evolution of the definition of these properties reflects their transformation from *locations of pollution* to *urban resource opportunities*. Looking back at government and media reports in the United States and Canada, the initial reference to these sites focused on the pollution or "contamination" issue. By definition, a *contaminated site* is generally one that has soil, groundwater, or surface water containing pollutants at levels that exceed those considered safe by regulators. The distinction was often made between *known* contaminated sites, which have undergone testing, and *potentially* contaminated sites, which are suspected of being contaminated because of the hazard potential of their previous land use (i.e., waste disposal, manufacturing, military, petroleum-based activities, former dry cleaners, etc.) or an event that occurred at the site, such as a chemical or fuel spill. Developers, investors, and consumers were extremely reluctant to build on these sites, regardless of whether they were known to be or suspected of being contaminated. Old industrialized cities were, therefore, left with extensive tracts of idle and stigmatized property throughout the core, while developers chose to build and residents chose to live in suburban greenfields. (See box 12.1.)

The term "brownfields" came to be used more widely in the mid-1990s in an effort to shift the emphasis away from the contamination issue and toward seeing the land as a resource to redevelop. The most commonly used definition of brownfield in both the United States and Canada at that time was the one posed by the federal US Environmental Protection Agency: "abandoned, idled, or under-used industrial and commercial facilities where expansion or redevelopment is complicated by real or perceived environmental contamination." The more recent definition put forward in 2002 in the US Small Business and Liability Relief and Brownfield Revitalization Act modifies the definition slightly, to "real property, the expansion, redevelopment, or reuse of which may be complicated by the presence or potential presence of a hazardous substance, pollutant, or contaminant." This definition considers both known and suspected contamination as issues complicating the reuse of the land resource.

There has been no systematic effort in the United States or Canada to catalogue the quantity and location of brownfields, which would be considered useful regardless of whether one was identifying pollution risks or resource opportunities. Estimates on the number of brownfields in the United States have ranged from 130,000 to as many as 650,000, while in Canada that number is between 2,900 and 30,000. Most effort has gone to cataloguing hazardous properties, such as known landfills and hazardous-waste facilities. To identify suspected brownfields, a historical land use approach is applied whereby different types of properties are inventoried based on the likelihood of their former land use causing contamination. For instance, vacant rural land and residential property have a low probability of contamination, but former coal-gas plants, metal-plating plants, landfills, vehicle-maintenance facilities, gas stations, dry cleaners, and urban vacant/abandoned land often have a range of pollutants that contaminate the soils. Such present and former land uses can be identified using historical land-use maps and databases and entered into a geographic information database to map out areas of risk and opportunity.

Box 12.1 Redeveloping Brownfields in Minneapolis

The city of Minneapolis provides an example of one city that has proactively supported the redevelopment of brownfields, particularly along the Mississippi River. The Mill District is the centerpiece of this transformation. Once considered the largest milling district in the world, its industries and infrastructure fell victim to deindustrialization. The last train crossed the majestic Stone Arch Bridge in 1978, and many buildings along the river stood vacant, like the former General Mills plant that was gutted by fire in 1991.

As with many projects that involve large geographic clusters of brownfields, this one was carried out incrementally with the support of many partners. In this case, the Minnesota Department of Transportation began transforming the unused bridge into a pedestrian and bicycle trail in the early 1990s, while the city built Mill Ruins Park along the riverbank in multiple phases (reopening of the historic canal and links to the bridge in 2001, restoring the historic mill features in 2002, reconstructing a 650-foot wood plank trail in 2003, construction of pedestrian paths and interpretive features in 2005, etc.). Various management techniques and institutional controls were used to manage contaminants.

These public projects helped spark a redevelopment boom throughout the district that includes commercial, residential, retail, arts and culture, and green-space projects. Many of the original flour mills have also been saved and renovated into elegant loft homes and office spaces. The fortified ruins of the Washburn "A" mill, the largest in the world at one time, have been transformed into the cornerstone of the Mill City Museum (see figure 12.1). Once considered a void in the heart of the city, this mixed-use neighborhood has resurfaced as the historical and cultural center of Minneapolis, loved by residents and visitors alike. Laying the foundation for this, however, has been a concerted effort by the state of Minnesota and other levels and branches of government in Minneapolis to address the procedural, legal, and financial costs and risks that inhibit brownfields' redevelopment and to push for more sustainable redevelopment.

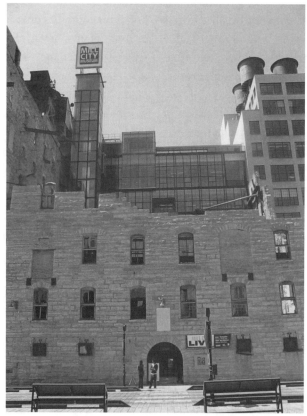

Figure 12.1   The redevelopment of Mill City Museum retains its old façade to celebrate its past. (Photo by Chris DeSousa)

Regulatory and administrative efforts to manage and redevelop brownfields have sought to address three key issues: (1) site assessment and cleanup; (2) legal liability; and (3) funding for cleanup. The initial desire was to clean up urban brownfields to background or pristine conditions, similar to those found in remote locations or parklands. But this proved too costly to do and left many properties sitting idle. Developers were reluctant to pay for such involved cleanups and worried they might be liable should remaining contamination cause problems years later. Today, two types of approaches are used to assess the extent of soil pollution and set cleanup goals:

1. Generic, numeric soil-quality criteria: these are numerical indexes derived from (eco)toxicological studies that identify pollution levels according to a tolerable health risk. Pollution levels considered to pose a risk can also vary according to how the land will be used (e.g., for housing, parks, industry). For example, soils must be cleaner if the reuse will be for schools or housing, less so if the reuse will be commercial or industrial; and
2. Risk-based corrective action: these are procedures for developing soil and groundwater criteria that consider tolerance and risk exposure levels associated with a specific site and/or land use to be implemented as part of the corrective action process (i.e., cleanup levels are tailored to the specific site and its proposed reuse).

Unless a contaminated site poses an immediate risk to human health and the environment, its cleanup and redevelopment typically takes place only when someone wants to develop the site. Those interested in acquiring, remediating, and redeveloping a brownfield typically go through the following course of action, most often with some oversight and support from government. First, a preliminary assessment of the site is carried out that involves a visit to the property, a review of historical records, and interviews with past and present occupants and owners. If this assessment identifies the potential for contamination, a second assessment is performed that includes sampling and testing of the soil and groundwater. If these conditions do not meet government standards, then another report is prepared outlining the cleanup approach to be used to make the site safe. A final report is then submitted once cleanup measures have been undertaken. As for remediation techniques, the most common way to categorize these is on the basis of whether contaminated soil and/or groundwater is treated in place (*in situ* technologies) or removed from the ground for treatment (*ex situ* technologies). The most common, and typically least costly, *ex situ* remediation method is "dig and dump," wherein contaminated soil is excavated from the site and placed in a suitable landfill facility. Other common options are to cover (or cap) the contaminants using an engineered barrier or to treat them using biological agent-, vapor-, heat-, or water-based technologies.

The second key issue that continues to be somewhat problematic in both countries is liability. Common legal questions posed by regulators, developers, and other parties involved in the brownfields issue are: Who is liable for the cleanup of a site? How should liability be assigned? Should there be protection against liability after a site has been cleaned to the standards of the day? With regard to who should pay for cleanup, most legal frameworks follow a "polluter pays" principle, which stipulates that the person responsible for polluting a site pays to have it cleaned up even if the release was legal at the time (retroactive liability). The problem is, however, that in many cases a polluter can no longer be found or the corporation is bankrupt and/or no longer exists. As for imposing liability, governments typically employ one of two approaches. Under the strict joint and several liability system in the United States, one particular party can be assessed liability for damages without requiring proof of negligence (i.e., responsible parties are financially liable even if the release was legal at the time), and parties who contribute to a site's pollution can each be liable as if they alone polluted the site (and government can recover all costs from any party regardless of causation). Under an allocated liability system, more often used in Canada, the different parties are held liable for cleanup in accordance with their individual contribution to the pollution problem. With regard to prospective liability, the fear of those conducting a cleanup is that they will have to bear the responsibility of making the site conform to new standards if those standards change in the future, so they want some guarantee that this will not be the case. Governments in both countries have made efforts to clarify liability rules and protect developers from prospective liability in order to allow brownfields to become developable resources.

The third key issue relates to managing the added cost associated with redeveloping brownfields (i.e., for environmental consulting, remediation, demolition, and legal fees). If the property market functions as it should and there is a high demand for a parcel, then the landowner is expected to reduce the cost of that parcel to cover the additional cost associated with brownfields management. In many cases, however, the value of land in a particular location and/or the profit generated from a permitted use is simply not enough to cover costs and entice private development capital. It is here where governments have intervened to assist with brownfield projects using various administrative and financial tools. These can include so-called offsets (e.g., technical assistance, procedural facilitation, and project support), which are indirect financial measures used to provide assistance, reduce bureaucratic delays, and minimize procedural challenges. Government tax incentive programs (i.e., credits, abatements, or forgiveness) have also been used to make investment capital available in weaker market areas and to promote specific types of economic development. Governments can also directly finance brownfield-related costs through grants, loans, and other means (e.g., revolving, low-interest, forgivable loans, tax increment financing, reduced land cost). These funds can be used to cover the front-end expenses associated with site assessment and can be applied to cleanup, demolition, and other site preparation activities needed to make the property ready for construction.

As the ability to manage the risks and costs associated with brownfields improves, more and more stakeholders are seeking to redevelop this resource in a way that achieves a broader range of environmental, social, and economic goals tied to sustainable urban development. Indeed, where better to put progressive models of sustainable and green development than on symbols of an unsustainable and brown past?

WATER POLLUTION

A fresh and dependable supply of water is critical to sustaining life and supporting healthy communities, economies, and environments. Every city faces two broad water issues: water supply and water quality, both of which rely on water infrastructure. Water supply infrastructure includes the systems of delivery (aqueducts, pipes). Water quality is an issue associated with pollution and the removal of contaminated or dirty water, and this infrastructure includes sewer systems and treatment facilities.

Water Supply

Drinking water comes from surface water or groundwater. It goes into a water treatment facility, where it is purified to certain standards. In cities, an underground network of pipes delivers drinking water to homes and businesses served by a public water system. The United States and Canada rank number one and number two in water consumption, compared with other highly developed countries. Canadians use over three hundred liters of water per person per day. Only the United States consumes more water per person, at 1,682 cubic meters per capita. In part, this is due to the lack of widespread water conservation practices and water pricing that does not promote efficiency.

In the United States, there are approximately 155,000 public water systems that range in size from small (serving populations in the hundreds) to extra large (serving populations greater than one hundred thousand). Each day water utilities in the United States supply nearly thirty-four billion gallons of water. Water suppliers use a variety of treatment processes to remove contaminants from drinking water. These processes include coagulation, filtration, and disinfection. Some water systems also use ion exchange and absorption. Water utilities select the treatment combination most appropriate to treat the contaminants found in the source water of their particular system. Water utilities must test their water frequently for specified contaminants and report these results to the states. If a water system does not meet the minimum standards, it is the water supplier's responsibility to notify its customers. Many water suppliers now are also required to prepare annual reports for their customers, and the use of the Web has allowed the public to stay better informed.

Both the federal government and states have responsibilities for providing safe water. The Safe Drinking Water Act was passed by the US Congress in 1974 to protect public health by regulating the nation's public drinking water supply. Canada passed a similar law. The EPA has also set standards for some ninety chemicals, microbes, and other physical contaminants in drinking water. The law was amended in 1986 and again in 1996; generally, amendments to an original law involve increasing standards, not lowering them.

While most cities in North America take safe drinking water for granted, there remain a number of threats to drinking water. Possible contaminants include lead, arsenic, and chromium. Improperly disposed-of chemicals, animal and human wastes, wastes injected underground, and naturally occurring substances also have the potential to contaminate drinking water. Drinking water that is not properly treated or disinfected or that travels through an improperly maintained distribution system may also pose a health risk. In the post-9/11 world, drinking water utilities find themselves facing new responsibilities resulting from concerns over water system security and threats of infrastructure terrorism.

The average American uses about ninety gallons of water each day in the home, and each American household uses approximately 107,000 gallons of water each year (compare this daily consumption to that of the average European, who uses fifty-three gallons, and the average citizen of sub-Saharan Africa, who uses three to five gallons). Today it costs about two dollars to provide one thousand gallons of clean water, which equates to approximately $300 per household per year. While this is a small cost compared with fueling our automobiles, the cost of making water safe continues to rise. In the United States and Canada, much of the existing drinking water infrastructure (the underground networks of pipes, treatment plants, and other facilities) was built during the late nineteenth century. This infrastructure is now more than one hundred years old and in many cases cannot handle the volume of demand caused by population growth, or the pipes may be leaking or deteriorating. A recent EPA *Drinking Water Infrastructure Needs Survey* estimated that US cities will need to invest $150.9 billion over a twenty-year period to ensure the continued source development, storage, treatment, and distribution of safe drinking water. In North American cities, clean and safe drinking water is a given, but there are still challenges ahead from protecting the supply and the need to upgrade or expand infrastructure.

Issues about water supply are often highly political. Take the case of Atlanta, which faces ever-increasing water problems because of its distance from major waterways. The metro area had a population of 2.9 million in 1990; it was 5.2 million in 2012. An increase in population impacts the city's daily draw on the water reserve; in 1990, the city consumed 320 million gallons; by 2010 it was 510 million gallons. With two million more residents projected by 2030, water use is expected to rise to more than seven hundred million gallons a day. In 2007, a major drought brought Atlanta's water supply to the brink of failure. Officials admitted that there was only three months left of stored fresh water to supply Atlanta. Many cites in the West such as Los Angeles, Las Vegas, and Denver have ushered in water conservation measures—including offering incentives, installing high-efficiency toilets and low-flow shower heads, and increasing monthly water bills for big water users— but Atlanta has been slower to enact such policies. Instead of reducing usage, Atlanta has focused its efforts on increasing supply. Since 1956, Atlanta's primary source of water has been Lake Lanier. But the city has met with resistance from the state of Georgia, which has attempted to limit the amount of water released from the lake. The river system also serves the states of Alabama and Florida. These states fear that Atlanta's increasing use of water upstream will harm ecosystems in their states. In 2009, a federal judge declared it illegal for Atlanta to use Lake Lanier for its drinking water supply. In June 2011, the Eleventh Circuit Court reversed the ruling, stating that the city could withdraw water from the lake. In early 2012, both Florida and Alabama petitioned the Supreme Court to review the decision and resolve the issue of water usage from the Lake Lanier system. The case is still under review, but if Atlanta is denied use of the lake, its water supply could be reduced by roughly 40 percent. While we tend to think of "water wars" in the arid West, this is an example of how increased demand for water, even in areas that tend to have high rainfall, can be politically charged issues.

Water Quality

Many cities in Canada and the United States built sewer systems to collect wastewater and wastewater treatment facilities in the nineteenth and early twentieth century. However, population growth has meant that today the volume of sewage and stormwater often exceeds the processing ability of most treatment plants. This is particularly noticeable during heavy rains.

Combined sewage overflow (CSO) refers to the temporary direct discharge of untreated water (see figure 12.2). CSOs occur most frequently when a city has a combined sewer system (CSS) that collects wastewater, sanitary wastewater, and stormwater runoff in various branches of pipes, which then flow into a single treatment facility. CSSs serve about 772 communities containing forty million people in the United States. Most communities with CSSs (and therefore with CSOs) are located in the Northeast and Great Lakes regions and the Pacific Northwest, affecting cities such as New York, Boston, Philadelphia, Toronto, Ottawa, and Vancouver. During dry weather, CSSs transport wastewater directly to the sewage treatment plant. However, rainwater or urban storm runoff is not directed separately but comingled with household wastes and industrial wastes. When it rains, few facilities can handle the sudden increase in the volume of water, and as a result, the excess volume of sewage, clean water, and stormwater is discharged untreated into rivers, lakes, tributaries, and oceans.

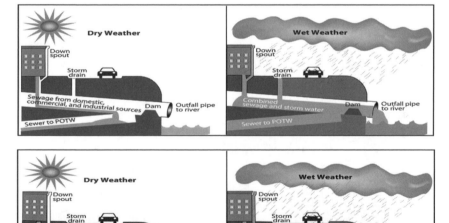

Figure 12.2 Combined sewer systems. In cities with combined sewer systems, shown in the top diagrams, stormwater runoff from rain combines with sewage in the same pipe system and is discharged, untreated, directly into rivers, creeks, or estuaries. The discharge consists of many pollutants, untreated sewage, and debris. In cities with separate sewer systems, shown in the bottom diagrams, stormwater is not mixed with other sewage, so it can be safely discharged without treatment. *Source:* US EPA, "Report to Congress: Impacts and Control of CSOs and SSOs" (2004), http://www.epa.gov/npdes/pubs/csossoRTC2004_chapter02.pdf.

As the joke goes, CSO doesn't stand for "crap spewing out," but it might as well. CSOs contain raw sewage from homes, businesses, and industries, as well as stormwater runoff and all the debris and chemicals that wash off the street or are poured into storm drains. This toxic brew is unappealing and quite dangerous. CSOs contain untreated human waste, oxygen-demanding substances, ammonia, pesticides (such as malathion sprayed on the city to fight West Nile virus), nutrients, petroleum products (from sources such as gas stations, auto repair shops, and garages), and other potential toxins and pathogenic microorganisms associated with human disease and fecal pollution. Forty types of disease-causing pathogens have been found in raw sewage that discharges into CSOs (see figure 12.3).

In 2010, approximately 850 billion gallons of raw sewage were discharged from CSOs into US waters. In addition, some fifty-one million pounds of toxic chemicals were released from municipal sewage treatment plants. In New York Harbor alone, more than twenty-seven billion gallons of raw sewage and polluted stormwater is discharged out of 460 CSOs each year. Although water quality in New York Harbor and throughout the Hudson River Estuary has improved significantly over the past few decades, many parts of the waterfront and its beaches are still unsafe for recreation after it rains. As little as one-twentieth of an inch of rain can overload the system. The main culprit is outmoded sewer systems that combine sewage from buildings with dirty stormwater from streets. Unless investment in reducing CSO events increases significantly, the EPA predicts that by 2025, sewage pollution will exceed 1968 levels—the highest in US history.

CSOs are among the major sources responsible for beach closings, shellfish restrictions, and the contamination of drinking water. Residents of cities that suffer CSOs are often warned to avoid contact with river water or beach water for several days after periods of heavy rainfall.

Figure 12.3   On the Cincinnati waterfront, residents are reminded that the Ohio River is subject to combined sewer overflows that create a danger to public health. (Photo by Lisa Benton-Short)

In 2012, the National Resources Defense Council (NRDC) issued a report noting that US beach water continued to suffer from serious contamination and pollutants by human and animal waste. As a result, America's beaches issued the third-highest number of closings or advisories in the report's history in 2011, with the second-highest number occurring one year before in 2010. Many of the worst beaches are found in Los Angeles, New York, New Jersey, Illinois, and Louisiana. Southern California beaches have struggled with water quality, mostly as a result of sewage pollution. The NRDC study found that fecal contamination at Los Angeles and Orange County beaches causes between 627,800 and 1,479,200 excess gastrointestinal illnesses each year. In Louisiana, the BP oil disaster, which began with the April 20, 2010, explosion on the Deepwater Horizon rig and ended when the well was capped on July 15, 2010, continues to affect beaches along the Gulf of Mexico in Louisiana, Mississippi, Alabama, and Florida. Oil spill inspection and cleanup efforts continued throughout 2011 and into 2012, even at beaches whose oil spill closures, advisories, and notices were lifted.

Waste Treatment Infrastructure

Once sewage has reached a treatment plant, physical processing can separate biological solids from wastewater. Primary treatment refers to screens or filters that catch raw sewage and debris, channeling them to sludge ponds, where the organic materials are broken down by bacteria. Often sludge that has dried is shipped to landfills.

Secondary treatment involves aeration and finer filtration and eliminates more than 95 percent of disease-carrying bacteria from the water. Box 12.2 outlines some of the current challenges to wastewater treatment.

Municipalities in Canada and the United States are undertaking projects to mitigate CSO and have been since the 1990s. For example, Ottawa has been working for many years to separate sewers from the remaining combined sewers (see figure 12.4). The city has spent some $750 million to upgrade its

---

Box 12.2 Challenges in Wastewater Treatment

- Many of the wastewater treatment and collection facilities are now old and worn and require further improvement, repair, or replacement to maintain their useful life;
- The character and quantity of contaminants presenting problems today are far more complex than those that presented challenges in the past;
- Population growth is taxing many existing wastewater treatment systems and creating a need for new plants as increasing urbanization provides additional sources of pollution not controlled by wastewater treatment;
- One-third of new development is served by decentralized systems (e.g., septic systems) as population migrates farther from metropolitan areas (particularly in the exurbs).

Source: EPA Office of Water. 2004. "Primer for Municipal Wastewater Treatment Systems." EPA Wastewater Management, http://water.epa.gov/aboutow/owm/upload/2005_08_19_primer.pdf.

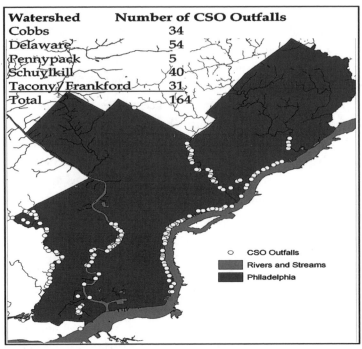

Watershed	Number of CSO Outfalls
Cobbs	34
Delaware	54
Pennypack	5
Schuylkill	40
Tacony/Frankford	31
Total	164

○ CSO Outfalls
▮ Rivers and Streams
▮ Philadelphia

Figure 12.4   A map of combined sewer overflows in Philadelphia. Philadelphia, like many older industrial cities in the Northeast and Great Lakes, has combined sewer systems in the older areas of the city. *Source:* Philadelphia Water Department, "The CSO Long Term Control Plan" (2011), http://www.phillyriverinfo.org/CSOLTCPU/CSOLTCP/pdf/LTCP%20Backgrounder%201105.pdf.

infrastructure. Prior to 1990, the quantity of untreated combined sewage discharged annually to lakes, rivers, and streams in southeast Michigan was estimated at more than thirty billion gallons per year. In 2005, after spending US$1 billion of a planned $2.4 billion on stormwater projects, untreated discharges were reduced by more than twenty billion gallons per year. This investment has yielded a 67 percent reduction in CSOs. It includes numerous sewer separation, CSO storage and treatment facilities, and wastewater treatment plant improvements constructed by local and regional governments. Many other cities are undertaking similar projects to address CSOs. But these are billion-dollar projects, and cities look to states and the federal government for help in funding these large-scale infrastructure projects.

Regulating Water Pollution

In 2012, the US EPA celebrated the fortieth anniversary of the 1972 Clean Water Act, which set the framework for water pollution policy. The Clean Water Act (CWA) is the cornerstone of surface-water quality protection in the United States. Similarly, in 1970, Canada passed the Canada Water Act. Since 1999, Environment Canada has been the federal ministry in charge of conserving and protecting Canada's water resources.

Both water acts established, for the first time, a single federal agency in charge of water pollution and responsible for establishing basic federal standards to which all states/provinces had to comply. The US Clean Water Act also requires reporting of discharge information and making it publicly available. This gives citizens a strong role to play in protecting water resources and the tools to help them do so. In today's information economy, discharge release and toxic release inventory are available to citizens using the Internet, and citizens have access to even more information, such as permit documents, pollution management plans, and inspection reports. The provision for public information also allows citizens to bring action (or sue) to enforce the Clean Water Act. This has proved instrumental in making progress in cleaning up water pollution.

In the United States, the CWA was highly ambitious: its major goals were to completely eliminate the discharge of water pollutants, restore water to "fishable and swimmable" levels, and completely eliminate all toxic pollutants. Today these three aspirational goals of the CWA of 1972 have *not* been achieved, yet they continue to provide the framework for how the federal government (and municipalities) deal with water pollution.

Pollution regulation has also been important because it has created federal financial assistance for municipal sewage treatment plant construction and has set out regulatory requirements that apply to industrial and municipal dischargers. Both of these are critical to understanding the relationship between cities and water pollution reform. With federal assistance, many cities were able to upgrade sewage treatment plants, adding secondary or tertiary treatment or increasing the volume the treatment plants could process. Water regulation has also targeted industrial

and municipal discharge, creating monitoring and management programs for point source pollution. The result is a decrease in industrial point pollution.

After forty years of implementation, there have been both successes and failures. Point source pollution from industrial sources has been reduced. In many rivers and lakes, oxygen levels have recovered due to the filtering out of organic wastes. Some pollutants have declined, but others are on the increase. In the United States in 1972, two-thirds of the lakes were too polluted for swimming or fishing; by 2012, two-thirds of the lakes, rivers, and waterways were safe for swimming and fishing. In 1970, more than 70 percent of industrial discharge was not treated at all; today, 99 percent is. Lake Erie, shared between Canada and the United States, was declared "dead" in 1969 but has since recovered. And in Cleveland's Cuyahoga River, once a stark symbol of the plight of America's rivers, the blue herons have returned, and the city now boasts new marinas lining a river walk and upscale sidewalk cafes (see box 12.3 for a look at the Cuyahoga forty years later).

In 1970, only eighty-five million Americans had a wastewater treatment plant. By 2008, 226.4 million people received centralized collection and wastewater treatment (more than 74 percent of the US population). Yet more than fifteen large cities continue to discharge some 850 billion gallons of untreated sewage and runoff each year during heavy rains and floods. In some cities, beach closures have increased in places where the combined sewers are older and inadequate for the population. And while the total releases of toxic pollutants has decreased (particularly with regard to mercury and DDT), more than forty-seven states still post fish consumption

Box 12.3 Cuyahoga Forty Years after the Fire

In June 1969, the Cuyahoga River in the city of Cleveland caught fire. The river, filled with kerosene and other flammable material, was probably ignited by a passing train that provided the spark. Although it burned for only thirty minutes, the incident and the famous photograph of the river on fire became a pivotal part of an emerging environmental movement. *Time Magazine* described the Cuyahoga as the river that "oozes rather than flows" and in which a person "does not drown but decays." The memorable 1969 fire sparked legislation for the Great Lakes Water Quality Agreement and the Clean Water Act of the 1970s. The federal government directed large amounts of money, dealt with industrial polluters, and enforced regulations: the river was on track to get cleaner.

The hundred-mile river is composed of the upper half and the lower half (near Cleveland). Today, the lower half of the river is no longer the incendiary sewer of the dark days of 1969. Industrial discharge has been controlled significantly. However, the river still receives discharges of stormwater, combined sewer overflows, and incompletely disinfected wastewater from urban areas upstream of the park. Nonpoint sources are the result of urbanization, more specifically suburbanization, in metro Cleveland. People are moving into suburbs that were once open spaces and farmland. And with suburban settlement comes an increase in impervious surfaces such as rooftops, driveways, parking lots, sidewalks, and lawns.

Although much healthier than forty years ago, some sections of the river are far from healthy. Most of the river remains unacceptable for recreational use because of high concentrations of *Escherichia coli* (*E. coli*), a fecal-indicator bacterium. Contaminant and bacteria levels can still be high, especially after periods of rain. Here is a summary of some of the river's lingering problems:

- Trash
- Toxics
- Bacteria
- Fish tumors
- Lack of aquatic diversity
- Beach closings

For these reasons, the Environmental Protection Agency recently classified portions of the Cuyahoga River watershed as one of the forty-three Great Lakes Areas of Concern.

On a more optimistic note, in 2009, a water quality analyst was the first person in more than half a century to find a living freshwater mussel in that long-polluted portion of the river. Somehow the freshwater mussel managed to survive the past century through the worst of the pollution on the Cuyahoga, and the mussel population is on the increase.

advisories for contamination due to mercury, PCBs, dioxins, and DDT.

However, much remains to be done. Almost half of US waters are still impaired—too polluted to serve as sources of drinking water or to support good fish and wildlife. Wetlands continue to be lost to pollution and development. Today, nonpoint source pollution—runoff from farms, suburbs, and cities—is the leading cause of water pollution but is inadequately addressed by the CWA.

The success of the CWA at controlling point pollution contrasts with its failure to address nonpoint sources of pollution. Nonpoint source pollution comes mainly from suburban runoff and urban stormwater runoff—where rainwater falls and collects numerous pollutants as it makes its way to rivers, streams, and bays. According to the EPA, by 2010, 43 percent of lakes and 37 percent of estuaries were impaired because of nonpoint pollution and municipal discharge. Addressing nonpoint pollution remains underfunded. Since 1990, the EPA has spent some $90 billion on water, but only 44 percent of that on nonpoint pollution. In addition, while the EPA has set aside $8 billion for water projects over the next several years, only $200 million is slated for nonpoint pollution. Today, debates about what to do with urban nonpoint pollution are part and parcel of larger debates about land-use planning, urban development, and sustainability.

AIR POLLUTION

Air pollutants are composed of either visible particulates (ash, smoke, or dust) or invisible gases and vapors (fumes, mists, and odors). The US EPA has identified more than 189 air pollutants; however, the regulatory measures are primarily directed at only a few. A dozen air pollutants account for a majority of the volume of air pollutants. Most of the air pollutants are generated when fossil fuels are used. Throughout the twentieth century, cities have increasingly relied on three primary fossil fuels—coal, natural gas, and petroleum—for energy and transportation. Because all fossil fuels are carbon based, they release carbon monoxide and carbon dioxide when combusted. Coal also contains sulfur oxides and nitrogen oxides that are released during combustion. New sources of pollution, combined with increased use of fossil fuels for a myriad of needs, means that air pollution for many cities has continued to increase despite regulatory efforts.

The Six Criteria Pollutants

Nearly all of the so-called most common or most prevalent pollutants are generated in urban areas. In the United States, the EPA has classified six "criteria pollutants" as those which pose the most ubiquitous threat to health and the environment (see box 12.4). These pollutants are called criteria pollutants because the EPA uses them as the basis for setting permissible levels. Almost all air-quality monitors are located in urban areas, so air-quality trends are more likely to track changes in urban emissions rather than changes in total national emissions.

Criteria pollutants are the most regulated air pollutants, and policy has focused on limiting (but not outlawing) their use and discharge into the environment. One of the most difficult aspects to limiting the production of criteria pollutants is that they are emitted from a variety of sources—the generation of

Box 12.4 The Common Air Pollutants

Ozone (ground-level ozone is the principal component of smog):

- *Source*—chemical reaction of pollutants; volatile organic compounds (VOCs) and nitrogen oxides (NO_x).
- *Health effects*—breathing problems, reduced lung function, asthma, irritated eyes, stuffy nose, reduced resistance to colds and other infections, may speed up aging of lung tissue.
- *Environmental effects*—can damage plants and trees; smog can cause reduced visibility.

VOCs, smog formers:

- *Source*—VOCs are released from burning fuel (gasoline, oil, wood coal, natural gas, etc.), solvents, paints, glues, and other products used at work or at home. Cars are an important source of VOCs. VOCs include chemicals such as benzene, toluene, methylene chloride, and methyl chloroform.
- *Health effects*—In addition to ozone (smog) effects, many VOCs can cause serious health problems such as cancer and other conditions.
- *Environmental effects*—In addition to ozone (smog) effects, some VOCs such as formaldehyde and ethylene may harm plants.

Nitrogen dioxide (an NO_x); smog-forming chemical:

- *Source*—burning of gasoline, natural gas, coal, oil, and so on. Cars are an important source of NO_2.
- *Health effects*—lung damage, illnesses of breathing passages and lungs (respiratory system).
- *Environmental effects*—Nitrogen dioxide is an ingredient of acid rain (acid aerosols), which can damage trees and lakes. Acid aerosols can reduce visibility.

Carbon monoxide (CO):

- *Source*—burning of gasoline, natural gas, coal, oil, and so on.
- *Health effects*—reduces ability of blood to bring oxygen to body cells and tissues; cells and tissues need oxygen in order to function. Carbon monoxide may be particularly hazardous to people who have heart or circulatory (blood vessel) problems and people who have damaged lungs or breathing passages.

Particulate matter (PM-10) (dust, smoke, soot):

- *Source*—burning of wood, diesel, and other fuels; industrial plants; agriculture (plowing, burning off fields); unpaved roads.
- *Health effects*—nose and throat irritation, lung damage, bronchitis, early death.
- *Environmental effects*—Particulates are the main source of haze that reduces visibility.
- *Property damage*—Ashes, soots, smokes, and dusts can dirty and discolor structures and other property, including clothes and furniture.

Sulfur dioxide (SO_2):

- *Source*—burning of coal and oil, especially high-sulfur coal from the eastern United States; industrial processes (paper, metals).
- *Health effects*—breathing problems, may cause permanent damage to lungs.
- *Environmental effects*—SO_2 is an ingredient in acid rain (acid aerosols), which can damage trees and lakes. Acid aerosols can also reduce visibility.
- *Property damage*—Acid aerosols can eat away stone used in buildings, statues, monuments, and so on.

Lead:

- *Source*—leaded gasoline (being phased out), paint (houses, cars), smelters (metal refineries); manufacture of lead storage batteries
- *Health effects*—brain and other nervous system damage; children are at special risk. Some lead-containing chemicals cause cancer in animals. Lead causes digestive and other health problems.
- *Environmental effects*—Lead can harm wildlife.

Source: US Environmental Protection Agency, "The Plain English Guide to the Clean Air Act," http://www.epa.gov/airquality/peg_caa/cleanup.html.

energy and the use and combustion of fossil fuels in various forms of transportation and agricultural activities. For many cities, however, much of the air pollution comes from motor vehicle exhaust, a problem that has increased as a result of more vehicles on the road and more miles driven each year. For example, hydrocarbons—the precursor to smog or surface-level ozone—come primarily from cars, motorcycles, trucks, and gasoline-powered equipment (such as lawn mowers and blowers). Diesel-powered vehicles and engines contribute more than half the mobile source of particulate emissions. Almost one-third of nitrogen oxides come from motor vehicles, and 95 percent of the carbon monoxide in US cities comes from mobile sources. The significant connection between vehicles and urban air pollution is well established.

A city that does not meet the primary standard for a given pollutant is called a non-attainment area. Cities in nonattainment must create an action plan for each pollutant in nonattainment. Action plans include targets for reduction of pollutants, ways to encourage use of public transportation and decrease the use of single-occupancy vehicles, securing of voluntary reductions, and development of a variety of outreach and educational tools. Although the EPA has been regulating criteria pollutants since the 1970 Clean Air Act was passed, many urban areas are still classified as nonattainment for a least one criteria pollutant. The American Lung Association's 2012 Report, *State of the Air,* examines three key pollutants—smog, short-term particulate matter (stays in the air for under twenty-four hours), and long-term particulate matter. The report shows that air quality in many cities has improved but that over 127 million people—41 percent of the nation—still suffer from pollution levels that are too often dangerous to breathe. Approximately 5.7 million Americans live in cities that received grades of F for all three pollutants.

Photochemical Smog

Smog occurs when volatile organic compounds (VOCs) react with nitrogen oxides and oxygen in the presence of heat and sunlight. Pollutants undergo reactions that form ground-level ozone, or smog. Hence smog is not emitted directly into the air but is created through a series of chemical reactions. It is produced by the combination of pollutants from many sources, including smokestacks,

cars, paints, and solvents. The EPA estimates that almost 60 percent of smog is produced by transportation sources—cars, trucks, and trains. Smog is found primarily in urban areas and is often worse in the summer months, when heat and sunshine are more plentiful. Table 12.1 lists the worst US cities for smog in 2012, and table 12.2 lists the worst cities in Canada. Many Californian cities lead the list, although the good news is that nearly all cities have improved air quality since 2000.

Ozone smog represents the single most challenging pollution problem for most US and Canadian cities. More than eighty-one million Americans live in urban areas that exceed air-quality concentrations for ozone, and progress on ozone reduction is the slowest for all criteria pollutants. But progress has been made. In 2012, twenty-two of the twenty-five cities with the most ozone pollution improved their air quality over 2011. Still, nearly four in ten people in the United States live in areas

Table 12.1   Ten Worst Ozone-Polluted Cities in the United States, 2011

2012 Rank	Metropolitan Area
1	Los Angeles-Long Beach-Riverside, CA
2	Bakersfield-Delano, CA
3	Visalia-Porterville, CA
4	Fresno-Madera, CA
5	Sacramento–Arden-Arcade–Yuba City, CA
6	Hanford-Corcoran, CA
7	San Diego-Carlsbad-San Marcos, CA
8	Houston-Baytown-Huntsville, TX
9	Merced, CA
10	Charlotte-Gastonia-Salisbury, NC-SC

Source: American Lung Association. 2011. *Annual Report.* http://www.stateoftheair.org/2011/city-rankings/most-polluted-cities.html (accessed July 2012).

Table 12.2 Worst Smog and Particulate Matter for Canadian Cities

Rank by Amount of Ground-Level Ozone		Rank by Amount of Particulate Matter
1	Kitchener, ON	5
2	Toronto, ON	7
3	Windsor, ON	3
4	Simcoe, ON	11
5	Hamilton, ON	10
6	Egbert, ON	4
7	Montreal, QC	1
8	St. Catharines, ON	6
9	Kejimkujik, NS	7
10	Oshawa, ON	22
11	Halifax, NS	13
12	Québec City, QC	18
13	Saint John, NB	7
14	Vancouver, BC	16
15	Calgary, AB	11

Source: "Blowin' in the Wind: Canada's Smoggiest Places," *Canadian Geographic*, May/June 2000, http://www.canadiangeographic.ca/magazine/mj00/alacarte.asp.

with unhealthful levels of ozone pollution. The situation is poor in Canada as well. More than half of all Canadians live where ground-level ozone can reach unacceptable levels in summer. Every major Canadian city has levels of airborne particles high enough to constitute a health risk.

Smog is highly corrosive to rubber, metals, and lung tissue. Short-term exposure can cause eye irritation, wheezing, coughing, headaches, chest pain, and shortness of breath. Long-term exposure scars the lungs, making them less elastic and efficient, often worsening asthma and increasing respiratory tract infections. Because ozone penetrates deeply into the respiratory system, many urban residents are at risk, including the weak and elderly but also those who engage in strenuous activity. For those who were born and have lived in smoggy cities such as Los Angeles, Houston, and Washington, DC, long-term exposure may be breaking down the body's immune system, increasing the chances of suffering respiratory illness and harming the lungs in later life. In many US cities, doctors are reporting increasing frequency of asthma in children. A recent Southern California Children's Health study looked at the long-term effects of particulate pollution on teenagers. Tracking 1,759 children between ages ten and eighteen, researchers found that those who grew up in more polluted areas face the increased risk of having underdeveloped lungs that may never recover to reach their full capacity. The average drop in lung function was 20 percent below what was expected for the child's age, similar to the impact of growing up in a home with parents who smoked.

Photochemical smog is one pollutant that is often exacerbated because of geography. Cities located in basins and valleys—such as Los Angeles and Denver—are particularly susceptible to the production of smog. Denver, the Mile High City, suffers from smog and other air pollutants that are made worse by its elevation in the Rocky Mountains. Because of Denver's high altitude, the city experiences frequent temperature inversions when warm air is trapped under cold air and cannot rise to disperse the pollutants across a wider area. As a result, smog may hover in place for days at a time, generating a "smog soup" that envelops the city. Denver has worked to turn around its air pollution problem, but despite these efforts, as of 2011, Denver remained out of compliance with EPA standards. Another issue of "smog geography" occurs in Montreal and Toronto. These cities are upwind of major industrial cities in the Midwest, and some of the air pollutants that generate smog in Toronto and Montreal originate across the border. Windsor, Toronto, Montreal, and Vancouver are cities where acceptable ozone levels are exceeded an average of ten or more days in the summer. Cities with high concentrations of fossil-fuel-burning power plants, metal smelters, and cement and fertilizer factories and those with high densities of cars and trucks are also likely to experience smog production.

Since the 1970s, the US and Canadian governments have taken steps to control pollution emissions from automobiles and factory stacks through legislation such as the Clean Air Acts. These have required the installation of catalytic converters to capture much of the automobile exhaust, while vapor traps on gas pumps prevent the evaporation of carbon dioxide into the air. Recent efforts to develop hybrid and zero-emission vehicles (such as electric cars) are other ways both private and public interests

are using technology to alleviate air pollution. However, new sources of pollution, combined with increased use of fossil fuels for myriad needs, has meant that air pollution for many US and Canadian cities has continued to increase despite regulatory efforts.

Most US and Canadian cities publish a daily "Air Quality Index" (see table 12.3). When ozone concentrations are high, smog alerts are issued to warn people with asthma and those with chronic respiratory disease to stay indoors and for healthy people not to exercise. For many urban residents, smog forecasts are part of their daily planning. On the worst smog concentration days in Washington, DC, officials encourage the use of public transportation by making the Metro and Metro buses free to all users. In most cities, major newspapers feature a daily "Air Quality Index," noting which air pollutants are likely to be above federal standards. An important change is the development of air quality apps for smartphones, which allow users to view their local air quality for a range of pollutants (see box 12.5).

Table 12.3   The US EPA's Air Quality Index

Air Quality Index (AQI)	Numerical Value	Meaning	Color
Good	0–50	Air quality is considered satisfactory, and air pollution poses little or no risk.	Green
Moderate	51–100	Air quality is acceptable; however, for some pollutants there may be a moderate health concern for a very small number of people who are unusually sensitive to air pollution.	Yellow
Unhealthy for Sensitive Groups	101–150	Members of sensitive groups may experience health effects. The general public is not likely to be affected.	Orange
Unhealthy	151–200	Everyone may begin to experience health effects; members of sensitive groups may experience more serious health effects.	Red
Very Unhealthy	201–300	Health alert: everyone may experience more serious health effects.	Purple
Hazardous	> 300	Health warnings of emergency conditions: the entire population is more likely to be affected.	Maroon

Source: US EPA.

Box 12.5 There's an App for That

New technologies are changing the way people access information about environmental quality. In the United States, for example, the American Lung Association offers State of the Air, a free smartphone app for iPhone and Android with current air-quality information. According to the association's website, it is considered "a life-saving resource for people living with lung disease like asthma and chronic obstructive pulmonary disease (COPD), people with heart disease or diabetes, as well as older adults and children." With State of the Air, users can enter their zip code or use the geo-locator function on their smartphones to get current and next-day air-quality conditions. The app provides levels of both ozone and particle pollution and sends out alerts if air quality is unhealthful. If the day's air pollution is particularly severe, the app will provide specific recommendations—advising that outdoor activities should be rescheduled or that people who work outdoors should limit extended or heavy exertion.

The EPA also offers a free app: its AIRNow mobile application provides real-time air-quality information that can be used to protect your health when planning your day. This app allows a user to get location-specific reports on current air quality and air-quality forecasts for both ozone and fine particle pollution (PM2.5). Air-quality maps from the AIRNow website provide visual depictions of current and forecast air quality nationwide, and a page on air-quality-related health effects explains what actions people can take to protect their health at different Air Quality Index levels, such as "code orange."

In Canada, the Asthma Society of Canada website posts air-quality reports. They too have an Asthma App to download to a smartphone.

Also under discussion is the idea of putting air-quality sensors in cell phones, with the idea that these would provide a crowdsourced way of gathering numerous location-specific, real-time air-quality measurements. If developed, this would be an innovative and interesting way for scientists to gather data at a microscale.

To download Air apps: American Lung Association, http://www.lung.org/healthy-air/outdoor/state-of-the-air-app.html; EPA air app, http://m.epa.gov/apps/airnow.html; for Canada, the asthma app is found at http://www.asthma.ca/widget/; similarly, air-quality reports for most cities and locations can be found at http://www.theweathernetwork.com/airquality/cancitiesaq_en/.

Indoor Air Pollution

Another type of pollution that is often overlooked, but a threat to public health nevertheless, is indoor air pollution. Radon is an example of an indoor air pollutant. It is a radioactive gas that results from a natural breakdown of uranium in soil, rocks, and water. Although radon gas can be found in any type of building, it is more likely that people will be exposed to it in their homes. The radon gas enters into a home primarily through the foundation and basement. It can come in through cracks in a basement floor, drains, sump pumps, and construction joints, among other places. Radon cannot be seen or smelled, so without testing, people may not realize they are exposed to unsafe radon levels in the home. This is of particular concern because the EPA estimates that radon is currently linked to twenty thousand lung cancer deaths a year, with the risk increasing substantially if the person smokes. Naturally occurring radon in indoor air has been identified as the second leading cause of lung cancer after tobacco smoking. The EPA estimates that one in fifteen homes has an elevated radon level.

Radon is a problem all over the United States and Canada, but it varies in prevalence and intensity. In Canada, for example, a 2010 report found that radon levels in Ottawa were three times the national average; cities in the provinces of Manitoba, Nova Scotia, and Saskatchewan have the highest proportion of homes estimated to be above the guideline, but there is great variation even within the cities and provinces. Radon measurements can vary as a result of geology, aerial radioactivity, soil permeability, and foundation type. The magnitude of the problem, its geographic variability, and the fact that it can vary in measurements in the short term and long term make it difficult to manage at the national and state level. States differ in their programs; some provide free radon testing kits or regulate providers of radon testing and mitigation.

Because the EPA has focused most on providing information and data and has not become involved with remediation, the obligation to test for radon lies with the homeowner and is particularly recommended when buying, building, or selling a house. Testing for radon can be done using charcoal canisters, alpha track detectors, ion detection

devices, and more advanced electrically powered devices.

In addition to radon, many of us are surrounded daily, in offices and in our homes, by products that outgas chemicals. Polyester shirts and water bottles contain toxic dyes and catalysts; computers, video games, and hair dryers all outgas teratogenic and/or carcinogenic compounds. Carpets, wallpaper adhesives, paints, insulation, and other items in our homes release chemicals, impacting indoor air quality. Allergies, asthma, and "sick building syndrome" are on the rise. Yet legislation establishing mandatory standards for indoor air quality is practically nonexistent, and there is no easy way for the average homeowner to test for the hundreds of possible chemicals in his or her home.

Air Quality Trends

The first US federal law dealing with national air-quality standards was the 1970 Clean Air Act (CAA). Canada passed its Clean Air Act in 1970 as well. Both laws initially focused on point source air pollutants such as energy plants, factories, and other stationary emitters. In Canada, the 1970s and 1980s focused most on the issue of acid rain. Since the 1970 US CAA there have been several amendments, including the 1990 and 1997 Clean Air Act amendments. The 1990 amendments have a direct impact on cities. For the first time, the EPA established five categories for cities in nonattainment (those that did not meet federal regulations for criteria pollutants). The categories were marginal, moderate, serious, severe, and extreme. Those cities originally classified as severe or extreme were mandated to become attainment areas by 2005. In 2010, no city had violations of SO_2, NO_2, and CO. Downward trends in annual NO_2, CO, and SO_2 are the result of various national emissions-control programs. For example, an abrupt decline in NO_x emissions was brought about by EPA's NO_x SIP Call program, which began in 2003 and was fully implemented in 2004.

Nonattainment areas for ozone have improved: between 2001 and 2010, ozone nonattainment areas showed a 9 percent improvement in ozone concentration levels. Nearly all US cities experienced fewer unhealthful days in 2010 compared to 2002. Today, ozone and particle pollution are the primary contributors to unhealthful Air Quality Index days. Los Angeles, labeled "extreme" in 1990, remains in nonattainment, although its notoriously smoggy air is the cleanest it has been in fifty years. Still, in one out of every three days, millions of Los Angelenos breathe in dirty air. In addition, the 1990 Clean Air Act amendment established stricter tailpipe standards, finally addressing the growing problem of nonpoint pollution. This downward trend in air-quality concentrations is expected to continue and will have profound health benefits for residents in US cities.

Yet more than four decades after the Clean Air Act, air pollution reform in US cities is as mixed as reform in water pollution. Some pollutants—primarily those coming from point sources—have decreased. For example, total emissions of toxic air pollutants have decreased by approximately 42 percent between 1990 and 2005. The EPA cites control programs for facilities such as chemical plants, dry cleaners, coke ovens, and incinerators as being primarily responsible for these reductions. The six criteria pollutants have also decreased. Air pollution was lower in 2010 than in 1990 for the following pollutants: ozone by

17 percent, particulate matter by 38 percent, lead by 83 percent, nitrogen oxides by 45 percent, carbon monoxide by 73 percent, and sulfur dioxide by 75 percent. Overall, according to the EPA, between 1980 and 2010, total emissions of the six criteria pollutants have decreased 67 percent. The trends are similar for Canada, which has reduced many of the criteria pollutants but remains challenged most to reduce ground-level ozone.

Similar to the situation with water pollution, the most significant air pollution problems today stem not from point sources but from nonpoint sources. While legislation in the 1970s and 1980s focused on point sources (such as factories and smokestacks), regulation today confronts increased nonpoint pollutants. Common nonpoint sources of air pollution include automobiles, trucks, buses, airplanes, lawn and garden equipment, and even charcoal-burning backyard grills. The most common nonpoint sources are mobile. Although twenty-first-century automobiles produce 60–80 percent less pollution than cars did in the 1960s, more people are driving more cars more miles. In 1970, Americans traveled one trillion miles in motor vehicles; by 2000, they drove more than three trillion miles. But there has been good news; vehicle miles driven seems to have flattened somewhat, peaking in 2008. In 2012, it was estimated that Americans drove approximately 3.05 trillion miles. But we walk, bike, and take public transit more often. Despite these positive developments, vehicle emissions remain a significant part of the air pollution picture.

Following decades of regulation and good intention, cities in North America remain a long way off from eliminating the threat of air pollution to both public health and environmental quality.

CLIMATE CHANGE

Cities today consume 75 percent of the world's energy and emit 80 percent of the world's greenhouse gases. North American cities are both the major generators of greenhouse gases and the key players in greenhouse gas reduction. There is growing attention to the relationship between cities and climate change.

Climate Science: The Basic Facts

Climate change is linked to greenhouse gases (GHGs). There are four principal greenhouse gases: carbon dioxide, methane, nitrous oxide, and fluorinated gases. Three of the four gases are naturally occurring, while fluorinated gases are man-made. Carbon dioxide, methane, and nitrous oxides are continuously emitted into and removed from the atmosphere by natural processes on earth. Anthropogenic (man-made) activities, however, can cause additional quantities of these and other greenhouse gases to be emitted or sequestered, thereby changing their global average atmospheric concentrations. Most anthropogenic emissions come from the combustion of carbon-based fuels, principally wood, coal, oil, and natural gas. According to the EPA (see figure 12.5), the primary sources of these gases are:

- Carbon dioxide (CO_2): Carbon dioxide enters the atmosphere through burning fossil fuels (coal, natural gas, and oil), solid waste, trees and wood products, and also as a result of certain chemical reactions (e.g., manufacture of cement). Carbon dioxide is removed from the atmosphere (or "sequestered") when it is absorbed by plants as part of the

biological carbon cycle. In 2010, CO_2 accounted for about 84 percent of all US greenhouse gas emissions from human activities.
- Methane (CH_4): Methane is emitted during the production and transport of coal, natural gas, and oil. Methane emissions also result from livestock and other agricultural practices and by the decay of organic waste in solid-waste landfills.
- Nitrous oxide (N_2O): Nitrous oxide is emitted during agricultural and industrial activities as well as during combustion of fossil fuels and solid waste.
- Fluorinated gases: Hydrofluorocarbons, perfluorocarbons, and sulfur hexafluoride are three synthetic, powerful greenhouse gases that are emitted from a variety of industrial processes.

Carbon dioxide emissions in the United States increased by about 12 percent between 1990 and 2010. Since the combustion of fossil fuel is the largest source of GHG emissions in

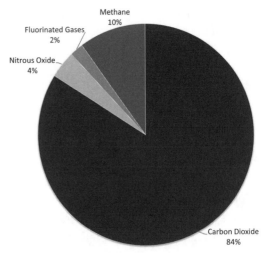

Figure 12.5   Greenhouse gases in the atmosphere by percentage volume. *Source:* US EPA.

the United States, changes in emissions from fossil fuel combustion have historically been the dominant factor affecting total emission trends. Methane is the second most prevalent greenhouse gas emitted in the United States from human activities. In 2010, methane accounted for about 10 percent of all US GHG emissions from human activities. According to the US EPA, methane's lifetime in the atmosphere is much shorter than carbon dioxide, but methane is more efficient at trapping radiation than carbon dioxide. Pound for pound, the comparative impact of methane on climate change is more than twenty times greater than carbon dioxide over a hundred-year period. Globally, about 40 percent of total nitrogen oxide emissions come from human activities. Nitrous oxide molecules stay in the atmosphere for an average of 120 years before being removed by a sink or destroyed through chemical reactions. The impact of one pound of nitrous oxide on warming the atmosphere is more than three hundred times that of one pound of carbon dioxide. Finally, fluorinated gases, unlike many other greenhouse gases, have no natural sources and come only from human-related activities. These gases represent the smallest amount of greenhouse gases in the atmosphere, but they are quite potent. Small atmospheric concentrations can have large effects on global temperatures. They can also have long atmospheric lifetimes—in some cases lasting thousands of years. Like other long-lived GHGs, fluorinated gases are widely diffused in the atmosphere, spreading globally after they are emitted. Each of these gases can remain in the atmosphere for different amounts of time, ranging from a few years to thousands of years. GHGs remain in the atmosphere long enough to become well mixed, meaning that the amount that is mea-

sured in the atmosphere is roughly the same all over the world, regardless of the source of the emissions. These four gases absorb some of the energy being radiated from the surface of the earth and trap it in the atmosphere, essentially acting as a blanket that makes the earth's surface warmer than it would be otherwise (see figure 12.6).

Greenhouse gases are necessary for life as we know it, because without them the planet's surface would be about sixty degrees Fahrenheit cooler than it is at present. But as the concentrations of these gases continue to increase in the atmosphere, the earth's temperature is climbing above its past levels. According to NOAA and NASA data, the earth's average surface temperature has increased by about 1.2 to 1.4 degrees Fahrenheit since 1900. The ten warmest years on record (since 1850) have all occurred in the past thirteen years. Most of the warming in recent decades is very likely the result of human activities. Other aspects of the climate are also changing, such as rainfall patterns, snow and ice cover, and sea level. The United Nations International Panel on Climate Change notes that if greenhouse gases continue to increase, climate models predict that the average temperature at the earth's surface could increase from 2.0 to 11.5 degrees Fahrenheit above 1990 levels by the end of this century. Warmer temperatures influence the patterns and amounts of precipitation, reduce ice and snow cover as well as permafrost, raise sea levels, and increase the acidity of the oceans.

Since 1990, both the United States and Canada conduct a yearly national greenhouse gas inventory and submit this to the United Nations in accordance with the Framework Convention on Climate Change. In 2011, the EPA reported that since 1990, US green-

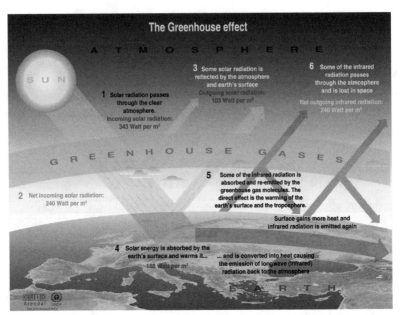

Figure 12.6   The greenhouse effect. *Source:* Philippe Rekacewicz, UNEP/ GRID-Arendal. 2005. "The Greenhouse Effect." http://www.grida.no/ graphicslib/detail/greenhouse-effect_f8f1.

house gas emissions have increased by 10.5 percent. In Canada, however, growth rates of greenhouse gas emissions have actually begun to decrease. From 1990 to 2000, the average annual growth in emissions was 2.1 percent, while in contrast, between 2000 and 2008, the average annual emission growth was 0.3 percent. The good news is that between 2009 and 2010, Canada's emissions remained steady despite economic growth of 3.2 percent.

The EPA reports that by 2100, the average US temperature is projected to increase by about four to eleven degrees Fahrenheit. An increase in average temperatures worldwide implies more frequent and intense extreme heat events, or heat waves. The number of days with high temperatures above ninety degrees Fahrenheit is expected to increase throughout the United States, especially in areas that already experience heat waves. For example, cities in the Southeast and South-

west currently experience an average of sixty days per year with a high temperature above ninety degrees. These areas are projected to experience 150 or more days a year above ninety degrees by the end of the century under a higher emissions scenario. In addition to occurring more frequently, these very hot days are projected to be about ten degrees hotter at the end of this century than they are today under a higher emissions scenario.

So is there a genuine "climate debate"? Yes and no. Scientists are certain that human activities are changing the composition of the atmosphere and that increasing the concentration of GHGs will change the planet's climate. But they are not sure by how much it will change, at what rate it will change, or what (and where) the exact effects will be. This level of uncertainty about impact is what climate change deniers have focused on in their effort to prevent regulation of energy use or to sign important international treaties to limit emissions. Extreme climate change deniers also question whether anthropogenic emissions are significant and point to the earth's history of fluctuating climate patterns. However, climate scientists and experts have proven that anthropogenic emissions are significant and that these concentrations do affect global average temperatures. Climate experts agree that man-made emissions of carbon dioxide and methane have rapidly accelerated since the nineteenth century as industrialization evolved and expanded.

Impacts of Climate Change

Climate change is impacting society and ecosystems in a broad variety of ways. Table 12.4 lists just some of the impacts of climate change. Climate change could have significant impacts on food production around the world. Heat stress, droughts, and floods may lead to reductions in crop yields and livestock productivity. Climate change also has the potential to exacerbate national security issues and increase the number of international conflicts over water and food.

In April 2011, the United States experienced record-breaking floods, tornadoes, drought, and wildfires, all within a single month. NOAA's National Climatic Data Center had already reported ten weather events from 2011 for which damages and/or costs reached or exceeded one billion dollars each, exceeding the previous annual record of nine events recorded over the entire year in 2008. NOAA estimated the total damage of property and economic impacts for all weather-related disasters during the spring and summer of 2011 at more than forty-five billion dollars. In the summer of 2012, record heat waves

and drought affected large areas of the US Midwest and East. In Washington, DC, for example, July set an all-time temperature record of three degrees Fahrenheit higher than any other July on record. The severe and costly losses suffered during recent extreme weather events demonstrate the importance of increasing the resilience of the United States to climate variability and change in order to reduce economic damages and prevent loss of life.

Until recently, much of the debate about climate change has been at the global or national scale. The urban scale was often ignored, but in the past ten years or so, this area of study has expanded significantly. Two major effects of climate change will be rising sea levels and rising global average temperatures. The major danger to human populations in cities will probably occur from extreme events such as increased storm surges (related to increasing mean sea levels) and temperature extremes (related to increasing average temperatures). In other words, climate change is not just about warming up; it also involves increases in and increased frequency of weather-related events such as rainfall patterns, snow and ice cover, and sea level.

At the urban level, cities also face different vulnerabilities to and geographies of climate change. For example, inland cities such as Las Vegas, Calgary, Edmonton, and Denver may see an increase in soil erosion and a loss of water availability. Summer heat waves and droughts may affect the type of yield of crops. Underground water sources may become stressed and overused, and competition for water may intensify. Cities in the Midwest and Northeast such as Chicago, Windsor, and Detroit may also experience wetter winters with heavier snowfall. Cities located on lakes

Table 12.4   Potential Climate Impacts

Water Resources	• Shift in the timing of spring snowmelt to earlier in the spring • Lower summer stream flows, particularly in snowmelt-dependent water systems in the western United States • Increased risk of drought • Increased risk of flooding • Increased competition for water • Warmer water temperature in lakes and rivers • Changes in water quality (varies by water quality parameter)
Recreation	• Increased opportunities for warm-season activities in milder regions of the United States • Decreased opportunities for warm-season activities during the hottest part of the year, particularly in the southern United States (e.g., from heat, forest fires, low water levels, reduced urban air quality) • Reduced opportunities for cold-season recreation due to decreased snowpack and/or reduced snow or ice quality • Increased reliance on snow making at ski areas • Shifts in tourism dollars within a community from one recreation sector to another or from communities losing recreational opportunities to communities gaining opportunities
Energy	• Reduced heating demand during winter months • Increased cooling demand during summer months • Increased or decreased hydroelectric generating capacity due to potential for higher or lower stream flows
Infrastructure	• Need for new or upgraded flood-control and erosion-control structures • More frequent landslides, road washouts, and flooding • Increased demands on stormwater management systems with the potential for more combined stormwater and sewer overflows • Reduced effectiveness of sea walls with sea-level rise
Public Health	• More heat-related stress, particularly among the elderly, the poor, and other vulnerable populations • Fewer extreme cold-related health risks • Increase in vector-born illnesses (e.g., West Nile) • Reduced summer air quality in urban areas due to increased production of ground-level ozone
Business	• Price volatility in energy and raw product markets due to more extreme weather events • Increased insurance premiums due to more extreme weather events • Fewer shipping disruptions associated with snow and ice • Impacts on business infrastructure located in floodplains or coastal areas • Shifts in business opportunities
Coastal Areas and Aquatic Ecosystems	• Increased erosion or damage to coastal infrastructure, dunes, beaches, and other natural features due to sea-level rise and storm surge • Loss of coastal wetlands and other coastal habitats due to sea-level rise, erosion • Increased costs for maintenance and expansion of coastal erosion control (natural or man-made) • Saltwater intrusion into coastal aquifers due to sea-level rise • Increased risk of pollution from coastal hazardous waste sites due to sea-level rise • Loss of cultural and historical sites on coastline due to sea-level rise and related impacts

Source: Adapted from Center for Science in the Earth System (The Climate Impacts Group), Joint Institute for the Study of the Atmosphere and Ocean, University of Washington, and King County, Washington. 2007. *Preparing for Climate Change: A Guidebook for Local, Regional and State Governments.* http://www.iclei.org/fileadmin/user_upload/documents/Global/Progams/CCP/Adaptation/ICLEI-Guidebook-Adaptation.pdf: 40-41 (accessed September 2012).

or rivers, such as Ottawa, Toronto, Kansas City, Cincinnati, Memphis, and Sacramento, may experience flooding in the spring as more snowpack melts but reduced flows late in the summer; the potential for summer water shortages could affect the supply of water for drinking, agriculture, electricity production, and ecosystems.

Climate Change and Water

A major emerging issue is the connection between climate and water. Climate change will have a big impact on water in terms of sea-level rise and flooding rivers. Changing climate patterns will affect the availability of freshwater both locally and regionally.

Several factors will impact cities and water. First is sea-level rise. Global average sea level rose at an average rate of around 1.7 ± 0.3 mm per year from 1950 to 2009. Two main factors contribute to sea-level rise. First is thermal expansion, which means that as ocean water warms, it expands in volume. The second is from the contribution of land-based ice (from glaciers and ice sheets) resulting from increased melting. Scientists report increased melting of ice at rapid rates in the Arctic Ocean. In 2007, the Intergovernmental Panel on Climate Change projected that during the twenty-first century, sea level will rise another seven to twenty-three inches (eighteen to fifty-nine centimeters). But at the climate conference in Copenhagen in 2011, scientists suggested that the 2007 report was a drastic underestimation of the problem and that oceans were likely to rise twice as fast. Recent satellite and other data show seas are rising by more than one-eighth of an inch (three millimeters) a year—more than 50 percent faster than the average for the twentieth century. There is a widespread consensus that substan-

tial long-term sea-level rise will continue for decades to come. Rapidly melting ice sheets in Greenland and Antarctica are likely to push up sea levels by three and one-half feet (one meter) or more by 2100.

Rising sea levels threaten already vulnerable salt marshes and other coastal habitats that provide storm protection to cities; heavy precipitation caused by more extreme weather events will increase sewer overflows, degrade water quality, and increase the likelihood of waterborne diseases. From more severe and frequent droughts to unprecedented flooding, many of the most profound and immediate impacts of climate change will relate to water. Impacts include sea-level rise, saltwater intrusion, harm to fisheries, and more frequent and intense storm events. Some climate modelers have even predicted large areas of coastal cities such as Seattle, Halifax, Vancouver, Miami, Charleston, and New York will be flooded by the increase in sea levels. Figure 12.7 shows a map of possible flooding in Charleston, South Carolina.

In addition to rising sea level, storms and storm surge may cause widespread flooding in coastal cities. Many climate experts predict that climate change will increase the number and intensity of storms and hurricanes. Cities may also face problems from impacts that include increased coastal erosion, higher storm-surge flooding, inhibition of primary production processes, more extensive coastal inundation, changes in surface-water quality and groundwater characteristics, increased loss of property and coastal habitats, increased flood risk and potential loss of life, loss of nonmonetary cultural resources and values, impacts on agriculture and aquaculture through decline in soil and water quality, and loss of tourism, recreation, and transportation functions.

Figure 12.7   Map of potential flooding in Charleston, South Carolina. For many coastal cities, sea level rise and increased storm events could mean that areas of the city could be underwater for extended periods of time. *Source:* NOAA Coastal Services Center, http://www.csc.noaa.gov/digitalcoast/_/pdf/chsflood.pdf.

Responding to Climate Change: Mitigation and Adaptation

Throughout the 1990s and early 2000s, much of the literature on climate change viewed mitigation and adaptation as two competing methods. An early emphasis on mitigation was the result of the United Nations Framework Convention on Climate Change (UN-FCCC) in 1992, one of the first international treaties that promoted policies to reduce GHG emissions, and the subsequent, more binding 1997 Kyoto Protocol (which Canada signed but the United States did not). Mitigation focuses on the reduction of GHGs in order to meet the ultimate objective of the UNFCCC, which is to achieve "stabilization of greenhouse gas concentrations in the atmosphere at a level that would prevent dangerous anthropogenic interference with the climate system." The International Panel on Climate Change,

for example, defines mitigation as "an anthropogenic intervention to reduce the sources or enhance the sinks of greenhouse gases."

While mitigation tackles the causes of climate change, adaptation, on the other hand, tackles the effects of the phenomenon. Adaptation refers to the ability of a system to adjust to climate change (including climate variability and extremes), to moderate potential damage, to take advantage of opportunities, or to cope with the consequences.

For many years, mitigation was a more popular focus, in part because adaptation carried with it a sense of fatalism and also an implicit critique that those nations such as the United States, Canada, and Russia were more responsible for high emissions. In recent years, however, there is a movement toward a blend of both mitigation and adaptation agendas. This has occurred for several reasons. One is that there are limits to the ability to adapt, so actions to mitigate climate change must continue at the same time as cities plan for adaptation. For example, the relocation of communities or infrastructure may not be feasible in many locations, especially in the short term. Over the long term, adaptation alone may not be sufficient to cope with all the projected impacts of climate change. Second, while climate change is inevitable and will need to be adapted to, it is still possible to mitigate the severity of this change by altering human behaviors. The past several years have seen more of a blend of agendas that focus on both reducing greenhouse gas emissions and preparing for inevitable changes.

Governments at all levels are implementing policies geared toward both mitigation and adaptation. But there still remain those who resist making changes, despite the overwhelming evidence. Some resist climate mitigation or adaptation actions because they believe it will be a significant economic drain.

Mitigation

Many cities in North America have confronted the challenge of climate change with a focus on mitigation. Mitigation focuses on reducing the concentrations of GHGs either by reducing their sources or increasing their sinks. There are several broad categories, including reduction of fossil fuel use (by using alternative energy sources), energy efficiency and conservation, and the promotion of carbon sinks. There are many ways to approach these through specific strategies and policies; a few are highlighted in box 12.6. Most mitigation efforts are in broad categories that include low-carbon energy, carbon storage, carbon science, and carbon policy. Recently, there is greater emphasis on mitigation that is seen to

have a multiplier effect. For example, green buildings are a fixture of sustainability and climate change discussions as they are linked to energy conservation and storm-water runoff. Also, because climate mitigation is essentially about reducing GHG emissions, mitigation efforts can also have positive side-effects on public health and ecosystems.

Adaptation

At one level, adaptation is about ensuring that the infrastructure of a city, from buildings and industrial facilities to roads and sewage systems, has as low a vulnerability as possible to likely future climate changes, and is as flexible as possible, with an ability to cope with the high level of uncertainty over the actual nature of future changes in climate. At another level, it involves putting institutional frameworks in place that are "adaptation friendly"—for example, urban planning offices that build adaptation requirements into a wide range of ongoing planning activities.

A 2011 National Research Council report, *America's Climate Choices*, notes that cities across the United States are already experiencing a range of climatic changes, including more frequent and extreme precipitation events, longer wildfire seasons, reduced snowpack, extreme heat events, increasing ocean temperatures, and rising sea levels. The 2011 survey of 396 mayors from all fifty states found that over 30 percent are already taking climate impacts into account within their planning and improvement programs, demonstrating growing local concern about climate risks. For example, the City of Chicago, anticipating a hotter and wetter future, is taking steps to adapt such as repaving alleyways with permeable materials to handle

Box 12.6 Selected Climate Mitigation Efforts

Use alternative energy sources:

- Renewable energy such as solar, hydroelectric, biofuels
- Nuclear power
- Carbon dioxide capture and carbon sequestration from power plants or industrial sources

Improve energy efficiency and conservation:

- Transportation:
  - Improve vehicle efficiency (including use of hybrid or zero-emission vehicles)
  - Reduce the number of miles traveled
  - Encourage bicycle use
  - Promote public transportation
- Urban planning and building design:
  - Encourage green buildings and green roofs
  - Increasing the energy efficiency of buildings

Sinks and conservation:

- Plant trees and promote reforestation

greater rainfall and reduce flood risks and planting trees that can tolerate warmer conditions. Even smaller cities are making adaptation plans. Greg Heartwell, mayor of Grand Rapids, Michigan, says:

The City of Grand Rapids is addressing various climate-related threats such as extreme heat and more intense precipitation events. We see these climate strategies as an extension of responsible governance and an imperative investment in the future prosperity of our city. As an inland watershed city, we have focused on restoring and maintaining a high quality of water in the Grand River with over $240 million in combined sewer separation investment. This prepares us for ever-increasing precipitation levels now and into the future.

Cities are now planning for climate adaptation, and these plans involve a range of examples and strategies, some of which are highlighted in table 12.5.

Although cities are taking the lead in climate adaptation, they will need federal governments to support the costs of many types of projects. For example, cities on the coast are developing plans to relocate water and sewer infrastructure to higher elevations. For smaller, lower-wealth cities, this could be a significant financial burden without grants from the federal government.

Table 12.5   Examples of Adaptation Approaches

Coastal City Adaptation	• Identify and improve evacuation routes and evacuation plans for low-lying areas to prepare for increased storm surge and flooding
	• Shore protection techniques and open space preserves that allow beaches and coastal wetlands to gradually move inland as sea level rises
Ecosystems Adaptation	• Protect and increase migration corridors to allow species to migrate as the climate changes
	• Promote land and wildlife management practices that enhance ecosystem resilience
Energy	• Increase energy efficiency to help offset increases in energy consumption
	• Harden energy production facilities to withstand increased flood, wind, lightning, and other storm-related stresses
Human Health	• Implement early warning systems and emergency response plans to prepare for changes in the frequency, duration, and intensity of extreme weather events
	• Plant trees and expand green spaces in urban settings to moderate heat increases
Water Resources	• Improve water use efficiency and build additional water storage capacity
	• Protect and restore stream- and riverbanks to ensure good water quality and safeguard water quantity
Infrastructure	• Relocate vulnerable water and sewer infrastructure

Source: US EPA. 2012. "Adaptation Overview." http://www.epa.gov/climatechange/impacts-adaptation/adapt-overview.html (retrieved August 2012).

There are signs that federal agencies are working with cities on climate adaptation. Southeast Florida cities such as Miami and Palm Beach are already experiencing the impacts of extreme weather and sea-level rise, compromising drainage systems and seawalls during high-tide events. With continued sea-level rise and the prospect of more intense hurricanes and heavy downpours, the region faces greater risks of flooding, safe water supply shortages, infrastructure damage, and natural resource degradation. In response, Broward, Miami-Dade, Palm Beach, and Monroe Counties entered into the Southeast Florida Regional Climate Change Compact in 2010 to address these threats collaboratively. Local and regional offices of federal agencies—including NOAA, USGS, and EPA—have supported these counties with regional adaptation planning. For example, the US Army Corps of Engineers and NOAA provided technical assistance to evaluate threats of future sea-level rise. USGS applied advanced hydrologic models and provided financial resources to support projects related to saltwater intrusion of groundwater supplies and flood risks. EPA provided coordination support, helping connect the compact partners with critical technical, planning, and programmatic resources.

Climate Plans

Many cities already have strong local policies and programs in place to reduce global warming pollution, but more action is needed at the local, state, and federal levels to meet the challenge. In March 2005, Seattle mayor Greg Nickles and nine other US mayors, representing more than three million Americans, joined together to invite cities from across the country to take additional actions to significantly reduce global warming pollution. Three months later in June, the Mayors Climate Protection Agreement was passed unanimously by the US Conference of Mayors. The Mayors Agreement on Climate Change is remarkable in that it occurred primarily because the United States has refused to ratify the Kyoto Protocol. In the absence of national leadership, cities have committed themselves to the agreement. The agreement tasks participating cities to take following three actions:

1. Strive to meet or beat the Kyoto Protocol targets in their own communities through actions ranging from anti-sprawl land-use policies to urban forest restoration projects to public information campaigns;
2. Urge their state governments and the federal government to enact policies and programs to meet or beat the greenhouse gas emission reduction target suggested for the United States in the Kyoto Protocol—7 percent reduction from 1990 levels by 2012; and
3. Urge the US Congress to pass greenhouse gas reduction legislation, which would establish a national emission trading system.

By 2012, the Mayors Agreement on Climate Change included 1,054 mayors from the fifty states, the District of Columbia, and Puerto Rico, representing a total population of over eighty-eight million citizens. Many US cities have also initiated local environmental legislation that exceeds EPA standards or, as in the case with the Mayors Agreement on Climate Change, occurs in the absence of national leadership.

Increasingly, local initiatives and partnerships are working to advance climate change policy. In 2007, the city of Montreal and the Province of Québec joined the Climate Group, an international organization dedicated to the promotion of federated state and large multinational corporation action in the area of climate change. Canadian cities have partnered to create the New England Governors/Eastern Canadian Premiers Climate Change Action Plan 2001, in which several cities pledge regional, national, and international collaboration in order to stabilize regional GHG emissions at 1990 levels by 2010 and lower them to 10 percent below 1990 levels by 2020. More than forty Canadian and US cities are also members of the Climate Registry. The Climate Registry is a nonprofit collaboration among North American states, provinces, territories, and Native sovereign nations that sets consistent and transparent standards to calculate, verify, and publicly report greenhouse gas emissions into a single registry. This registry aims to become a component of a North American GHG emissions cap-and-trade market. Other examples include the Western Climate Initiative (WCI), which is a group of North American states working together to implement a GHG emission cap-and-trade system for certain economic sectors that are heavy GHG emitters.

One outcome from these networks and agreements is the creation of city climate plans. Most climate plans address both mitigation and adaptation. In its 2007 climate plan, New York City established the goal of reducing citywide GHG emissions by 30 percent below 2005 levels by 2030. In 2009, it reported that citywide GHG emissions were lower than in 2008, the first year a decrease in GHG emissions has been recorded. As with many cities, New York's greenhouse gas emissions are dominated by energy consumed in transportation and energy consumed in buildings. Roughly 78 percent of New York City's GHG emissions are related to heating, cooling, powering, and lighting buildings, and 20 percent are related to transportation. Not surprisingly, its climate plan focuses on ways to reduce energy use. Similarly, Chicago adopted its Chicago Climate Action Plan in 2008. The broad goal is to eliminate GHG emissions by 80 percent of their 1990 level. Divided into five main strategies, the plan mostly deals with ways to mitigate climate change and pays less attention to adaptation. Chicago proposes to reduce GHG emissions by retrofitting older buildings with more energy-efficient technology, investing in clean and renewable energy sources, and reducing waste and industrial pollution. In order to improve transportation, the Chicago Transit Authority has introduced over two hundred hybrid buses that now comprise nearly 13 percent of the city's fleet. The plan also considers adaptation focusing on what the city sees as the two main effects of climate change: extreme heat and decreased precipitation. To combat an increased urban heat island, the city has pledged to plant more than ten thousand trees. Since 2008, the city has also added fifty-five acres of permeable surfaces. Similarly, Toronto adopted its climate plan in 2007. The plan calls for initial funding of $42 million for energy conservation measures, $20 million for renewable energy projects, and $22 million for retrofitting city facilities.

The development of city climate plans is relatively recent, and many of these are initial blueprints for action. Over the next several years, it is likely that cities will further develop their climate plans to include a better balance of mitigation and adaptation strategies. Climate change is inextricably linked to cities, and this is an area of research and policy that will continue to be of critical importance in the years to come.

CONCLUSIONS

As this chapter has shown, the impact of cities on their natural environment is significant and far ranging. Human activities impact land, air, water, and climate. These remain important challenges for cities to address as they try to reduce risk and vulnerability to disasters and as they envision a more sustainable future.

SUGGESTED READINGS

Aerts, J., W. Botzen, M. Bowman, P. Ward, and P. Dircke, eds. 2011. *Climate Adaption and Flood Risk in Coastal Cities*. London: Routledge.

Bicknell, J., D. Dodman, and D. Sattherwaite, eds. 2009. *Adapting Cities to Climate Change: Understanding and Addressing the Development Challenges*. London: Earthscan.

Biswas, A., C. Tortajad, and R. Izquierdo-Avino. 2009. *Water Management in 2020 and Beyond*. Berlin: Springer.

Brimblecombe, P., ed. 2003. *The Effects of Air Pollution on the Built Environment*. London: Imperial College Press.

Bulkeley, H. 2013. *Cities and Climate Change*. London: Routledge.

Cisneros, B. J., and J. B. Rose. 2009. *Urban Water Security: Managing Risks*. Leiden: Taylor & Francis.

Craig, R. K. 2009. *The Clean Water Act and the Constitution: Legal Structure and the Public's Right to a Clean and Healthy Environment*. 2nd ed. Washington, DC: Environmental Law Institute.

Girardet, H. 2008. *Cities People Planet: Urban Development and Climate Change*. 2nd ed. Chichester: Wiley Academic Press.

Gumprecht, B. 2001. *The Los Angeles River: Its Life, Death and Possible Rebirth*. Baltimore: Johns Hopkins University Press.

Jones, J. A. A. 2010. *Water Sustainability: A Global Perspective*. London: Hodder Education.

Karvonen, A. 2011. *Politics of Urban Runoff: Nature, Technology, and the Sustainable City*. Cambridge, MA: MIT Press.

Melosi, M. V. 2011. *Precious Commodity: Providing Water for America's Cities*. Pittsburgh: University of Pittsburgh Press.

Rosenzweig, C., W. D. Solecki, S. A. Hammer, and S. Mehrotra, eds. 2011. *Climate Change and Cities: First Assessment Report of the Urban Climate Change Research Network*. Cambridge: Cambridge University Press.

Solomon, S. 2010. *Water*. New York: Harper Perennial.

Stone, B., Jr. 2012. *The City and the Coming Climate: Climate Change in the Places We Live*. Cambridge: Cambridge University Press.

Watt, J., J. Tidbald, V. Kucera, and R. Hamilton. 2009. *The Effect of Air Pollution on Cultural Heritage*. New York: Springer.

World Health Organization and UNICEF. 2012. "Progress on Sanitation and Drinking-Water." WHO and UNICEF Joint Monitoring Program, http://www.wssinfo.org/fileadmin/user_upload/resources/JMP-report-2012-en.pdf. Accessed July 2012.

CITIES ON THE WEB

American Lung Association. 2012. "Key Findings, State of the Air 2012." Retrieved June 2012 from http://www.stateoftheair.org/2012/key-findings/.

For up-to-date information on ozone/smog and interactive maps, go to www.epa.gov/air/ozone pollution.

Scorecard, the Pollution Information Site, www.scorecard.org, allows you to profile the air, land, and water pollution in your state, city, or community in the United States.

Watch an interesting short video on combined sewer overflows at http://www.riverkeeper.org/campaigns/stop-polluters/sewage-contamination/cso/.

13

Urban Hazards
JOHN P. TIEFENBACHER

Cities are hazardous places. Despite the amenities that cities provide, there are inherent problems. The dangers arise from the locations chosen for settlements. For most American cities, original settlement sites were often places with characteristics that met certain needs: they provided natural resources (e.g., access to abundant water, transportation modes, energy sources, marketable goods [timber, fish, or coal], or places for refuge) or economic advantages. As settlement populations grew, agriculture was driven from land that became more valuable (or more profitable for the land owners if sold) for housing, transportation networks, or industrial uses than for growing food. Local fisheries also lost vitality, in part because of overexploitation, but also because local development reduced water quality and fish habitat. People still reside in places that provide access to many of these resources, though today access to distant sources has become easier and residential location is less directly tied to meeting basic needs because of improved urban and global transport systems and trade. In the United States and Canada, we are intellectually and spatially separated (and often consciously disconnected) from the impacts of our lives.

What we "need" has changed dramatically throughout history and other factors such as employment, local economies, social relationships, politics, social preferences, and environmental amenities increasingly drive contemporary residential "choices." For instance, *interesting* landscapes, *peaceful* settings, and *beautiful* views are pull factors in decision making among willingly relocating populations. Unfortunately, such attractions correlate with the most dynamic of natural environments: rivers that flood; coasts prone to storms, erosion, and tsunami; seismically and volcanically active mountain ranges with unstable slopes; or forested landscapes prone to fire. Or they may be places where economically active human landscapes contain certain dangers such as heavy traffic, industrial activities, or extraction of resources and/or people (criminals, terrorists, or enemies) or lifestyles and conflicts (such as with socially and politically alienated communities, drug users, or the mentally ill). For those with few options, these locations might be left over from the choices of the free, wealthy, or powerful segments of society. Each of these places holds some potential for "bad" things to happen.

In the twenty-first century, North American cities are susceptible to many environmental hazards, including droughts, floods, heat waves, earthquakes, ice storms, and volcanic eruptions. At first glance, many "natural disasters" in cities seem like natural disasters, forces of nature. But these events have impacts and effects that were mediated through the prism of socioeconomic power structures and arrangements. While there are certainly physical forces that can wreak havoc on our cities, disasters are first and foremost social experiences that often affect the poor more than the rich and reveal economic inequality, social injustice, and poor planning efforts. For example, following Hurricane Katrina's 2005 flooding of New Orleans, scholars Chester Hartman and Greg Squires wrote their 2006 book *There Is No Such Thing as a Natural Disaster*. The flooding of the city was a result of the poorly designed levees, a result of inadequate funding of public works. They argued that the effects of Hurricane Katrina were socially and racially determined: flooding disproportionately affected the poorest neighborhoods of the city, and the hardest hit neighborhoods were nonwhite. The racial and income disparities in the city were reflected in the spatial patterns of the flood damage. More than seven years after the disaster, vast areas in the Lower Ninth Ward, a predominantly African American neighborhood, remain unrestored (see figure 13.1).

North American cities face changing patterns and challenges of hazards and disasters. Advances in infrastructural engineering and notions of preferred landscapes generate technological issues that also change hazard patterns. There are general landscapes of risk in cities generated by natural processes (river and coastal flooding, hurricanes and other storms, and earthquakes), and at the same time there are ways urbanization augments hazards technologically and socially. Disasters reveal our social fault lines as well as our polit-

Figure 13.1   Several years after Hurricane Katrina, vast areas of the Lower Ninth Ward are still not recovered and remain vacant. The lack of rebuilding suggests that political and social issues often underlie recovery efforts. *Source:* Google Maps.

ical failings. The primary aim of urban hazard management today is the quest for resilience.

CONCEPTS

The "bad things" that happen might be regarded as "risks," but risk simply refers to a probability (a "chance") that something negative could occur as processes occasionally become extreme or move beyond typical circumstances and present challenges. Box 13.1 lists a range of "extreme events." When negative outcomes vary spatially and affect people, we refer to them as "hazards." In scholarly terms, "hazard" is actually the probability that an "extreme" event will negatively impact people, their property, or their economic interests and is usually qualified by the extent, depth, or quantity of the impacts. Alternatively, a hazard's measure reflects the disaster potential. Here we define a disaster as an outcome of a hazardous event that exceeds a person's, place's, or system's ability to absorb it without upset.

Box 13.1 Assorted Urban Hazards in North American Cities

NATURAL HAZARDS

Geophysical

Earthquakes	Subsidence
Erosion	Tsunamis
Landslides	Volcanic eruptions
Sinkholes	Wildfires

Meteorological

Atmospheric inversions	Haboobs
Blizzards	Heat waves
Coastal inundation	Hurricanes and tropical storms
Derechos	Ice storms
Droughts	Severe thunderstorms
Fog	Tornadoes
Floods	

Biological

Infestations	Plant and animal disease outbreaks
Invasive species	Vicious and disease-carrying pets and wildlife

TECHNOLOGICAL HAZARDS

Air pollution	Industrial accidents
Automobile accidents	Internet failures
Blackouts	Levee failures
Bridge collapses	Occupational hazards
Building collapses	Pesticide exposures
Building fires	Plane crashes
Chemical spills and airborne releases	Radiation releases
Communication system failures	Sunspots and solar activity
Dam failures	Train derailments
Electrical system failures	Ultraviolet radiation exposure
Energy crises	Water pollution

SOCIAL HAZARDS

Carjacking	Riots
Consumer product tampering	Road rage
Contagious disease outbreaks	Serial killers and serial rapists
Domestic violence	Terrorism
Epidemics	Theft
Handgun violence	Vandalism
Poverty	Violent crime

Geographical analyses of the probabilities that extreme events coincide with human landscapes identifies the places most in need of actions to reduce (or mitigate) disaster potential. These locations may or may not be distinguished as having the densest populations or the poorest neighborhoods. They also may *not* be closest to a risk-generating feature such as a coastline, fault line, riverbank, nuclear plant, interstate highway, or mental hospital. Spatially, the intensity of the impacts generated by extreme events may not reflect the geography of the sources of hazard because localities can have characteristics that cause them to respond differently to events, and therefore the geography of potential impacts must be examined carefully. Similarly, the communities in impacted locales might experience events differently because of their proximity to the "energy" of the event, individuals' personal characteristics, their economic and social wherewithal, their status in society, the built landscape surrounding them, and even a government's emergency response preparedness. These so-called vulnerabilities influence the distribution and the significance of impacts from extreme events.

Vulnerabilities associated with culture, religion, or education might influence how people perceive, interpret, or understand what is happening in an emergency. The relationships between and status of social groups might influence choices they make (or think they *can* make) in response to immediate and long-term threats. For instance, urban homeowners' associations, in order to maintain neighborhood property values, might restrict homeowners' choices or options for structural or spatial remedies to wildfire or seismic risks. Residents of poorer neighborhoods may have little control over the hazardousness of their neighborhoods because they may lack the economic wherewithal to manage it or the decision-making power associated with property ownership. The quality and strength of buildings, power grids, highways, or railroads can make elements of infrastructure more or less likely to be damaged or destroyed by specific events, and this influences the potential for disasters and disruption of a community. Training and practice by police, fire, or rescue personnel and emergency management agencies can diminish the impacts of events, and preparedness can vary over space and time. While vulnerability management can be used to manage hazard, it might have inadvertent negative consequences.

Cities tend not to wait passively for disasters to occur. Rather, they often attempt to manage hazard to mitigate disasters. People respond in diverse ways as they are guided by cognition or awareness and understanding, which may be incomplete or even wrong. Responses can prompt adaptation, minor or major adjustments, evacuation, planning and preparedness, permanent relocation, or even measures that attempt to eliminate the threat completely. For example, such measures could include straightening and deepening river channels, fortifying coastlines with seawalls, or passing laws to prevent "accidents." In few cases have hazards been eliminated. Such "elimination" efforts, however, tend to fall short and usually only change the geographies of risks or redistribute the risk to others. The exceptions are most apparent in locations where people (or whole communities) have been removed or economic activities have ceased and are no longer exposed to the hazard. For instance, the small community of Soldiers Grove (population 653 in 2000) in southwestern Wisconsin decided in 1977 to relocate the entire community above the floodplain and flood hazard zones associated with the Kickapoo River. The effort was completed by 1983, and the result was enhanced by a coincidental conversion to solar electrification. Similarly, residents of Gays Mills (population 625), a Kickapoo River neighbor to Soldiers Grove, committed to a similar relocation project in 2010 in order to remove the flood hazard from their midst. In these places, the potential for disaster has been eliminated because the hazard has been attenuated—but the risk has not.

Throughout the twentieth century, urban growth produced "hazards" by increasing human interaction with biophysical, geophysical, and ecological processes. This is a dialectical process. As people interact with natural processes, they cease to be natural, becoming a hybridized set of humanized natural pro-

cesses. Labeling events as "natural disasters," in fact, mistakenly assigns their causes to nature. Hazards and disasters are caused by people, regardless of the source of the threat. Natural processes, technological processes, and social processes can generate hazards, but they are hazards because of human actions. Nature (even a "wild" animal) is dispassionate toward human beings. It is impartial in our interactions with it except insofar as an element of nature might strive to protect its own interest; it neither intends to harm people nor seeks to eliminate us. Disasters are entirely produced by *somebody's* actions, though they may not have been prompted by the actions of those disasters' victims. Often, the desires and actions of socially, politically, and economically powerful interests may generate riskscapes. Riskscapes are landscapes of probabilities for an extreme event. They impact marginalized populations, the politically or economically weak, or simply bystanders. Thus, the real roots of hazard are not biological, geological, or chemical processes but are the activities of actors who are often members of societies' elite groups. Disasters occur when people, health, or property are negatively impacted by extreme events or conditions. Without people and development, the potential for damage or loss of human life and/or property does not exist as extreme events would affect nothing of value to us. Without people, natural processes would simply continue as they have throughout time.

NATURAL, TECHNOLOGICAL, AND SOCIAL HAZARDS

Technological processes such as industrial and other activities can generate acute events that are of high energy, are discrete in time, and have an intense effect on the surroundings. Such processes can also generate chronic situations in which events are less intense, occurring over a long period of time, and produce constant, low-grade, and less apparent exposure to victims. Examples of acute events are releases of radioactivity from nuclear power facilities, intentional and accidental releases of toxic materials from industrial and commercial enterprises, explosions from many types of activities, and even deadly automobile accidents. Chronic problems include air and water pollution, exposure to pesticide residues, and first-, second-, and thirdhand tobacco smoke exposure, among many others. It is only when a death or a case of disease or injury is recognized as unusual, is suspiciously clustered in time, or is becoming too common do people go looking for its causes. Chronic exposures have, for the past half-century or so, come to be regarded as "environmental problems." Impacts are often delayed, unexpected, and unpredicted, but they diminish human health and cause long-term degradation of nature and ecosystems. They might clearly impact only a few people scattered over a region, which for most people mentally unlinks the impacts from their causes. By contrast, acute events are commonly regarded as technological hazards and may be managed in very different ways because of cognitively clear, direct links between events and negative impacts.

Natural and technological processes have traditionally been the object of study for hazard and disaster researchers. Studies of social processes that produce "social hazards" have been less common for this group of scholars. However, with the recent rise in awareness that terrorism can produce a hazard, social hazards have begun to be regarded as deserving of attention by hazards scholars and emergency managers. After countless centuries of death and destruction caused by man's inhumanity to man (as in wars, by murderers, by violence wrought by gun owners, and others), the terrorism acts committed on September 11, 2001, have compelled scholars to consider social problems as hazards. Though terrorism is relatively rare, other causes of social hazards are not. North American cities, in fact, force the "melting pot" of social relationships onto the front burner of the "stove of problems" with which managers must contend, through the concentration of people, the competitive motives of cultures in America, personal pursuits of power, and the augmentation of prejudice by self-interested actors. The resulting conflicts generate social friction and stress and lead to clashes and antisocial behaviors that are hazardous and complicate urban natural and technological hazard management.

URBAN HAZARDS AND DISASTERS IN NORTH AMERICA

Cities are rarely constructed in arbitrary locations with clear designs that reflect social goals or intentioned desires. The organic process of development of most cities is based on internal forces (investment and innovation) that spawn economic growth and external forces that spawn population growth, like in- or out-migrations between cities, between cities and the countryside, or between countries (immigration). More recent development in most cities has been premised on past patterns established for economic, strategic, and functional reasons but not on the patterns of risk that were established long before people came to occupy these places.

Floods

North American landscapes have always experienced floods, as have the cities that came to fruition on them. Settlers used the best available information about locations they could gather. Unfortunately, flood frequency and distribution, typical weather patterns, and climate extremes were (and still are) often very difficult to discern from recent conditions, and even long-term, detailed weather records could not enable perfect knowledge or prediction of future flood conditions. While locating settlements in floodplains is problematic, settlements also create flood problems where they may not have previously existed.

From 1840 to 2011, major flood disasters have occurred in American and Canadian towns and cities at least seventy-eight times (table 13.1). This undoubtedly underestimates the pattern of urban flood hazards today, at least in part because the definition of "city" has evolved over the past two centuries. Major floods continue to occur in smaller cities, but they have not tended to be dramatically catastrophic in terms of either mortalities or monetary losses and have therefore been less noteworthy or simply not widely reported. Of the seventy-eight flood events in the table, fifty-four were produced primarily by prolonged or heavy precipitation. Many, thirty-five, were early spring (January through April) floods in which rain-melted snow added to the high rainfall amounts that occurred. Five hurricanes also played a role in ten urban floods in the US South and East. Furthermore, six dam, dike, and levee failures contributed to

floods in fourteen more cities in the eastern, northern, and western United States and Canada. Each urban flood site possesses unique locational and situational characteristics, but occupants have played a major role in modifying the patterns, creating distinctly different flood riskscapes. The frequency of flood disasters in fact reveals how people have enhanced flood hazard in cities. Eleven flood disasters occurred prior to 1900. Twenty more occurred between 1900 and 1950. Thirty-two major floods struck North American cities between 1950 and 2000. And at least fifteen more disasters already occurred in the first eleven years of this century.

Every flood is different. Even when a specific city experiences two or more events, the distributions of the impacts of the events are never identical. Rainfall patterns, rates, and intensities might be dramatically different. Rainstorms might have followed extended periods of either drought or wetter-than-usual conditions. Soils, in places with absorptive soils that can store water, might be saturated and instead enhance runoff. As vegetation similarly slows runoff, its condition and abundance can also be a factor. All of these factors produce riskscapes.

But people also constantly change their urban landscapes, reducing the permeability of its surfaces and the absorbability of the built environment. These factors are constantly changing upstream and down, and predicting the next big storm (and its spatial extent, location, speed, and characteristics) is challenging because of the constantly evolving hazardscape. Some cities are becoming not only flood prone but flash-flood prone, in part because of economic interests that drive development of undeveloped land.

Table 13.1   Major Urban Floods in the United States and Canada, 1840 to Present

Location	Year	Primary "Cause"	Location	Year	Primary "Cause"
St. Louis, Missouri	1844	Heavy rain	Lawrence, Kansas	1951	Heavy rain
New Orleans, Louisiana	1849	Heavy rain	Kansas City, Kansas	1951	Heavy rain
Des Moines, Iowa	1851	Heavy rain	Kansas City, Missouri	1951	Heavy rain
Concord, New Hampshire	1852	Heavy rain	Salem, Oregon	1964	Heavy rain
Georgetown, District of Columbia	1852	Heavy rain	Clinton, Iowa	1965	Heavy rain
Philadelphia, Pennsylvania	1869	Hurricane	Rapid City, South Dakota	1972	Dam failure
Washington, District of Columbia	1869	Hurricane	Lansing, Michigan	1975	Heavy rain
			Flint, Michigan	1975	Heavy rain
Williamsburg, Massachusetts	1874	Dam failure	Kansas City, Missouri	1977	Heavy rain
			Linda, California	1986	Heavy rain
Omaha, Nebraska	1881	Heavy rain	Thornton, California	1986	Heavy Rain
Council Bluffs, Iowa	1881	Heavy rain	Grand Forks, North Dakota	1987	Dike failure
Johnstown, Pennsylvania	1889	Dam failure			
Hepner, Oregon	1903	Heavy rain	East Grand Forks, Minnesota	1987	Dike failure
Lansing, Michigan	1904	Heavy rain	Fargo, North Dakota	1987	Dike failure
Kalamazoo, Michigan	1904	Heavy rain	Moorhead, Minnesota	1987	Dike failure
Pittsburgh, Pennsylvania	1907	Heavy rain	Wahpeton, North Dakota	1987	Dike failure
Albion, Michigan	1908	Heavy rain	Breckenridge, Minnesota	1987	Dike failure
Austin, Pennsylvania	1911	Dam failure	Lewiston, Maine	1987	Heavy rain
Columbus, Ohio	1913	Levee failure	Rumford, Maine	1987	Heavy rain
Dayton, Ohio	1913	Heavy rain	Mexico, Maine	1987	Heavy rain
Chillicothe, Ohio	1913	Heavy rain	Jay, Maine	1987	Heavy rain
Taylor, Texas	1921	Hurricane	Hartford, Connecticut	1996	Heavy rain
Lowell, Massachusetts	1936	Heavy rain	Olivehurst, California	1997	Levee failure
Cincinnati, Ohio	1937	Heavy rain	Arboga, California	1997	Levee failure
Louisville, Kentucky	1937	Heavy rain	Wilton, California	1997	Levee failure
Owensboro, Kentucky	1937	Heavy rain	Manteca, California	1997	Levee failure
Paducah, Kentucky	1937	Heavy rain	Modesto, California	1997	Levee failure
Aurora, Indiana	1937	Heavy rain	Fort Collins, Colorado	1997	Heavy rain
Columbus, Ohio	1937	Heavy rain	San Marcos, Texas	1998	Hurricane
Dayton, Ohio	1937	Heavy rain	New Braunfels, Texas	1998	Hurricane
Los Angeles, California	1938	Heavy rain	Wilmington, North Carolina	1999	Hurricane
Manhattan, Kansas	1951	Heavy rain			
Topeka, Kansas	1951	Heavy rain	Bound Brook, New Jersey	1999	Hurricane

Location	Year	Primary "Cause"	Location	Year	Primary "Cause"
New Brunswick, New Jersey	1999	Hurricane	New Ulm, Minnesota	2010	Heavy rain
			Mankato, Minnesota	2010	Heavy rain
Houston, Texas	2001	Hurricane	St. Peter, Minnesota	2010	Heavy rain
Beaumont, Texas	2001	Hurricane	Savage, Minnesota	2010	Heavy rain
New Orleans, Louisiana	2005	Hurricane and levee failure	Shakopee, Minnesota	2010	Heavy rain
			Henderson, Minnesota	2010	Heavy rain
Atlanta, Georgia	2009	Heavy rain	Brandon, Minnesota	2011	Heavy rain
Warwick, Rhode Island	2010	Heavy rain	Minot, North Dakota	2011	Heavy rain
Cranston, Rhode Island	2010	Heavy rain			
Johnston, Rhode Island	2010	Heavy rain			

Box 13.2 "Flash-Flood Alley"

The Austin to San Antonio (Interstate 35) corridor in central Texas contains some of the fastest-growing US communities of the past decade. The population of the five-county region (Williamson, Travis, Hays, Comal, and Bexar) has grown from about 2.6 million to more than 3.4 million from 2000 to 2010, and the Round Rock-Austin-San Marcos Metropolitan Statistical Area is the eighth-fastest growing region of the country. While not a shocking fact, the implications might surprise. Population growth needs land development. This region straddles a geologic feature known as the Balcones Fault, and this is seen in a landscape feature: the Balcones Escarpment. The escarpment is uplifted limestone; its prominence separates the Blackland Prairie region (a southern extension of the Midwest prairies) from the Edwards Plateau (the southeastern portion of the high plains province called the "Texas Hill Country"). Because the Edwards Plateau is limestone and because climate and vegetation don't foster it, soil does not form quickly. Little soil is present in the eastern part of this region, and the land has little capacity to absorb rainfall or runoff.

The inactive fault is not the source of hazard in the region: the uplifted land creates the risk. The uplift (gradual in some places, abrupt in others) causes an elevation rise of up to three hundred feet. This small difference orographically lifts air masses moving westward off the Gulf of Mexico when cold fronts approach from the west. The more humid (and warmer) Gulf air contrasts with the arid, cooler desert air. A clash between the two often generates very heavy precipitation events of short duration. When Gulf air masses are weakening tropical weather systems (like hurricanes), the amount of precipitation in one storm can be extreme. It often equals the annual average precipitation of the region.

This has always occurred and is natural. However, new residents and their development must contend with this flash flooding, and hazards are abundant. More people mean a greater probability that people and property will be affected. Add the transformation of land as vegetation is removed for road, subdivision, and business construction and as impervious (nonabsorbent) cover is added. Rainfall runs off even faster. The runoff crosses the new developments and the road networks built across natural ephemeral stream channels. The channels turn into the occasional rivers that formed them, and fast-flowing water several feet deep can cross a road perpendicular to the traffic. Inattentive and overly confident drivers can find themselves floating downstream, and if they are lucky, they can escape with their lives (but probably not their cars). Some are not so lucky.

Between 1990 and 2004, more than 190 major flood events occurred in these counties, leading to at least thirty-five deaths caused by encounters with flooded roadways. An "un-tolled" (they are not often reported or even recorded by authorities) number of drivers and passengers have averted personal catastrophe by surviving their encounters. This region has seen neither major nor minor flooding (not even much precipitation) since 2008 because of a multiyear drought, and this is ominous. Flood risk has continued to increase as a result of landscape development over the past five years, and flood hazards will also climb as new residents (and new and youthful automobile drivers) will not know where to expect flooded properties and flooded roadways. Many will see "new" floodplains revealed for the first time.

Surface-water management has evolved throughout North America's development. Eighteenth- and nineteenth-century approaches primarily avoided floods and drained flooded lands. Innovations, such as mechanical dredges and pumping systems, aided such efforts later in the nineteenth century, but management simply attempted to move water out of or away from cities and into the countryside. Dams controlled some dynamic rivers by impoundment but were often primarily intended to generate energy. Not until the late twentieth century were dams used to protect cities. By contrast, levee enhancement and artificial levees in and around the Midwest, the South, and the West in the late nineteenth and early twentieth centuries was used to mitigate flood hazards. St. Louis and Kansas City, Missouri, and Brownsville, Texas, for instance, grappled with levee issues during the past century as these "improvements" were built to signal that these cities

were safe and ripe for investment. Figure 13.2 shows a seawall in Galveston, Texas.

Commercial rivers received the most attention in the early twentieth century. The Ohio and Mississippi Rivers, for example, experienced numerous floods. The catastrophic Mississippi River flood of 1927 not only was a major watershed event in flood management but had major social and cultural ramifications as well. The most revealing element of the 1927 flood, however, was the dynamiting of levees downstream of New Orleans in order to "save" the city. Of course, the city that was saved was not really the people, but rather the economic interests of powerful local investors. The spaces of the poor and rural residents of Plaquemines Parish were sacrificed to the inundation. The Ohio River flood of 1937 also had significant impacts on river cities from Cincinnati to Paducah. The numerous major floods of the middle of the twentieth century led one geographer, Gilbert White, to delve

Figure 13.2   Seawall and beach, Galveston, Texas, ca. 1910.
Source: Library of Congress.

into American flood management, questioning the efforts to engineer floods from rivers and encouraging better decision making by floodplain occupants.

At the time, national policy toward flood disasters emphasized "bailing out" the victims of disasters rather than preventing disasters. After several decades of great expense, federal flood policies evolved to discourage risk taking (by reducing flood hazard). By the 1970s, the federal government encouraged loss protection through insurance rather than federal relief and reconstruction. Today, floodplain residents are "taxed" by compulsory participation in the National Flood Insurance Program. Unfortunately, this tax applies only to property buyers acquiring federally insured mortgages for flood-susceptible property. Those who owned and occupied floodplain properties before the program are not required to have flood insurance, so many at-risk floodplain residents are the next flood away from personal disaster and probable reliance on federal, state, private, and nonprofit relief. Indeed, countless millions of urbanites reside in locations of high flood risk today, and only by the luck inherent in probability have they not been impacted.

Hurricanes

In southeastern, midwestern, and eastern cities of North America, the annual season of tropical cyclone development raises the specter of flood disaster. Dozens of atmospheric low-pressure centers develop over warm subtropical waters of northern oceans during the summer and fall. Some evolve into so-called tropical depressions, tropical storms, and hurricanes. Paths and life spans of these storms are dictated by complex atmosphere-ocean interactions. Guessing where storms will go requires predictive models that are constantly fed data from monitoring and surveillance. Currently, these models are moderately successful.

North America's greatest death toll from any disaster was produced by a hurricane that struck Galveston, Texas, in 1900. At least six thousand people are believed to have died. While our technological capacity has evolved to detect and monitor hurricanes to allow time for warning of communities in their paths, precise and accurate prediction is still elusive. Only advancements in atmospheric science offer the improved prognostication of movements and strength of hurricanes. In the meantime, cities in cyclone-exposed regions must remain vigilant during hurricane "season" and should remove people from hazard-exposed locations.

Since 1842, hundreds of hurricanes and tropical storms have made landfall in the United States or Canada (figure 13.3). As with other natural processes, the patterns of hurricanes of the past do not determine future patterns of hurricanes. Examination of the list of past hurricanes reveals the chaotic temporal and spatial pattern of hurricanes and

their tendencies over the past 160 years (table 13.2). For instance, 60 of the 167 (category 2 or stronger) land-falling hurricanes occurred between 1850 and 1900. In the next fifty years (up to 1950), only thirty-eight more made landfall on Atlantic and Gulf coasts. Forty-five more made landfall between 1951 and 2000, and eleven more have crossed North American coasts in the past twelve years. Not all of these hurricanes struck urban areas, but each storm had a potential to impact many small and large cities. Urbanization has expanded the area of potential exposure. The population of coastal regions has climbed dramatically during the past century and a half as well, and it is easy to understand that the hazard is ever greater. Today, twenty-one million North Americans live in urban areas along coasts at elevations ten meters or less above sea level, while more than 50 percent of the US population lives in coastal counties today. Coastal

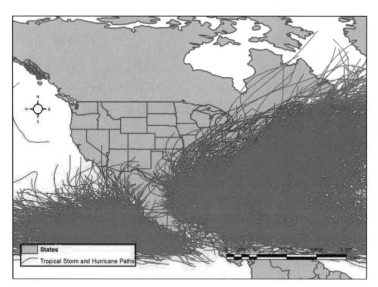

Figure 13.3   Paths of hurricanes and tropical storms in North America from 1842 to 2010. *Source:* International Best Track Archive for Climate Stewardship, National Climatic Data Center, National Oceanic and Atmospheric Administration. http://www.ncdc.noaa.gov/oa/ibtracs/index.php?name=ibtracs-data. Accessed April 26, 2012.

Table 13.2   "Strong" (Category 2 or Higher) Hurricanes in the United States and Canada, 1850–Present

Date*	Name	Category**	States Affected***
8/23/1851	Unnamed	3	Florida
8/25/1852	Unnamed	2	Louisiana
8/26/1852	Unnamed	3	Alabama, Mississippi
10/9/1852	Unnamed	2	Florida
9/8/1854	Unnamed	3, 2	Georgia, South Carolina
9/18/1854	Unnamed	2	Texas
8/16/1855	Unnamed	3	Mississippi
9/16/1855	Unnamed	3	Louisiana
8/11/1856	Unnamed	4	Louisiana
8/31/1856	Unnamed	2	Florida
8/11–12/1860	Unnamed	3, 2	Louisiana, Mississippi, Alabama
9/15/1860	Unnamed	2	Louisiana, Mississippi
10/2/1860	Unnamed	2	Louisiana
9/1/1865	Unnamed	2	Louisiana
10/23/1865	Unnamed	2	Florida
7/15/1866	Unnamed	2	Texas
10/4/1867	Unnamed	2	Louisiana
8/17/1869	Unnamed	2	Texas
9/8/1869	Unnamed	3	Massachusetts
10/4/1869	Unnamed	2	Maine
8/16/1871	Unnamed	3	Florida
8/25/1871	Unnamed	2	Florida
10/7/1873	Unnamed	3	Florida
9/16/1875	Unnamed	3	Texas
10/20/1876	Unnamed	2	Florida
10/3/1877	Unnamed	3	Florida
9/10/1878	Unnamed	2	Florida
10/23/1878	Unnamed	2	North Carolina
8/18/1879	Unnamed	3, 2	North Carolina, Virginia
8/23/1879	Unnamed	2	Louisiana, Texas
9/1/1879	Unnamed	3	Louisiana
8/13/1880	Unnamed	3	Texas
8/29/1880	Unnamed	2	Florida

(continued)

Table 13.2 (*continued*)

Date*	Name	Category**	States Affected***
8/28/1881	Unnamed	2	Georgia
9/9/1881	Unnamed	2	North Carolina
9/10/1882	Unnamed	3	Florida
9/15/1882	Unnamed	2	Louisiana
9/11/1883	Unnamed	2	North Carolina
8/25/1885	Unnamed	3	South Carolina
9/25/1885	Unnamed	2	North Carolina
6/14/1886	Unnamed	2	Louisiana, Texas
6/21/1886	Unnamed	2	Florida
6/30/1886	Unnamed	2	Florida
8/20/1886	Unnamed	4	Texas
10/12/1886	Unnamed	3, 2	Louisiana, Texas
9/21/1887	Unnamed	2	Texas
8/16/1888	Unnamed	3	Florida
10/11/1888	Unnamed	2	Florida
8/28/1893	Unnamed	3	Georgia, South Carolina
9/7/1893	Unnamed	2	Louisiana
10/2–3/1893	Unnamed	4, 2	Louisiana, Mississippi, Alabama
9/25/1894	Unnamed	2	Florida
10/9/1894	Unnamed	3	Florida
7/7/1896	Unnamed	2	Florida
9/29/1896	Unnamed	3, 2	Florida, Georgia
10/2/1898	Unnamed	2, 4	Florida, Georgia
8/1/1899	Unnamed	2	Florida
8/18/1899	Unnamed	3	North Carolina
10/31/1899	Unnamed	2	South Carolina, North Carolina
9/9/1900	Unnamed	4	Texas
9/27/1906	Unnamed	2	Florida, Alabama, Mississippi
10/18/1906	Unnamed	3	Florida
6/29/1909	Unnamed	2	Texas
7/21/1909	Unnamed	3	Texas
9/20–21/1909	Unnamed	3, 2	Louisiana, Mississippi
10/11/1909	Unnamed	3	Florida

Date*	Name	Category**	States Affected***
9/14/1910	Unnamed	2	Texas
10/18/1910	Unnamed	2	Florida
8/28/1911	Unnamed	2	South Carolina
10/16/1912	Unnamed	2	Texas
8/17/1915	Unnamed	4	Texas
9/29/1915	Unnamed	3, 2	Louisiana, Mississippi
7/5–6/1916	Unnamed	3, 2	Mississippi, Alabama, Florida
7/14/1916	Unnamed	2	South Carolina
8/18/1916	Unnamed	4	Texas
10/18/1916	Unnamed	2	Alabama, Florida
9/29/1917	Unnamed	3, 2	Florida, Louisiana
8/7/1918	Unnamed	3	Louisiana
9/10/1919	Unnamed	4	Florida
9/14/1919	Unnamed	3	Texas
9/21/1920	Unnamed	2	Louisiana
10/25/1921	Unnamed	3	Florida
7/27/1926	Unnamed	2	Florida
8/21/1926	Unnamed	3	Alabama
8/26/1926	Unnamed	3	Louisiana
9/18/1926	Unnamed	4	Florida
8/8/1928	Unnamed	2	Florida
9/17/1928	Unnamed	4	Florida
9/28/1929	Unnamed	3	Florida
8/14/1932	Unnamed	4	Texas
8/7/1933	Unnamed	2	Texas
8/23/1933	Unnamed	2	North Carolina, Virginia
9/4–5/1933	Unnamed	3	Florida, Texas
9/16/1933	Unnamed	3	North Carolina
6/16/1934	Unnamed	3	Louisiana
7/25/1934	Unnamed	2	Texas
9/3/1935	Unnamed	5	Florida
11/4/1935	Unnamed	2	Florida
7/31/1936	Unnamed	3	Florida
9/21/1938	Unnamed	3	New York, Connecticut, Rhode Island, Massachusetts

(*continued*)

Table 13.2   (*continued*)

Date*	Name	Category**	States Affected***
8/7–8/1940	Unnamed	2	Louisiana, Texas
8/11/1940	Unnamed	2	Georgia, South Carolina
9/23/1941	Unnamed	3	Texas
10/6/1941	Unnamed	2	Florida
8/30/1942	Unnamed	3	Texas
7/27/1943	Unnamed	2	Texas
9/14–15/1944	Unnamed	3, 2	North Carolina, Virginia, New York, Connecticut, Rhode Island, Massachusetts
10/19/1944	Unnamed	3	Florida
8/27/1945	Unnamed	2	Texas
9/15/1945	Unnamed	3	Florida
9/17–19/1947	Unnamed	4, 3	Florida, Louisiana, Mississippi
10/15/1947	Unnamed	2	Georgia, South Carolina
9/21/1948	Unnamed	3	Florida
10/5/1948	Unnamed	2	Florida
8/26/1949	Unnamed	3	Florida
10/4/1949	Unnamed	2	Texas
9/5/1950	Easy	3	Florida
10/18/1950	King	3	Florida
8/31/1954	Carol	3	North Carolina, New York, Connecticut, Rhode Island
9/11/1954	Edna	3	Massachusetts
10/15/1954	Hazel	4, 2	South Carolina, North Carolina, Maryland
8/12/1955	Connie	3	North Carolina
9/19/1955	Ione	3	North Carolina
9/24/1956	Flossy	2	Louisiana
6/27/1957	Audrey	4	Louisiana, Texas
9/27/1958	Helene	3	North Carolina
9/29/1959	Gracie	3	South Carolina
9/12/1960	Donna	4, 3, 2	Florida, North Carolina, New York, Connecticut, Rhode Island
9/11/1961	Carla	4	Texas
8/27/1964	Cleo	2	Florida
9/10/1964	Dora	2	Florida
10/3/1964	Hilda	3	Louisiana
10/14/1964	Isbell	2	Florida

Date*	Name	Category**	States Affected***
9/8–10/1965	Betsy	3	Florida, Louisiana
6/9/1966	Alma	2	Florida
9/20/1967	Beulah	3	Texas
10/19/1968	Gladys	2	Florida
8/17/1969	Camille	5	Louisiana, Mississippi
8/3/1970	Celia	3	Texas
9/16/1971	Edith	2	Louisiana
9/8/1974	Carmen	3	Louisiana
9/23/1975	Eloise	3	Florida
9/3–4/1979	David	2	Florida, Georgia, South Carolina
9/13/1979	Frederic	3	Alabama, Mississippi
8/10/1980	Allen	3	Texas
9/18/1983	Alicia	3	Texas
9/13/1984	Diana	3	North Carolina
9/1–2/1985	Elena	3	Florida, Alabama, Mississippi
9/27/1985	Gloria	3, 2	North Carolina, New York, Connecticut, New Hampshire
11/21/1985	Kate	2	Florida
9/22/1989	Hugo	4	South Carolina
8/19/1991	Bob	2	New York, Connecticut, Rhode Island, Massachusetts
8/24–26/1992	Andrew	5, 3	Florida, Louisiana
9/12/1992	Iniki	4	Hawaii
8/31/1993	Emily	3	North Carolina
8/3/1995	Erin	2	Florida
10/4/1995	Opal	3	Florida
7/12/1996	Bertha	2	North Carolina
9/6/1996	Fran	3	North Carolina
8/27/1998	Bonnie	2	North Carolina
9/25/1998	Georges	2	Florida, Mississippi
8/23/1999	Bret	3	Texas
9/16/1999	Floyd	2	North Carolina
9/18/2003	Isabel	2	North Carolina
8/13/2004	Charley	4	Florida
9/5/2004	Frances	2	Florida
9/16/2004	Ivan	3	Florida, Alabama

(*continued*)

Table 13.2   (*continued*)

Date*	Name	Category**	States Affected***
9/26/2004	Jeanne	3	Florida
7/10/2005	Dennis	3	Florida
8/29/2005	Katrina	3	Louisiana, Mississippi
9/24/2005	Rita	3	Texas, Louisiana
10/24/2005	Wilma	3	Florida
9/1/2008	Gustav	2	Alabama, Louisiana
9/13/2008	Ike	2	Florida, Texas, Louisiana, Mississippi, Alabama

* Dates indicate the day of landfall. A range indicates the dates the storms entered new states.
** Category listed is determined by the strength of the hurricane as it made landfall or crossed into the next state or states listed.
*** States listed are those that experienced category 2 or higher sustained winds and are in order of the storm's passage.

counties comprise 17 percent of US land area, and most of this space is on the Atlantic and Gulf coasts, where hurricanes occur at least annually (on average). There is therefore significant potential for disaster.

Hurricanes can bring a range of problems to urban areas. While tropical storms can also cause major flood events, hurricanes add the hazards of high sustained winds (anything above seventy-four miles per hour creates a "hurricane"), tornadoes, and storm surge. Passage of the storm does not necessarily end the event. Transportation, power, and emergency response can all be debilitated by the storm. Box 13.3 describes New York City's experience with Superstorm Sandy and the complex risks associated with all phases of the hurricane event.

Box 13.3 New York Hurricane Hazard and Inundation Risk: Superstorm Sandy

New York City and its metropolitan region is a so-called megacity (an urban system with at least ten million people and a density exceeding two thousand people per square mile). The challenges of managing risk and hazard in such large cities (of which there are more than twenty today) often exceeds the capacity of local governments and regional management agencies.

In late October 2012, a tropical cyclone formed in the western Atlantic and quickly grew to a very large and destructive hurricane. Hurricane Sandy was the tenth hurricane of 2012, and the second major hurricane of that year. It made landfall first near Kingston, Jamaica. It moved back into the Caribbean Sea and strengthened, making landfall in Cuba as a category 3 storm. Several days later, Sandy curved north-northwest, gathered strength again, and merged with a storm moving over the eastern United States. The merge made it turn northwest, turning it into the Northeastern Seaboard. It was a category 2 when it made landfall along the coast of the northeastern United States on October 30 (see figure 13.4). In the

Figure 13.4   Superstorm Sandy makes it way to the northeastern
United States, 2012. *Source:* NOAA.

United States, Hurricane Sandy affected twenty-four states but wrought most of its damage
in New Jersey and New York. Damage in the United States was estimated at over seventy-one
billion dollars. The severe and widespread damage the storm caused, as well as its unusual
merge with a frontal system, led the media to nickname the hurricane "Superstorm Sandy."

In New York City, its storm surge flooded streets, tunnels, and subway lines, cutting
power in and around the city. Flooding would be produced not because of the heavy rainfall
rates or runoff from inland areas that can be expected but because hurricanes circulate
counterclockwise in the northern hemisphere, and their greatest flood threat is found in
the upper-right quadrant of the storm, where sustained winds and the low pressure of the
atmosphere in the storm system lift and push the surface of the ocean forward, ahead of
the storm. Storm "surge" is a major threat to coastal islands, bays behind barrier islands,
and estuaries where freshwater rivers enter the salty ocean. If the path of a storm is oriented "just right" relative to the coast, it can cause devastating flooding, and this can be
exacerbated further by coincidence with a period of high tide.

Several days before the storm hit, government weather forecasts noted that there was
a 90 percent chance that the East Coast would be impacted by the storm. The governor
of New York declared a state of emergency, as did New Jersey. The Federal Emergency
Management Agency (FEMA) coordinated with state and other emergency management
partners in states along the coast. Preparations began in New Jersey when residents on
barrier islands were told to evacuate and the Atlantic City casinos were closed. In New

York and Pennsylvania, major airline carriers cancelled all flights into and out of major airports, and some of the railroads suspended service. In New York City, schools, bridges, tunnels, and subways were closed, and emergency management worked to evacuate low-lying portions of the islands of the city while people could still do so safely. Even the New York Stock Exchange closed for two days.

The storm caused widespread flooding and power outages. Some 4.8 million people were without power in the first days after the storm. A week later, nearly a million were still without power. Lines were down, and many substations were flooded by storm surge. One explosion at a substation on the East Side of Manhattan plunged the lower third of that borough into darkness for days. In New Jersey, the city of Hoboken flooded; and many coastal communities were devastated. At least thirty-seven people in New Jersey were killed. In New York, the East River overflowed its banks, flooding large sections of Lower Manhattan. Battery Park, for example, had a water surge of almost fourteen feet. Seven subway tunnels were flooded. The storm also damaged or destroyed more than one hundred thousand homes on Long Island. Several months after the storm, significant recovery work remained. Sandy highlighted the fragility of the aging American infrastructure, particularly the electricity network. In many Northeast communities, utilities have not buried power lines, which means that falling trees, branches, and debris from heavy winds can easily knock out power lines.

Superstorm Sandy helped reignite debate about the relationship between climate change and intense weather events. Sandy may be little more than the coincidental alignment of a tropical storm with another storm. But many believe that the storm was enhanced by global warming because of the abnormally warm sea surface temperatures offshore the East Coast of the United States. Warming oceans and greater atmospheric moisture are intensifying storms, while rising sea levels are worsening the effects of storm surge.

The track of this hurricane could have generated a worse disaster for New York City. It may be only a matter of time until a category 3 or stronger hurricane makes landfall in a region of very high population. Storm surges of storms greater than a category 3 will devastate the region, particularly when the surges are enhanced not only by a contemporaneous high tide but also by sea-level rise generated by climate change. Damages caused by hurricane winds and tornadoes spawned by hurricanes will make conditions even more dangerous. Mitigation by residents is vital to prevent disasters, but this always becomes especially difficult when many residents have developed dismissive attitudes to the warnings and suffered no consequences from doing so. Megacities possess megachallenges that are made even more complicated by the many people who cling to their beliefs of invincibility. Perhaps people have to experience disasters before they adopt attitudes that promote safety and self-preservation.

Although among climate scientists climate change is regarded as a certainty, how climate change will alter the geography of hurricanes is difficult to predict and diminishes scientific confidence about future hurricane predictability. This is publicly expressed as *uncertainty*. Fewer hurricanes might form (lowering risk), or more will form (heightening risk). They might be stronger (heightening risk) or weaker (lowering it). We may see a significant northward shift of these storms. Fewer might strike land (hazard might be lowered), or more might (heightening hazard). Perhaps the hazard will intensify as larger cities to the northeast (such as New York, Philadelphia, Toronto, Montreal, or Boston) or even on the West Coast (San Diego or Los Angeles, for instance) experience more and stronger hurricanes, some maybe for the first time. Because of their inexperience with full-strength hurricanes (rather than tropical storm or even tropical depressions), these cities may experience catastrophes. These cities are not likely to have developed hurricane disaster management plans, nor to have required building codes for these events.

Coastal Erosion

While the atmosphere is highly dynamic and constantly changing in its redistribution of heat and moisture around the globe, oceans are also dynamic and in constant motion; visible changes along coastlines may seem less abrupt to terrestrial residents. The most dynamic zone of the earth's surface however, is where land interacts with ocean. Ports were established on North American coasts to promote trade, facilitate naval power, and extract ocean resources. These cities depend upon regularity of the near-shore ocean

bottom to enable safe passage of ships. The physical shape of most coastlines is unfortunately dictated by the supply and distribution of sediments (sands and finer-grade materials) derived from eroding lands and the entrained load transported seaward by rivers, from coastal zones "upstream" (laterally along the coast from the direction of longshore currents) or from offshore ocean sediments driven ashore by wave action. These sources of sediment vary over time, and major shifts in any can suddenly change the near-shore bottom, causing sedimentation of shipping lanes near a coast. Changes of the amount of sediment carried in rivers that flow into either bays behind barrier islands or directly into the ocean can change coastal beaches and wetlands that receive that sediment. In some coastal areas, beaches and wetlands provide buffers against land-falling hurricanes for the cities that may be located inland (see box 13.4).

Unwilling to accept prevailing environmental conditions, some cities have also attempted to engineer "their" coastlines to solve "their" problems. Unfortunately, they tend to only change their problems, not eliminate them, often disturbing downstream beaches. For instance, cities dredge ship channels through breaks in barrier islands to achieve sufficient depth for boat traffic. Dredging requires substantial monetary investment to sustain. The passage of major storms often rearranges sediments because of increased erosion onshore (upslope from the coast) and wave transport from offshore. Some cities build jetties (one or even a pair of long piles of stones dropped in lines jutting into the sea perpendicular to the coastline) instead of or in addition to dredging, intending to block or impair the flow of sediment laterally

Box 13.4 New Orleans, Katrina, and Coastal Erosion

Hurricane Katrina in 2005 unfortunately revealed, among myriad social and political problems, the socially constructed geography of inequity in exposure and social vulnerabilities of the residents of the city of New Orleans, as well as the structural vulnerabilities of the engineered environment that was built to protect New Orleans, Louisiana, from the ravages of hurricanes and Mississippi River floods. Levees were breached east of the city as a powerful storm surge flowed up the channel referred to as the Mississippi River Gulf Outlet (or MR-GO). Drainage and ship channels within the city were also inundated by storm surge from Lake Ponchartrain and the Industrial Canal as the hurricane passed just east of the city and winds drove the lake and river waters from the east and north into the "bowl" occupied by New Orleans. This disaster generated the largest loss of life (1,836 deaths) in the United States related to a natural phenomenon (as opposed to epidemics, acts of terrorism, or wars) since a 1928 cyclone that devastated Puerto Rico and southern Florida (killing more than three thousand Americans).

Katrina was a powerful hurricane. As it approached the coast of Louisiana in late August 2005, it was a category 5 hurricane with sustained winds exceeding 175 miles per hour. The storm surge predicted for the coast was expected to be twenty-nine feet or higher. Fortunately, during the early morning hours of August 28, before the hurricane made landfall in Louisiana, the sustained winds had diminished to 125 miles per hour, and the 120-mile-wide storm was recategorized to "only" a category 3 status.

While New Orleans occupies a high-risk position (in terms of flooding) as much of the city lies one to two feet below sea level and the height of the Mississippi River levees as the river passes through the city is twenty feet above sea level, its exposure to hurricanes and tropical storms from the Gulf of Mexico has been mitigated by the downstream deposition of the sediment that is carried past the city by the river. New Orleans is about fifty miles northwest of the Gulf of Mexico, and coastal beaches, barrier islands, estuarine wetlands, and thousands of square miles of marshes, swamps, and rural agricultural land established on riverine sediment help to buffer the city from storms off the Gulf. The sediment has poured from the channels of the bird's-foot delta over the ages. The entrained sediments are driven back toward the coastline by ocean waves, and they circulate in the littoral system. Historically, the intervening land south and east of New Orleans had been growing at accelerating rates over the past two centuries (enhanced by farming-generated erosion throughout the Mississippi-Missouri-Ohio River system). However, that trend has slowly reversed during the past few decades by efforts to manage the rivers' flows.

Levees, flood-control structures, dams, and locks all reduce the capacity of any river to carry sediment. Slower flow cannot carry as much sediment, and the result of the construction of these technologies is that less has been reaching the Mississippi's mouth at the Gulf. To this sediment starvation of coastal Louisiana, we must factor in the impacts of resource extraction activities in the coastal plain. The pumping of oil and natural gas from subsurface geological structures, the displacement and pumping of saltwater from local groundwater in order to improve land for agriculture, and the pumping of freshwater for consumption by small towns and cities in the region have collectively led to subsidence of the land surface and saltwater inundation of the coastal plain. Estuarine vegetation has a limited resistance to saltwater exposure, and it can be destroyed by constant and even permanent exposure to ocean water. Wave action increasingly erodes the vulnerable coastal land, and the Gulf creeps northward toward New Orleans. And adding future changes to the height of sea level resulting from climate change augments flood risk and several hazards that result from less coastal buffering capacity.

New Orleans is losing its protective cushion. It is believed that the impacts of Katrina may have been worsened by diminished natural mitigation capacity. As coastal wetlands shrink, so does the region's capacity to absorb the blow of hurricane landfall. As the coast-line "moves" closer to New Orleans, the power unleashed by strong tropical cyclones will be less attenuated, and New Orleans will become less habitable.

along the shoreline. Jetties create "swirls" upstream of the jetties that dump the sediment offshore, starving the downstream coastline, which is then eroded by normal wave action. The coast downstream of the jetty wastes away as the beach retreats inland. In response, downstream residents often construct groins, shorter hydraulic structures comprising rock piles set at strategic angles to the coast and cemented with concrete designed to catch the eroding sediment and thereby save their beach or shoreline. These create pocket beaches that are periodically enriched artificially with dredged sand from offshore, satisfying local residents but, of course, starving downstream beaches of sediment. Contagious reactions continue to echo as the original decision reverberates on and on down the coast. Eventually, people on some segment of coast decide that the loss by erosion is too great a risk to their properties as the sea floods or threatens coastal properties, and they attempt to harden "their" shore to "eliminate" erosion of "their" coastline. Often communities will

construct a seawall, a concrete abutment that is built vertically above the mean waterline to prevent direct wave action on the properties along the coastline. Galveston, Texas, did this, for example, after the infamous hurricane of 1900. Seawalls accomplish what coastal dunes might do naturally, but they provide no sand for accretion into a beach. Construction and periodic nourishment of an artificial beach is expensive and must be repeated *ad infinitum*. If not, the seawall will eventually receive the full energy of ocean-generated waves, and the near-shore bottom will deepen. Ultimately, the seawall could be undercut, requiring the battle to start anew with costly renewed vigor.

Add to this "normal" battle against the sea the impact of climate change. Atmospheric warming causes ocean warming. Warming water expands. Add freshwater melt from ice caps and glaciers, and the result is sea-level rise. Rising seas translate into coastal-zone flooding and shrinking land surface. Approximately twenty-one million urbanites in North America reside within about thirty feet of current-day sea level. As discussed in the previous chapter, significant climate-change-induced magnifications of coastal flood hazards will occur and will be very difficult to manage as they evolve. Among the exposed cities at great risk, the New York, Los Angeles, and Miami metropolitan areas are the most likely to experience extensive coastal inundation.

Aside from the direct impacts to buildings and to residential spaces and the permanent displacement of people, seawater floods will also destroy infrastructure and urban infrastructure through corrosion caused by saltwater. Roads, railways, and subways could be flooded, damaged, or destroyed by rising seas. Airports, seaports, and trucking facilities in low-lying areas might also be submerged. Dikes may be the only recourse to holding back the sea, and cities (like New Orleans, Miami, and New York) already poised for greater catastrophe given that they are at or below sea level will endure epic challenges unless they somehow adapt or adjust to predictions.

Severe Weather: Tornadoes, Blizzards, and Heat Waves

Among the most dramatic natural hazards of the atmosphere are extreme weather events that produce tornadoes, ice storms, blizzards, and heat waves. While these can occur anywhere and occur preferentially in no special types of landscapes, the city does magnify their threats.

Destructive windstorms, for example, cannot be prevented, but their effects are manageable. One great twentieth-century achievement is technology enabling detection and tracking of tornadoes. Increased warning time and advance communication of imminent storms has saved many lives. Improved radar

and preparedness have made mass casualties from tornado outbreaks less likely. Destruction caused by storms, however, is not easy to avoid. Though generally moving west to east, the path of a tornado is rather arbitrary from the perspective of residents, as tornadoes are seemingly guided mostly, if not entirely, by atmospheric dynamics rather than by the characteristics of the landscape. Windproofing efforts such as hurricane clips on the roofs of houses can prevent damage in weaker storms, but a direct "hit" by a tornado frankly makes windproofing of most structures irrelevant. Education programs that encourage wind-resistant design of shelters or construction of safe rooms in homes for refuge are probably the most effective activities for mitigation of damages and prevention of deaths and injuries from tornadoes in cities and their surroundings.

The damages wrought by blizzards and ice storms that interrupt transportation, collapse power lines, or prevent emergency response can be mitigated by prestorm emergency response planning. Having working and effective equipment to plow snow from roads or restore power quickly is vital and requires not just financial resources but also adequate foresight by city managers. Ironically, it is not the cities prone to blizzards, ice storms, or windstorms that are most likely to experience disasters. The communities having little experience will be less prepared for response. Cities in the southeastern United States, for instance, are far less experienced with regard to unusual winter storms. It may not be realistic or financially feasible for all cities to prepare for rare events, so usually, many simply take their chances and weather the consequences.

Heat waves are defined as extended periods of unusual, constant, and extreme heat and are most often associated with cities. Development replaces natural land cover with artificial surfaces that behave differently when sunlight falls on them. City surfaces are made of unnatural heat-absorbent materials like concrete and blacktop macadam (covering parking lots, airports, and road networks) and roofing materials (such as dark shingles and tar). Increased absorption enhances the normal amount of solar radiation that will be converted from the high-energy, shorter wavelengths of incoming solar radiation (or insolation) into longer wavelengths as they are reradiated to the lower atmosphere, thus warming it. In this way, cities effectively create "heat islands" in local and regional weather patterns. The urban heat island is the distinct warming of urban areas compared with surrounding rural areas. In the average US metro region, for example, urban areas are 4 to 18 degrees Fahrenheit (2 to 10 degrees Celsius) warmer than surrounding rural areas. Warmer cities also mean hotter buildings that may be insufficiently ventilated or cooled without technology. Air conditioning is usually used to respond to this these days, but using more air conditioning raises the urban demand for electricity and can result in blackouts that ironically disable the cooling systems used to make such places livable. The city of Chicago, for example, has an active policy of encouraging the vegetation of commercial roofs through grants, tax breaks, and other financial inducements to developers and builders.

Heat waves are particularly dangerous in homes and buildings that can't staunch the heat or for residents who can't afford to cool them. The most likely to suffer are the most vulnerable: the elderly, the infirm, the poor, and those who are socially isolated from public assistance. Heat waves affect people in rural areas as much as in urban areas, but

recent heat waves in Chicago (1995), New York and the cities of the Middle Atlantic states (1999, 2001), the entire eastern half of Canada and the United States (2002, 2006), and Los Angeles and much of California (2006) produced mass casualties among their vulnerable populations. The 1995 heat wave that struck the city of Chicago lasted for over a week with temperatures that reached over one hundred degrees every day. By July 20, more than seven hundred people had died. It was referred to in the press as a "natural disaster," an unfortunate outcome of a freak meteorological condition. But in his 2002 book *Heat Wave*, Eric Klinenberg found that deaths were greatest among elderly people living on their own. The tragedy was not simply a natural disaster but the outcome of the social isolation of seniors, retrenchment of public assistance, and declining neighborhoods. Most victims were seniors who lived alone with few visits from public health officials. This underscores a key theme in this chapter: the disaster was not the result of high temperatures but of high temperatures as mediated through a complex set of social and political relationships.

The problem of heat in cities will worsen with global climate change. Nighttime low temperatures are expected to rise as the atmosphere also humidifies resulting from increased evaporation caused by rising temperatures. Physiological stresses caused by daytime heating will increase because of the lack of nighttime relief. Heat-related death rates in cities will rise and may be magnified, particularly by air pollution.

Earthquakes

Although "where" earthquakes will strike is easier to predict than where weather events will occur, the *timing* of earthquakes is unpredictable; there also seems to be no presaged warning. The scientific understanding of the workings of the earth's crust has improved exponentially since the 1850s, and detection and monitoring technologies and networks have improved our understanding of the risk patterns. Fault lines in the crust reveal stressed zones at the interfaces of earth's tectonic plates. These are usually seismically active areas and provide information about the direction and speed at which the plates are moving above the mantle. These tend to indicate something about the potential for an earthquake. Occasionally, however, faults that are located near the edges of plates are not visible at the surface, and this leaves us blind to their existence. These blind faults pose significant danger, particularly for urban areas in places like the Pacific Northwest. Past earthquakes and volcanic features are indicators of seismic regions produced by convergence of plates or by midplate "hot spots." These spots are usually far from plate boundaries and have caused major earthquakes in the US mid-South and coastal southeast. Plate movement is not smooth and constant, however, and plates do not generate quakes with any apparent temporal or spatial regularity. Therefore, releases of built-up pressures on faults are not predictable, and the best management responses we can take are avoiding development in earthquake-prone areas, engineering the city to adapt to the risk, and mitigating the impacts of earthquakes.

Earthquakes have been important in the histories of several North American cities (table 13.3). While seismic zones have generated disasters infrequently in our region, they are very important to our cities. Today, Seattle, Washington, Vancouver, British Columbia,

Portland, Oregon, and Memphis, Tennessee, are poised for unprecedented disasters should the "big ones" occur, as seismologists suggest. The damages depend on the progress of mitigation and activities to retrofit existing infrastructure. Other Pacific Coast cities including Anchorage, Alaska, San Francisco, California, and Los Angeles, California, have had earthquakes relatively recently. One earthquake does not completely eliminate the potential for another in the same region soon after the first, and in some regions of the world, large earthquakes are relatively frequent. The second greatest "natural" disaster in the United States in terms of loss of life occurred in San Francisco in 1906 (see figure 13.5). The city was devastated not only by earthquake but also by uncontainable conflagration. The same city experienced another destructive but weaker earthquake in 1989. If events similar to our past earthquakes were to occur today, the impacts could be devastating. And if the past reveals risk, cities of the East and the Rocky Mountains should be prepared: major earthquakes struck Charleston, South Carolina (1886), and Denver, Colorado (1873).

Today, most North America cities have earthquake risk, but most are rather low probabilities and involve only weak earthquakes. The only region unlikely to see a strong earthquake is north-central North America, where the bedrock is an igneous formation known as the Canadian Shield (figure 13.6). The perimeter of this region has experienced a number of sizable earthquakes, for instance, in the St. Lawrence Valley of Canada, but significant quakes to the north and west are rare. The biggest threat today seems to be in the Pacific Northwest, where residents face the prospects of a quake that could be greater than a 9.0 Richter-scale magnitude (see box 13.5).

Table 13.3   Major (> 6.0 Richter Magnitude) Earthquakes in the United States and Canada, 1800–Present

Location	Date	Magnitude	Location	Date	Magnitude
New Madrid, Missouri	12/16/1811	7.0	Lompoc, California	11/4/1927	7.1
New Madrid, Missouri	12/16/1811	7.7	Grand Banks off Newfoundland	11/18/1929	7.2
New Madrid, Missouri	1/23/1812	7.5			
New Madrid, Missouri	2/7/1812	7.7	Eureka, California	6/6/1932	6.4
San Bernardino County, California	12/08/1812	6.9	Long Beach, California	3/11/1933	6.4
			Parkfield, California	6/8/1934	6.1
Ventura, California	12/21/1812	7.1	Helena, Montana	10/19/1935	6.3
Northeast Arkansas	1/5/1843	6.3	Helena, Montana	10/31/1935	6.0
Fort Tejon, California	1/9/1957	7.9	Timiscaming, Ontario	11/1/1935	6.1
Hayward, California	10/21/1868	6.8	San Francisco Bay, California	6/10/1936	6.5
Lake Chelan, Washington	12/14/1872	7.4			
California/Oregon Coast	11/23/1873	7.3	Maui, Hawaii	1/23/1938	6.8
Denver, Colorado	11/08/1882	7.3	San Francisco, California	6/11/1938	6.8
Charleston, South Carolina	9/1/1886	7.3	Imperial Valley, California	5/19/1940	7.1
Imperial Valley, California	2/24/1892	7.8	Vancouver Island, British Columbia	6/23/1946	7.3
Vacaville, California	4/19/1892	6.4	Haida Gwaii, British Columbia	8/22/1949	8.1
Charleston, Missouri	10/31/1895	6.6			
Calaveras fault, California	6/20/1897	6.3	Puget Sound, Washington	4/13/1949	7.1
Mendocino County, California	4/15/1898	6.8	Kona, Hawaii	8/21/1951	6.9
			Kern County, California	7/21/1952	7.3
Eureka, California	4/16/1899	7.0	Fallon-Stillwater area, Nevada	7/6/1954	6.6
San Jacinto, California	12/25/1899	6.7	Stillwater, Nevada	8/24/1954	6.8
Parkfield, California	3/3/1901	6.4	Eureka, California	12/21/1954	6.5
Cook Inlet, Alaska	12/31/1901	7.1	Prince William Sound, Alaska	3/28/1964	9.2
Fairbanks, Alaska	8/27/1904	7.3			
San Francisco, California	4/18/1906	7.8	Puget Sound, Washington	4/29/1965	6.5
Calaveras fault, California	7/1/1911	6.5	Parkfield, California	6/28/1966	6.1
San Jacinto, California	4/21/1918	6.8	San Fernando, California	2/9/1971	6.6
Vancouver Island, British Columbia	12/6/1918	7.2	Sitka, Alaska	7/30/1972	7.6
			US-Mexico border, Imperial Valley, California	10/15/1979	6.4
Eureka, California	1/31/1922	7.3			
Parkfield, California	3/10/1922	6.1	Humboldt County, California	11/8/1980	7.2
Humboldt County, California	1/22/1923	7.2			
			Loma Prieta, California	10/18/1989	6.9
Charlevoix, Quebec	3/1/1925	6.2	Landers, California	6/28/1992	7.3
Santa Barbara, California	6/29/1925	6.8	Northridge, California	9/1/1994	6.7
Monterey Bay, California	10/22/1926	6.1			

Figure 13.5   San Francisco after the earthquake and fire of 1906.
(Photo by Arnold Genthe, 1906, courtesy of Library of Congress)

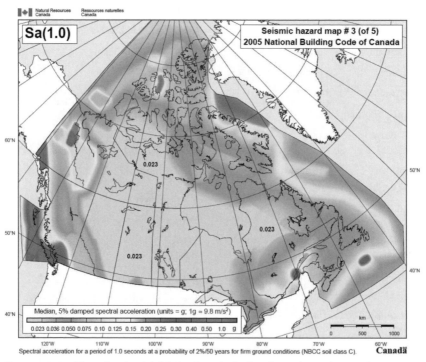

Figure 13.6   Map of seismic risk in Canada indicating where there exists a 2
percent probability that an earthquake producing peak ground acceleration of
one Hz (or a wave of one cycle per second) will occur in the next fifty years.
Source: Natural Resources Canada. http://www.earthquakescanada.nrcan.gc.ca/
hazard-alea/zoning/NBCC2005maps-eng.php. Accessed April 26, 2012.

Box 13.5 Earthquake Hazards in Seattle, Washington, and Victoria and Vancouver, British Columbia

On January 26, 1700, the greatest known earthquake to strike Canada and one of the strongest to strike North America in modern times occurred along the undersea Cascadia thrust fault off the west coast of Vancouver Island, British Columbia. The earthquake has been retrospectively measured as having had a magnitude of 9.0 on the Richter scale and is considered a "great quake" (of which there have been thirteen over the past six thousand years). The primary hazard that an offshore earthquake of this size would pose is a tsunami risk for coastal cities of the Pacific Basin. A similar quake striking in the same proximity today would certainly cause great destruction in cities and towns throughout the Puget Sound region of the United States and southwestern British Columbia, Canada.

An even greater hazard to this region than such great quakes (which are almost certain to occur again in the very near future) is the probability of weaker, though still very destructive, earthquakes that originate along faults located beneath the cities of Seattle and Vancouver. These onshore earthquakes can be shallow or deep in the crust and can release Richter magnitude 7 levels of energy. Five have occurred within about four hundred miles of Seattle and Victoria during the past 130 years: in 1872 (a shallow quake) and then in 1918, 1929, 1946, and 1970 (deeper quakes). In 2001, a 6.8 magnitude earthquake called the Nisqually Quake caused two billion dollars in damage to Seattle. This was a deep quake that did not hit Seattle as strongly as the others, but it was felt over a much wider area. The proximity of the moving Pacific, North American, and Juan de Fuca crustal plates (that generate deep and megathrust events) and hundreds of faults (that generate very strong shallow quakes) to the built environment makes the Pacific Northwest (and Canada's Southwest) extremely likely to suffer a significant catastrophe in the near future. (It is said that there is an 84 percent chance that an earthquake of 6.5 magnitude or greater will occur here in the next fifty years and a 21 percent chance that a "structurally damaging" earthquake will impact the southern end of Vancouver Island in the same time frame.)

As has been discussed, the presence of people makes hazard from the natural risk. Seattle, for instance, currently has a population exceeding six hundred thousand and is surrounded by urbanized areas of more than eight thousand square miles that contain more than 3.4 million people. Similarly, Vancouver has about six hundred thousand residents, and its metropolitan population is almost 2.9 million people spread over only 1,100 square miles. Victoria, the capital of British Columbia, has a population of about eighty thousand and a metropolitan population of nearly 350,000 in an area of about 270 square miles. These cities were established during the latter half of the nineteenth century in this active and seismically complex region. The most important questions that must be faced are related to efforts to improve seismic engineering and safety of structures in the built environment and the preparation of residents should the expected occur.

The Seattle Fault is an east-west trending fault line that generated a very large earthquake a little more than a millennium ago. It runs through Seattle from Bremerton to Issaquah beneath areas that have very loose sediments overlying the bedrock. Unconsolidated earth and rock debris have the tendency to move when shaken violently, and this causes them to behave much like a liquid. This process is called liquefaction. The implications of liquefaction were most clearly seen in the effects of the 1989 Loma Prieta earthquake in the Marina district of San Francisco. Aside from loss of structural stability for buildings, particularly in places where urban space was created with artificial fill, slopes can fail (chiefly in places where structures have been constructed above the slope), and landslides can rearrange the land surface, particularly in areas like the Pacific Northwest that have significant topographical relief. The humid environment will also contribute to this liquefaction and the slide susceptibility of these urban areas.

The most critical challenges involve the collapse of structures and breakage or failure of, in particular, critical infrastructure. Fortunately, communities, states, and provinces in this portion of both countries have aggressively undertaken mitigation. Seismic retrofits of homes (particularly low-income residential structures), redesign, retrofitting and reconstruction of critical infrastructure (like fire stations, fire boats, bridges, automatic gas shut-off valves, the water system, dams), and upgrading of building codes have been supported logistically and financially by the city of Seattle in the past few years. Community preparedness has also been a focus, not only among the general population, but among the most vulnerable populations (the elderly and disabled, linguistically isolated populations, and the poor) as well. Since 2004, Vancouver has completed more than 137 seismic mitigation projects to schools and many other buildings as well. The provincial government updated its earthquake response plan (in 2008), coordinating the responsibilities of individuals, communities, the province, First Nations, and the federal (Canadian) government. City building codes, provincial building codes, and national building codes are in effect throughout the province. A national building code for earthquake mitigation, in particular, was promulgated in 1995. British Columbia adopted the national code in 1998 and amended it to fit unique BC circumstances. And the city of Vancouver adopted and modified these into the city's seismic building code in 1999. The overall effect of these efforts will be determined only when the next strong tremor hits. Officials and some residents of the region can say, whatever the outcome of the next event, that they did not wait to take action. It seems the region is taking the earthquake hazard seriously.

Tsunamis are ocean waves generated by displacement of water either through changes in the shape of the sea floor or by large landslides into the ocean, sometimes caused by earthquakes under the ocean floor. The potential impacts of tsunamis (that are seismically generated) add substantial risk of powerful, fast-moving inundation of coastal cities by long-wavelength waves, as demonstrated in rather recent disasters: for example, in northern Japan in 2011, the coastlines surrounding the Indian Ocean in 2004, and the Chilean coast in 1960. Most coastal cities of the United States and Canada have been relatively untouched by tsunamis, but historically, tsunamis have devastated Anchorage, Alaska, the Hawaiian Islands, Newfoundland, and other North American regions (table 13.4). While these events presage what can happen, they do not necessarily dictate the impact locations of future tsunami. Virtually every city that fronts on a coastline possesses tsunami risk. Future coastal inundations will depend on the strength and location of earthquakes, the geophysical impacts of these events, and the degree that the ocean attenuates sudden displacement. The population distribution along the coastlines in the United States certainly magnifies the hazard. Technological advancements in detection of wave energy transmission within the Atlantic Ocean and Pacific Ocean basins are the only tools we have to enable evacuation of coastal regions to high ground inland, but in very dense and normally traffic-choked regions, this may mitigate only a small number of the deaths caused by a future tsunami disaster.

Table 13.4   Known (and Possible) Historic Tsunamis Affecting the United States and Canada, 1700–Present

Location of Tsunami Impact	Cause of Tsunami	Date
Vancouver Island, British Columbia	9.0 M_w Cascadia earthquake	1700
Delaware River "swell"*	?	11/14/1840
Island of Hawaii, Hawaii	Landslide on Mauna Loa triggered by 7.5–8.0 M_w	1868
Maine	earthquake on island	11/17/1872
Longport, New Jersey*	?	6/9/1913
Puerto Rico	?	10/11/1918
Rockaway Park, Queens, New York*	?	8/6/1923
Coney Island, New York*	?	8/8/1924
Maine	?	1/9/1926
Burin Peninsula, Newfoundland	?	11/18/1929
Atlantic City, New Jersey*	7.2 M_w Grand Banks, Atlantic Ocean earthquake	8/19/1931
Aleutian Islands, Alaska/Hilo, Hawaii	?	4/1/1946
Lituya Bay, Alaska**	7.8 M_w Aleutian Islands earthquake	7/9/1958
Hilo, Hawaii	8.3 M_w Alaska Panhandle earthquake	5/22/1960
Alaska, British Columbia, Washington,	9.5 M_w Valdivia, Chile earthquake	3/27/1964
Oregon, and California	9.2 M_w Anchorage, Alaska earthquake	5/19/1964
Northeastern United States*	?	5/18/1980
Spirit Lake, Washington (freshwater)**	Landslide created by eruption of Mount St. Helens	7/4/1992
Daytona Beach, Florida*	?	

M_w: moment magnitude

* Possible tsunami

** Denotes "megatsunami," a tsunami that has initial wave heights much larger than normal tsunamis and that originate not from tectonic activity but from landslides or volcanic eruption

Fires

Fire has always been vital to living in cities, particularly for cooking and the heating of dwellings. The Industrial Revolution greatly enhanced the role of combustion in urban growth and improved the lives of many by using combustion of fossil fuels for manufacturing, in high-temperature refining and smelting furnaces, and eventually in the internalizing of combustion in engines. Both industrialization and faster transportation aided urban population agglomeration, employment opportunities, and improved quality of life. The extraction of energy from fossil materials from the earth diminished our reliance on wood and brought us into the high-energy industrial world of today. Coal (in the eighteenth and nineteenth centuries) and petroleum and natural gas (in the twentieth) were new sources of energy enabling the use of new materials and the development of new processes that built cities.

Fire was also a major problem for North American cities from their beginnings. At least seventy-seven times, major multibuilding, extensive fires dating from the earliest European settlements in North America burned cities; at least eleven of these fires were intentionally set (for a number of reasons during wars) (table 13.5). As early settlements had comparatively low density, dwellings, outbuildings, and commercial operations were usually separated enough that fires in wooden structures were not contagious. Only seven of the seventy-seven extensive, major fires occurred during more than a century prior to the beginning of the nineteenth century. As settlements grew and towns and cities emerged, central business districts intensified construction and commercial and industrial activities. Eight fires occurred between 1800

and 1849. In landscapes of wood and brick structures, urban fire hazards increased. As long as cities were constructed of combustible materials, widespread fire was problematic. Communities began to address this problem with fire brigades that were motivated to fight to contain the fires, and thus the damages, and prevent greater disasters.

While firefighting as an institution can be traced back to the Roman Empire, modern firefighting began during the eighteenth and nineteenth centuries. Early American approaches to fire prevention included materials management such as the outlawing of wooden chimneys and thatched roofs and the establishment of volunteer surveillance teams and fire brigades, which usually moved water in buckets toward a fire. After the creation of pressurized city water systems and then the introduction of pumper trucks, fitted with coal-fueled, steam-powered pumps and able to transport equipment to the conflagrations, the business of professional firefighting emerged. Cincinnati, Ohio, became the first American city to employ full-time firefighters in 1853; creating a regular roster of experienced firemen who were more efficient and adept at suppressing fire. Throughout the nineteenth century, however, brigades remained voluntary and were often committed to particular neighborhoods, to particular ethnic groups, or even to particular political parties and politicians. Despite increasing vigilance, twenty-one major fires burned North American cities between 1850 and 1899. Citywide fire departments did not formally emerge until the twentieth century.

One of the most famous fire epics occurred in Chicago in 1871. Although Mrs. Catherine O'Leary and her cow were publicly blamed for starting the fire, the exact cause and origin

Table 13.5   Major Deadly Urban Fires in the United States and Canada, 1600–Present

Location	Year (and cause if not accidental)	Location	Year (and cause if not accidental)
Jamestown, Virginia	1608 (burned purposely during war)	Vancouver, British Columbia	1886
Jamestown, Virginia	1676 (burned purposely during war)	Seattle, Washington	1889
		Bakersfield, California	1889
St. John's, Newfoundland	1696	Lynn, Massachusetts	1889
Montreal, New France	1734	St. John's, Newfoundland	1892
New York City, New York	1776	Hinckley, Minnesota	1894
New Orleans, Louisiana	1788	Windsor, Nova Scotia	1897
New Orleans, Louisiana	1794	New Westminster, British Columbia	1898
Detroit, Michigan	1805		
Buffalo, New York	1812 (burned purposely during war)	Ponce, Puerto Rico	1899
York, Upper Canada	1813 (burned purposely during war)	Sandon, British Columbia	1900
		Jacksonville, Florida	1901
Portsmouth, New Hampshire	1813	Baltimore, Maryland	1904
Washington, District of Columbia	1814 (burned purposely during war)	Toronto, Ontario	1904
		San Francisco, California	1906
St. John's, Newfoundland	1817	Chelsea, Massachusetts	1908
St. Louis, Missouri	1849	Oscoda/Au Sable, Michigan	1911
Toronto, Ontario	1849		
Montreal, New France	1852	Salem, Massachusetts	1914
Troy, New York	1862	Matheson, Ontario	1916
Atlanta, Georgia	1864 (burned purposely during war)	Halifax, Nova Scotia	1917
		Atlanta, Georgia	1917
Columbia, South Carolina	1864 (burned purposely during war)	Tulsa, Oklahoma	1921 (burned during riot)
		Astoria, Oregon	1922
Richmond, Virginia	1865 (burned purposely during war)	Timiskaming District, Ontario	1922
Portland, Maine	1866	Berkeley, California	1923
Chicago, Illinois	1871	Lillooet, British Columbia	1931
Peshtigo, Wisconsin	1871	Texas City, Texas	1947
Port Huron, Michigan	1871	Brentwood-Bel Air (Los Angeles), California	1961
Boston, Massachusetts	1872		
St. John, New Brunswick	1877	Boston, Massachusetts	1964
Ocala, Florida	1883	Chelsea, Massachusetts	1973

(continued)

Table 13.5   (continued)

Location	Year (and cause if not accidental)	Location	Year (and cause if not accidental)
Chelsea, Massachusetts	1974	Malibu, California	2007 (wildland-urban interface fire)
Lynn, Massachusetts	1981 (caused by a bombing)	Los Angeles, California	2008 (wildland-urban interface fire)
Buffalo, New York	1983		
Philadelphia, Pennsylvania	1985 (authorities dislodging an anti-government group)	Corona, California	2008 (wildland-urban interface fire)
		Chino, California	2008 (wildland-urban interface fire)
Oakland Hills, California	1991 (wildland-urban interface fire)	Yorba Linda, California	2008 (wildland-urban interface fire)
Highland, California	2003 (wildland-urban interface fire)	Anaheim Hills, California	2008 (wildland-urban interface fire)
San Bernardino, California	2003 (wildland-urban interface fire)	Brea, California	2008 (wildland-urban interface fire)
San Diego, California	2003 (wildland-urban interface fire)	Altadena, California	2008 (wildland-urban interface fire)
San Diego, California	2007 (wildland-urban interface fire)	Los Angeles, California	2009 (wildland-urban interface fire)
Los Angeles, California	2007 (wildland-urban interface fire)	Bastrop, Texas	2011 (wildland-urban interface fire)
Orange, California	2007 (wildland-urban interface fire)		
Temecula, California	2007 (wildland-urban interface fire)		

of the fire remains uncertain. On October 8, a small fire started in an alley and quickly turned into a widespread conflagration. The spread of the fire was accelerated by the overuse of wooden structures, a recent drought, and strong winds. The fire lasted until the morning of October 10, when a light rain helped douse the remaining flames. The fire killed three hundred people and left more than one hundred thousand homeless. Much of the downtown was destroyed. Yet within five years, the city was rebuilt and celebrated by hosting the 1893 Columbian Exhibition that showcased the rebuilt city. Chicago survived the great fire of 1871 to come back

bigger and more confident than ever, creating insurance and fire companies and instituting new building codes that planned for and negated a repetition of the tragedy. Cities that survive disasters often respond by creating better institutional arrangements that mitigate a repeat of the fire hazard.

Though numerous cities established professional fire departments by the *fin de siècle*, most used horse-drawn trucks. Communication and transportation were vitally needed improvements but were in their infancy, particularly in newer cities. The city of San Francisco, for instance, was said to have had the most modern firefighting organizations in the country in 1906. Their system alerting teams to fires was noteworthy as telegraphs were linked to local stations, and they were able to arrive at the scenes with sufficient speed to extinguish the blazes. At the time of the magnitude 7.9 earthquake in 1906, responders were disabled from response as the tremor destroyed the city's water system and no water emerged from neighborhood hydrants. Furthermore, collapsed buildings blocked access throughout the city. Anything that wasn't destroyed by the earthquake succumbed to fire; most of the city burned to the ground.

Telegraphs, though widely distributed by 1900, did not reach private residences or every neighborhood. Telephone systems were coming into vogue but did not reach the urban middle and lower classes. Critical to effective urban fire suppression was speed: speed of detection, rapid communication to responders, and swift arrival of firefighters at a scene reduced damage and limited disruptions. These abilities improved during the first two decades of the 1900s. By the end of World War I, most fire trucks were motorized, and most cities had telephonic coverage. But despite these improvements, seventeen more major urban fires occurred between 1900 and 1949.

The spatial extent of major fires in cities was shrinking, but the problem was not so much under control as it was changing. Only eight more spatially extensive urban fires occurred prior to 2000, but the problem was replaced by structure fires.

Two technological developments altered the geography of the fire hazard in North American cities: development of iron- (and later steel-) framed structures providing vertical construction and the improvement of the elevator. The heights of all wooden and stone structures were constrained by stability and strength issues, but iron girding allowed stories to be placed above the traditional four- or five-floor limit. Potential users of buildings also set a limit: few desired to climb more than three or four flights of stairs, particularly if they were carrying possessions. Elevators changed the practical issues impeding acceptance of taller buildings and enabled the skyscraper.

Skyscrapers challenged firefighting anew. Fighting fires in the upper stories of ten-story (or more) buildings required significant modifications of fire suppression strategies, equipment, and evacuation plans. Fires tended to spread upward. Getting water and fire-suppressing chemicals to upper stories was challenging. Building occupants were growing exponentially in number with the height of the buildings, and moving them rapidly past fires and out of buildings was tricky. Climbing down stairs is slow and increases exposure to heat and flames. The elevator, which enabled vertical construction of housing, was not the alternative for escape. People were unwittingly opting for "risky" places for residence or employment as they were enamored with solutions for their need for space in cities, views provided by elevation in buildings, or the seclusion that height provided (table 13.6).

A more recent development of urban fire risk has emerged at the perimeter of many cities. While North America's urban systems have dramatically increased in population over the twentieth and twenty-first centuries, the areal extent of cities has also grown. Both exposure and vulnerability to fires ignited in wildlands have risen dramatically in recent years.

The North American appreciation of nature has grown over the twentieth century. North American suburbs hark back to the gardens of the royalty of Europe, and per-

Table 13.6   Major Deadly Structure Fires in the United States and Canada, 1800–Present

Structure	Location	Year
Richmond Theater	Richmond, Virginia	1811
The White House and Capitol	Washington, DC	1814
US Patent Office, Blodget's Hotel	Washington, DC	1836
Building	Mayagüez, Puerto Rico	1841
Sts. Michael and Augustine Roman Catholic Churches	Philadelphia, Pennsylvania	1844
Brooklyn Theater	Brooklyn, New York	1876
US Patent Office	Washington, DC	1877
Washburn "A" Flour Mill	Minneapolis, Minnesota	1878
The Rotunda, University of Virginia	Charlottesville, Virginia	1895
Windsor Hotel	Manhattan, New York	1899
Hoboken Docks	Hoboken, New Jersey	1900
Iroquois Theater	Chicago, Illinois	1903
Collinwood School	Cleveland, Ohio	1908
Parker Building	New York City, New York	1908
Rhoads Theater	Boyertown, Pennsylvania	1908
Friedlander Leather Remnants Factory	Philadelphia, Pennsylvania	1910
Triangle Shirtwaist Factory	New York City, New York	1911
Equitable Life Assurance Building	New York City, New York	1912
Factory	Binghamton, New York	1913
St. John the Baptist School	Peabody, Massachusetts	1915
Centre Block of Parliament Buildings	Ottawa, Ontario	1916
Norman State Hospital	Norman, Oklahoma	1918
Mayagüez Theater	San Juan, Puerto Rico	1919
Cleveland School	Camden, South Carolina	1923
Babbs Switch Schoolhouse	Oklahoma	1924
Laurier Palace Theater	Montreal, Quebec	1927
Cleveland Clinic	Cleveland, Ohio	1929
Study Club	Detroit, Michigan	1929
Ohio Penitentiary	Columbus, Ohio	1930
Terminal Hotel	Atlanta, Georgia	1938
Rhythm Night Club	Natchez, Mississippi	1940
Cocoanut Grove	Boston, Massachusetts	1942
Knights of Columbus Hotel	St. John's, Newfoundland	1942
Gulf Hotel	Houston, Texas	1943

Structure	Location	Year
Hartford Circus	Hartford, Connecticut	1944
Empire State Building	New York City, New York	1945
LaSalle Hotel	Chicago, Illinois	1946
Winecoff Hotel	Atlanta, Georgia	1946
St. Anthony's Hospital	Effingham, Illinois	1949
Mercy Hospital	Davenport, Iowa	1950
Littlefield Nursing Home	Largo, Florida	1953
Charles Berg Laboratories	Philadelphia, Pennsylvania	1954
Larkin Warehouse	Buffalo, New York	1954
Warrenton Nursing Home	Warrenton, Missouri	1957
Our Lady of the Angels School	Chicago, Illinois	1958
Fretz Building	Philadelphia, Pennsylvania	1963
Golden Age Nursing Home	Fitchville, Ohio	1963
Hotel Roosevelt	Jacksonville, Florida	1963
Surfside Hotel	Atlantic City, New Jersey	1963
Dale's Penthouse Restaurant	Montgomery, Alabama	1967
Florida State Prison	Jay, Florida	1967
Pioneer Hotel	Tucson, Arizona	1970
Blue Bird Café	Montreal, Quebec	1972
Hotel Vendome	Boston, Massachusetts	1972
National Archives	St. Louis, Missouri	1973
Upstairs Lounge	New Orleans, Louisiana	1973
Gulf Refinery	Philadelphia, Pennsylvania	1975
Barson's Overbrook Restaurant	Philadelphia, Pennsylvania	1976
Retirement Home	Goulds, Newfoundland	1976
Beverly Hills Supper Club	Southgate, Kentucky	1977
Younkers Department Store	Des Moines, Iowa	1978
Opémiska Community Hall	Chapais, Quebec	1979
Extendicare Ltd. Nursing Home	Mississauga, Ontario	1980
MGM Grand Hotel	Las Vegas, Nevada	1980
Keansburg Boarding Home	Keansburg, New Jersey	1981
Dorothy Mae Apartments	Los Angeles, California	1982
Northwestern National Bank	Minneapolis, Minnesota	1982
Dupont Plaza	San Juan, Puerto Rico	1986

(continued)

Table 13.6   *(continued)*

Structure	Location	Year
Ford Automobile Dealership	Hackensack, New Jersey	1988
First Interstate Tower	Los Angeles, California	1988
Happy Land	Bronx, New York	1990
One Meridian Plaza	Philadelphia, Pennsylvania	1991
Worcester Cold Storage	Worcester, Massachusetts	1999
World Trade Center	New York City, New York	2001
Charleston Sofa Super Store	Charleston, South Carolina	2007
Alma College	St. Thomas, Ontario	2008
Quebec City Armory	Quebec City, Quebec	2008
Governor's Mansion	Austin, Texas	2008
Deli	Buffalo, New York	2009

haps that is the status to which suburbanites aspire. The fear of nature-dominated spaces has diminished for many North Americans, and the greening of cities and expansion into less-developed landscapes for seclusion and peace demonstrate this. The outcome of this is that it has led to unintentional exposure to wildfire, producing tens of billions of dollars in property loss and equivalent expenditures for fire suppression. Since 2000, sixteen major, historic fires originated and burned within the so-called urban fringe.

Widespread residential wildfire threats are a recent development resulting from traditional American forest fire management. Suppression of fire was practiced by federal and state agencies throughout the twentieth century largely to protect forest resources. Economics motivated agencies to spot and extinguish fires in forests as quickly as possible to save timber resources and profits. Over time, management learned to appreciate other forest values in managing for wildlife and other wildland uses. Unfortunately, fire exclusion served to stockpile fuel for future fires.

Fire risk has risen and continues to rise every year there is no fire. The most recent fires have been more intense and more difficult to control than past "natural" fires. It is now apparent that building near public or private forestlands is unwise, and analysis of current development reveals that the wildfire hazard is extraordinarily high around some cities. From 1990 to 2007, sixteen catastrophic wildfires have destroyed more than twelve thousand residential dwellings. Many additional smaller fires (with proportionate impacts on smaller communities) have occurred as well. While past fires seem heavily biased toward California and the western states, it should be noted that the risk is high throughout the eastern United States as well. Fires in Florida during the first decade of the twenty-first century have threatened smaller communities, and other cities in the East will be impacted by wildfires eventually (see figure 13.7). Fire is now being managed under a new regime that not only recognizes the ecological role it plays in making healthy ecosystems but also manages the stock of fuels in forests.

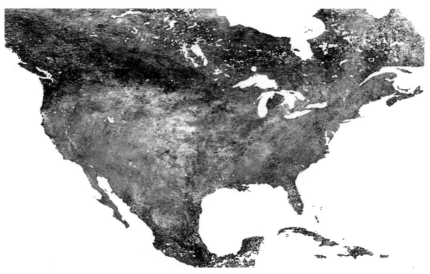

Figure 13.7   In this NASA map of land-surface temperature anomalies, the intensity and scope of the heat wave in the western United States is clearly visible (shown in lightest gray/white)—especially over Colorado, southwest Nebraska, and parts of Wyoming. *Source:* NASA map based on data gathered from June 17–24, 2012, from the Moderate Resolution Imaging Spectrometer (MODIS) on NASA's Terra satellite.

Enhancing this hazard in the urban fringe are vulnerabilities built into the landscapes over the past few decades. Box 13.6 discusses how society has created such hazards. Curvilinear streets in suburban subdivisions with limited ingress and egress are intended to enhance exclusivity and promote seclusion. They inadvertently make evacuations difficult and complicate firefighting. Heavy vegetation also limits residential fire awareness and vigilance, leaving it more susceptible to fast-moving fires. Furthermore, developments in areas with complex terrain and a lot of relief (i.e., with hills, canyons, or valleys) can be very dangerous for similar reasons, but the risk there is heightened by wildfire dynamics and local conditions produced by fires. Because of the diversity of geographies of residential development throughout North America, there can be no single one-size-fits-all approach to managing the urban-fringe fire problem short of completely removing the exposed from places of high risk.

Box 13.6 Geographic Perspectives on Urban Hazards

Many urban hazards result from endeavors for private profit that ignore the costs (or externalities) to others, from actions that are temporally shortsighted, or from behaviors that are ignorant of the long-term implications. The lack of spatial awareness, spatial thinking, or spatial planning is revealed in the negative social outcomes of disasters and catastrophes. While some human actions can be discouraged or even made illegal, many are simply problems when they are undertaken in certain contexts. As discussed in this chapter, it is both individuals and society that create hazard by participating in natural, technological, or social processes in ways that threaten health, welfare, or property; many of these processes are tied to the landscapes and locations in which they occur. For example, human occupancy of places where flooding, seismic and volcanic activities, drought, and frost can occur or are commonplace ought to be avoided or "occupied" very carefully. Built landscapes that possess hidden vulnerabilities (like structures that are built of highly flammable materials or that house potentially incendiary or explosive activities) ought to be publically identified, reorganized, restricted, or managed with heightened vigilance in order to diminish the likelihood of disaster. But human demands are unceasing, and there is usually significant reticence to "surrender" to nature or geography, particularly if a space or place has economic value.

Geographers often strive to reveal the patterns of activities and processes (both natural and human, visible and invisible) that occur on earth. Through geographical analysis using geographic tools such as geographic information systems, remote sensing, spatial statistical analysis, and geographical insights, geographers can expose and clarify the implications of present-day decisions and prospects for future disasters. Geographers can illuminate the places where future disasters might occur, identify the locations more likely to experience disasters sooner and places that might be more severely impacted, and uncover the most vulnerable populations, places, systems, and processes in a region of heightened risk.

Because cities tend to be defined by the spatial reach of the urban political unit in which management decisions are (or can be) made, they can be regarded as a purposeful system that organizes its own internal operations. Ideally, a city can rectify recognized problems and may be able to avoid disruptions and disasters. However, cities of North America are organic systems that have evolved in place over decades or centuries; they do not exist in vacuums, and they have historical inertia in their political, economic, and social systems that tends to slow down solutions to recognized spatial problems (hazards, vulnerabilities, exposures). Hazard management may require years or decades of unraveling of past spatial decisions before commencing with effective hazard mitigation and sustainable redevelopment. Geographers possess skills to sort out the legal, social, political, and economic resistance to spatial change and can, theoretically, encourage urban systems to evolve toward safer, less expensive, and more efficient organization. Geographers do this by gathering spatial data, analyzing the patterns of geophysical, meteorological, biological, technological, and sociological processes and their interactions, and providing decision-making guidance to planners and others in urban, state, and national governmental agencies. By fostering the development of spatial awareness, understanding the workings of complex systems, sensitivities to manifold issues and social problems, and effective communication skills, geographers can actively contribute to the solutions of many urban hazard problems.

CONCLUSIONS: URBAN VULNERABILITY AND URBAN RESILIENCY

Ultimately, the age-old notion that the city is an effective refuge from the threats of nature (or enemies of any type) is constantly disproved. Indeed, there are many threats derived from natural processes that are in some way or another intensified by urban development. Nature infuses cities with the raw materials of civilization, but the resources come with costs. Hazards are the cost of "living" that can be magnified or attenuated by our choices.

The distribution of risks from flooding, severe storms, earthquake activity, and wildfires, among the many other things that can do harm, is constantly changing spatially and temporally, and the idea of eliminating risk completely is impractical. What can be managed is the hazard. We can reduce the implications of events that occur with planning and preventive decisions. Vulnerability intensifies the impacts of hazard events if our differential characteristics are ignored. The susceptibility of cities and their populations to hazards can be managed as well.

Recently, urban hazard managers have become more focused on managing urban vulnerabilities. Their goal is to reduce destructive impacts and limit disruption caused by extreme events. Reducing exposure of hazard-vulnerable people, communities, systems, infrastructures, or even government agencies to hazards will assist this effort. Whereas twentieth-century hazard managers sought urban disaster *resistance* by creating hardened, theoretically impenetrable systems and structures, the twenty-first-century manager now strives for disaster *resilience*.

Resilience is accomplished by enabling the capacities of people, communities, infrastructure, and systems to absorb the impacts of extreme events so that hazards impinge less on lives, social systems, and urban infrastructure. Resiliency building suggests that we can preferentially control disaster impacts so that our communities will quickly return to normal after an event.

In the twenty-first century, urban planners are challenged to develop hazard management plans that involve the following stages of disaster management:

- Emergency response to quell the emergency and rescue the victims during the period from the occurrence of the event to days or weeks afterward;
- Restoration of infrastructure, systems, and services over the next few weeks to months in order to make the disaster-impacted region at least livable for the emergency-sheltered populations and returning evacuees;
- Reconstruction of the destroyed buildings and urban infrastructure to at least predisaster quality during the first few months to first few years of the post-disaster period to "recover" from the disaster; and
- Redesign, reorganization, replacement, and redevelopment of the city with rebuilding projects to mitigate future hazards, to eliminate social and structural vulnerabilities, and to create a resilient city undertaken during the few years or decade following the disaster.

Such "resilient" cities express the power of hope and opportunity in the face of adversity.

North American systems are designed for and primarily driven by capitalist economics. The understanding of the problems (and the hazards we face) is filtered through a capitalist (neoliberal) perspective. Hazard mitigation choices are also limited by the values inherent in this perspective; therefore, places tend to change only incrementally and only after disasters. Prevention is known to be less costly economically (and certainly in terms of mortalities and casualties) than is reaction, recovery, reconstruction, and after-the-fact mitigation, but our society tends to play the odds. The vulnerable, the marginalized, and the powerless often experience the consequences of the decisions made by elites and the powerful. Urban disasters in North America will continue to occur according to the geographies of economics and ethics, and only when preventive actions and fundamental restructuring of urban spaces are undertaken will they begin to diminish. That time is unlikely to come soon, at least willfully, before disaster.

SUGGESTED READINGS

Burby, R. J., ed. 1998. *Cooperating with Nature: Confronting Natural Hazards with Land-Use Planning for Sustainable Communities*. Washington, DC: Joseph Henry Press.

Kates, R. W., and I. Burton, eds. 1986. *Geography, Resources and Environment, Volume 1: Selected Writings of Gilbert F. White*. Chicago: University of Chicago Press.

Leichenko, R. M., and K. L. O'Brien. 2008. *Environmental Change and Globalization*. New York: Oxford University Press.

Mileti, D. 1999. *Disasters by Design: A Reassessment of Natural Hazards in the United States*. Washington, DC: Joseph Henry Press.

Mitchell, J. K., ed. 1999. *Crucibles of Hazard: Mega-Cities and Disasters in Transition*. New York: United Nations University Press.

Oliver-Smith, A. 2009. "Sea Level Rise and the Vulnerability of Coastal Peoples: Responding to the Local Challenges of Global Climate Change in the 21st Century." InterSecTions 'Interdisciplinary Security ConnecTions' Publication Series of UNU-EHS. Bonn: United Nations University, paper no. 7.

Rodríguez, H., E. L. Quarantelli, and R. R. Dynes, eds. 2007. *Handbook of Disaster Research*. New York: Springer.

White, G. F., ed. 1974. *Natural Hazards: Local, National, Global*. New York: Oxford University Press.

Wisner, B., J. C. Gaillard, and I. Kelman, eds. 2011. *The Routledge Handbook of Hazards and Disaster Risk Reduction*. New York: Routledge.

14

Urban Sustainability
GEOFF BUCKLEY

Sustainability is a term we hear often these days, but just what does it mean? The standard response is to dust off the definition first proffered by the United Nations World Commission on the Environment and Development nearly thirty years ago, the one that admonishes us to meet the needs of the present "without compromising the ability of future generations to meet their own needs." In *Hope and Hard Times: Communities, Collaboration and Sustainability*, Ted Bernard provides us with a more eloquent and satisfying definition. Simply stated, sustainability means "putting in place the age-old desire to live richly, equitably, and peaceably with each other and with our natural surroundings so that our 'home' may offer itself to the imaginations and tables of generations to come." This requires a new consciousness, one that allows humans to make a living without depleting social and natural capital while ensuring equity between and across generations. As James Gustave Speth points out in his recent book, *The Bridge at the Edge of the World: Capitalism, the Environment, and Crossing from Crisis to Sustainability*, sustainability is also about keeping options "alive" so that we are better equipped to handle future contingencies.

What about urban sustainability? For many, sustainability in an urban setting conjures up images of solar panels, green roofs, bamboo floors, and smart cars. Occasionally buying items off the "green" products shelf at the local grocery store—compact fluorescent lightbulbs for instance—instead of where we normally shop. Throw in some bicycle lanes, a weekly farmers market, and some neon-orange recycling bins, and the picture is complete. To journalist David Owen, however, "Sustainability is a context, not a gadget or technology." Indeed, for far too long, the goal of achieving urban sustainability has been treated merely as a "technomanagerial endeavor"—one that involves upgrading and retrofitting existing infrastructures so that they are more efficient; developing policies and regulations that promote reducing, reusing, and recycling materials; encouraging the use of alternative fuels; and so on. Not that these are unimportant activities. However, urban sustainability entails much more than the pursuit of "ecological modernization" (see box 14.1).

As the foregoing paragraphs suggest, sustainability is not just about living our lives in a way that is more environmentally benign. It is about a new way of seeing the world and our place in it. Certainly, this new vision calls for us to tread more softly, but it also involves taking advantage of new

Box 14.1 What Is Sustainability?

The term "sustainability" is used so often today it has come to mean both everything and nothing. At one end of the spectrum, it is used by marketers to sell "green" items and technologies that promote a way of life that is clearly *unsustainable*. At the other end, sustainability is linked to an emerging worldview that aims to protect and conserve resources, build resilient human communities, and strengthen our connection to the natural world. Ask ten people on the street what the definition of sustainability is, and be prepared for ten different responses.

Generally speaking, we can divide definitions of sustainability into two categories—strong and weak. Strong sustainability seeks to sustain natural capital. Here, the priority is to protect and conserve the natural environment. It encourages a shift away from ever-increasing material consumption and anticipates changes in human values, lifestyles, and behaviors. Weak sustainability, on the other hand, prioritizes long-term economic growth. Natural capital may be consumed as long as substitutes are available. Both fall under the umbrella of sustainability but represent very different ways of living in the world.

Frustrated with the way the term has been co-opted by business and industry, some planners and environmentalists prefer the term "thrivability." They argue that thrivability goes beyond sustainability—even so-called strong sustainability—by incorporating social justice concerns more explicitly into the mission. Moreover, it offers a more optimistic approach, one that pushes us toward a future we desire as opposed to avoiding a future that frightens us. In this way, critics maintain, it is more visionary and hopeful.

When we think of sustainability in an urban context, we think of a city which is designed, retrofitted, and managed in such a way as to minimize consumption of energy, water, and other critical "inputs" such as food while at the same time cutting back on generation of air and water pollution, excess heat, and other harmful "outputs." Although there is no one-size-fits-all definition for what a sustainable city should look like, the goal, ultimately, is to create the smallest ecological footprint possible. In her recent book, *Emerald Cities: Urban Sustainability and Economic Development*, Joan Fitzgerald reminds us that there is more to urban sustainability than simply minimizing our environmental impact. Indeed, she notes that there is a "tacit radicalism" associated with the sustainability agenda in that it offers a political critique of the "ecological damage and economic inequality created by free-market capitalism." Thus, sustainability—the strong variety at least—requires us to consider our actions in relation to others and, further, to pursue a more democratic civic politics.

Cities offer both challenges and opportunities when it comes to meeting society's sustainability goals. On the challenges side of the equation, cities consume approximately 75 percent of the world's energy and are responsible for about 80 percent of global greenhouse gas emissions. With respect to opportunities, cities possess the potential to be the greenest places on the planet because of their density. This density not only contributes to greater energy efficiency but also greater creativity. Concentrating people in a particular place—especially highly educated and skilled people—often results in greater innovation and higher productivity.

economic opportunities and, equally important, ensuring that environmental and economic benefits are distributed equitably among all citizens. In this chapter, we will use the "three e's"—environment, economy, and equity—as organizing principles to explore the concept of urban sustainability in all its complexity. The underlying premise is that cities, especially those that are densely settled, permit us to utilize resources more efficiently, generate economic activity more effectively, and enjoy healthy, meaningful lives. Considering that more than 80 percent of the population in the United States and Canada now lives urban, the chance to make the vision a reality is within our grasp.

ENVIRONMENT

For centuries, cities have been viewed as the antithesis of nature. During the nineteenth and early twentieth centuries, for instance, if someone uttered the word "nature" in the same sentence as the word "city," the reference was probably to a park or an undeveloped parcel of land. In fact, many of these parks—including Central Park in New York and San Francisco's Golden Gate Park—were originally designed to counter what were perceived as the dehumanizing effects of the Industrial Revolution. At the time, park advocates believed that exposing urban dwellers to fresh air and open space was the perfect antidote for a variety of social ills plaguing our cities, including crime and juvenile delinquency. In much the same way that cities today build stadiums and other amenities to lure residents and businesses back to the urban core, cities in the nineteenth century built parks. A city without a major urban park during the second half of the nineteenth century was clearly out of step with the times.

Of course, nature abounds in our cities—and not just the kind one finds in urban parks. From the volunteer species that colonize vacant lots to the street trees we plant to beautify our neighborhoods, more than a quarter of urban land is covered by tree canopy. In some cases, there is more tree canopy shading our cities than there is in adjacent suburban or rural areas. Add to this the expansive acreage of public and private green spaces that many cities possess, including playgrounds, greenways, schoolyards, and cemeteries, and the boundary between urban and rural blurs even further. Although the arbitrary distinction between urban and rural—and between humans and nature—is gradually giving way to more nuanced interpretations, these perceptions still resonate in the minds of many. Increasingly, however, cities are treated as hybrid landscapes. Rather than think in terms of nature *in* cities, we think of the nature *of* cities. We also acknowledge that cities function as ecosystems, complete with energy flows and nutrient cycling. When suburban residents add fertilizer to their lawns in the spring, for example, surface runoff carries excess nitrogen and phosphorus far and wide via stormwater sewer systems that mimic the "natural" drainage network that once existed. Contrary to popular belief, the laws of ecology still apply within the city limits!

The Urban Footprint

That the boundaries separating our cities from the wider world are fluid should come as no surprise. On a daily basis, cities require enormous inputs of energy, food, and water. Plummeting transportation costs throughout the nineteenth and twentieth centuries, coupled with technological innovations such as refrigeration and reinforced concrete, allowed growing cities to look beyond their hinterlands to meet their needs. Today, Wyoming coal from the Powder River Basin lights up homes in Ohio, fruits and vegetables from around the world end up in the produce section of grocery stores in Philadelphia, and water from as far away as Mono Lake and the Colorado River quenches the thirst of Los Angelinos. And then there is petroleum. Whether stuck in commuter traffic in Boston, attending a conference in Houston, or vacationing in Miami, you are connected to oil. If it is not produced domestically—and more than 60 percent of what we consume annually in the United States is not—then it has to be imported. Canada and Mexico are America's biggest foreign suppliers, but we also receive significant shipments from more distant locations, including Saudi Arabia, Nigeria, and Venezuela. Without oil, life as we know it in our cities would grind to a halt.

Cities also generate a lot of waste and pollution. During periods of economic boom and bust, often referred to as the Kuznets cycle, the demand for raw materials rises and falls. So, too, does the demand for space to send construction and demolition waste. Here again, declining transportation costs come into play, permitting cities to ship solid and hazardous waste to distant locations. With regard to domestic refuse, which has increased steadily since 1960, New Jersey ships more than half of its waste out of state. Meanwhile, Pennsylvania is now United States' biggest importer of other people's trash. Cities also generate a lot of sewage waste. As urban populations grew throughout the nineteenth century, the need to dispose of this waste while protecting

drinking water supplies drove many cities to construct elaborate sewer systems and treatment facilities. Long after most major cities had modernized in this way, Montreal continued to rely on the swift current of the St. Lawrence River to carry its effluent downstream. Only in 1994 did the city discontinue this practice, the same year New York stopped dumping sewage sludge offshore. One important consequence of these developments is that the vast majority of urban and suburban residents have only a very vague idea where their resources come from or what happens to their wastes once they are discarded.

In recent years, geographers and others have tried to restore these connections by applying the concept of the ecological footprint. The first academic publication about the ecological footprint was by William Rees in 1992. Rees developed the ecological footprint as a quantitative tool that estimates humanity's ecological impact on the ecosphere in terms of appropriated ecosystem (land and water) area. The footprint links resource consumption with waste production to calculate how much land is required to support human activities in a given location. For example, a city that is more reliant on private autos than public transport has greater energy needs and thus has a larger footprint. In cities, individual and national footprints combine and interact to produce distinctly urban regional effects. The city of Calgary in Canada undertook a survey and found that the city's footprint was between 9.5 and 9.9 global hectares (gha) per person. High energy use was the single biggest contributor. As a result of the study, the city government of Calgary delayed greenfield developments and moved toward greater use of renewable sources. The city's light rail system is now powered entirely by wind-generated energy.

While we tend to think of cities as "unsustainable" and rural areas as being more self-sufficient, Edward Glaeser, professor of economics at Harvard University, reminds us that this is not necessarily true, noting, "Manhattan, not suburbia, is the real friend of the environment. Those alleged nature lovers who live on multi-acre estates surrounded by trees and lawn consume vast amounts of space and energy. If the environmental footprint of the average suburban home is a size 15 hiking boot, the environmental footprint of a New York apartment is a stiletto-heeled Jimmy Choo. Eight million New Yorkers use only 301 square miles, which comes to less than one-fortieth of an acre a person. Even supposedly green Portland, Oregon is using up more than six times as much land a person than New York."

By virtue of their heavy consumption of energy and other resources, Americans—rural and urban—have one of the largest ecological footprints in the world, requiring approximately twenty-five acres of biologically productive land or sea per capita to support our lifestyles. Nowhere is the contrast between ecological footprint and area occupied more pronounced than in our cities. Although cities take up relatively little room, their ecological footprints are large because urban residents consume huge amounts of energy and generate prodigious amounts of waste. Ironically, it is just this relationship—large numbers of people squeezed into relatively small spaces on the earth's surface—that make cities more efficient and, potentially, more sustainable. "If the future is going to be greener, then it must be more urban," writes Edward Glaeser. "For the sake of humanity and our planet, cities are—and must be—the wave of the future."

KEYS TO SUSTAINABILITY

So what is it about urban living that makes cities potentially more sustainable than surrounding suburban and rural areas? A closer look at New York City explains. First, packing so many people into such a relatively small space has forced New Yorkers to build up instead of out (see figure 14.1). This is especially true on the island of Manhattan. Building skyscrapers not only permits the city to add tremendous floor space using the same amount of ground area, it compels residents and businesses to be much more energy efficient. Stacking apartments on top of one another saves energy in the wintertime because excess heat from one unit helps warm surrounding units, including those on

Figure 14.1 Downtown Manhattan. High-density living is one of the keys to sustainability. (Photo by Alexandra MacColl Buckley)

the next floor. Second, urban dwellers tend to consume less electricity than suburbanites, with the average suburban household consuming 27 percent more electricity than its urban counterpart. Even among cities, electricity consumption can vary (see box 14.2). Third, high rents in New York cause most people to occupy small living spaces. Living smaller means New Yorkers accumulate fewer material goods. Finally, big cities mean less driving and, by extension, less fossil fuel consumption and air pollution. When buses and vans use cleaner-burning fuels such as natural gas, air quality in the city improves even more (see figure 14.2). In New York, high population density and an efficient public transportation network make car ownership unnecessary. With 82 percent of employed residents walking, biking, or taking public transit to work, the average commuter in Manhattan today consumes petroleum at the same rate as the average American did back in the 1920s. All that walking and biking has another benefit: New Yorkers tend to weigh less and live longer than the average American today. That city living may hold the key to sustainability should come as welcome news to anyone living in North America.

Box 14.2 Staying Cool in Toronto

Urban dwellers consume less electricity than their suburban counterparts—this much we know. However, the actual amount of electricity consumed per capita in any given city can vary tremendously. The most important factor that helps to explain the difference is summer heat. Whether it is Houston, Texas, or Miami, Florida, when temperatures spike in July and August, people reach for the thermostat. Even in more northern locations, such as Boston, Massachusetts, and Minneapolis, Minnesota, high summer temperatures and humidity can make our lives miserable, if only temporarily. They can also wreak havoc with monthly utility bills. Among North American cities, Vancouver, British Columbia, is often lauded for its sustainability achievements and eco-friendly lifestyle. The reputation is well deserved. In this case, however, it is Toronto that has taken a creative and bold step in the direction of sustainability.

While many cities rely on fossil fuels to generate the electricity that cools our homes in summer, the City of Toronto has taken a different approach. In 1990, the Canadian Urban Institute—an organization dedicated to promoting economic and environmental sustainability—along with numerous other interested parties began to investigate the possibility of drawing cold water from the bottom of Lake Ontario to modify air temperatures in government buildings, office high-rises, hotels, and other structures in Toronto's downtown. A unique collaboration between the Enwave Energy Corporation and the City of Toronto soon turned the dream into a reality. After an environmental assessment for the deep lake water cooling (DLWC) project was approved in 1998, design and construction began in earnest. The system was officially commissioned in 2004. Today, Toronto's DLWC is the world's largest lake-source cooling system. It has been deemed a stunning success, distributing steam and chilled water to slightly more than half the potential market in Toronto, while at the same time lowering utility bills, attracting environmentally conscious businesses to the urban core, and significantly reducing emissions of carbon dioxide and other air pollutants associated with the burning of coal.

How does the system work? Essentially, Torontonians take advantage of a permanent reservoir of cold water that collects at the bottom of Lake Ontario. During the winter months, the lake's surface temperature cools to about four degrees Celsius (thirty-nine degrees Fahrenheit). As the surface water's density increases, it begins to sink to the bottom. In summer, the situation is reversed. Water at the surface of the lake warms up, but because its density does not increase, it does not sink. The result is that cold water remains trapped at the bottom year round. Regardless of how high the mercury rises in the summer, water at the bottom of the lake is always frigid. To take advantage of this phenomenon, Enwave sank three intake pipes to a depth of eighty-three meters along the slope of the lake bottom to a distance of about five kilometers offshore. Water is pumped to a filtration plant, where it is processed and then redirected to Enwave's energy transfer station. Here, an energy transfer takes place between the cold water drawn from the lake and the company's closed chilled water supply loop. Once this process is complete, the water flows to the city's potable water system. How cool is that?

Figure 14.2   City bus in Washington, DC, powered by natural gas. Vehicles such as these generate less air pollution than more conventional models. (Photo by Geoff Buckley)

The Rising Tide of Urban Sprawl

Unfortunately, New York City is the exception rather than the rule when it comes to population density. In cities such as Nashville, St. Louis, Las Vegas, Phoenix, Edmonton, and dozens more, urban form was not constrained by physical geography. Moreover, it was influenced by the automobile, which has dominated transportation in the United States and Canada since the 1950s (see figure 14.3). Thanks in part to federal highway subsidies and favorable housing policies, cities across the United States spread outward instead of upward (see figure 14.4). As more and more people traded apartments and row houses in the city for detached housing in the suburbs, our metropolitan areas "sprawled." From a sustainability perspective, the results have been disastrous. To begin with, the movement from urban to suburban has eroded municipal tax bases and discouraged investment in urban infrastructure, including public transportation. Sprawling low-density suburban development has also dispersed employment, which means more people drive more cars, increasing fuel consumption, compounding congestion problems, and adding to the air pollution load. In the United States, southern cities in particular have very high driving levels. The situation in Atlanta is emblematic of the problem. At 8,500 square miles, Atlanta is

Figure 14.3   Cars entering Las Vegas, Nevada. As the multiple lanes and signage suggest, this city was designed with the automobile in mind. (Photo by Geoff Buckley)

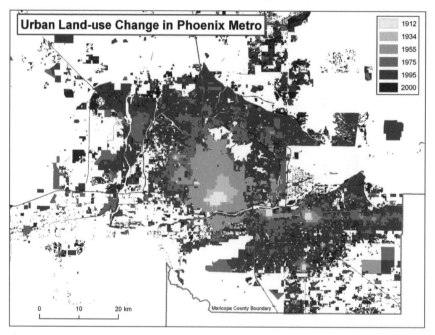

Figure 14.4   Expanding urban land use in central Arizona, 1912–2000. Phoenix is one of the most "sprawling" cities in the United States. *Source:* Central Arizona-Phoenix Long-Term Ecological Research.

Figure 14.5 Urban sprawl on the outskirts of Columbus, Ohio. Curvilinear streets and cul-de-sacs discourage public transportation. (Photo by Geoff Buckley)

one of the country's "biggest sprawl bombs." Unlike New York City, where less than a third of residents drive to work, 94 percent of Atlanta's inhabitants commute by car.

The damage inflicted on cities by car culture is even more far reaching. Cars have done more than jam boulevards and intersections. They have altered the social and cultural fabric of these once-vibrant places. For many urban scholars, mixed-use zoning, which combines commercial and residential land uses, is one of the attributes that make cities interesting and exciting places to live and work. In many cities, cars and highways changed this dynamic because low-density sprawl actually promotes the segregation of land uses, making everything from shopping and dining to visiting a doctor or a friend more difficult to accomplish using anything other than a car for transportation. Design elements such as curvilinear streets and cul-de-sacs render walking, biking, and even bus travel impractical (see figure 14.5).

Toward a More Sustainable Future

Numerous strategies have been employed in recent years to keep urban sprawl in check. In the 1970s, for instance, Portland, Oregon, established an urban growth boundary. Though not a permanent barrier against automobile-dependent sprawl, it has protected valuable open space while at the same time made in-filling a more desirable and lucrative option for developers. In Baltimore County, Maryland, efforts to preserve farmland and control sprawl go back even further, to 1967, with the adoption of an Urban Rural Demarcation Line. In general, however, urban growth boundaries and other similar fixes such as greenbelts have proven either too restrictive or too controversial to replicate widely. In 1997, the state of Maryland unveiled its Smart Growth Initiative, which sought to manage growth using a variety of financial incentives and planning tools. The goal was to encourage developers to protect rural areas by building more compact residential subdivisions. But it still meant growth would take place on the urban periphery. Smart growth may be an improvement over sprawl, but is it really smart?

Since the early 1980s, "new urbanists" have taken a different approach to the problem, with architects and planners like Andres Duany, Elizabeth Plater-Zyberk, and Peter Calthorpe seeking to create more livable communities by promoting designs that favor walking and biking over driving. Characterized by small lots, narrow mixed-use streets, front porches, and an easily navigated grid pattern, new towns like Seaside, Florida, have proven both popular and financially successful. More encouraging still, applying new urbanist principles to downtown districts has rejuvenated neighborhoods in cities such as Vancouver, British Columbia, and Portland, Oregon. Despite the best efforts of new urbanists and advocates of smart growth, however, the situation has deteriorated in many parts of the country. Since 1970, average house size in the United States has increased 50 percent while per capita electricity consumption has shot up 70 percent. Worse, 80 percent of new home construction since 1994 has been "exurban," a term that describes leapfrog development occurring at the farthest reaches of the urban-rural interface As the preceding discussion suggests, compact living is good because it allows us to take advantage of economies of density. This is one of the cornerstones of urban sustainability. Greater population density translates into more tax dollars, less driving, and cleaner air. But this is only part of the equation. Building taller and living smaller should not come at the expense of parks and trees. Nor should it cause us to sacrifice historically and culturally significant buildings and neighborhoods in favor of tall apartment buildings. While in many cases it makes sense to replace older low-rise buildings with taller, more efficient structures, this is not always the case. We must remember that historic neighborhoods, cultural landmarks, and scenic vistas are amenities that draw people to live in cities in the first place. So, too, are trees and parks.

Trees and parks in particular offer social and ecological benefits that are difficult to replace in an urban setting. In the summer, trees provide shade and energy savings to urban residents. They also store carbon, improve air quality, mitigate the effects of the urban heat island, and contribute to higher real-estate values. Citing the benefits, cities throughout the United States and Canada are developing plans to increase their urban tree canopies (see box 14.3). Parks accomplish many of the same things but are also valued for the recreational opportunities they provide. This is an especially important topic today given the high percentage of children and adults in the United States suffering from obesity and type 2 diabetes. Finally, urban green spaces, from large parks to private backyards, provide valuable habitat to a remarkable variety of species, both native and introduced. In places like East Los Angeles or sections of New York City, where there is demand for green space but little room to build or expand a park, planners and community groups have come up with novel ways to "green" neighborhoods. New York's high line—an abandoned elevated railway turned into a linear park in the city's former Meatpacking District—is an extraordinary example of such an effort (see figure 14.7).

Box 14.3 Reforesting Baltimore

Henry Ford once famously remarked that the only way to "solve the City Problem" was to leave the city: "Get the people into the country, get them into communities where a man knows his neighbor, where there is a commonality of interest, where life is not artificial, and you have solved the City Problem. You have solved it by eliminating the City." Of course, Ford was hoping that all those people fleeing the city would be driving brand new Model T Fords. But this misses the larger point. The problem with this way of thinking is that it ignores the natural elements that exist in cities, even in the densely built-up downtown areas. Yes, as Betty Smith's 1943 novel reminds us, trees really do grow in Brooklyn. They also grow in Baltimore. More than a quarter of urban land is covered by urban tree canopy.

Baltimore's experience with professional forestry dates to 1912, when the city passed its first street tree law. Ordinance No. 154, as it was known, authorized the city engineer "to regulate the planting, protection, removing and controlling of all trees, growing, planted and to be planted in the streets of Baltimore, not under the jurisdiction of the Board of Park Commissioners, and to appoint a City Forester and such other employees and assistants as may be necessary to carry out the provisions of this ordinance." Although not the first city in North America to embrace the planting of urban trees, Baltimore's experience is illustrative of the problems cities face today as they struggle to maintain, let alone expand, their tree canopies. Despite opposition to tree planting in some quarters, Baltimoreans have generally been enthusiastic supporters of tree-planting efforts (see figure 14.6). Getting trees to grow in what can prove to be a hostile environment demands more than enthusiasm, however. That's where TreeBaltimore comes in.

Figure 14.6   Faculty and children at Franklin Square Elementary School in Baltimore, Maryland. Recently, the school replaced 1.39 acres of asphalt with grass and trees, giving children a safer—and eventually shadier—place to play. (Photo by Christopher G. Boone)

Led by the Baltimore City Department of Recreation and Parks, TreeBaltimore is a program that seeks to expand the city's tree canopy through the planting, management, and protection of trees. Recognizing that municipal resources are limited and that the city's urban tree canopy has been on the decline in recent years, TreeBaltimore aims to reach its goal of doubling the city's tree canopy in the next twenty-five years through tree planting, improved care for existing trees, natural regeneration, and instilling a sense of pride and stewardship among residents. Perhaps this statement from the TreeBaltimore website best captures the spirit of sustainability that lies at the heart of the initiative: "The TreeBaltimore campaign is a 'call to action' to residents to plant a tree. By planting and caring for a tree at your home, business or park, you are helping to clean our air and water. Trees also help reduce summer air temperatures, save energy, buffer noise and increase the economic stability of Baltimore." To underscore the value of the urban forest, TreeBaltimore reminds citizens that each year the city's 2.8 million trees store upwards of 527 tons of carbon, capture 244 tons of ozone, and provide an estimated $3.3 million in energy savings.

Figure 14.7 New York City's popular "high line." In neighborhoods with little room for parks, such creative features offer recreational opportunities for residents. (Photo by Alexandra MacColl Buckley)

Over the past decade, sustainability has emerged as a major theme in urban policy and resource management circles. Across the United States and Canada, cities are developing sustainability plans and charting progress toward established benchmarks (see box 14.4). As many of these plans clearly show, politicians and residents alike are con- cerned not only about environmental issues but about economics and equity as well. We explore these topics in the sections that fol- low, bearing in mind that for a city to truly move down the path of sustainability, it must maintain or recapture economic relevance and strive to ensure that everyone shares in the wealth.

Box 14.4 Green Phoenix

Phoenix is no stranger to sustainability efforts. In some respects, this desert city has been at the forefront of the movement for decades, spearheading sustainability efforts long be- fore the term came into vogue. As far back as 1968, for example, Phoenix was recycling tires and incorporating rubber into new road surfaces. Thanks to the city's water conservation program, per capita water usage has declined by 20 percent since 1986. The city also re- ceives kudos for reusing approximately 90 percent of its wastewater. In 2005, Phoenix began requiring that all new city buildings meet basic LEED (Leadership in Energy and Environ- mental Design) specifications. Other initiatives include the cleanup of hundreds of acres of contaminated brownfield sites, the use of alternative fuels in the city's fleet of vehicles, an in-filling program that has been active since 1994, and construction of a light rail system.

On the other hand, anyone familiar with Phoenix's problems knows the obstacles that stand in the way of a more sustainable future. Temperatures in the city reach or exceed one hundred degrees Fahrenheit (thirty-seven degrees Celsius) 110 days per year, which, of course, ratchets up the urban heat island effect. Low precipitation rates and periodic droughts threaten water supplies. Many residents, especially those in low-income brackets, suffer from some of the worst air pollution in the country. Add to the mix a high total population (1.4 million in 2010) and low population density (2,785 people per square mile)—a combination that has earned Phoenix the dubious moniker "poster child of Sun Belt sprawl"—and one begins to appreciate the magnitude of the problem. Nevertheless, city officials and their partners are not shying away from the challenge.

In 2009, Mayor Phil Gordon announced a seventeen-point plan to make Phoenix the most sustainable city in the United States. Developed in collaboration with Arizona State University, Green Phoenix, as the plan is known, seeks to build on past conservation efforts while stimulating the local economy and improving quality of life for the city's residents. A significant first step toward implementation was taken in early 2009, when Mayor Gordon and Michael Crow, president of Arizona State University, secured funding from the federal government through the American Recovery and Reinvestment Act (ARRA). As of December 2010, Phoenix has received $429 million in federal stimulus funding. In keeping with the six main priority areas identified in the plan—greener neighborhoods, solar city, greening homes and businesses, public buildings LEED retrofit, renewable energy, and efficient city lights—ARRA-funded projects include green retrofitting of public housing, adding solar panels to city facilities, making street and transportation improvements, replacing aging water infrastructure, and restoring eight miles of the Salt River. According to the Green Phoenix webpage, "Phoenix is committed to reduce air pollution, greenhouse gases, conserve energy and water resources. Their support includes conducting sound water and land use planning, providing recreational opportunities, preserving open space and wildlife, and restoring blighted land and riparian habitat." How the plan will fare in the aftermath of the recent housing collapse and with global climate change posing greater risks is difficult to say. Despite the best of intentions, the outcome of Phoenix's sustainability efforts is by no means assured.

ECONOMY

From an economic perspective, the goal of urban sustainability is to create decent jobs, boost incomes, and build the tax base of the city—all with an eye toward securing long-term stability. At the same time that we work to build the urban economy, we must safeguard those aspects of urban living that attract people to the city in the first place. This includes protecting the city's natural environment, preserving historically significant buildings and neighborhoods, reducing or eliminating pollution, and improving quality of life for all citizens. Balancing the three e's—environment, economy, and equity—is not easy, but it is absolutely imperative if cities are to realize their long-range sustainability goals.

The housing bubble burst in 2008 showed that crises affect cities in different ways. What happened in Phoenix and Miami was very different from what played out in San Francisco and Boston. The effect the crisis had on city centers and inner-ring suburbs compared to fringe suburbs was also quite different, with housing prices holding steady for the former while dropping precipitously for the latter in most places. How cities respond to adversity depends on a number of factors. What is the nature of the challenge they face? How diversified is their economy? How educated are their residents? How skilled are their workers? Human capital, even more than physical infrastructure, explains which cities succeed and which languish. Many studies suggest that skilled people are better at adapting to changing circumstances and that "skilled cities" are better equipped to weather economic crises.

The Urban Challenge

Cities in North America face a variety of economic challenges. One that rises to the top of the list is shifting demographics. Many of the most populous cities in the United States back in 1950 have lower populations today than they did sixty years ago, with Cleveland, Detroit, and St. Louis suffering losses of well over 50 percent. It is difficult for cities to build a more solid tax base and take advantage of economies of density if they are losing residents. So where are all these people going? While there has been a general population shift to the South and the West in the United States over the past several decades, there has also been a steady movement of people from urban to suburban areas. This migration has been driven in part by the movement of corporate offices from urban locations to suburban campuses. Recapturing at least part of this tax base is a goal for many cities, prompting many to redevelop or reclaim their "natural environment" to attract reinvestment. Waterfront developments, cleaning up brownfields, and reusing factories have dominated urban economic development schemes across the United States and Canada (see figure 14.8).

Another challenge cities face is closely related to the first. Massive amounts of energy and money are invested in buildings and roads as part of a rhythmic cycle of construction that cities in North America experience every fifteen to twenty-five years. But new buildings and roads are only part of the story. Time and energy—and money—are needed to *maintain* buildings and roads as well as the parts of a city's infrastructure we either do not see or take for granted, such as telecommunications, sewer and stormwater systems, parks, and street trees. This is where cities face a conundrum. Many municipalities cannot afford the infrastructure they now possess. The extreme example, of course, is New Orleans, where an elaborate network of levees and pumps requires constant upkeep and repair. Coming up with creative and environment-friendly alternatives to the highly engineered solutions of the sanitary city era is a must for today's cash-strapped cities. Instead of spending millions of dollars replacing stormwater sewers and treatment facilities, for example, cities need to find cheaper solutions that address pollution problems at the source rather than at the end of the pipe (see figure 14.9). Focused on pollution prevention and informed by the precautionary principle, such an approach necessarily entails changes in consumer behavior and, in some cases, changes in governance.

Figure 14.8   "Greening" of the riverfront in Pittsburgh, Pennsylvania. Once a center of industry, the city has remade itself into a financial hub. (Photo by Geoff Buckley)

Figure 14.9   Curb extension in Baltimore, Maryland. Replacing concrete and asphalt with more permeable surfaces reduces stormwater flow. (Photo by Meghan Rodier)

Finally, while change creates economic opportunities for some cities, it throws a monkey wrench in the works for others. A city that once thrived as a break-of-bulk center, for instance, may find itself at a distinct disadvantage if a new transportation technology favors another location. Similarly, a city whose economy is tied to a single industry may find itself vulnerable if a city somewhere else can manufacture the same item cheaper and faster. To remain competitive, cities must figure out ways to remain economically relevant in a world where the pieces on the chessboard are constantly moving. New York City lost its edge as an important center of manufacturing decades ago but retooled and is thriving today. Pittsburgh, once a major hub of industrial activity, is now a center of finance and technology. What will happen in cities like Cleveland,

Detroit, and St. Louis only time will tell. One thing is certain—there is no shortage of ideas. Box 14.5 discusses a reenvisioning of Detroit.

Jobs and the Environment in Portland

If there is a poster child for urban sustainability, Portland, Oregon, is it. Well known for its progressive planning and "outdoors" lifestyle, the city consistently receives top honors—or close to it—in green city rankings. According to Sustainlane.com, which used a variety of metrics to rank order the fifty most populous cities in the United States, Portland's high marks can be explained by the fact it has had a "thirty-year jump" on the competition. The survey notes that "city-planners in Portland have been thinking green since the 70s, when the rest of the country was still embracing

Box 14.5 A Leaner, Greener Detroit

When one thinks of the many problems plaguing cities in the old manufacturing belt of the United States—plummeting populations, staggering unemployment, and decaying infrastructure—one cannot help but think of Detroit. Since 1950, the Motor City's population has dropped by more than 60 percent. Unemployment, especially among African Americans, hovers well above the national average. In many ways, sections of the city still have not recovered from the riots of 1967. Today, more than one-quarter of the 138-square-mile city is vacant, including vast stretches of former industrial land. Although Detroit sounds like a lost cause, its mayor, city council, and citizens are not throwing in the towel. Two recent initiatives suggest that a brighter and more sustainable future may be just ahead.

First, Detroit's Sustainable Design Assessment Team (SDAT) has come up with a set of recommendations to deal with the myriad problems facing the city, especially those related to economy, land use, transportation, energy, and food security. One suggestion calls for Detroit to adopt an "urban villages" model. Proponents maintain that such a strategy would increase density and connectivity, promote the development of pedestrian- and bicycle-friendly neighborhoods, and facilitate a transition to alternative energies, such as solar and wind. At the same time, as many as ten thousand acres of abandoned land could be converted to commercial agricultural operations over the next decade. The plan also anticipates new jobs opening up in the manufacturing sector, including retrofitting homes and businesses for greater energy efficiency and manufacturing and installing wind turbines, solar arrays, and other renewable technologies. Finally, and perhaps most significantly, the report urges Detroit to come to terms with the fact that it is now a smaller city than it once was and that it should "reconsider its land use, economy, and transportation network around that reality."

The second initiative, the Detroit Works Project, was unveiled as a process by which city officials and residents could create a shared vision for Detroit's future—one that seeks to restore the physical, social, and economic fabric of the city. The effort is divided into "Short Term Actions" and "Long Term Planning." The Short Term Actions component seeks to bring meaningful change to neighborhoods that need it most today. As the name suggests, the goal of Long Term Planning is to develop "a comprehensive and action-oriented blueprint for near and long-range decision making" that the city can follow as it blazes a path toward a more sustainable future.

Although the "blueprint" has not yet been completed, the city's website lists the following as priorities based in part on citizen input: improving job and economic growth; improving efficiency of city system networks; improving neighborhood stability; defining "quality of life" ingredients for healthy and sustainable neighborhoods; creating strategies for vacant land; retaining and attracting population; and leveraging public and private investments for greater impact.

While some may question the efficacy of urban agriculture, particularly in a former industrial zone, Detroit's new approach signals a willingness to break from the past and chart a course that leads to a more realistic and sustainable future—one that is smaller, denser, and more connected.

the strip mall. The city enacted strict land-use policies, implementing an urban growth boundary, requiring density, and setting a strong precedent for sustainable development. The city's natural beauty is hard to beat, too." As successful as Portland has been at implementing a variety of sustainability measures, its economy has remained its Achilles heel. Hampered by a high unemployment rate relative to the rest of the nation, creating jobs has long been a challenge. A new economic development strategy released in 2009 identifies several niche sectors where Portland could take advantage of its strengths. These include streetcar production and bicycle manufacture and repair.

With respect to public transportation, Portland is the first city in the United States to reduce vehicle miles traveled. The city's streetcar lines, in particular, have proven very popular with residents and tourists alike, carrying twelve thousand riders per day and reducing annual vehicle miles traveled by seventy million. Since construction began in 2001, 55 percent of development in the central business district has taken place within one block of the route. The streetcar is also credited with spurring construction of thousands of new housing units, including low- and moderate-income homes, as well as attracting hundreds of new businesses. Add to this the fact that residents have three times voted to expand the system, and you have the makings of a success story. Although the transit system itself provides jobs, Portlanders hope that United Streetcar, a subsidiary of local manufacturer Oregon Iron Works (OIW), will expand that base. Rather than simply import streetcars manufactured in the Czech Republic, OIW recently acquired the rights from the

Czech firm Skoda-Inekon to manufacture the streetcars locally. Currently, dozens of cities across the United States are considering adding new streetcar systems. If they do, there may be plenty of business opportunities—and jobs—opening up in Portland. Another potential growth area that holds promise for Portland is also related to transportation—bicycles (see figure 14.10). Currently, the city possesses more than three hundred miles of bike lanes and trails. Well integrated with the "transportation mix," more workers commute to the office by bike than in any other city in the United States. All these bikers on the road—and the numbers continue to climb—have opened the door to dozens of new businesses, from manufacturers of precision components and custom frames to helmet makers like Nutcase, a home-grown company which also caters to the needs of skateboard, in-line skating, and scooter enthusiasts. Of course, bicycle miles add up, increasing the demand for maintenance and repair shops.

The Future

What works in Portland will not necessarily work in Cleveland, or Detroit, or St. Louis. Every city in the United States and Canada has its own set of challenges and, just as important, its own unique assets. Taking advantage of these building blocks, regardless of whether they are physical, social, cultural, or historical, is a good place to start. Developing an educated and skilled workforce, rethinking infrastructure, involving the public in the visioning process (as is happening in Detroit), and diversifying the urban economy so that it can weather the storms that are sure to come are also critical. Of course, there are no

Figure 14.10   Cyclists in Amsterdam, capital of the Netherlands. Bicycles are a safe and efficient form of transportation in many European cities. Several cities, including Portland, Oregon, are seeking to integrate bicycles more effectively into their transportation planning. (Photo by Geoff Buckley)

guarantees. Taken together, however, these measures point to the future and not the past.

EQUITY

The final component of urban sustainability is equity. Put simply, the distribution of environmental "goods," such as parks and street trees, and environmental "bads," such as polluting industries and waste facilities, should be just. According to the US Environmental Protection Agency, environmental justice is defined as "the fair treatment and meaningful involvement of all people regardless of race, color, national origin, or income with respect to the development, implementation, and enforcement of environmental laws, regulations, and policies." Thus, an environmental injustice may exist if "goods" and "bads" are distributed inequitably across space *or* if residents are shut out of the decision-making process.

The Environmental Justice Movement

Although urban residents have been dealing with locally unwanted land uses for a long time—from the stench of tanning and rendering operations to the smoke of factories and steam locomotives—environmental justice, as both an academic endeavor and a vehicle for activism, has a much shorter history. Starting in the 1980s with the General Accounting Office's study on landfill siting and the United Church of Christ's report on toxic waste disposal in the United States, researchers began to notice that waste disposal sites were often located in or near minority neighborhoods. Over the next twenty years, social scientists and environmental activists sought to determine whether locally unwanted land uses such as these were intentionally placed in minority and low-income areas or whether minority and low-income residents were attracted to these areas because of the availability of inexpensive housing and jobs. More recently, "white privilege" has emerged as a way to explain how residents in affluent and predominantly white neighborhoods are able to deflect unwanted land uses to other parts of town.

Two recent developments in the field have shifted research agendas in important ways. First, social scientists have broadened the scope of the field, turning their attention increasingly to the inequitable distribution of environmental amenities and how the quality of these amenities varies across space in cities like Edmonton, Los Angeles, and New York. Driven by concerns over rising type 2 diabetes and obesity levels, especially among inner-city children, researchers have also begun to study "food deserts" and access to recreational space and, further, to frame these as public health as well as environmental justice issues. Another significant development has been a renewed effort to introduce a historical perspective to equity studies. These "process" equity studies cast light on the social institutions and uneven power relations that create the patterns we see on the map, helping us to recognize the legacy effects of past decisions and to appreciate the context within which those decisions were made.

The View from Phoenix and Baltimore

When it comes to studying environmental justice, two particularly good places to focus attention are Phoenix, Arizona, and Baltimore, Maryland. While both cities have very different histories and face different environ-mental challenges, they are similar in that they both belong to the National Science Foundation's Long-Term Ecological Research (LTER) network. As the only urban LTERs in the network, much attention has been devoted to learning how these cities function as socio-ecological systems.

In Phoenix, a combination of zoning and "persistent and diverse forms of racism" have permitted hazardous industries to concentrate their activities in Latino and African American neighborhoods. Although decisions to place noxious facilities in the midst of minority communities were not made with the intent to inflict harm, the net effect over the past century has been to place a disproportionate share of environmental burdens on low-income, minority neighborhoods in South Phoenix. That Latino and African American residents have not benefitted economically from this arrangement only makes matters worse. Although citizen activism since the 1990s has met with some success, the legacy of past zoning decisions has left an imprint on the urban landscape that will be difficult to efface.

Making amends for past environmental injustices may drop from the city's list of priorities, however, if officials and residents cannot figure out a way to recover from the housing collapse of 2008. How warmer and drier climatic conditions will affect residents who already live in a water-stressed region of the country is also open to speculation. Of course, here Phoenix is not alone. In addition to developing sustainability plans, numerous cities have produced or are in the process of producing climate action plans. An important component of these plans is to make sure that climate change mitigation does not protect some groups of people at the expense of others (see box 14.6).

Box 14.6 Taking Climate Action in Chicago

As discussed in chapter 12, one of the most difficult challenges cities across North America—and throughout the world—will face in coming decades is developing strategies to deal with global climate change. Whether it is hotter temperatures, increased storminess, or rising sea levels, planners and policy makers worry about the ability of urban residents—and urban infrastructure—to withstand the presses and pulses associated with greater climatic instability. For city officials tasked with ensuring the health and safety of urban inhabitants, the terms "vulnerability" and "resilience" have become part of their everyday lexicon. Unlike the era of the "sanitary city," however, when engineered "fixes" were both technologically and economically feasible, cities today must find a different way forward. Even if money were not an issue, engineered solutions cannot completely eliminate risk, as the experience of New Orleans with destructive storms plainly shows.

Chicago is no stranger to extreme weather events. In *Heat Wave: A Social Autopsy of Disaster in Chicago*, Eric Klinenberg gives us a blow-by-blow account of the deadly heat wave that battered Chicago in 1995. Particularly disturbing is the effect it had on elderly, low-income residents. Cooped up in small apartments, with little shade and without air conditioning, they were defenseless against the heat. Worse, the city was ill equipped to help them. Fast-forward fifteen years, and the city of Chicago is in a very different position. With an average temperature that has increased 2.6 degrees since 1980 and a growing concern that severe weather events could become more frequent under a different climatic regime, the city convened a climate task force to study the problem. They invited leading scientists to offer their visions of Chicago's climate future and to speculate on how higher temperatures and increased precipitation down the road might affect not only the city's economy and health but its native ecosystems as well. (Long-range predictions suggest that Chicago's plant hardiness zone may look more like northern Alabama's by the end of the twenty-first century.) According to the group's website, the scientists demonstrated "that we need to act now to reduce our emissions while preparing for climate changes that cannot be avoided." The city responded with its Climate Action Plan in 2008.

To deal with anticipated changes, the task force developed a plan with five main strategies. Acknowledging that buildings are responsible for 70 percent of all city emissions, the first strategy focuses on improving energy efficiency. The second strategy emphasizes the importance of using cleaner sources of energy and, to a greater degree, relying more heavily on renewables. The third and fourth strategies concentrate on improving transportation options and reducing waste and industrial pollution, respectively. Taken together, these are the mitigation strategies. The final strategy calls for adaptation, that is, adopting measures that "will help reduce the impact of the changes that can be expected even if we greatly reduce emissions." Ultimately, the goal of the plan is to "reduce our emissions and prepare for change." As with any such endeavor, success is possible only if everyone with a stake in the city's future is willing to play a role in implementing the plan.

Turning to Baltimore, two examples drawn from research conducted in support of the Baltimore Ecosystem Study challenge assumptions about the patterns we typically associate with environmental justice. The first example focuses on the distribution of toxic release inventory (TRI) sites and their proximity to African American neighborhoods. Whereas studies conducted in other cities indicate that industrial sites and hazardous facilities are often located in or near minority communities, a recent Baltimore study shows just the opposite—that such facilities are more closely associated with white working-class communities. Historical evidence shows that the unusual distribution is not the result of a twentieth-century concern for equity. Rather, exclusionary housing practices and segregationist policies—Baltimore was the first major city in the United States to pass a segregation ordinance—forced African Americans to live far away from their place of work. Long before exposure to industrial pollution was a concern, white workers took advantage of both de jure and de facto segregation so that they could live closer to jobs.

The second example focuses on parks and park access. A simple distributive study reveals that black Baltimoreans today have a very high access to parks and other recreational facilities compared with blacks in other cities in the United States. While this may be true, historical analysis reveals that the city's park system was not created with them in mind. Despite park literature and rhetoric to the contrary, Baltimore's park system has a long history of discriminating against African Americans (see figure 14.11). For decades, Baltimore's small black population was confined to overcrowded ghettos just outside the downtown. During the 1940s

and 1950s, thousands of African Americans from the South migrated to the city just as large numbers of whites began their exodus to the suburbs. The result was that Baltimore's black population began to spread out, occupying areas that were previously off-limits to them. In essence, black Baltimoreans' high access to parks can be explained by the simple fact that they inherited a system that was not intended for them. From our present vantage point, it may appear that Baltimore's current distribution of parks is just, but if one takes into consideration the city's history of segregation and the limited role African Americans played in the decision-making process, then perhaps we might reach a different conclusion (figure 14.12).

Transportation Justice

Yet another way that issues of social and environmental justice play out in an urban context has to do with transportation. Walking may be a desirable option for people living in a neighborhood with narrow streets, slow-moving traffic, and mixed-use zoning, but for others who are compelled to get around on foot in a landscape clearly designed for the automobile, it's a very different story. According to the nonprofit safety advocacy group Transportation for America, urban sprawl is not just bad for the environment, it is downright dangerous for pedestrians forced to navigate its wide swaths of asphalt. The decades-long neglect of pedestrian safety in the design and use of American streets is exacting a heavy toll on our lives. In the past decade, from 2000 through 2009, more than 47,700 pedestrians were killed in the United States, the equivalent of a jumbo jet full of passengers crashing roughly every month. On top of that,

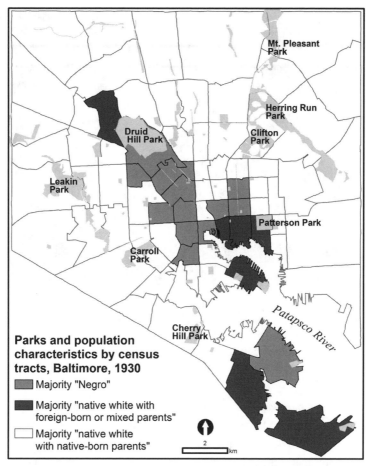

Figure 14.11   Parks and park access in Baltimore, Maryland, 1930.
For the most part, residents in the majority white census districts
enjoyed a higher access to parks. *Source:* Map by Christopher G.
Boone.

more than 688,000 pedestrians were injured
over the decade, a number equivalent to a pedestrian being struck by a car or truck every
seven minutes.

A recent report released by the group
ranked four Florida metropolitan areas as the
most dangerous places to walk in the country.
The Orlando-Kissimmee region came in first
out of fifty-two, with more than 550 pedestrians killed between 2000 and 2009 (see table
14.1). By contrast, New York City-Northern
New Jersey-Long Island is considered one of

the safest metropolitan areas for walking, an
area which, not coincidentally, possesses the
highest number of people who walk to work.

How is this a social and environmental justice issue? As the report notes, African American and Hispanic residents suffered the highest
pedestrian fatality rates. They are also the least
likely to own a vehicle. A report in the *New
York Times* identifies bus riders as a particularly
vulnerable group "because bus stops are often
between intersections on long, wide roads and
are far from stoplights. People race across to get

Figure 14.12   Baltimore mayor Thomas D'Alesandro, to the right of the plaque, at the dedication of a new playground in 1949. Like many cities at the time, Baltimore's park facilities were segregated. *Source:* Reproduced courtesy of the University of Baltimore, Langsdale Library, Special Collections, Thomas D'Alesandro, Jr. Collection: Series IV-C, Box 4.

to the other side, rather than walk (in steamy weather or after a long day's work) a quarter- or half-mile to a stoplight. . . . The problem is especially acute for children and the elderly, who have greater difficulty judging distances and speed." One bright spot is that Orlando appears to be taking the report seriously, building miles of sidewalks, installing audible pedestrian signals, introducing a variety of traffic-slowing measures, modifying bus stops, and making lighting improvements.

Pattern and Process

Environmental injustice has many faces. While the siting of a noxious facility in a Latino neighborhood in South Phoenix offers us a textbook example of an environmental injustice, the two examples from Baltimore are more complex. They remind us that as-

sumptions can be dangerous and, further, that looks can be deceiving. We cannot assume that environmental "bads" are always associated with low-income minority communities or that white residents always have greater access to parks and recreational facilities. With regard to the justice issues surrounding transportation, we cannot presume that in a country with more than 250 million registered passenger vehicles, everyone has access to a car. Nor can we jump to the conclusion that if walking is so easy and convenient for New Yorkers, it must be easy and convenient for everyone.

Each of these cases provides an example of an injustice, but it may not be the one we suspected at first, yet another reminder that cities are incredibly complex places—socially, culturally, politically, and economically. Only by paying attention to pattern *and* process are

Table 14.1 Deadly Cities for Pedestrians, 2000–2009

Metro Area	Total Pedestrian Fatalities	Average Annual Pedestrian Fatality Rate (per 100,000 people)	Pedestrian Danger Index (PDI)
Orlando-Kissimmee, FL	557	3	255.4
Tampa-St. Petersburg-Clearwater, FL	905	3.5	212.7
Jacksonville, FL	342	2.8	177.8
Miami-Fort Lauderdale-Pompano Beach, FL	1,555	2.9	167.9
Riverside-San Bernardino-Ontario, CA	938	2.5	139.2
Las Vegas-Paradise, NV	421	2.5	135.2
Memphis, TN-MS-AR	266	2.1	132.6
Phoenix-Mesa-Scottsdale, AZ	867	2.3	132.4
Houston-Sugar Land-Baytown, TX	1,024	2	128.2
Dallas-Fort Worth-Arlington, TX	942	1.6	119.4

Source: Transportation for America. 2011. "Dangerous by Design." http://t4america.org/resources/dangerousbydesign2011/states/worst-metros/.

we able to come up with plausible explanations. This necessarily involves making sure that our environmental justice studies include both distributive and procedural components. Only then will we be able to account for the legacy effects of past decisions and, just as important, monitor how these decisions play out over time and at different scales. Here is one thing we know for sure, however: disadvantaged communities rarely possess the political and economic power to contest the decisions that affect them.

CONCLUSIONS

Another way to think about sustainability is to imagine what a more "humane metropolis" might look like. Developed to help solve the planning and design problems that confront us, it is a "vision" with five key parts:

- Green: protection and restoration of ecological services;

- Restorative: promotion of physical and mental health and safety of residents;
- Efficient: conserve energy, matter, water, and time;
- Equitable: inclusive, being socially and environmentally just; and
- Neighborly: maintain a sense of community and a sense of place.

The aims are laudable, but making them a reality will be challenging. Progress has been uneven at best. Yet there are indications that an important shift in thinking and behavior is already under way. Two examples illustrate what may be an important trend.

The first example focuses on automobile culture. Data from the Federal Highway Administration indicate that Americans' love affair with the car may be cooling off. According to a recent report, just 46.3 percent of potential drivers nineteen years old and younger possessed a driver's license in 2008 compared with 64.6 percent twenty years earlier. Likewise, drivers in the twenty-one- to thirty-year old age bracket drove 12 percent fewer miles. While driving a fuel-efficient vehicle is better than driving a gas guzzler, the best option for the environment is not driving at all. Perhaps a more telling indicator is that "brand" recognition and preference with respect to cars is exhibiting signs of decline among young consumers.

The second example concerns suburban living. In a recent editorial titled "The Death of the Fringe Suburb," author Christopher B. Leinberger notes that in the 1990s, most of the United States' expensive housing was located in the high-end outer suburbs, but today it is found in the city center and inner suburbs—a consequence of the 2008 housing collapse. At the same time, demand for the "suburban fringe houses that are in such oversupply" continues to drop, virtually guaranteeing further price declines. "The good news is that there is great pent-up demand for walkable, centrally located neighborhoods in cities like Portland, Denver, Philadelphia and Chattanooga," writes Leinberger. "Those retail centers and subdivisions will never be worth what they cost to build. We have to stop throwing good money after bad. It is time to instead build what the market wants: mixed-income, walkable cities and suburbs that will support the knowledge economy, promote environmental sustainability and create jobs." To what degree the outer suburbs recover is difficult to say. That homeowners in these far flung automobile-dependent subdivisions suffered terribly during the crisis shows their vulnerability.

To ensure progress toward sustainability, we need policies that promote density and efficiency in our cities. We need creative urban designs to serve as magnets that lure people and jobs to the abandoned spaces that haunt our downtowns. We need to reduce pollution, protect green spaces, and ensure that everyone has an opportunity to live a healthful and productive life. We also need to reduce consumption and limit the negative impact cities have on the faraway places that supply their needs. More than anything, however, we need the behavior shifts outlined in the examples above to spread and gain momentum. Only then will cities be able to fulfill the promise of sustainability.

SUGGESTED READINGS

Benton-Short, L., and J. R. Short. 2013. *Cities and Nature*. 2nd ed. New York: Routledge.

Bernard, T. 2010. *Hope and Hard Times: Communities, Collaboration and Sustainability*. Gabriola Island, BC: New Society Publishers.

Birch, E. L., and S. M. Wachter, eds. 2008. *Growing Greener Cities: Urban Sustainability in the Twenty-First Century*. Philadelphia: University of Pennsylvania Press.

Boone, C. G., and A. Modarres. 2006. *City and Environment*. Philadelphia: Temple University Press.

Fitzgerald, J. 2010. *Emerald Cities: Urban Sustainability and Economic Development*. Oxford: Oxford University Press.

Glaeser, E. 2011. *Triumph of the City: How Our Greatest Invention Makes Us Richer, Smarter, Greener, Healthier, and Happier*. New York: Penguin.

Jacobs, J. 1961. *The Death and Life of Great American Cities*. New York: Vintage.

Karvonen, A. 2011. *Politics of Urban Runoff: Nature, Technology, and the Sustainable City*. Cambridge, MA: MIT Press.

Kunstler, J. H. 1993. *Geography of Nowhere: The Rise and Decline of America's Man-Made Landscapes*. New York: Touchstone.

Owen, D. 2009. *Green Metropolis: Why Living Smaller, Living Closer, and Driving Less Are the Keys to Sustainability.* New York: Riverhead Books.

Platt, R. H., ed. 2006. *The Humane Metropolis: People and Nature in the 21st-Century City.* Amherst: University of Massachusetts Press.

Rees, W. E. 2003. "Understanding Urban Ecosystems: An Ecological Economics Perspective." In *Understanding Urban Ecosystems*, edited by Alan R. Berkowitz, Charles H. Nilon, and Karen S. Hollweg. New York: Springer.

Rees, W. E., and M Wackernagel. 1996. *Our Ecological Footprint: Reducing Human Impact on Earth.* Gabriola Island, BC: New Society Publishers.

Speth, J. G. 2008. *The Bridge at the Edge of the World: Capitalism, the Environment, and Crossing from Crisis to Sustainability.* New Haven: Yale University Press.

Spirn, A. W. 1984. *The Granite Garden: Urban Nature and Human Design.* New York: Basic Books.

CITIES ON THE WEB

Baltimore Ecosystem Study: http://www.beslter.org/.

Central Arizona—Phoenix Long-Term Ecological Research: http://caplter.asu.edu/.

The Humane Metropolis: http://humanemetropolis.org/.

Sustain Lane: http://www.sustainlane.com/us-city-rankings/.

Sustainable Cities Institute: http://www.sustainablecitiesinstitute.org/view/page.home/home.

US EPA, Environmental Justice: http://www.epa.gov/environmentaljustice/.

Index

About the Editor and Contributors

Matthew Anderson is a university lecturer of geography at Montana State University, Billings. He teaches courses in human geography, political geography, urban studies, and GIS. His research interests focus on the political economy of the neoliberal city, the politics and dynamics of urban growth and redevelopment, and critical social and spatial theory. Current research examines the temporal dynamics of redevelopment governance in Chicago, its emergence and recent evolution, and the ways in which governance actors are responding to rapidly changing sociopolitical conditions and economic realities.

Lisa Benton-Short is associate professor of geography at George Washington University. She teaches courses on cities and globalization, urban planning, and urban sustainability. As an urban geographer, she has research interests in urban sustainability, environmental issues in cities, parks and public spaces, and monuments and memorials.

Geoff Buckley is professor of geography at Ohio University. His research interests include management of public lands, especially state forests and city parks; urban sustainability; environmental justice; and the evolution of mining landscapes.

Christopher DeSousa is associate professor and new Director of the School of Urban and Regional Planning at Ryerson University in Canada. Prior to joining Ryerson, he was the chair of Urban Planning at the University of Wisconsin-Milwaukee as well as a member of the Geography and Urban Studies faculty. His research activities focus on various aspects of brownfield redevelopment, urban environmental management, and sustainability reporting in Canada and the United States

Bernadette Hanlon is assistant professor of city and regional planning at the Austin E. Knowlton School of Architecture at the Ohio State University. Her research interests include suburban decline and growth, urban policy and planning, and state and local government.

Amanda Huron is assistant professor of interdisciplinary studies at the University of the District of Columbia in Washington, DC. She holds a doctorate in earth and environmental sciences/geography from the Graduate Center of the City University of New York and a master's degree in city and regional planning from the University of North Carolina, Chapel Hill. She teaches courses on cities, world geography, and the history of Washington, DC. She is an urban geographer with interests in housing, cooperative economic structures, and participatory city planning.

Yeong-Hyun Kim is an associate professor of geography at Ohio University. Her research interest includes globalization, world-city politics, urban immigrant communities, and international labor migration. She teaches urban geography, world economic geography, and globalization and the developing world. She is currently working on a research project examining the return migration of ethnic Koreans from Northeast China to South Korea.

Deborah Martin is associate professor of geography at Clark University. Her research interests are place representation, place identity, urban politics and activism, and qualitative methods. Her current research projects include the legal dimensions of land-use conflicts and urban politics and the socioenvironmental impacts of, and neighborhood and policy responses to, the Asian longhorned beetle infestation in central Massachusetts. She has published in journals such as *Annals of the Association of American Geographers*, *Antipode*, *Gender Place and Culture*, *Environment and Planning A*, *International Journal of Urban and Regional Research*, *Mobilization*, *Professional Geographer*, and *Urban Geography*.

Nathaniel M. Lewis is a Canadian Institutes of Health Research (CIHR) Postdoctoral Fellow in the Gender and Health Promotion Studies Unit within Dalhousie University's School of Health and Human Performance. His dissertation research, recently completed at Queen's University, focused on gay men's migration decisions and the production of gay space in Ottawa, Canada, and Washington, DC. As a social and health geographer, he is interested how the policies and practices of place affect access to health services and broadly conceived health outcomes, particularly among marginalized populations. His work can be found in *Health & Place*, *Gender, Place & Culture*, *Social & Cultural Geography*, and other journals.

Robert Lewis is a professor of geography at the University of Toronto. His main teaching responsibilities lie in the historical geographies of urban development and social inequality. His research examines the industrial history of American cities, with particular focus on Chicago between 1880 and 1960, and the social geographies of colonial Bombay and Calcutta.

Lindsey Sutton is a broadly trained human geographer with an interdisciplinary background in international affairs, human development, and Latin American studies. Currently, she teaches as an adjunct associate professor for Western New Mexico University. She is committed to supporting human development through education, research, and outreach and is currently engaging in socially conscious yoga outreach projects to support charities and communities.

John Tiefenbacher is professor in the Department of Geography at Texas State University in San Marcos, Texas. Dr. Tiefenbacher's research has focused on environmental geography, or the relationship between people and their natural environments. He has published on a diverse set of topics that examine perception and behaviors of people with regard to natural and technological hazards, environmental problems, and personal preconceptions about the places they inhabit. He has undertaken studies throughout the United States and Mexico. His current research pertains to the challenges of urban hazards and evacuating cities, adaptation to climate change, and the responses of agricultural industries (particularly wine growing) to climate changes in several regions (principally South America, the United States, and Europe) of the world.

Thomas J. Vicino is associate professor in the Department of Political Science and core faculty of the School of Public Policy and Urban Affairs at Northeastern University in Boston, Massachusetts. He is the chair of the Master of Public Administration program and teaches courses on public policy issues in the urban arena. His research focuses on the political economy of cities and suburbs and the related issues of metropolitan development, housing, and demographic analysis.

Kathryn Wells received her PhD in geography at Syracuse University in 2013. She is currently in a postdoctoral fellowship at Virginia Tech College of Architecture. Her current research examines housing policy, social movements, and urban change in Washington, DC.

David Wilson is professor of geography and the unit for criticism and interpretive theory at the University of Illinois at Urbana-Champaign. His current work focuses on the material and discursive impacts of globalization on the North American city, city politics and urban political movements, and contemporary city restructuring. His latest books are *Race and Housing: America's New Black Ghetto* (2007) and *Inventing Black-on-Black Violence: Discourse, Space, and Representation* (2005). He currently sits on the editorial boards of *Urban Geography, Social and Cultural Geography, Professional Geographer, Syracuse University Book Editor Board*, and *Acme: the International Radical E-Journal*.